HOME OF THE TEMPERATE.

HOME OF THE INTEMPERATE.

FIFTY YEARS HISTORY OF THE TEMPERANCE CAUSE.

INTEMPERANCE

THE GREAT NATIONAL CURSE, THREATENING THE PURITY AND STABILITY OF OUR INSTITUTIONS, SECULAR AND RELIGIOUS; THE FRUITFUL SOURCE OF POVERTY, MISERY, CRIME, AND DEGRADATION OF THE INDIVIDUAL AND FAMILY.

DESCRIBING

THE PROCESS OF MANUFACTURING LIQUORS; POISONOUS INGREDIENTS USED IN ADULTERATION; OFFICIAL REPORTS OF REVENUE RECEIPTS FROM ITS SALE.

HISTORICAL SKETCH

OF THE VARIOUS MEANS ADOPTED FOR ITS SUPPRESSION THROUGH LEGISLATION, OPEN AND SECRET TEMPERANCE SOCIETIES; WASHINGTONIANS; GOOD TEMPLARS; GOOD SAMARITANS; DAUGHTERS OF SAMARIA, ETC., FROM THE FIRST ORGANIZED SOCIETY TO THE PRESENT TIME.

CAREFULLY PREPARED FROM THE MOST RELIABLE AND EMINENT AUTHORITIES.

BY J. E. STEBBINS,

AUTHOR OF MOSES AND THE PROPHETS, CHRIST AND THE APOSTLES, FATHERS AND MARTYRS; GLORY OF THE IMMORTAL LIFE, ETC.

WITH

A FULL DESCRIPTION OF THE ORIGIN AND PROGRESS OF THE NEW PLAN OF LABOR BY THE WOMEN UP TO THE PRESENT TIME.

BY T. A. H. BROWN,

REPORTER FOR THE CINCINNATI GAZETTE, WHO HAS BEEN CONSTANTLY IN THE FIELD.

ILLUSTRATED.—SOLD BY AGENTS, ONLY.

HARTFORD:

PUBLISHED BY L. STEBBINS.

CINCINNATI, OHIO:—HENRY HOWE.

M. A. PARKER & CO., 163 AND 165 CLARK ST., CHICAGO, ILL.

1874.

PREFACE.

In order to insure efficient action in any direction, it is highly important there should be a full understanding of all those things which have a practical bearing on the subject in hand. In general, there is a vague sort of recognition of the claims of Temperance — a thoughtless assent to their transcendent importance; and yet there is a deplorable apathy and indifference among the mass of the people with reference to the whole matter. With a want of consideration, and perhaps a want of knowledge, they are, in great measure, ignorant of the gigantic proportions intemperance is assuming in the land, and the impending danger, in consequence, to all the dearest and best interests of humankind. They are not aware of the startling facts, which are as so many revelations of the power and extent of a mighty evil that is working ruin in society, and impoverishing and degrading, not only individuals and families, but even the nation itself. They do not know how long is the procession that is marching on under the black banner of a most determined foe, nor of the blight and desolation the enemy is spreading in its course. They are but slightly moved by the stirring appeals that are now and then made to them by a passing lecturer, for they have no intelligent appreciation of the broad, urgent, and pressing need for action. To meet this condition of the common people, is the design of the present volume, and in its preparation access has been had to the best and most reliable authorities of this country and of Europe.

It aims to give a faithful representation of the *drinking system*, in its every aspect. It shows what it does and must inevitably do in the case of any person who allows himself to come under the influence of it, in any degree. It gives a record of the alarming results that attend it, and pictures the fearful end of the tippler — darkly shaded, indeed, but true, as too many can testify. The story needs to be told; told until the people — as the heart of one man — shall awake to the tremendous issues, and be moved to take part in the stern conflict; told until the eyes and ears of all mankind shall be open to see and hear the sights and sounds that are associated with this phase of public and private life; told until it shall reach the remotest hamlets, and inspire with courage and earnestness that shall be as a universally popular sentiment to resist the assaults of a dreaded invader. *Temperance* or *Intemperance* is the question. Shall the benignant reign of the one give us peace and prosperity, or the wasting desolation of the other be our grief and our curse? The answer belongs to the people. Then, let none turn away from these candid and impartial statements. Let no prejudice deter any one from a deliberate survey of the important work. Let no one shut his heart against the conviction these truths are calculated to awaken. It is a vital subject. It touches man's interest at every point. It appeals to every attribute of his nature, his affection, his honor, his ambition, his dignity, and as he regards his salvation, in all these and more, he should take heed to the call.

For such an end as this we would send this volume into every family. We would introduce it into every home, and say to its inmates — it was meant for your highest weal; take and read it. Let fathers and mothers give it to their sons as they go out into the world, and bid them ponder and practise; so shall it be to them as a shield in the time of temptation, and fortify them in the hour of danger; and thus there shall be a good beginning in the work of reform, that shall gladden the homes and hearts that are to add to the stability and glory of the American Republic.

J. E. STEBBINS.

List of Illustrations.

LIST OF ILLUSTRATIONS.

TABLE OF CONTENTS.

CHAPTER V.

Origin of the Evil.

CHAPTER VI.

What is the Stimulant?

CHAPTER VII.

Ale and Beer.

CHAPTER VIII.

Rum and Brandy.

CHAPTER IX.

Where is it found?

CHAPTER X.

Probability of Reform.

CHAPTER XI.

Blighting Effects upon Society.

CHAPTER XII.

National Loss.

CHAPTER XIII.

What is the Remedy?

CHAPTER XIV.

Temperance Workers.

CHAPTER XV.

Temperance Societies.

CHAPTER XVI.

Adulteration of Liquors.

CHAPTER XVII.

License and Prohibition.

CHAPTER XVIII.

Legislative Action.

WOMEN'S TEMPERANCE CRUSADE.

INTRODUCTION. By Dio Lewis.

CHAPTER XIX.

CHAPTER XX.

CHAPTER XXI.

CHAPTER XXII.

CHAPTER XXIII.

CHAPTER XXIV.

CHAPTER XXV.

CHAPTER XXVI.

CHAPTER I.

INTEMPERANCE — THE NATION'S CURSE.

OUR FAIR HERITAGE. — THE CURSE UPON IT. — NATURE AND EXTENT. — UNITED STATES TAX. — CAPITAL INVESTED. — FIRST DISTILLATION. — DRINKING IN HIGH PLACES. — ORDINATION BILLS. — FIRST SOCIETIES. — TOTAL ABSTINENCE. — THE CRISIS.

A FAIRER heritage is not to be desired than that which is given to the dweller upon American soil. Whether we look at the munificence of nature, or that which hath been wrought out by the agency of men in their onward march to civilization, we are compelled to say that ours is a goodly land.

From the forest-crowned hills of New England's remotest corner to the sunniest slopes on the Pacific shore, there are countless forms of beauty and grandeur to challenge admiration, besides an equal display of those things which develop into the more substantial utilities of life; making the country what it is — rich and prosperous. The enthusiast in every direction may find in the rock-ribbed hills, the winding streams, the smiling meadows and broad prairies, the wild and picturesque valleys, the snow-clad mountains and the stretch of ocean, that which will meet his every want, foster his wildest ambition. The adventurer pushes on to new and unexplored regions, and at every step opens up new wonders to the gaze of the world.

The speculator, in his search for more of treasure, turns over the stones which hide the golden dust and the shining metals, and he finds that Nature opens her veins and rewards him with a lavish hand. They who would look above these material considerations, and desire the elevation of mankind in a higher sense, find their wishes met and their hopes strengthened in the universal diffusion of knowledge, the number and variety of the institutions which have for their object the accomplishment of these very ends.

The social, political, and religious advantages which are denied to so many of the nations of the earth, are open to the mass of the people; and altogether, we are constrained to say, it is a goodly heritage. With these God-given conditions, that were designed to make mankind happier and better, we yet fail to come up to the requisite standard of goodness and virtue. The original paradise, we know, was dismantled by the fall, and since then there is no portion of the world without its dark features; but enough was preserved from the wreck and ruin to remain as a rich legacy, had it been cherished and kept as it should be. No one can look abroad at the present time, and not be painfully conscious that there is a fearful curse upon us — that there is a blighting influence at work — a canker eating into the very heart of society, and sapping the foundations of our dearest and best institutions. This gigantic evil, this cruel monster, is Intemperance; and its frightfully increasing power and prevalence are enough to startle a world from its lethargy and indifference, and incite to active measures for the suppression of that which is becoming a terrible and wide-spread devastation. Were a foreign foe to invade our country, and arrogate to themselves superior power by dictating laws in opposition to those of our own beneficent government, with what earnest and decisive measures would they be met! How strongly would the spirit be rebuked! No means would be left untried to quell the disturbing forces. No sacrifice would be counted too dear to win the result, and restore harmony, by sending back the threatening invaders, and looking well to internal fortresses. But more to be dreaded than the wiliest and most determined external foe is this modern Giant of Intemperance that is stalking through the length and breadth of our land, leaving misery, poverty, crime, and every species of ruin in its path. The rebellious hordes may attempt invasion and raise their own issues, and all this will be met, for at the clarion call of the country thousands will rush to the scene of conflict, armed, equipped, and nerved for a mighty onset; but the stronger and more seductive influences that are unceasingly at work, preying upon the vital interests of the nation, are left comparatively unchecked, and altogether without means commensurate with the necessities of the case. A want of consideration, it may be, is one prominent reason for the neglect. Many perhaps deplore it as it comes within their own narrow range of observation, perhaps within the circle of their acquaintance; but a thoughtful, intelligent, broad view reveals the fact of a nation in peril — a nation in so much danger that it calls for the wisest and most careful legislation, that, if possible, the imminent and threatened evil may be averted, and the cloud lifted that encircles us with so much of gloom.

Sad as the contemplation of these things may be, it is nevertheless a duty of every lover of his race, every citizen who is interested in maintaining a fair and prosperous condition of things in the country, to look the startling and alarming facts in the face, that they may be prepared for intelligent co-operation in the great work that needs to be done. To say nothing of the countless forms of wretchedness that is induced by the Demon of Drink, it is like a desolating scourge, that is impoverishing our land, robbing its inhabitants of everything that should be their glory and their pride. Estimates made with regard to the consumption of spirituous liquors are perfectly appalling. It has been said by one interested in these calculations that "there is a sufficient quantity of fermented and distilled liquor used in the United States, in one year, to fill a canal four feet deep, fourteen feet wide, and one hundred and twenty miles in length." "The liquor saloons and hotels of New York city" alone, he says, "if placed in opposite rows, would make a street like Broadway eleven miles in length." The statement is intensified in the assertion that "the places where intoxicating drinks are made and sold in this country, if placed in rows in direct lines, would make a street one hundred miles in length. If the victims of the rum traffic were there also, we should see a suicide at every mile, and a thousand funerals a day." Could "the drunkards of America," he continues, "be placed in procession five abreast, they would make an army one hundred miles in length." And all this vast company, under the influence of that which is nothing less than soul-destroying fire, are continually adding to the long catalogue of crimes which unrestrained human passion is capable of committing; and thus it is that our public records are stained with the recital of the most atrocious and daring deeds of cruelty that fiendish malice can perpetrate. They carry the flaming torch of the incendiary in one hand, and the knife of the murderous assassin in the other; and the fire and the bloodshed create a momentary sensation, and it has gone. Theoretically, public sentiment is against all this. It deplores the existence of so tremendous an evil; but practically the great part of the people have been soothing themselves to sleep when they ought to have been awake and in earnest to meet the emergencies of the age in this direction.

A long, sad wail comes up from desolated homes, broken hearts, crushed hopes, and squandered fortunes, all over the land; and with it there is borne on the breeze the despairing cry, "Is there no help for us?" To-day there seems a disposition to heed the cry, and haste to the rescue; and thrice happy will be the day when these efforts shall be crowned with success. It is no trifling issue. It is not the work of any limited period of time, but an unceasing and persistent warfare waged against it will eventually do much towards subduing it. Philanthropists and good men need to be on the alert. Evil and selfish principles are active under the dominion of the enemy.

The investment of capital and the enlistment of energy in these departments are strikingly at variance with the enginery for good. In the single State of New York, where there are over seven thousand churches, there are over twenty-one thousand licensed dram-shops. There are no computations for the practical sorrows which flow out of this extended traffic. The sighs and tears, the groans, miseries, and woes, cannot be told; yet statistics enable one to form some idea of what these may be, when it is considered what the nature of the cause is which produces the effect. The amount of tax collected by the United States on spirits for a single year of recent date, with the amount in quantity which it represented, aggregated a money interest of over $400,000,000. The corresponding tax upon beer for the same time, with the same representation, showed a money value of $300,000,000 more. Added to this was the interest of the wine trade, of about $75,000,000. This, together with the import trade of liquors, beer, and wine, presented a total of nearly $165,000,000. This has nothing to do with the vast amount of capital invested in the requisite buildings and machinery to carry on the stupendous work, nor with the expense involved in the various demands in the prosecution of the trade. This swells the figures far beyond those we have given. Nor does the cost stop here. Back of all this is a story of loss which no money can supply. It has been said, if one were to take a final count of even this sum, at twenty thousand dollars a day, it would take more than an ordinary lifetime to complete the task; that, if it were in gold, and loaded in wagons, it would fill more than a thousand wagons of a ton each, and, if in silver, it would require more than fourteen thousand, while the procession would extend over seventy-five miles; and all this would be but the representation of a single year of the terrible traffic.

It is estimated that there are those so confirmed in the habit of intemperance as to bear the name of drunkard, as to make an army of 600,000 in the United States; 60,000 of these annually pass out of sight, filling dishonored graves, "unwept, unhonored, and unsung," because every trace of their manhood had been obliterated, and every promising hope blasted, by their mad career. Notwithstanding this lamentable fact, the places they knew are filled by others; and the unbroken ranks pursue their march, to re-enact the same fearful tragedies, and reach the same untimely end. Those who pander to the wants of this vast multitude are selfish and unscrupulous in their measures, and unceasingly ply their ruinous arts, regardless of the consequences. Others may seek to advance the moral and spiritual interests of the country, but they are everywhere met by this mighty obstacle.

The unequal contest is observed in the calculation that while $12,000,000 are annually spent in keeping watchmen upon the hills of Zion, $700,000,000 are employed in ministering to the depraved appetites of men, inducing morbid conditions of mind and body, thus bringing into action a host of counteracting influences, which hinder the salvation of the country. Could the money that is appropriated in this direction be diverted from its accustomed channel, and go to swell the tide of human interests, churches, schools, colleges, libraries, and every benevolent institution would dot every portion of our land; life and health giving streams would flow through all its borders; and from countless homes and hearts would issue such a jubilant anthem as was never before sung upon earth.

It may be asked, "Is it worse now than in the days of old?" However that may be, it certainly ought to be better; but a glimpse of the past may give some satisfaction to the propounder of such a question. Fashion and custom throw about these things, as in all others, their various forms at different periods, so that we find things regulated by another standard entirely as we go back.

A thousand years of the world passed away in blissful ignorance of the nature and power of alcohol. Even its existence, as extracted from fermented liquor, was unknown. Then the people of Arabia wrought out the discovery which has proved such a curse, not only to this nation, but to almost every other. When the process was first accomplished, "no one knew what this product of distillation was, nor was there any language that had for it even a name. They, however, called it alcohol, and that is now the chemical name in every country. The word had been previously used in Arabia as the name of a fine powder, which the ladies had used to give brilliancy to their complexions. It was soon ascertained to be a poison, and no one thought of using it for a drink. About the year 1230, it began to be used in the south of Europe as a medicine; and from thence its use gradually extended for that purpose over various parts of the civilized world. Judging from its *immediate* effects," it was thought to be a valuable boon to the human race, cheering, strengthening, and prolonging existence, intensifying all the enjoyments of mankind, adding those that were hitherto unknown, until it came to be denominated "the water of life." The most extravagant things were written extolling its peculiar and wonderful properties. Said a writer of the times, in the quaint language of the period, "It sloweth age, it strengtheneth youth, it helpeth digestion, it abandoneth melancholie, it relisheth the heart, it lighteneth the mind, it quickeneth the spirits, it keepeth and preserveth the head from whirling, the eyes from dazzling, the tongue from lisping, the mouth from snaffling, the teeth from chattering, and the throat from rattling; it keepeth the stomach from wambling, the heart from swelling, the hands from shivering, the sinews from shrinking, the veins from crumbling, the bones from aching, and the marrow from soaking."

With such ideas of its transcendent virtues, it is not strange that the indulgence of it as a beverage became more and more common. Ignorant of its physiological effects, and glorying in the exhilaration of the draught, many came to think they could not live without it. More and more extensive became its use; and in 1581, during the Netherland war, we find the English giving it to their soldiers, to fit them better, as they supposed, for their work, and kindle anew their warlike propensities. It was not until the year 1700 that the people of our own country became interested in the matter of distillation, and then a distillery was opened at Boston. From that time the business rapidly increased, and spread through various parts of the United States, so that in 1815 the number of distilleries had come to be numbered by thousands, sending out millions of gallons of the fiery stimulant for a waiting people. "With the mass of the people," it is said, "distilleries were for a long time considered a blessing to the country. They furnished, it was thought, a ready market for the surplus grain; they gave a new value to the orchard, whose superabundant fruit could at once be converted into brandy; they brought ready employ to the carpenter, the cooper, the carrier, and furnished the nation with an excellent article, which it was importing from Holland and the West Indies at great cost. Pious men, deacons of churches, owned and labored in them, without loss of character. It is even affirmed that one of New England's strongest divines, filling one of the best pulpits in the land, ministering to the spiritual wants of a large congregation, was during the week employed in perfecting the operations and superintending the affairs of a distillery, which was adding to his material gain.

If a convention of ministers was to be held, the exhilarating element was the chief attraction. Among the curious items of history at the present day, are some such bills, where brandy and cider were by far the largest appropriation. The following bills in connection with a church in Hartford, Ct., will serve as characteristic specimens of these times. On the back of the first bill is written, "Ordination: eight pounds allowed, and order given on treasurer in full."

THE SOUTH SOCIETY, IN HARTFORD,

TO ISRAEL SEYMOUR, DR.

1784.				
May 4th.	To keeping ministers, &c.			
	2 mugs tody,	£0	2	4
	5 segars,	0	5	10
	1 pint wine,	0	3	0
	3 lodgings,	0	9	0
May 5th.	To 3 bitters,	0	0	9
	3 breakfasts,	0	3	6
	15 boles punch,	1	10	0
	24 dinners,	1	16	0
	11 bottles wine,	3	6	0
	5 mugs flip,	0	5	10
	3 boles punch,	0	6	0
	3 boles tody,	0	3	6
		£8	3	11

This was the year that Hartford was first incorporated as a city.

Still another, on a similar occasion, of a later date, illustrates the peculiarity of the times:—

SOUTH SOCIETY

TO THOMAS SEYMOUR, DR.

For the expenses attending the Ordination of Mr. Flint, April 19 and 20, 1791.*

To 50 lemons, at 10*s*.,	£0	10	0
3 gallons of wine of D. Bull,	0	16	10
1 gallon of ditto of G. Burnham,	0	6	6
1 ditto of cherry rum,	0	10	0
1 gallon of best spirits,	0	6	0
2 quarts of brandy,	0	3	0

* This was for sixteen men to dine one day, and forty the second.

		£	s.	d.
To	1 large loaf of sugar, 16 lbs., at 1*s.* 6*d.*,	£1	4	0
	1 brown sugar, half quarter, 10*s.*,	0	10	0
	half barrel best cyder,	0	6	0
	60 wt. of best flour,	0	12	0
	24 lbs. of butter,	0	18	0
	10 doz. eggs, at 6*d.*,	0	5	0
	1 bushel of apples,	0	3	1
	spices,	0	6	0
	raisins,	0	3	0
	3 lbs. of coffee,	0	2	4
	1 lb. of tea,	0	8	0
	18 lbs. best beef,	0	6	0
	2 qrs. veal, &c.,	0	15	10
	1 turkey,	0	6	8
	1 doz. fowls,	0	12	0
	3 hams, at 6*d.*,	0	18	6
	vegetables,	0	8	6
	pickles, 2*s.* 6*d.*,	0	2	6
	pipes, 1*s.* 6*d.*,	0	1	6
	tobacco, 4*s.* 3*d.*,	0	4	3
	2 bushels oats,	0	3	0
	hire of attendance,	1	16	0
	hire house cleaned,	0	4	0
	walnut wood,	0	8	0
	extra trouble,	3	0	0
	Total,	£16	15	7

The generous mixture went the rounds, until sparkling wit and brilliant sarcasm were in full play. At one time, for the greater refreshment of the whole man, a little cracker was put in the cup. At a certain gathering of these ministerial dignitaries, the tender conscience of one of the brethren became somewhat disturbed by the indulgence, and tasted the cracker, while he refused the accompanying potion, whereupon a reverend brother remarked, in tones of sarcastic rebuke, "You will eat the devil, but not drink his broth."

For a long time, ministers were wont to prepare themselves for their morning exercises on the Sabbath by an extra dram. The wedding and the funeral were alike occasions for its use. School committees took their seats at the last day among the juvenile crowd; and the flowing bumper was there, to call out all the goodly qualities of their natures, and bring the social current into lively exercise. In short, the use of the alcoholic stimulant became general among the American people. It came to be considered the grand panacea for all the ills of life, a necessity for all classes of people and all conditions of being. It fortified one against the heat of summer and the cold of winter. The "glass" was associated with every object and interest of life. Seldom was a bargain ratified without it, and a social party or visit was never complete aside from it. It was the parishioner's welcome to his pastor, an important part to a friendly greeting. The decanter, with its usual accompaniments, was an essential feature of house-furnishing. At stated times it was regularly resorted to, until custom marked the morning dram as indispensable, one at eleven and at four o'clock, and still another to prepare for the slumbers of the night. These were necessities. Those interspersed were governed by inclination and convenience, or by the peculiarity of circumstance. During the war of the American Revolution, government furnished the soldiers a regular allowance of the article, under the mistaken apprehension that it would make them better soldiers. When the war closed and the men disbanded, carrying the habits of the barrack to their homes, it was found that the custom of drinking intoxicating liquors was becoming so universally prevalent in all classes of society, that the more thoughtful and intelligent began to wake up to the subject, and consider the importance of doing something to check what seemed to them a rapidly growing evil. Licensed by the government, and sanctioned, as it had been, by the Christian church, the public mind had failed to grasp it in its true bearings. Neighborhoods and communities had hailed the distillery as a means of blessing to them. It enhanced the value of their hard-earned products, and filled their otherwise scanty coffers with wealth. Altogether, it had become a mighty and complicated enterprise; but no candid observer could shut his eyes to the fact that, whatever might be said for it, it was nevertheless a prolific source of wretchedness and want. The conviction pressed itself home upon the strongest and best minds that something must be done. The yeomanry of the land would not be likely to begin the work of reform; for, while those in higher walks and circles were saying, by their example, it was good for them, they felt justified in its use themselves. If it was good for the minister in his work, it was not less so for the weary tiller of the soil. The ablest and best talent of the times became enlisted in the cause, and the inevitable tendency of the widespread habit was held up to view. The public mind, once aroused to the contemplation of the subject, became thoroughly in earnest. Agencies were set in motion, societies formed, pledges drawn up and signed, and the people called to take a decided stand against that which experience denounced as a great wrong. From time to time, earnest speeches were made, and the work of reform went steadily on. The decanters were withdrawn from the sideboards of the higher and more influential circles.

The tide of public sentiment turned against the practice. Some began to be more shy and reserved in its use. But, while the stronger concoction was put out of sight in good measure, cider became the common beverage. Ordinary families filled their cellars with barrels of this article for their winter use, and not a meal of the day was complete without it. At every neighborly call, the mug of cider went the rounds, and it was not uncommon that forty and fifty barrels were little enough for the demands of a common household. As in Massachusetts the work of distillation had commenced, so there were inaugurated some of the first reformatory movements of the times. In 1813 a society was formed that had for its object the suppression of intemperance; but, inasmuch as this had only to do with what was considered the "*too free use*" of the corrupting drink, it fell short of the demand. The views of some prominent Englishmen found their way to our shores, in which total abstinence was set forth as the only true basis of action. Dr. Lyman Beecher, Dr. Edwards, and some of the leading spirits of New England, fell in with the doctrine, and lent their powerful arguments to the new issue. Gradually the leaven permeated society, renovated the church, and from that time temperance became one of the leading questions of the age. Societies rapidly multiplied; organizations were effected that had for their sole object the mitigation of an evil which was acknowledged to be the greatest curse of the nation.

Notwithstanding all the effort that has been made, the curse still remains, and the question is still before the people, "What shall be done to uproot the social evil?" for such is the phase it assumes. The voice of the people crieth out against the use of the deadly stimulant. A stigma rests upon the sale of it; and thousands, impelled by the love of gain, and yet fearful of losing their respectable standing, will resort to every trick of artifice and every form of secrecy to carry on their unhallowed trade unbeknown to the world. It is smuggled in every manner, labelled with every conceivable device, paraded by numberless mysterious signs; and private entrances and curtained rooms in all our

DRINKING PUNCH AND FLIP.

DRINKING CIDER.—(*See page* 32.)

cities and villages lure the unwary youth, until they are under the dominion of the tempter before the watchful eye of even the family has discovered the danger.

A certain phase of American life doubtless tends to foster this unhealthy and unhappy condition of things. The rapid and extended communication among our people, the exciting chase for wealth, the eager determination to rise above their fellows, and the propensity to ignore the slow methods of accumulation, have all won for us the reputation of a fast-going people. This unnatural excitability demands an artificial stimulus. It will have it. The youth of the country cannot bide the plodding necessities of their condition, and they rush to the cities to realize their brilliant ideal of life. A large part of them enter the arena, and engage in the contest, before their characters are formed and their principles are established; and, without the restraints of home, they fall an easy prey to the seducer, and are in the meshes of the destroyer ere they are hardly conscious of their position themselves. Retreat then seems impossible, and they rush on in reckless indulgence and extravagance, until they meet the end of their fate; and too often it is a sad story of ruin and disgrace. Thus it is that intemperance is becoming fearfully manifest among the young men of the land. Could something be done to place an effectual check upon these buddings of evil, and hinder their rapid working and development, it would be a glad day for the American people. A crisis is upon us. It is a grave, complicated, and momentous question. The social and moral bearings of the subject demand attention. Political and religious influence needs to be exerted in its behalf. A revolutionary movement of right impetus and character is loudly called for. The wretched system of adulteration that prevails at the present time, with its vast proportion of poisonous compounds, makes the habit of drinking now more pernicious in its effects upon soul and body than it was in the days of the fathers.

The mass of the people are ignorant of these things to a great extent. Let them carefully look into these things; candidly trace the origin, workings, and results of the whole matter; and then study out, if they can, the solution of the mighty problem, What shall be done to secure the salvation of our country from the curse of Intemperance?

CHAPTER II.

Physiogloical View of Intemperance.

AFFINITY OF NATURAL AND MORAL. — DEFACES THE HUMAN FORM. — THE DOCTOR'S EXPERIMENT. — A PHILOSOPHER'S APHORISMS. — ALCOHOL NO PROTECTION AGAINST COLD. — ASSERTION OF AN ENGLISH SAILOR. — STATEMENT OF PROFESSOR SILLIMAN. — DR. JEWETT'S TESTIMONY AS A MEDICINE.

The variety, beauty, and harmony of the natural world are due to certain laws and conditions, and these latter are realized in proportion to the natural order and working of the first. So it is with man. He is placed in his appropriate sphere on the earth, subject to conditions and laws also, and without the recognition and observance of these he stands a jarring element in the moral world, never coming to answer the end of his creation. Could we expect the beautiful alternation of sunshine and shadow; the warmth, freshness, and life of summer; the silence, frost, and vigor of winter, with all the attendant advantages and pleasures of the different seasons, if the laws of the universe were to be deranged, and act contrary to their original design? As well might we expect this as to suppose that man could retain his wonted activity and power, when every part of his body was under the influence of a demoralizing element, the direct tendency of which was to weaken, depress, and undermine the whole constitution. In the early history of alcoholic indulgence, thousands violated the laws of their physical being, without being conscious of what they were doing. The people had not an intelligent conviction of the effect of the powerful stimulant upon the human system. They were not aware of the injury that was constantly being done by the unnatural interference with the stomach, brain, and, indeed, every organ of the body. It is to be feared that even at this enlightened day there is a want of knowledge — at least of consideration — with reference to this phase of the matter. It involves the vitality of the whole system, and, that disturbed and weakened, man is shorn of his strength, and robbed of his power in every direction. "Alcohol," says an English physician of eminence, — and the same profession of our own country concur in the opinion, — "is primarily and essentially a lessener of the power of the nervous system." No one who has watched the gradual transformation of a man from his first cup in the morning to the perpetual and insatiable calls of a diseased and depraved appetite at the last, cannot fail to come to a like conclusion. Every step of the way betokens less and less of the power of resistance, — of nervous force and energy. Humanity is disfigured by thousands of living instances of this sad truth. All the dignity and beauty of the human form become wasted in them. The story is written on every line of their countenance, so that all the world may read as they pass. The brightness of the eye becomes dimmed; the vacant look and the meaningless stare take the place of the thoughtful, inquiring gaze of intelligence. The face becomes bloated, the hands nerveless, the whole figure bent and powerless, the step unsteady; and the whole man, like a stately ship that has been stranded upon the waters, is dismantled and useless.

In order to prove the depressing nature of the stimulant, a certain physician subjected himself to its operation, and thus writes concerning it: "Some years ago," he says, "I purposely placed myself under the influence of alcohol. At eight o'clock P. M., and three and a half hours after partaking of a light tea, I took one ounce of rectified spirits of wine diluted with two ounces of water; ten minutes afterwards I repeated the dose. The first perceptible effect was a sensation of warmth in the region of the stomach, followed immediately by a chilliness over the whole surface of the body, though the temperature in the room was at 68° Fahrenheit. This was speedily followed by reaction. The pulse indicated arterial excitement, and I breathed more rapidly than usual. As soon as the spirit rose to the brain, the cheeks became flushed, the eyes sparkled, and the temporal arteries throbbed. I then felt an irresistible tendency to talk, and became very loquacious. This was attended with an involuntary screwing of the mouth, a meaningless laughter, and an attempt to sing. In fact, I felt 'jolly.' But, together with this, there was an unsteadiness in my gait; my legs felt very light. There was a giddiness in my head, and a strange confusion in my mental powers. The ability to fix the attention upon any subject was greatly impaired, but the imagination was excited, and the fancy wild and restless. Ideas came and went, and I had no power to retain them. As I had not partaken of alcohol for many years, its action upon me was very striking and rapid, and soon became almost overpowering." The causes of these various symptoms he thus describes: "The sense of heat and warmth in the region of the stomach was undoubtedly owing to the acrid property of alcohol irritating the mucous membrane of that delicate organ. The sense of chilliness, extending over the whole surface of the body, was clearly due to an interference with the capillaries of the surface and the functions of the skin. But were not the exhilaration and jollity, the brightening of the eyes, and the glowing of the countenance, indicative of increased activity of the circulation in the brain? If so, alcohol must be a stimulant. But I remember that this state was attended by other symptoms, indicating not stimulation, but depression. There were lightness of the head and of the legs, unsteadiness of gait and movement, with a certain bewilderment and obtuseness of the mental powers. I then saw that two of the properties of alcohol were concerned in producing these symptoms. The unsteadiness of gait and motion was to be attributed to the narcotic action of the drug just then coming into operation, depressing the cerebellum, which regulates voluntary motion, and also the cerebrum, the seat of the intellectual powers. The excitement was owing to the irritant property of alcohol affecting principally the base of the brain. The alcohol being rapidly absorbed from the stomach, and carried to the brain, its acrid properties at once come into play. The delicate tissues of the brain, at its base, are irritated, and blood flows to this part; yet not sufficient at first to produce congestion, but only increased activity in the circulation. The region of the brain which is the seat of the reasoning and moral faculties, is the first to suffer, leaving the other part (the seat of the animal propensities) excited, while its functions are uncontrolled by reason and conscience. After this, even the cerebellum becomes narcotized, and the whole nervous system oppressed. On the whole, we concluded that the symptoms we experienced were produced by the combined volatile, acrid, and narcotic properties of alcohol."

The practical working of it everywhere, and in all classes, demonstrates beyond a doubt that it is antagonistic to the human constitution. Some have been possessed with the idea that the use of it, as a drink, was a material aid in the process of digestion; but a variety of experiments makes it plain that it renders it more difficult. "A tonic is that which gives tone or firmness to an organ, and therefore is the opposite of that which, by exciting an organ to extra action, is certain to impair its tone, and therefore no such property can be ascribed to the alcoholic stimulant, so called. A philosopher of long ago contradicted the statement that this could have anything to do as an aid, and with his name are associated the aphoristic remarks, "Water-drinkers have keen appetites," and that "Hunger is abated by a glass of wine."

Some of the lovers of the article would fain assert that it is food in itself; that it is extracted from the nourishing grains of the earth, and its final condition retains some of its nutritive qualities still; but scientific analysis has exploded this theory, and common observation has confirmed it.

It is also urged that there is a benefit accruing from the warmth it gives to the body, thus giving it power to resist the cold; but this, though a wide-spread, is still a mistaken apprehension. All experience of travellers in the coldest and severest climates prove, beyond a question, that it hides within itself none of this power. The voyager in the arctic regions bear unequivocal testimony to the injuriousness of spirits on this very account, when used to any extent in the high latitudes. It lowers the vital temperature, rather than increases it. A healthful flow and condition of the blood are the life of the system, and this becomes poisoned and diseased by the introduction of the fiery liquid, and there is no power of resistance in any direction. It is well nigh impossible to combat disease with this to contend with. Health-producing remedies cannot have their legitimate action when swept away by a current of impure blood.

Says one, in writing upon these things, "As soon as the alcohol makes its way into the organism and diffuses through the fluids, so soon there is depression, so soon respiration falls, carbonic acid gas from respiration decreases, and muscular strength, consciousness, and sensibility decline. Speaking honestly, I cannot admit the alcohols through any gate that might distinguish them as apart from other chemical bodies. I can no more accept them as foods than I can chloroform or ether. That they produce a temporary excitement is true; but as their general action is quickly to reduce animal heat, I cannot see how they can supply animal force. To resort for force to alcohol is, to my mind, equivalent to the act of searching for the sun in subterranean gloom, until all is night."

An English sailor asserts that "A Danish crew of sixty men, well supplied with provisions and *these fiery waters*, attempted to winter in Hudson's Bay; but fifty-eight of them died before spring. An English crew of twenty-two men, *destitute* of these *waters*, and obliged to be almost constantly exposed to the cold, wintered in the same bay, and only two of them died."

It has been said that, "If the human body were transparent, and the operations of its organs in sustaining life visible, every man might see that nature itself teaches that the drinking of alcohol cannot be continued by a man without hastening his death." From the first formation of the habit a physical malady has commenced, and nothing can control or avert it but an entire removal of that which induced the condition. The maddening thirst which it engenders has nothing natural about it. None of the natural and God-given provisions of the earth meet its demands, or assuage the intensity of its cravings. By the activity and arrangement of the organs of the human system, they have as much to do "as is consistent with permanently healthful action, and with the longest continuance of human life, when men take nothing but suitable food and drink."

Notwithstanding all that has been said of the physiological aspect of the case, and all that has been declared of its inevitable results in arresting vitality, a large number of physicians still deal largely in its use with their patients, professedly to secure just the oppoposite effect. A distinguished chemist of our own country, Professor Silliman, pronounces it of the same nature as chloroform and ether; and no one would think of giving either to a weak and sinking patient as a *restorative.* Some, who are in the habit of visiting the sick and the dying, declaim loudly against this practice of thus giving the stupefying potion, thus beclouding the intellect and obscuring the vision of those who should see and feel clearly and rationally.

Dr. Jewett thus quotes a conversation on this point: "'In what state of mind did the man die?' asked a gentleman of a Christian brother, who, the day previous, had spent some time with a dying friend. 'I cannot tell you anything about his state of mind, whether cheered by Christian hopes or otherwise,' said the friend; 'for he was, for the last twenty-four hours of his life, completely intoxicated by the large quantity of liquor given him, with a view to support him in his sinking condition; and,' added the gentleman, who was a faithful and devoted Christian, and often in the chambers of the sick to speak words of comfort and Christian counsel to the suffering, 'I cannot, *these days*, get any comfort or do any good by visiting the sick and the dying, for a large portion of them die drunk. So much brandy is given them that the feeble brain reels under its influence, and they have no realizing sense of their condition.'"

For all sorts of diseases, and all conditions of being, it is the universal and favorite prescription with some. Either from ignorance, or a want of due respect to hygienic laws, it is the same thing for heat or for cold, for the want of a thing or its superabundance. Says the above writer, "A good lady some time since asked me if I thought it likely that the drinking of ale or milk punch by a nursing mother would affect the child. 'Of course, madam,' I replied. 'But why did you ask the question?' This was her answer: 'Why, all the while my daughter followed the prescription of her doctor, and drank milk-punch, we could scarcely keep the little one awake, even while dressing it. It slept nearly all the time, day and night.' 'Yes, madam,' I replied, 'and it was precisely the same sleep that the poor drunkard enjoys when we find him stretched by the fence or on the sidewalk.'"

A great work will be done for the coming age if the false impressions of the nature and tendency of these things shall be corrected, and something be introduced that shall add to the power of the human system, instead of diminishing and wasting its force and energy. The physiological argument for the cessation of strong drink as a beverage is urgent and strong, to say nothing of its extensive use by the medical profession. The body is the temple of the soul, and for the sake of the sacred thing enshrined within it, Temperance should be written upon every portal, and made guardian of the sacred interests.

CHAPTER III.

Intemperance as related to Heart and Intellect.

RELATION OF MIND AND BODY. — KINGLY POWER OF INTELLECT. — DOOM OF TALENTED MEN. — QUEEN CITY STATESMEN. — THE WANDERING BEGGAR. — POWELL'S OPINION. — EPICURUS. — HUGH MILLER'S TESTIMONY. — THE MORAL NATURE. — EFFECTS OF MORAL BLIGHT.

"My mind to me a kingdom is," was an immortal strain of one of the poets; and when he uttered the fervid exclamation, he paid a glowing tribute to the distinctive feature of man — to that which raises him high above all the lower orders of creation, and makes him first, chiefest, and best among all the creations of the Infinite. Mind is the glory of man, and the wealth of a kingdom but faintly shadows forth its scope and destiny. Its aspirations are as high as heaven, and its existence commensurate with that of the great Eternal himself. The body is the casket which holds the priceless thing, and no philosopher may be able to tell just how they are bound together — to tell precisely how the mysterious union, the subtle relations, and the hidden springs are adjusted; but one thing is certain, they act and re-act, and the harmony or friction of one produces corresponding conditions in the other. It therefore follows that, if, from any cause whatever, the machinery of the body becomes powerless and inert, the higher faculties of the soul are retarded accordingly, hindered in their growth and development, and narrowed down in their capacities for action in every way. If the body be constantly under those depressing influences which are inseparably connected with the physiological conditions of intemperance, it cannot be a fit ally for the mind within. It cannot be a help to it. From the very necessity of its relation, it must affect its coloring and character; and if it does not build up, it will pull down; if it does not elevate and soften, it will degrade and harden. Who shall count the loss? Who sum up the fearful aggregate of the mental waste that has come to the world by reason of this single habit alone? Some of the brightest intellects the world has known have gone out in obscurity and darkness; their light has been quenched in rayless, starless gloom, and they sleep in dishonored graves, living, if at all, in the memories and hearts of men, only as standing monuments to proclaim against the folly of excessive drinking. Names that might have graced the pages of history in every department of science, letters, and art, find no place there, because their rare endowments were slighted and perverted by their own reckless and unhallowed indulgence.

We declaim against the folly and ignorance of the heathen, who gloat over the oracles of superstition, building their altars, and bringing their offerings to the strange gods of their own fancy; but the countless devotees that flock to the shrine of Bacchus in our own civilized land, and in our own enlightened age, is vastly more to be wondered at. To see men, who were made to reflect the image of the Divine, deliberately, wantonly throw away their birthright — men who are fully conscious of their responsibility, duty, and destiny, to spurn it all, and pander to the cravings of a diseased appetite which they themselves have taken pains to create — is a greater sin than heathenish folly has yet committed.

Poets, with brilliant imagination, who might have sent out their thrilling melodies into the heart of a saddened world, dispelling many shadows and lifting many burdens, have foregone their privileges, and given themselves to drink, which has become to them a demon, that has hushed all the sweet cadences of song, making themselves miserable and the world more sad.

Historians have used the destroying stimulant, until the unsteadiness of their hands has compelled them to lay down the pen, which might have recorded the incidents of a passing age in such a manner as to insure the gratitude of their posterity in all coming time; but their career has been cut short, and their influence brought to an end, because they had wound about themselves the galling chains of intemperance, and could not again be free. Men of clear perception and keen intellectual vigor are fitted to become philosophers, and there are many of these who might have enriched the world's thought, and shed light and knowledge upon the intricate problems of moral and mental working; but they have failed, because their perceptions have been dimmed and their vigor diminished before the work was done.

Statesmen have been lost to the country in this way, and an endless amount of talent crushed and lost sight of in the wreck and ruin involved in this the curse of our land. Intellect would hold kingly sway, if it might. The gigantic evil has crept into the councils of the nation; and there, where wisdom, prudence, and moderation should rule and reign; where the gravity, weight, and importance of arguments and decisions affect the interest and destinies of nations, — there have been found representatives of the people, singled out from all others for their superior ability, who yet were unfit to sit in judgment, because the faculties of their minds were deranged and impaired, their judgment warped and clouded, by unduly imbibing the exciting and poisonous draught. In the Queen City of the West is a young man of rare ability and promise. The people have not been slow in the recognition of his statesman-like qualities, and have conferred upon him some of the highest honors of the state. His clear understanding of legislative working, and his broad and comprehensive views of legislative demand, have won for him an enviable distinction, and given him a large place in the appreciation of an intelligent public. Nothing stands between him and the high road to congressional fame but the habit of intemperance, which is coiling itself about him, and bids fair to hold him in its anaconda-like embrace. There are times when, for days together, he gives himself up to the fatal indulgence, and all his powers of intellect are as though they were not. Without a revolutionary movement to hold him in check, his doom is sealed. His mind will fail, his intellect droop, and he is gone. And this is but a single instance of a countless list of similar cases. Several years since, a man called at the door of the writer, a wandering beggar. Forbidding in every aspect of his appearance, one felt an involuntary shrinking from his presence. Aimless, homeless, and friendless, he went hither and thither, fulfilling none of the duties he owed to himself as an individual, and of course wholly regardless of those incumbent upon him as a citizen. Spurned from the doors of men, he hated and cursed them all. He added nothing to the stock of human happiness, and his life was a miserable failure with himself; and yet that man was a graduate of one of the most prominent colleges of New England. He entered the institution with high hopes and flattering prospects. His friends fondly imagined that such fine talent must meet with more than ordinary success, and they looked to see him come out in the foremost ranks of the honored. But in an evil hour he yielded himself to the spell of the tempter, and he went down, until his once soaring intellect was gone, the dignity of his manhood sacrificed, the strength of his character lost, and every trace of his noble ambition had vanished. The stories of faded intellects are sad ones. The annals of intemperance are full of them, and history, observation, and experience are confirming the mournful truth continually.

Says Frederick Powell, a noted English writer, —

"The drunkard is a degraded man intellectually. Our Creator has endowed us with mental faculties that we may work out the higher purposes of life, and fulfil our grand destiny. He has endowed us with judgment and understanding, that we may inquire into the causes of things, and, by comparing one thing with another, arrive at the truth. He has also endowed us with imagination and fancy, that we may, as it were, revel in a world of beauty of our own creation. He has endowed us with memory, that we may treasure up events and facts, and thus garnish our minds with mental wealth. Now, intemperance obscures the judgment and weakens the understanding, so that a man is unable to discover or to appreciate truth. It distorts the imagination, and fills the chambers of the soul with pictures obscene and foul. It perverts and paralyzes the memory, which, instead of treasuring up useful knowledge, becomes a receptacle for the dregs of knowledge, and thus only adds to the soul's pollution."

Thus it is that degradation is stamped upon the highest and best part of being, and the distinctive glory of man departs. There has been a prevalent notion among some that one could think and write better under the influence of an exciting stimulant; but numberless testimonies of professional men go to corroborate the statement that, so far from being an aid, it seriously detracts from the working power of the brain. Almost all the great and continuous thinkers of every age have united in this one conclusion, that alcoholic action is a sure and certain hinderance to intellectual progress. The philosophers of antiquity set a good example in this respect. Epicurus, the great founder of a philosophical system, urged temperance as the only passport to the enjoyments of life, and the only means of attaining to the performance of its virtues. Over his gateway he kept the following inscription: "Passenger! here thou wilt find good entertainment; it is here that pleasure is esteemed the sovereign good. The master will receive thee courteously; but take note, thou must expect only a piece of cake and thy fill of water. Here hunger is not provoked, but satisfied; thirst is not excited, but quenched." How different this from the many costly and elaborate entertainments of the rich at the present day, where wine and spirits fill the goblets of the feaster and the feasted, and the sparkling mixture is quaffed, the exhilaration begins, and deeds and sayings are recorded that bring them down to a level with the lowest circles, if it be they escape a positive disgrace to humanity! In Egypt wine was forbidden to both priest and king, because it was deemed prejudicial to the interests of clear-headed reason, and the welfare of the nation demanded the full exercise of this.

Hugh Miller, so well known as one of Scotland's intellectual workers, thus speaks of an occasion when two glasses of whiskey were presented to him. "It was considerably too much for me," he says; "and when the party broke up, and I got home to my books, I found, as I opened the pages of my favorite author, the letters dancing before my eyes, and that I could no longer master the sense. The condition into which I had brought myself was, I felt, one of degradation. I had sunk by my own act, for the time, to a lower level of intelligence than that on which it was my privilege to be placed; and, though the state could have been no very favorable one for forming a resolution, I in that hour determined that I would never again sacrifice my capacity of intellectual enjoyment to a drinking usage, and with God's help I was enabled to hold by the determination."

Dr. Hitchcock, of Amherst College, has left on record his testimony to the fact that mental labor can be performed vastly better when one is free entirely from artificial stimulus. While making a geological survey in Massachusetts, which involved peculiar and long-continued exertion, he says, —

"I was usually employed from sunrise until ten o'clock at night, with little interruption; yet, during all my wanderings, I drank not one drop of alcohol, and I found myself more capable of exertion and fatigue than in former years, when I was in the habit of taking occasionally stimulating drinks."

Mr. S. C. Hall, a well-known author, says, —

"I live by the labor of my brain, and can testify that, since I have become a teetotaler, I have had an increase of intellectual power, and can work three times longer than when I indulged, *even moderately*, in the use of strong drink."

Statements might be multiplied, were it necessary; but no one can look into the subject at all without being convinced of the truth of these things as a principle. Besides all these intellectual considerations, there is still another side to the picture. Man has a moral constitution. There is *Conscience*, that faithful monitor in the human breast. When we attempt to do wrong, Conscience says, "Beware! and think of the divine law and its consequences." When we walk uprightly and do well, then we seem to hear her sweet voice crying, "Well done!" There is also that keen appreciation of the good, the beautiful, and the true, and those noble affections that so adorn and bless human nature. But intemperance hurls Conscience from her lofty seat, and her voice ceases, or sounds unheeded; those noble sentiments of rectitude and purity are weakened; the kindly affections of the human breast become withered; whilst every evil passion and vile propensity are fostered into frightful development and ruinous exercise. Thus the man who drinks to excess, and gives up the key to the citadel of reason, is a lost man. It matters not how rich the endowments of his nature may be, he is poverty-stricken in every respect.

"The great and essential evil of intemperance," says Dr. Channing, "is the voluntary extinction of reason. The great evil is inward, or spiritual. The intemperate man divests himself for a time of his rational and moral nature, casts from himself self-consciousness and self-command, brings on frenzy, and, by repetition of this insanity, prostrates more and more his rational and moral powers. He sins immediately and directly against the rational nature, that divine principle which distinguishes between truth and falsehood, between right and wrong action, which distinguishes man from the brute. This is the essence of the vice, what constitutes its peculiar guilt and woe, and what should particularly impress and awake those who are laboring for its suppression. All the other evils are light compared with this, and almost all flow from this; and it is right, it is to be desired, that all other evils should be joined with and follow this. It is to be desired, when a man lifts a suicidal arm against his higher life, when he quenches reason and conscience, that he and all others should receive solemn, startling warning of the greatness of his gullt; that terrible outward calamities should bear witness to the inward ruin which he is working; that the handwriting of judgment and woe on his countenance, form, and whole condition should declare what a fearful thing it is for a man, God's rational offspring, to renounce his reason and become a brute."

A man with a blighted moral nature is a sad spectacle; no sadder sight in all the world. Every avenue to good is closed. However fine his sensibilities may have been, they become blunted. Arguments are powerless. He will not be convinced. Tears, sighs, entreaties, are without avail. The most affectionate pleadings are as nothing. The offices of love are all unheeded, and there is but little hope that salvation will come to such a one. Surely it is enough to excite the pitying tears of even the angels in heaven, if they are permitted to take a look into the ways of the sons of men. To see creatures so gifted of Heaven, capable of rising ever nearer and nearer to the one great central idea of all perfection, yet abandon all aspiration and effort, and effectually bar the door against all progress, — surely they must count it an anomaly in the universe, and force the exclamation, Verily it is a fallen world.

CHAPTER IV.

SOCIAL AND RELIGIOUS OUTLOOK.

NO PART OF BEING UNTOUCHED. — HOME, THE HEART OF THE SOCIAL WORLD. — THE YOUNG MAN. — CASE IN WESTERN NEW YORK. — POVERTY NOT THE GREATEST CURSE. — LOSS TO SOCIETY. — BLIGHT UPON THOSE FACULTIES WHICH BUILD UP RELIGIOUS CHARACTER.

THERE is no one isolated stand-point where we may take our position, and with one sweeping glance take in the whole effect of the mighty evil we are considering. The complicated nature of mankind forbids this. They who have traced its influence upon the physical part of being, and seen how surely and effectually it degrades the moral and intellectual, will also be prepared to behold the completion of the work in its social and religious aspect. Could it be seen that there was any part of the man that could escape the ravages of the destroyer, that some little corner of the being somewhere would preserve its natural conditions, and remain the same, we might say there was some redeeming feature in the case; but it is apparent, beyond a doubt, that nothing is left untouched by the blighting, withering influence of intemperate indulgence. There were harmony and adaptation at the beginning, and it was meant they should be preserved. To ignore the requisite conditions is to blast the whole scheme. The divinely-appointed institutions of the world, for the happiness of mankind, involve the necessity of a social nature; and the perfection and development of this are clearly connected with mind and heart. With the powers of these weakened and blunted, there is no more capacity for true social enjoyment. There is no more blessed boon given to man for his earthly condition than *home*. There is no one provision which so completely meets the varied wants of his nature as this; and he who allows the tendrils of his heart to spread the farthest, and take the deepest, strongest hold of this, is the man who is most secure against all the temptations and evils of a siren world. It is here that all the social affections bud and blossom. It is here that their richest and sweetest fragrance is shed. "Here," it is said, "is the heart of the social world." Men are what their homes are; children what their homes make them.

It is the place where all the social qualities of the nature should be unfolded, cherished, and enjoyed; a place where the intermingling of thought and affection should be constantly making one happier and better; and if allowed its practical and legitimate working, it will tend to the realization of this end. It is true, those who are wont to quaff the wine when it is red, base their arguments for its use strongly upon its social qualities and influence; but who does not know that it destroys all the finer feelings of humanity, and makes the once cheerful and pleasant spirit of the household its most dreaded foe?

The demon of drink has been permitted to enter thousands of homes in our land, and wherever it has gone, it has hushed every song of joy, killed out every hope, and brought only poverty, wretchedness, and every form of misery in its train.

We need no other evidence of its transforming power of the social affections, than to see what it hath wrought here. It banishes domestic peace, for there is nothing left for it to feed upon. The sharpest agonies and the keenest pangs are associated with this phase of the question. The lives of wives, mothers, and sisters are cruelly embittered all the way through, because husband, brother, and son are all lost — are meaningless terms, when their hearts have been made callous, and their social nature robbed of its beauty. Says the eloquent Dr. Kitchell, "Much of this is concealed from the public gaze as long as concealment is possible. Back of the visible ravages of intemperance, and deeper than all these, there lies a field of devastation which has never been fully explored, and can never be more than partially reported. It is the wasted realm of the social affections, the violated sanctuary of domestic peace." "It is here that the higher and inner life of woman is marred and tortured, her most sacred and cherished affections crushed and blighted. These are private sorrows, that her most intimate confidant must not know, so anxious is she to sustain the good character of those so dear to her. But from this inner world of suppressed wretchedness there will occasionally burst forth to the ear of human pity a piercing cry of those who writhe under the slow torments of a desolate heart and the overflow of misery. It is merely what inadvertently escapes through chasms violently rent open, and tells sadly of a sea of anguish that is stifled forever in its secret recesses. The bursting hearts of mothers for their ruined sons; of wives from whose life all joy and hope, all love and tenderness, have been blotted out; of daughters' shame, crushed and doomed to penury and disgrace — could we look on all these grief-stricken females, some of whom have been well off, happy, and respected, now doomed to brutality and want, each with her own peculiar history of woe, we should ask no further witness to the heinous guilt of the rum traffic, or the righteousness of law against the destroyer of all these." He who was designed to be the friend and protector of woman is in no wise fitted for his place when he is under the debasing influence of strong drink. The observation of every one will furnish examples of those who have dethroned the dearest friends of their hearts, and sundered every social tie, rather than forego the so-called pleasures of the exhilarating beverage.

It is not many years since a young man in Massachusetts went to the grave of a drunkard in the very vigor of his youth. Nurtured in the bosom of an affectionate family, he was the object of fond solicitude, and bright hopes were entertained of his future success in life. In an evil hour he yielded to the fascinations of the cup, and when it became apparent that the habit was taking fast hold of him, an earnest effort was made to save him. But parental counsel, sisterly entreaty, and friendly advice were nothing. If he stayed in his career long enough for conscience to whisper of the wickedness of his course, he speedily silenced the voice of the monitor, by imbibing the poison still more deeply. His father thought to expostulate with him once more, and promised to set him up in business and provide handsomely for his starting, if he would seek to free himself from the habit that was upon him, and which would surely end in his destruction. But the susceptibility and ambition of even that youthful spirit were gone, and he replied to the touching appeal, with heartless indifference, "I had rather have my drink;" and the broken-hearted father followed his son to a drunkard's grave at the early age of twenty-three. Love and kindness, that are so potent under other circumstances, have but little effect here. The innocent and eloquent pleadings of a child that would soften and subdue the most obdurate heart in a man that was sober, make no impression here, for all that distinguishes man is scorched, burned out, and all the distinctive attributes of his nature are dead, and he stands like a withered tree, only awaiting its time to fall.—An instance that came under the observation of the writer, in Western New York, illustrates the case in hand; and yet it is but one of the many that are acted over and over again every day in every part of the land. Ralph W—— was a young man of prepossessing appearance and marked ability. Affable and courteous in his manner to an unusual extent, brilliant and gay in his conversation, sparkling in wit and repartee, he was the life of every company, and no circle was considered complete without him, in the community where he lived. He paid his attentions to an estimable and worthy young lady, and when it was known that the engagement was ratified that bound them together, she was congratulated as having won a rare prize. Up to this time he had only sipped a little now and then to please his gay acquaintances; but the insidious habit worked on insidiously until it became a confirmed thing. Meantime he was married and settled down in a quiet and attractive home. In the course of time a son and daughter were added to his family, and he still maintained his reputation as a kind and tender husband, a thoughtful and loving father; but all the while the appetite for strong drink had been gaining ground, until it overtopped all other considerations, and it became known that he was frequently intoxicated. For a long time his social popularity covered a multitude of sins, and his family sought in every way to shield him from public disgrace; but there is no way for these things when the man becomes thoroughly wedded to his cups. Dead to all feelings of shame himself, he cares for nothing but how he may quell the maddening thirst. Yielding to this, he went reeling through the streets, carrying untold misery and anxiety into his home, breaking the hearts that otherwise would have been as dear to him as life.—Sometimes reason is dethroned by causes altogether beyond human control, and persons turn against their dearest and best friends, and it is sad; but it is far less aggravating in its conditions than where people deliberately and wilfully pervert their higher nature, and render themselves incapable of exercising ordinary thought or affection. Even woman has buried all her gentler qualities in this remorseless grave. It is a humiliating fact that she has laid aside every endearing virtue of wife and mother, sister and daughter, and gone into the depths of degradation which the indulgence will inevitably produce. In country places this may not be seen or known; but the miserable hovels, the wretched abodes of squalor and want in all our large cities, tell the mournful tale, and are the unmistakable signs of what rum will do. Crowds of neglected and forsaken children show how utterly dead to every social instinct and affection those have become who should have been their guardians and protectors. So true is it that all that is good will die out of the heart, in either man or woman who gives up to the debasing influence of strong drink. There have been those who have been ready to sing to the praises of the "flowing bowl," but no one was ever enticed to drink of the foaming, sparkling mixture but found, all too late, that a venomous serpent lurked at the bottom, which poisoned the life of his manhood, and gave warrant of his death at the beginning. Says a writer already quoted, "Intemperance is to be pitied and abhorred for its own sake much more than for its outward consequences. These consequences owe their chief bitterness to their criminal source. We speak of the misery which the drunkard carries into his family. But take away his own brutality, and how lightened would be those miseries! We talk of his wife and children in rags. Let the rags continue, but suppose them to be the effects of an innocent cause. Suppose the drunkard to have been a virtuous husband, and an affectionate father, and that sickness, not vice, has brought his family thus low. Suppose his wife and children bound to him by a strong love, which a life of labor for their support, and of unwearied kindness, has awakened; suppose them to know that his toils for their welfare had broken down his frame; suppose him able to say, "We are poor in this world's goods, but rich in affection and religious trust. I am going from you, but I leave you to the Father of the fatherless, and to the widow's God." Suppose this, and how changed those rags! How changed those cold, naked rooms! The heart's warmth can do much to withstand the winter's cold; and there is hope, there is honor, in this virtuous indigence. What breaks the heart of the drunkard's wife? It is not that he is poor, but that he is a drunkard. Instead of that bloated face, now distorted with passion, now robbed of every gleam of intelligence, if the wife could look on an affectionate countenance, which had for years been the interpreter of a well-principled mind and faithful heart, what an overwhelming load would be lifted from her! It is a husband whose touch is polluting, whose infirmities are the witnesses of his guilt, who has blighted all her hopes, who has proved false to the vows which made her his; it is such a husband who makes home a hell, not one whom toil and disease have cast on the care of wife and children. Drunkenness brings poverty, but this is not the greatest curse. Could the sweet influences of love and trust be restored, thousands would take all the inconveniences and privations of this without a murmur. Were any new disease to come into the land, that had anything like the power, that showed anything like the deadly working of intemperance, how would it be dreaded! How its nature would be studied, and remedies be sought to lessen its power, and ameliorate the condition of its victims! But hardly a conceivable disease could maintain its perpetuity like this, or be so wide-spread and devastating in its effects; and yet it goes on, annually slaying its thousands and tens of thousands, while only a few are trying to arouse the slumbering people.

The man is not only lost to himself and his family, but he is lost to society. He is fitted for none of the duties which devolve upon him in this respect. The high privileges of citizenship, like every other good, are disregarded and forgotten. Could the blight and waste now produced by drinking be reversed, and the refreshing, invigorating, and life-giving principles of temperance have full sway, what a tide of blessing would be poured upon the social institutions of our country! The day of millennial glory would come in a thousand times sooner.

There is woe enough written upon the nature of man, could we stop here; but there is another shading to the picture, before it is complete. The religious element of man's being gives him claim to kinship with the Eternal. The spiritual within him is traced by the finger of a divine Architect, and when the superscription became visible and manifest, it read, "Thou art *immortal;* thy being shall be co-extensive with the Infinite, and thou shalt reign when the dust of ages has ceased to be." With this dignity stamped upon his nature, man stood alone, a thinking, rational, immortal creature; the highest, best, and crowning glory of all God's creations. More of the divine perfections were to be reflected from his being than from any other. It was meant that he should illustrate God's ideal of good more fully than all the world beside. So strongly did this desire enter into his plan, that when man turned aside from his high destiny, and by wilful transgression forfeited his original birthright, the costliest sacrifice that heaven or earth could devise was instituted to restore him to his lost possibilities. Redemption wrought out new phases, and reinstated mankind in a position of glorious opportunity, where all the capabilities and demands of his threefold nature might be fully met and exercised. These were as broad as the world, and as vast as eternity; but there was no limit or discouragement in the work as long as the given faculties were allowed their legitimate play, and made to fulfil their appropriate ends. It is not a light thing to have a soul in charge. When God sends men into the world, he sends them with this gift, and he says, "Take care of it for me, and I will give thee thy wages." "Thou shalt live and reign with me if thou do it well. All thine earnest efforts in this direction I will crown with success, and own at the last." A work like this, it is clear, demands the fullest play of the best faculties. If a man stupefies himself with drink, or anything else, he cannot think; and if thought is quenched, he cannot reason; and if reason do not act, there can be no wise judgment; and without this there is no decision, which, in its turn, fails to bring any real achievement; so that it may truly be said, that "intemperance is the mightiest force that clogs the progress of all good," in whatever phase it be viewed, social, moral, intellectual, or religious.

In estimating the ravages of alcohol, another thus sums up the results: —

"It has taken the glory of health from the cheek, and placed there the reddish hue of the wine-cup.

"It has taken the lustre from the eye, and made it dim and bloodshot.

"It has taken beauty and comeliness from the face, and left it ill-shapen and bloated.

"It has taken strength from the limbs, and made them weak and tottering.

"It has taken firmness and elasticity from the steps, and made them faltering and treacherous.

"It has taken vitality from the blood, and filled it with poison and seeds of disease and death.

"It has taken the impress of manhood from off the face, and left the marks of sensuality and brutishness.

"It has bribed the tongue to madness and cursing.

"It has turned the hands from deeds of usefulness, to become instruments of brutality and murder.

"It has broken the ties of friendship, and planted seeds of enmity.

"It has made a kind, indulgent father a brute, a tyrant, and a murderer.

"It has transformed the loving mother into a very fiend of brutish incarnation;" and besides all this that happens to the individual and family, there is yet the broader and national view, which will be considered as we proceed.

CHAPTER V.

Origin of the Evil.

MODERATE DRINKING. — EFFECT OF A SINGLE GLASS. — SUPPOSITION OF ITS LIFE-LONG INFLUENCE. — MODERATION INVOLVES THE GREATER DANGER. — THE MEETING. — THE PAUPER'S STORY. — LITTLE BY LITTLE.

While enumerating and considering the tremendous consequences of so destructive a habit, we are constrained to ask, Where is the beginning of these things? How is it that it is started and fostered, until it gains such relentless hold, that there is no escape from it? No more important question can be propounded at the present time, if it be asked with a view of finding a remedy that shall meet the emergencies of the case, and check the prevalence of a habit that is becoming so universal and prevalent. Learned men may discourse long and eloquently upon the origin of the races; but it is not half as important as to discover the application of means that shall free them from chains which keep their bodies and souls in slavish bondage. Scientific men will brave any amount of hardship and fatigue; will encounter the dangers of the most inhospitable regions and the fiercest climates, while following the obscure windings of some stream that may, perhaps, lead them to its hidden source, and all to satisfy the curiosity of an eager and speculative people; but there is yet a mightier problem to solve than these, and they who give the best practical solution may uplift, and perchance save, a nation.

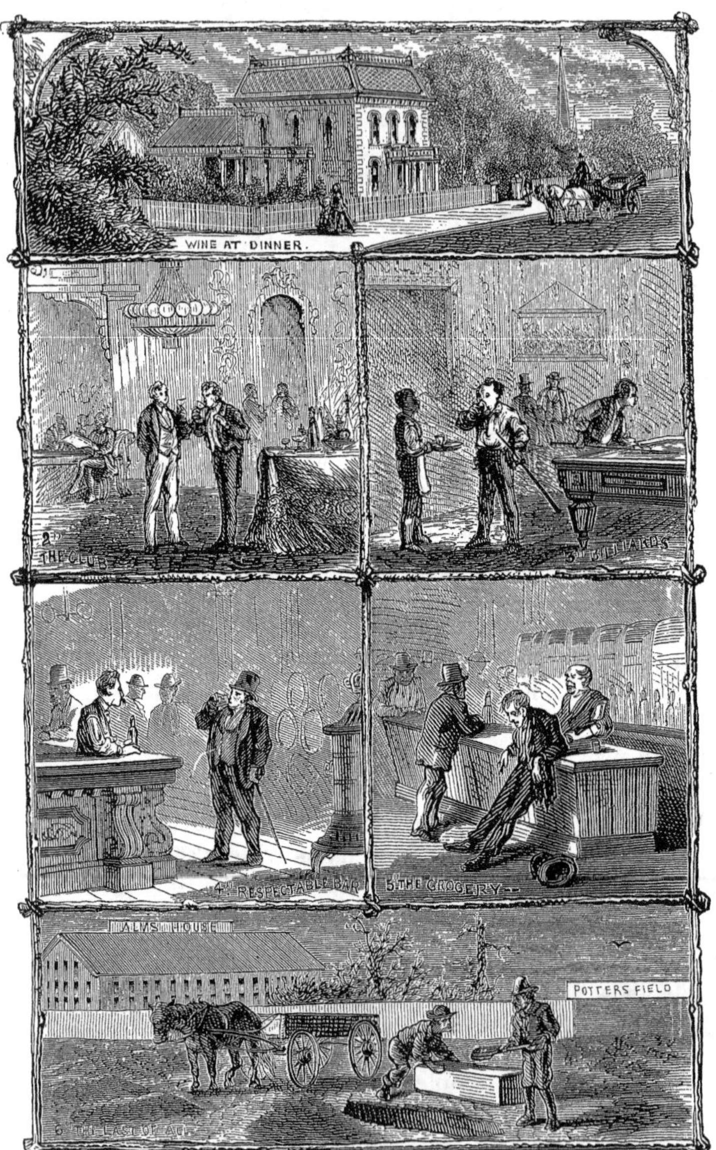

THE BEGINNING AND THE END.

The beginning of a thing is sometimes disproportionate to the ends accomplished; yet in everything there is a starting-point, around which clusters the main feature of interest, and with which is associated all that comes of it. Almost everything in nature is small at the first. It is the bud, the leaf, the stem, the branch, the trunk, the unfolding and developing process all the way; and a similar law controls and determines the conditions and habits of men. It is emphatically true with the habit of drinking; it begins with a little,— just a little now and then, — and he who takes it never dreams of going beyond the bounds of moderation. Mankind are wont to glory in their power of resistance, and they spurn the warning with indignation that possibly that "little" may weaken that power. A moderate indulgence can do them no harm, they think; and yet it is the way in which all drunkards are made. This first stage of intoxication is considered by some to be its worst phase. A physician of the present times, who has written upon "moderate drinking," as the "worst phase of intemperance," says that the most fearful consequences of this state is, "that it deprives a man of that calm reflection and sagacious foresight so essential to the correct performance of his duties in every relation of life. If the privation of reason is only partial, then the victim is not the same person he would be if in a natural condition, and a very large proportion of our public men are stunted and distorted in this way. The passions and emotions are more easily aroused, and are less under the control of the will.

"From this it will be perceived no man is safe after having drank one small glass. He is a changed man, and will say and do things that he would not say or do unaffected by liquor. He has parted with a portion of his discretion, which is among the higher attributes of his manhood. He has lost some of his reason. While his passions are more readily provoked, he has become weakened in the power of self-control. He is not only more inclined to do wrong, but is less liable to restrain himself from wrong doing. He has, therefore, undergone a very serious transformation; and if not ready for an evil deed, he is certainly more liable to be led into vice and crime. Such is the effect of the most moderate use of alcoholic beverages," and "in order to obtain a clear comprehension of the injury to the brain and nervous system, which is caused by one drink of any kind of liquor containing alcohol, we have only to suppose the effect or fuddle, however slight, to be as lasting as life itself; that Nature was not kind enough to relieve its victim, in due time, of the maudlin and perplexing burden; that there was no balm in Gilead for such a case, and no means under heaven by which he could become a sober man again. Could we conceive of a greater affliction, short of the entire wreck of reason, than a mortal thus doomed to carry in his blood and in his brain that one portion of alcohol, during all the days and nights of his earthly existence? Would not such a wretch cross the seas, and wander to the uttermost parts of the earth for his relief? Would he not sigh continually for deliverance, and long for sobriety or death? and if the intoxication of one glass would be such a horrible calamity, in case it was permanent and hopeless, it must *be equally bad while it lasts*."

People declaim loudly against the lower and baser forms of intoxication; but the same writer continues his statement by saying, that while these have been censured and paraded, "the evils of *moderate*-tippling, of themselves, and apart from all tendency to excess, have never been adequately depicted." "Extreme drunkenness," he says, "with all its pains and horrors, is a condition that carries with it a salutary disgust and a wholesome warning; it is, therefore, a blessed thing, compared with moderate drinking, in every light in which it can be viewed. It is a blessing to the drinker, because it punishes him for the violation of his moral and physical nature. It makes him stupid, and unable to do the mischief he would be more likely to do in a moderate state of intoxication. It presents a striking lesson to all, of some of the miseries inseparable from the drink fashion. The lowest class of drunkards would be ashamed to drink, if they were not sustained by the example of their more respectable and moderate associates; they would not be seen at a place where none but their own tribe were admitted; the liquor traffic is kept up by moderate drinkers; no human being could be found base enough to keep a den for the exclusive accommodation of sots. The sots are relieved of self-disgust by mixing themselves up with moderate drinkers as much as possible. If there could be no tippling without vulgar excess; if every man that uses alcohol as a drink would imbibe a sufficient quantity to make him beastly drunk every time he tasted it; if there were but two classes in the country — helpless sots and consistent teetotalers, our condition would be vastly better than it is now, and it would continue to improve rapidly. The sober class would increase and tho sots diminish, until this greatest of all evils would disappear. The second stage of drunkenness may be a sorer affliction to the individual and to his family; but the greatest calamities and the saddest disasters come from moderate, and not from immoderate intoxication. A man with a moderate quantity of alcohol in his brain will often be super-serviceable and over-officious in the transaction of business, and will be very apt to blunder; and the blunder may, owing to his position and the nature of his duties, be of such a character as to destroy the lives, property, and happiness of hundreds of his fellow-beings; whereas, if more deeply intoxicated, he would not attempt anything of the kind, and if he did he would be arrested in his temerity by others. His trust would be forfeited, his position lost, and his power to vex and trouble extensively would be gone The evil, of course, will be greatest where it affects the greatest and most influential minds. Such, if topers, must necessarily be moderate, because they move in a sphere from which the poor sot is excluded, and have charge of interests with which he is not permitted to meddle; and it is among these, the master spirits and controllers of human affairs, that alcohol does the most harm."

Could an effectual check be given to this habit of so-called moderation, would men of respectable standing cease to begin with the glass of occasional cheer, it would be comparatively easy to arrest this vice of the age. This has been called the "devil's railroad, with a steep downward grade to the depot of destruction;" and it is certain that the multitudes who throng the highway of intemperance, or, at least, most of them, took their first steps very moderately. The first glass, in thousands of instances, has been taken hesitatingly and shrinkingly; but the sense of shame and the power of resistance have been less with the second, and still less with the third, and so on until there is no more trace of pride or honor left.

In a volume compiled by E. C. Delevan, of New York, he narrates the following thrilling scene; and as it illustrates in a forcible manner the present phase of the subject, we give the story as he records it. The people of a certain town were gathered together to discuss the merits of the license question, and decide whether to authorize any one to deal out the article among them or not.

"The town had suffered greatly from the sale and use of intoxicating liquors. The leading influences were opposed to total abstinence. At the meeting, the clergyman, a deacon, and the physician were present, and were all in favor of continuing the custom of license, — all in favor of permitting a few men of *high moral character* to sell alcohol, — for they all agreed in the opinion that alcohol in moderation, when used as a beverage, was a good creature of God; and also, to restrict the sale or moderate use was an unjust interference with human liberty, and a reflection upon the benevolence of the Almighty. They all united in the belief that, in the use of alcohol as a beverage, *excess* alone was to be avoided. The feeling all appeared to be one way, when a single teetotaler, who was present by accident, but who had been a former resident of the town, begged leave to differ from the speakers who had preceded him. He entered into a history of the village from its early settlement; he called the attention of the assembly to the desolation moderate drinking had brought upon families and individuals; he pointed to the poorhouse, the prison-house, and the graveyard for its numerous victims; he urged the people, by every consideration of mercy, to let down the flood-gates, and prevent, as far as possible, the continued desolation of families by the moderate use of alcohol. But all would not do. The argument of the clergyman, the deacon, and the physician, backed by station, learning, and influence, were too much for the single teetotaler. No one arose to continue the discussion, or support him, and the president of the meeting was about to put the question, when all at once there arose from one corner of the room a miserable female. She was thinly clad, and her appearance indicated the utmost wretchedness, and that her mortal career was almost closed. After a moment of silence, and all eyes being fixed upon her, she stretched her attenuated form to its utmost height, then her long arms to their greatest length, and raising her voice to a shrill pitch, she called upon all to look at her.

"'Yes,' she said, 'look upon me, and *then* hear me. All that the last speaker has said relative to moderate drinking as being the father of all drunkenness, is all true. All practice, all experience declares its truth. All drinking of alcoholic poison as a beverage, in health, is *excess*. Look upon me. You all know me, or *once* did. You all know I was once the mistress of the best farm in this town. You all know, too, I once had one of the best, the most devoted of husbands. You all know I had five noble-hearted, industrious boys. Where are they now? Doctor, where are they now? You all know. You all know they lie in a row, side by side, in yonder churchyard; all, every one of them, filling the drunkard's grave! They were all taught to believe that moderate drinking was safe, — excess alone ought to be avoided; and *they never acknowledged excess*. They quoted *you*, and *you*, and *you* — pointing with her shred of a finger to the priest, deacon, and doctor — as authority. They thought themselves safe under such teachers. But I saw the gradual change coming over my family and prospects with dismay and horror; I felt we were all to be overwhelmed in one common ruin. I tried to ward off the blow; I tried to break the spell — the delusive spell — in which the idea of the benefits of moderate drinking had involved my husband and sons. I begged, I prayed; but the odds were greatly against me. The priest said the poison that was destroying my husband and boys was a good creature of God; the deacon (who sits under the pulpit there, and who took our farm to pay his rum bills) sold them the poison; the physician said that a little was good, and *excess* ought to be avoided. My poor husband and my dear boys fell into the snare, and, one after another, were conveyed to the dishonored grave of the drunkard. Now look at me again. You probably see me for the last time; my sand has almost run. I have dragged my exhausted frame from my present abode, your *poorhouse*, to warn you *all* — to warn you, deacon! — to warn you, false teacher of God's word,' — and with her arms high flung, and her tall form stretched to its utmost, and her voice raised to an unearthly pitch, she exclaimed, — 'I shall soon stand before the judgment seat of God; I shall meet you there, ye false *guides*, and be a swift witness against you all.'

"The miserable female vanished; a dead silence pervaded the assembly: the priest, deacon, and physician hung their heads. The president of the meeting put the question, 'Shall we have any more licenses to sell alcoholic poisons, to be drank as a beverage?' The response was unanimous, 'No!' and such would be the verdict of all Christendom, could they unitedly listen to similar tales of suffering and woe, that are written, if not on the visible page, on the sensitive tablets of the human heart, in letters of fire." These stories have almost invariably the same beginning. It is little by little. A few sands washed from the base of a strong dike may seem as nothing; but a little more, and this repeated, may send the rushing waters on beyond control; and so it is a glass here, and a glass there, that creates the remorseless craving which knows no bounds. But who offers that glass? and what is it? Let the next chapter tell.

CHAPTER VI.

WHAT IS THE STIMULANT

CLEOPATRA. — THE FIRST STEP. — SOCIAL PARTY. — NEW YEAR'S CUSTOM. — THE CREEK INDIAN. —ANECDOTE OF HENRY WILSON. — CHEMICAL TESTS. — PORT AND MADEIRA, SO CALLED. — WINE DEALER'S CONFESSION. — PROF. BUTLER'S TESTIMONY. — HORACE GREELEY'S. VOICE FROM PERSIA. — DR. HOLLAND. — CALIFORNIAN IDEAS. — BIBLE STAND-POINT.

IT is said of the beautiful, accomplished, and queenly Cleopatra that she dissolved a precious gem in a glass, and drank it, at one of her royal banquets, that she might show her proud retinue of attendants there was nothing too dear and costly to minister to the pleasure and contribute to the aggrandizement of one of her rank and position. Strange and foolish as this may seem, it is, nevertheless, less strange and less foolish than the conduct of those who press the glass to their lips, into which they throw ambition, honor, reputation, and every good that makes life a joy and a blessing. This is to throw away every possibility and privilege of manhood, and make the whole history a long and significant blank which should be a record of virtuous and worthy deeds. It is none too easy to build up a high and noble character, amid the difficulties and allurements of a wayward world, if the best conditions of being are regarded; but it is utterly impossible when one is under the dominion of decidedly adverse influences. To trace these to their source, in connection with this subject, is to find them hid in the bosom of the family.

"Tell me," said a gentleman to one who had become a miserable, wretched inebriate, in the days of comparative youth, —"tell me, where and what was it that first led you into this course of intemperance?"

"It was wine at my father's table, sir," replied the doomed and unhappy man. "Before I left the shelter of the paternal roof, I had learned to love the drink that has been my ruin. The first drop that ever passed my lips was handed to me by my now broken-hearted mother."

Doubtless many would make a similar confession, if pressed with the same inquiry. There are a great many homes in the land where a choice collection of spirits is considered an indispensable part of their domestic economy. The amount of these determines, in great measure, their wealth and standing. They form a part of the regular furnishing of the table, and the strength and qualities of these various compounds are the subject of enthusiastic comment among the honored guests of the household. The younger and unsuspecting members grow familiar with the thing, and the practice may not be associated in their minds with anything that is low. This is the beginning of the downward course of many. The habitual use of cider and wine at the table has led thousands into the open sea of intemperance. They go out into the broader theatre of public life, where temptation is thicker and fiercer, — where companions of kindred tastes and habits are only too glad to excuse themselves by seducing others, — and they fall an easy prey to the tempter. The social party presents its attractions, and there, too, sparkling wine is considered an indispensable requisite for the occasion. The ruby cup goes the rounds, and the unnatural light is kindled in the eye, an unwonted ardor is imparted to conversation, and the general hilarity betokens the power of that which is upon them. These things become rooted in the social system until they are a prevalent evil. The customs of fashionable society stamp them with a dignity and importance which the majority come to feel they must imitate, or forfeit their claims to respectable standing, not dreaming that the imitation threatens those claims more disastrously than the neglect of them could possibly do.

It has been customary, in years past, for the fashionable circles of the city, and of the country too, to open their doors on the first day of the new year, and extend the hospitalities of their homes to their numerous friends. Men from every profession turn out to do honor to the reception of many a distinguished and generous hostess; and congratulations are exchanged over the dainty wine-cup very politely, and sometimes, it may be, heartily. This is repeated again and again through the day, here and there a little, until they seek their rooms at night flushed, excited, dispirited beings, more inclined to drown their discomfort in a fresh draught than to seek to free themselves from it by a total refrain. In a recent discussion of a certain committee among the officials at Washington, one of the honored disputants thus spoke: —

"I heard last night a statement from one of the Creek Indians. There the United States has a law with a severe penalty for selling liquor to the Indians. This man, well educated, of five and thirty years of age, stated that in all their community he scarcely saw a drunken man; that once in a while, as they went down on the line of the railroad, one would be tempted, but, as a general rule, there was no part of their whole territory where a drop of intoxicating liquor could be found; and that, if a man brought in a keg or bottle of it, and it could be found, it was immediately destroyed. And

YOUNG LADY OFFERING HER LOVER WINE.

THE RESULT.

this man stood up as a specimen of a savage who had grown up without the use of intoxicating drinks, for he said, —

"'To this hour, there has never a drop of alcoholic drink passed my lips, and I never was really tempted but once in my life, and that was in the city of New York, three years ago, when our delegation was taken there. We were invited to a gentleman's house and into his parlor, and the lady of the house passed round a waiter with wine-glasses, and came to me and offered me a glass of wine, and I for the moment was tempted.' It was a lady in an elegant house in New York. 'But,' said he, 'I thanked her, and said I would prefer a glass of water.'"

Had all our young men the moral courage of the Indian, there would be little to fear, but most of them are unwilling to offend the fair lady who so graciously offers it, though their judgment condemns the custom, and they know it is tightening the chains that bind them to a fearful habit. Sad and humiliating as the confession may be, it is too true that ladies are responsible for many a poor drunkard's beginning. They do it in this way, under the cover of politeness and the sanction of fashion. Young ladies and gentlemen mingle together in rides and various amusements, and, rather than wound the sensitive gallantry of their attendants, the girls will sip of the wine, and thus strengthen the propensity in their brothers and friends.

A party of college students invited some young ladies to take a ride to a neighboring town for an evening's enjoyment. The contents of the flowing bowl were deemed necessary to promote it. They all drank of it, and before they could reach home their jollity attracted the attention and merited the rebuke of every lover of sobriety in their way.

"O thou invisible spirit of wine! if thou hast no name to be known by, let us call thee—Devil." So sang Shakspeare long ago; and let any one take his stand-point from American social life and manners, he would utter the same exclamation with equal emphasis now. The beverage has a large place at the tables of the wealthy, and no entertainment can be given in honor of distinguished personages or occasions but the toasts and sentiments must find their point in the cheery wine. It speaks but poorly for the moral courage of men that they will not frown upon the custom, when they know it to be injurious to the highest interests of those concerned. There is only now and then one who is strong enough to stand up, and openly adhere to his convictions of right, when the temptations of these flattering circumstances surround him. Henry Wilson, of Massachusetts, and the Vice-President of the nation, was such a man, and the people honor him for the integrity of his principles, and the manliness and decision of his course at the beginning. Twenty years ago he went to Washington with a petition to Congress from the people of his native state. Although comparatively young, his rising fame had singled him out as one eminently fitted for the important commission. While there, he received an invitation to dine with John Quincy Adams. His name had long been associated with the highest offices in the country, and it was no small honor to the newly-fledged statesman to be counted worthy of a place among the established dignitaries of the land. He had been poor, and was then a mechanic in moderate circumstances, and altogether unused to the ways and appearances of official dignity and style, and his name and place he had yet to win. Great men sat at the table—the greatest in the land; and should not the youthful aspirant for political distinction imitate the example of his superiors? The trying moment came when Mr. Adams extended to him the invitation, —

"Will you drink a glass of wine with me, sir?"

Temperance was one of the acknowledged virtues of the young man. He had planted himself firmly against everything that could intoxicate. But the eyes of many greater than he were upon him, and would it be best to risk his reputation upon so small a thing as the refusal of a glass of wine? It was not easy to decline such a request from his venerable host. Those about him, older and in some respects much wiser than himself, drank, and it all conspired to produce embarrassment; but amid his blushes and hesitation his manhood asserted itself, and he replied, —

"Sir, I never take wine."

It has been said that Massachusetts heard that answer, and set him down for a trusty servant forever after. Whatever influence the act may have had upon the brilliant assemblage at the time, it has found its place among the incidents of history, and made his name, together with the subsequent consistency of his conduct in this direction, a power to the cause of temperance everywhere.

There are those who think that wine is the least objectionable of all the so-called exhilarating drinks; that it is the purest, the most healthful and innocent beverage, aside from that which nature itself has provided, that can be had. They feel comparatively safe in its indulgence. But who does not know that, in these days of modern avarice, there is scarcely anything left that is pure? Addison told us long ago of philosophers who were daily employed in the transmutation of liquors, and, "by the power of magical drugs and incantations, raising, under the streets of London, the choicest products of the hills and valleys of France, squeezing claret out of the sloe, and drawing champagne out of an apple." The present system of adulteration leaves nothing untouched. Quoting from one having authority, he says, —

"Who does not know that nine tenths of the wine consumed is but brandy, or something worse, under another name? In France and other European countries are extensive establishments for the *manufacture* of all the choicest varieties of wines; and you may as well know that, when you have paid a round price for wines *imported direct from the wine-growing districts* and in *original packages*, you are yet most likely paying for what never smelt a grape. I do not say," he continues, "that there are *no* pure wines; but I say that adulteration is the law, and purity the exception, and that wines are so skilfully 'doctored' with well-selected drugs as to escape even chemical tests as to their quality. An able writer goes so far as to affirm that 'wine has become a myth, a shadow, a very Eurydice of life. *There is no such thing, we verily believe, as honest grape-juice wine remaining; nothing but a vile compound of poisonous drugs and impurely obtained alcohol.* And all our beautiful Anacreontics are merely fables, like the rest; for wine hath died out from the world, and the *laboratory is now the vineyard.*'"

It is said "that there is perhaps nearly a hundred times as much Port wine (so called from Oporto) sold and drank as can be made from all the grapes raised in the region of Oporto, including the whole Douro Valley." And another writer declares that, "if the Douro River were a thousand miles long, instead of only sixty, it could not furnish grapes enough to make all this ocean of 'Port' wine. The whole world of fashionable topers, invalids, and imbeciles are drinking wine made out of the little handful of grapes grown on the banks of a small creek in Portugal! The miracle of feeding five thousand souls from 'five loaves and a few small fishes,'" he says, "is as nothing compared to this."

This is only one feature of the case, only one branch of the trade, and that foreign. But our own country is pronounced the largest "wine-growing district" in the world! It is asserted that "here are furnished a *million times* more baskets of champagne (with exact imitation of foreign brands) than are put up of the pure juice in all the champagne districts of Europe! By passing the oil of whiskey through carbon, a Madeira is made, at a profit of five hundred per cent., which few can tell from the genuine." Madeira grows thirty thousand barrels of wine yearly, while America alone boasts of the annual consumption of fifty thousand barrels of the same article. These wines are produced at a very trifling cost by the use of neutral spirits, or even with "whiskey, vinegar, sulphuric acid, beet-root, alum, lead, logwood, potash, cider, copperas, and the like." Of these and other wines, the city of New York manufactures to the value of eight million dollars every year, and these go out to be employed largely in the mere formation of intemperate habits, that by and by must and will have something stronger for their support.

"It is a notorious fact," says one of the daily journals, "that even the California champagnes have been driven from the market by 'doctored wines,' or have themselves been 'doctored' to meet the popular demand."

A wine dealer, in the bitterness of his penitential sorrow, made the acknowledgment, on his death-bed, that "he had often seen his customers wasting away around him, poisoned by that he had meted out to them; and *that same wine*, which was the cause of their decline, was often prescribed by their physicians as a means of their recovery."

There is a lamentable ignorance among the mass of the people upon this whole subject. If, by any enlightening process whatever, the scales can be made to fall from their eyes, a brighter and better condition of things will be inaugurated, unless men persistently take the position which compels us to say, "None are so blind as those that *will* not see."

The voice of antiquity is clear and distinct upon this question. Far back in the history of the early ages, long before the birth of Christ, a Chinese emperor declared, "in a solemn assembly of states, that wine must be forbidden to his subjects, because it was the fruitful source of evil, and all manner of social disturbance." In the year 600, Mohammed prohibited the use of wine among his followers, "because it was the prolific cause of vice and crime." And Plato approved "the Carthaginian law that *no sort of wine* be drunk in the camp, nor anything save water," by reason of its inevitable tendency to produce drunkenness and insubordination. The laws of Sparta were made rigid on this point, and the most stringent measures resorted to, to put an end to the drinking of wine. "Slaves were made drunk, and *exhibited in this condition to youth*, in order to inspire them with abhorrence of this filthy vice."

It is to be remembered that all this comes down to us from centuries when the people were vastly better fitted to give decided issue upon the power of wine to promote or hinder temperance, for to them even the art of distillation was unknown.

There has been a widely-spread notion that native wine is not intoxicating in its nature; that in wine-producing countries, where it was used as a common and almost exclusive beverage, intemperance was comparatively unknown. But the testimony of modern travellers has nearly exploded the theory. If it be not so apparent to the American as he is passing through these countries, it is because these are shut out from the higher and better conditioned class; and in all the public means of conveyance, and in all the circumstances in which he is naturally thrown, he does not come in contact with this phase of life. Prof. Butler lived several years in Europe, both in city and country, and was therefore better qualified to give a correct judgment of the matter than those who formed their impressions from a hasty transit through the region.

"We have heard Americans assert," he says, "that there is no drunkenness in any country where wine takes the place of stronger liquors. Now, we have sifted this matter thoroughly, both in Italy and Switzerland, and are bound to deny the truth of this statement. Why is it, then, that so little drunkenness is seen by strangers? Because Italian laborers rarely begin their potations until the day's work is over. They carouse from about nightfall until midnight, when, money spent or credit exhausted, they reel home, and the cries and groans of wives and children soon tell of the fury and brutality which mark the drunkard the world over. Thinking it probable that brandy did most of the mischief, I inquired as to this point. In every case, my questions caused surprise, and the answers were always the same: 'No, no! it is wine — always wine.'"

Rev. E. S. Lacy, of San Francisco, spent several months in Switzerland, and thus writes: —

"I have just spent six months in a country place, where the people do nothing but work in the vineyards; where wine is cheap and pure, and far more the beverage of the laboring classes than water; where none think of making a dinner without a bottle of wine; where all the scenery is of the most elevating and ennobling character. *Here more intoxication was obvious than in any other place it was ever my lot to live in.* On holidays and festal occasions, you might suppose all the male population drunk, so great are the numbers in this deranged and beastly condition. On Sunday afternoons young men go shouting along the streets. Intelligent Germans inform me that this is the great social evil of their country, a place where wine, if not very cheap, is never adulterated, and where great quantities of it are drunk."

Louis Philippe, the King of France, in an interview with one of our own countrymen in 1838, described the intemperance of his people as very great, and declared that wine was its producing cause.

The Duke of Orleans made the statement to Mr. Delavan, the person referred to, and also said that, in those districts where the most wine was made, there was the greatest wretchedness, and the most frequent appeals to government for aid."

When Horace Greeley was travelling in France, he made these observations from her gay capital: —

"Wine *will* intoxicate — *does* intoxicate. That there are confirmed drunkards in Paris and throughout France is notorious and undeniable. You can hardly open a French newspaper that does not contain some account of a robbery perpetrated upon some person stupefied by over-drinking; a police case growing out of a quarrel over the wine-cup; or a culprit, when asked to say why the sentence of the law should not be pronounced against him, reply, 'I was drunk when this happened, and know nothing of the matter.' That journeymen are commonly less fitted for and less inclined to work on Monday than on other days of the week, is as notorious here as it ever was in any rum-drinking city that could be named."

The testimony of other travellers, equally prominent

and reliable, all concur in establishing the same conclusion. We give but one more observation with reference to the French people, and that is from the pen of Charles Dickens: —

"The wine-shops are the colleges and chapels of the poor in France. History, morals, politics, jurisprudence, and literature, in iniquitous forms, are all taught in these colleges and chapels, where professors of evil continually deliver those lessons, and where hymns are sung nightly to the demons of demoralization. In these haunts of the poor, theft is taught as the morality of property, falsehood as speech, and assassination as the justice of the people. It is in the wine shop the cabman is taught to think it heroic to shoot the middle-class man who disputes his fare. It is in the wine shop the workman is taught to admire the man who stabs his faithless mistress. It is in the wine shop the doom is pronounced of the employer who lowers the pay of the employed. The wine shops breed, in a physical atmosphere of malaria and a moral pestilence of envy and vengeance, the men of crime and revolution. Hunger is proverbially a bad counsellor, but drink is worse."

A voice comes to us from Persian lands, in the testimony of those who have lived and labored there, and are familiar with all the customs and manners of the native population. Mr. Labaree, who has long been a missionary in that land, writes to this country after this manner: —

"If I had any sentiments favorable to the moderate use of wine when I left America, my observations during the seven years I have resided in this paradise of vineyards have convinced me that the principle of total abstinence is the only safeguard against the great social and religious evils that flow from the practice of wine drinking."

Describing the scenes between vintage and Lent, he says, —

"As you might suppose, drunkenness in its various grades becomes too common to excite surprise. Priests apologize with the greatest coolness for irregularity of conduct by stating that they were, at the time, under the influence of wine.

"Carnival week, preceding Lent, is especially noted for the amount of wine consumed. The devotees of the bowl now give themselves up to the greatest excesses. Midnight orgies, low songs, and boisterous quarrels resound from almost every street. Multitudes, at other times moderate drinkers, are drawn almost irresistibly into this vortex of drunken revelry. A fellow-missionary tells me that on visiting, at the carnival season, last year, a large Christian village of eight or nine hundred inhabitants, he found, on inquiry, that from two to three hundred were drunk, and that some one was in similar condition in all but about twenty houses out of one hundred and thirty." And he adds, "There is scarcely a community to be found where the blighting influences of intemperance are not seen in families distressed and ruined, property squandered, character destroyed, and lives lost."

Dr. Holland sums up the whole thing when he writes, from the sunny land of the vine, his convictions upon this important subject. These ideas have been embodied in various forms into the temperance literature of the country; but they furnish so strong a declaration against the utility of domestic wine, and its power to diminish the evil of intemperance, we give it a place here.

"There is no question," he says, "that the people would be better, healthier, and happier, and much more prosperous, if there were not a vineyard in the canton.

We have been told in America — and I fully believed it — that, if a people could be supplied with a cheap wine, they would not get drunk; that the natural desire for some sort of stimulant would be gratified in a way that would be not only harmless to morals, but conducive to health. I am thoroughly undeceived. The people drink their cheap white wine here to drunkenness. A boozier set than hang around the multitudinous cafés here it would be hard to find in any American city; even here they enjoy the license of the Maine law. The grand difference in the drunkenness of an American and Swiss city is found in the fact that the man who has wine in him is good-natured, and the man who is equally charged with whiskey is a demon. There is no murdering, no fighting, no wrangling. The excitement is worked off in singing, shouting, and all sorts of insane jabber. Then the steady, old white-wine topers come into blossom. If you can imagine a cauliflower of the color of the ordinary red cabbage, you can achieve a very adequate conception of faces that are not uncommon in all this wine-growing region. So this question is settled in my mind. Cheap wine is not the cure of intemperance. The people here are just as intemperate as they are in America; and, what is more, there is no public sentiment that checks intemperance in the least. The wine is fed freely to children, and by all classes is regarded as a perfectly legitimate drink. Failing to find the solution of the temperance question in the Maine law, failing to perceive it in the various modes and movements of reform, I, with many others, have looked with hope to find it in a cheap and comparatively harmless wine; but, for one, I can look in this direction hopefully no longer. I firmly believe that the wines of Switzerland are of no use, except to keep out whiskey, and that the advantages of the wine over the whiskey are not very obvious. It is the testimony of the best men in Switzerland — those who have the highest good of the people at heart — that the increased growth of the grape has been steadily and correspondingly attended by the increase of drunkenness. They lament the planting of a new vineyard as we at home regret the opening of a new grog shop. They expect no good of it to anybody. They know, and deeply feel, that the whole wine-producing enterprise is charged with degradation for their country. A large amount of land in this canton of Vaud is surrendered to the cultivation of the grape; and, as the wine of Switzerland is never heard of out of Switzerland, it is plain that it is all drunk here. Indeed, I have been assured that the wine produced in this canton is drunk mainly in the canton itself. Now, from Villeneuve to Morges — a distance of twenty-five miles, as I guess somewhat at random — the entire lakeside, averaging half a mile in width, is a vineyard. One can say, with literal truth, that, throughout the entire territory I describe to you, no crop but grapes is grown. For the last three weeks, the whole working population, men and women, have been in these vineyards gathering the crop. The teams are employed in transporting the immensely large casks of new wine from the presses to the cellars of their owners, to the vaults of the owners who have purchased it, and to the railroad depot, for transportation to the storehouses of speculators in other quarters.

"There is an endeavor on the part of these people to throw a romantic interest around their vintage. The casks go through the streets with gay bouquets of flowers in their bung-holes; but, from what I have seen here of the effect of wine, the show is all a sorry farce.

"I was told, before leaving America, that I should be obliged to drink wine or beer in Europe. One good clerical friend assured me that I could not get through Great Britain safely without drinking beer. As I did not like beer, the prospect was not pleasant. Indeed, I felt about as badly discouraged as Brigham Young declares he did when the duty of polygamy was made known to him by heavenly revelation. Well, I did not drink beer, and I got through Great Britain very comfortably indeed. None of my party drank beer, and all survived, not only, but improved, upon cold water — the terribly poisonous water of Great Britain! In Paris I took the ordinary red wine. In Switzerland I continued it with great moderation, until I was thoroughly satisfied that every glass I drank damaged not only my health, but my comfort. Now I drink no wine at all; and that member of my party who has drank nothing but water from the time of leaving America, has experienced not one particle of inconvenience from the practice. We have all concluded that wine-drinking in Europe is just as unnecessary as in America, and that there was never a greater mistake than the supposition that alcohol in any form is necessary as a daily beverage for any man or woman."

What is true with reference to the subject is equally true in our own land. A voice comes to us from the sunny climes of the grape in our own country, testifying to the same thing. At a state convention of the friends of temperance in San Francisco, in 1866, the following resolution was adopted: —

"*Resolved*, That we consider the project of banishing intemperance from California by introducing the general use of wine as a beverage, to be a delusion and a snare. Even were it possible to exclude ardent spirits, and substitute the fermented juice of the grape, there is no reason to look for any other results than followed in the ages of antiquity, when wine was the only intoxicating beverage, and when the drunkenness of wine-drinking nations provoked the wrath of God, and the denunciations of Holy Writ."

Then and there they denounced the manufacture of wine "as destructive to the highest political and religious interests of the commonwealth."

Said the Rev. Dr. Stone, —

"I had entertained a sort of hope that the manufacture of pure wines, and their introduction into general use, would crowd out the gross and strong liquors, and diminish intemperance. *I am now fully convinced that this hope was groundless and delusive.* It is in evidence that full two thirds of all the wine is converted by the manufacturers into brandy. It also appears that in the wine-growing districts intemperance is on the increase, extending even to the youth of both sexes. *There is no way but to take ground against the production of grapes for all such manufacture.* This touches a large and growing pecuniary interest, and will provoke strenuous opposition; *but we must save this state, if it can be done, from such investment of capital and labor, and from the unavoidable result of drunkenness, profligacy, and crime.*"

An editor of a California paper thus writes: —

"Through some parts of these mountains, as well as in the valleys, there is arising one species of production fraught with dire evil to the producers and the country. It is that of wine-making. Already wine has become as cheap as milk, and is as freely drank, till many once sober men are growing habitually intoxicated. In one wine-growing neighborhood, we are told that young girls seventeen years of age reeled through the streets under the intoxication of pure California wine. Men once of worth now are, through wine, lost to society, and becoming a fear and disgrace to their families. One leading man enumerated to us five of his acquaintances who, once noble men, are now to be called drunkards through wine. Many of the temperance men who followed the wine-growing delusion are now returning to their proper senses. We know of some whose sons are drunkards; of others who have fallen victims themselves to the curse of appetite. We are not romancing in these statements; we know whereof we affirm, and can name not a few who were forced to choose between the alternatives of a drunken family or an abandonment of the wine business. One of these related to us personally this fact in these words: 'Myself and my whole family were fast becoming drunkards upon our wine; and the daily quantity drunk by each increased so rapidly as to threaten to consume the profits of the business.'"

Notwithstanding this and a host of similar testimony, there are those who yet fail to be convinced, and fly from it all to the shadow of Holy Writ, thinking that there they are shielded from the attacks of the would-be temperance reformer, who would rob them, as they think, of their cherished pleasures. Although they be confronted with the declaration there that "wine is a mocker," they pass that by, to linger at the marriage feast in Cana, whence an incontestable argument in their favor is supposed to be drawn. If miraculous agency was deemed worthy to supply the deficiency on this cheerful occasion by the highest of all authority, then was it not unquestionably a good thing? There are elaborate and learned discussions by men of reputation and talent to prove that the wines used on this and other solemn occasions were not fermented wines at all; that, when Christ used it as a significant emblem at the last touching memorial with his disciples, it was the simple "fruit of the vine," without any intoxicating element at all. We propose not to enlarge here upon this topic. There is something in the idea that "the word 'wine' occurs in the Bible two hundred and sixty-one times. One hundred and twenty-one times it contains warnings; seventy-one times it contains warnings and reproofs; twelve times it denounces it as poisonous and venomous; and five times it totally prohibits it." It sums up the whole thing in one broad and sweeping assertion — "No drunkard shall enter the kingdom of heaven."

We have dwelt thus long upon wine and its influence because a love for the weaker leads to the stronger — because here the first downward step is so often taken in the path that leads, in the end, to disaster and ruin. Dash the wine cup, and you save multitudes.

CHAPTER VII.

ALE AND BEER.

MANKIND SEEK SELF-GRATIFICATION. — WILL BEER INTOXICATE? — "LOST OR STOLEN." — BEER OF GERMAN ORIGIN. — THE BEER-LOVING NEIGHBOR. — "THE LITTLE THING." — BEER BILL IN ENGLAND. — DUKE OF WELLINGTON. — FRUIT OF INDULGENCE. — BEER-BREWERS' CONVICTION.

MANKIND have long been seeking "the philosopher's stone," that should turn everything into "gold." They have been trying to find something that would make ordinary hard things in their way lighter, easier, and more fanciful; something that would meet all their wants and passions, their desires and appetites, so as to cause less trouble to conscience, and preserve them from the haunting conviction that they were sacrificing their manhood to a forbidden indulgence. So, after this manner, they have been trying to persuade themselves that the milder form of stimulant might minister to their craving necessities, and yet keep them in the path of safety, and expose them to less censure; for before the faculties are benumbed by artificial means, the good opinion of fellow-men is a strong incentive to action. It is to be doubted if man experiences keener pangs than those which come to him in the first knowledge that he has forfeited the esteem of those about him by the open committal of that which they denounce. For fear of this the man who loves stimulating drink will hesitate, will carefully and cautiously enter the secret place, and drop his head and avert his gaze if he thinks there is any danger of recognition from those whom he would have remain in ignorance of his deed. For this reason, men who would not be seen drinking a glass of brandy will unhesitatingly take the foaming beer, and think they have done a light thing; but observation, as well as the conclusions of science, fully demonstrate the folly of those who imagine that ale and beer are among the wholesome and inoffensive drinks. Like many other inconsistent questioners, they go to work to prove the question, "Will lager beer intoxicate?" when experience, observation, and testimony have decided it beyond controversy. "As well ask me if two and two make four," says one. It is true that the percentage of alcohol in this is smaller, by far, than in most other compositions of the kind, and it takes larger quantities to insure intoxication; but nevertheless the spirit is there, and does its work. A short time since the following striking paragraph appeared in print: —

"LOST OR STOLEN.

"Through the agency of villains, under the disguise of friends, the undersigned has lost within the few past years the following items of property, viz.: —

An unencumbered estate;
A vigorous constitution;
A fair moral character;
A good standing in society;
An active, healthful conscience.

Also, at the same time, or soon after, the affection of a wife, of children and friends. The miscreants who have thus robbed me are members of one family. Their names are Rum, Gin, Brandy, Wine, and Ale. Another base fellow, a recent emigrant from Germany, named *Lager*, it is supposed had a hand in the robbery, as he is much in the company of the above-named brotherhood of thieves, and appears to be of kindred character. The villains are still lurking in the city. Whoever will apprehend them and bring the culprits to justice shall receive the thanks of those most interested, and a cup of cold water."

This beer is a drink of German origin, the saloon for its vending a distinguishing characteristic of their country. They are fitted up in fine style, and the proprietors allure a crowd of customers by the attractions of music, by spreading tables with tempting luxuries, and providing for every form of gay festivity. Hither the people resort continually, and on the Sabbath, men, women, and children flock to these scenes of hilarity, and may be seen, each with their glass of beer, in the various stages of excitement which the drink is calculated to produce. Among the things that have come to us through the influence of German immigration is the re-production of this same custom. Wherever a German settlement is found, the sign of beer is prominent. They take the brewery with them wherever they go, and it is heralded on the corners of all the streets. There they act over and over again the scenes of their fatherland; and they who know anything about it know that the end thereof is riot and confusion. A beer-drinker is nothing less than an intemperate man. His appearance indicates the same marks of dissipation as others. There is the same bloated and disfigured aspect; the look of the face degenerates into the same sensual expression as is written there by stronger mixtures. It may be slower in doing its work, but it is, nevertheless, essentially the same. Because of its slow working, many mistake its character altogether, and the keg of beer finds its way, regularly, into many families that would scorn the idea of bearing anything else but a reputation for temperance. Those in the lower walks of life, who drink largely and constantly, exhibit the same disposition that the intoxicated man always does. A neighbor of the writer was addicted to the habit of drinking, and it was almost always confined to *lager beer*. The contents of a beer cask would suffice but for a day or two, and at the times of these inordinate indulgences, he was in the lowest depths of intoxication. Morose in his family, when in his sober moments he was remarkably kind; neglectful of his business, when otherwise he was industrious — and altogether brutish and insensible. The glass of ale and the draught of beer, prescribed for health, and drank until it is considered a daily necessity, have kindled an irresistible appetite with a great many — an appetite the insatiable cravings of which could not be met without something far stronger; and that stronger potion has unmanned the individual and destroyed the man. A clergyman once remarked, "One of the smartest young men we ever raised in our place fell out of the midst of his college course a drunkard. Why? He took lager beer. Rank, pride, education, elevated society, ambition, and religious influences, — every motive that could lead him to refrain, — held back the young man;" "and who," he says, "shall measure the power of that passion for drink which ruined him?"

"A glass of ale is a 'little thing,' a 'small affair,'" says John B. Gough, that mighty worker in the cause of temperance; "but I care not what it is holds a man, so long as he is held by it." "Some men," he says, "play with this 'little thing' until they are in the position of the poor fellow outside the lines, when he called out, "I've got a prisoner." "Bring him in." "He won't come." "Well, then, you had better come in without him." "He won't let me."

A certain man had a son who became so addicted to the frequent use of the cup, that it threatened to hold him fast in its slavish chains; for there is that beneath the foaming surface that is like unto a binding fetter to

GERMAN BEER GARDEN—SUNDAY ENTERTAINMENT.

the body and soul of every man who imbibes so freely. Awaking to the consciousness of his condition, he resolved to begin the work of reformation, and for eighteen months he adhered to his resolution, and his friends exulted in the hope that he was safe. Happening one day to be at a public house, where he saw a clergyman call for a glass of beer, the sleeping demon within him awoke, and he said to himself, "If he can take a glass of beer, why cannot I?" With that he did take, and the flood-gates were open — the power of resistance was gone. He took another, and another, until hope and effort, pride and ambition, died out, and he became a miserable sot, and his death was the death of the drunkard.

The same arguments are urged with reference to beer that have been urged in connection with wine. Many have supposed that it would lighten the ravages of intemperance; that it would diminish its sad results a thousand fold, because its quality and nature were less baneful. The English Parliament enacted what was termed "the beer bill," on this assumption, in 1830. Some of the strongest minds of the realm supported the measure, with the avowed conviction that it would furnish the people with a "wholesome beverage," and "preserve their morals from contamination." After the passage of the bill, the Duke of Wellington declared it to be "a greater achievement than any of his military victories." But the result of its action was sad enough. In less than a year the strongest supporters of the measure were surprised by the sudden and general demoralization produced. Among others, the Rev. Sydney Smith had looked to the passing of the bill as one of great importance — an omen for good; but only two weeks after it came into effect, he wrote, "The new beer bill has begun its operations. *Everybody is drunk.* Those who are not singing are *sprawling*. The sovereign people are in a beastly state." Another writer declares, that, "from his own knowledge he could positively assert that these beer shops had made many who were previously sober and industrious now drunkards, and many mothers had also become tipplers."

Another argument of the beer supporters is, that its evolution from nourishing grains make it eminently conducive in repairing the waste of the human system, but Professor Chandler, of Columbia College, in subjecting the whole to a rigid chemical analysis, has dissipated this theory, and shown that the nutritive qualities of its distilled condition are meagre indeed.

So, in whatever light we look at it, from whatever point of observation we consider it, there remains nothing favorable to the adoption of beer as a favorite and wholesome beverage. All theories that tend to this crumble and fall before the tragic scenes of history and experiences. If any doubt it, let them visit the shops and the saloons where this liquid draught is constantly dealt out and consumed, and behold the invariable and inevitable tendency of the whole thing. Let them witness the bacchanalian revelry of those who tarry long at the beer, and then say, if they can, wherein lies the innocence and harmlessness of the drink. It is there that every low and debasing influence is at work; there that every low amusement is resorted to, and there the enginery of evil kept in motion — the fires kindled, and the flames fed by men whose baser passions are stirred to the unhallowed work by the unnatural pressure that is upon them. Then we feel like taking up the sentiment of the poet of the past, in another sense, and exclaiming, "O thou invisible spirit of 'beer,' had we no other name to call *thee* by, we should christen thee as the Bard of Avon baptized the spirit of wine long ago, and recognize in this the grim portrait of him who presides over the world of woe."

There is now and then a ray of hope that comes athwart the gloom. Some are awaking to the consideration of the consequences which the custom of beer drinking involves. A sensation has recently arisen, by the conviction and corresponding action of a prominent brewer in Newark, N. J. He was one of the largest and wealthiest dealers in the place, had been in the business twenty-five years, and amassed a fortune estimated at half a million. All through the city of New York his beer was in popular demand. A few weeks since, under the conviction of duty which pressed upon him, he abandoned the pursuit which had engrossed his mind for a quarter of a century; discharged those whom he had in his employ; and declared his work, in the ordinary direction, to be at an end. Thus he tells his story: "Three years ago I stopped drinking any kind of beer or liquor, and have not tasted a drop since. Latterly I began to think that it was inconsistent for me to make for others what I deemed hurtful to myself. When I finally came to the conclusion that my business was wrong, and that to continue in it would simply be to outrage my conscience, I promptly resolved to stop; and I have done it. I intend that this building, if used at all in future, must be devoted to other purposes. I resolved not to sell my business; I wanted it stopped. My action is not the result of religious excitement or conversion, but a conviction of what was my duty. I suppose that a good many Germans will take offence at what I have done; and I am very sorry. The brewers, too, will be offended; but, once convinced, as I am, that intemperance is the great curse of the world, I shall never again have anything to do with beer making. The Germans are sensitive on this question; but I guess, on second thought, they will admit my right to hold my own views; I certainly would not interfere with theirs.

Since getting out of the traffic, I have felt like a new man, — as though a load had been lifted from my conscience." Would similar resolutions be acted upon by those in like circumstances, and engaged in the same business, what burdens would be lifted from thousands of human hearts that now lie crushed and bleeding, with hope and gladness all gone out of them! Not only would those immediately concerned share in the delightful sense of relief, but the crowd of those more remote, over whom the rushing tide of woe has swept, would lift up their heads, and breathe more freely under the new condition. When conviction shall have taken a wider range, and duty a broader sweep, there will not be so many wagons passing through our streets, piled up with the casks which contain the elements of disease and death, and are suggestive of all manner of unpleasant things. Even now they are passing the window, bent on their sad mission — and where are the hearts and hands that are waiting to stay the blighting curse? Where are those who would stay the filling of the cup, ere it be lifted to the lips of those who wipe out every symptom of a healthy taste in draining the fiery contents?

The times demand that they lurk no more in their hiding-places, but come forth with courage and strength, and wage open war with the formidable tyrant that leadeth so many captive at his will.

CHAPTER VIII.

Rum and Brandy.

STEPPING DOWNWARD. — TEMPERANCE PILLARS DISREGARDED. — WIFE'S METHOD OF REFORM. — THREE STAGES OF DRINK. — ALCOHOLIC DERANGEMENT OF THE STOMACH — OF THE BLOOD. — THE INEBRIATE'S CONFESSION. — THE PHYSICIAN'S STORY. — RICH AND POOR ALIKE FALL. — WILKES BOOTH. — CASE OF DELIRIUM TREMENS. — THE MAN WHO THOUGHT HIMSELF SAFE. — THE MANIAC'S SHRIEK.

We read of "stepping heavenward," and as all the beautiful possibilities of such a course dawn upon us, everything that is good and true within us bows before it. We see how all the discipline of such a life tends to the exaltation of the soul; how all surrounding circumstances and attendant providences are so many refining processes to lift up and ennoble the heart; how the secret and mysterious working of the invisible good shines out through the eyes, and reveals itself in every line of the face, until we, too, discover the rounds of the ladder of light up which such are climbing, and which is lost in the depths of the blue ether beyond.

By the law of association we are borne upward, also. We trace the history of such ones with those feelings of intense satisfaction which we imagine the watchful guardians of the celestial world to feel when those whom they have been commissioned to "bear up," and minister unto, upon the earth, are obedient unto the heavenly vision, and wake to the harmonies of their angelic touch. But who shall turn from this to give an adequate description of the one *stepping downward* —

downward to the very brink of perdition, recklessly nearing the verge of remediless ruin, and all the while writing the direst prophecies for himself? Meantime, the shadows which precede coming events, are settling down into the "blackness of darkness" forever.

O, it is enough to make the angels weep, if they are ever permitted to look down from their abodes of celestial purity and blessedness, and behold the multitude who are stepping, yea, rushing on, in this broad highway of intemperance. To see those who should be reflecting the glory of their creation, wilfully blotting out every trace of that which divinity stamped upon them, and prostituting all their gifts before an unholy and unhallowed shrine, is enough to stir even heaven with pitiful indignation. There is no language strong enough to denounce the folly of such a course; and yet the sad truth is acted out a thousand times, over and over, every day and every year. We are so familiar with the recital of all this waste and perversion; so accustomed to the story of guilt and wretchedness — the wrongs and woes involved, that they too often fail to excite more than a sigh of commiseration, or, at most, the silent tear of pity. We have followed these unhappy beings while taking the first steps in their downward course, and we come now to the last station of their "Black Valley Railroad," just ahead of which is the Depot of Destruction, and beyond, the track is lost in the shadows of the Infernal. We have seen them begin thoughtlessly — take the first steps remorsefully and shrinkingly, and we have seen them grow gradually bold and defiant, until they have reached the abandonment of every worthy impulse, and provoked the fury of a tempest which they knew would leave them a wrecked and stranded thing on the shores of time, with scarce a ray of hope that they could ever again be restored or refitted for the position they had lost — if, indeed, they go not out of sight entirely.

This is the point where the strongest of alcoholic mixtures will alone suffice to meet the want; where the slow steps of the first grade have passed into the rapid strides of a steep declivity that knows no resistance. One by one the pillars of Temperance, against which he may have leaned in time past, have been swept away, and there remains nothing more for his support or his safety. He is impelled onward and downward by the momentum of his own deeds. Reason, Science, Revelation, and Experience are said to be the guide-boards in the way of every man, each pointing, with unerring finger, to the gate of the wise, and warning against the path of the destroyer; but what are all these, and what the evils to which they point to him, who is controlled by rum and brandy, and every sensibility stupefied thereby? What to him are the calm deductions of reason, when the proper functions of his judgment have no more play?

What to him are unfoldings of science when the faculties of perception have been dimmed and bleared until there is no more power of vision remaining? And what the monitory tones of revelation and experience, when conscience is deadened to every sound? when hope ceases to allure, and fear stirs no compunction? There seems no avenue by which the confirmed inebriate can be reached. His soul is effectually barred against all warning and entreaty. Now and then, it may be, there comes a lucid interval, when the memory of what is lost comes over the mind, and there comes a humiliating sense of the degradation that rum has occasioned, accompanied by a momentary desire to be free from the galling bondage. The right treatment, at such a time, doth sometimes work a change. "What brings you here, Mary?"

said a man to his wife, as she entered the saloon where he had been leaving his money and his mind. She had pondered the fact over and over, until, in her desperation, she resolved to risk the attempt of a daring deed, and follow him to his well-known haunt. "It is very lonesome at home," she replied, "and your business seldom allows you to be there." There was a touching look of grief on that face, a plaintive sorrow in her tone as she said, "To me there is no company like yours; and as you cannot come to me, I must come to you. I have a right to share your pleasures, as well as your sorrows."

"But to come to such a place as this!" expostulated the husband. "But no place can be improper where you are," said the poor, discouraged wife. "Whom God hath joined together, let not man put asunder." Taking up the glass of spirits which the keeper of the saloon had poured out for him, who had become his frequent customer, she raised it to her lips.

With a look of unutterable astonishment he exclaimed, "Surely you are not going to drink that?" "Why not?" said she; "you say that you drink to forget sorrow, and surely I have sorrows to forget." Her children stood by her side in all their wondering innocence, and she gave to them what their father had called the cup of blessing. "Woman! woman!" cried the father, in great excitement, "you are not going to give that stuff to the children?" "Why not? Can children have a better example than their father's? Is not what is good for him good for them also? It will put them to sleep, and they will forget they are cold and hungry;" and, resolutely holding the cup, she said, "Drink, my children; this is *fire*, and *bed*, and *food*, and *clothing*. Drink: you see how much good it does your father." It was enough. With seeming reluctance she suffered her husband to lead her home, and all that night all the powers of good and evil within him were struggling for the mastery. He thought of all that had brought him and his family to where they were; to what a height of anguish his devoted wife had risen to inspire her with daring for such an act; what depths of despair she must have fathomed ere she determined upon that first step — that dreadful, doubtful lesson. To have appropriated that one more glass, which she had snatched from his grasp, might have made it too late to comprehend and escape the situation. As it was, he resolved, if there was any help for him, on earth or in heaven, he would reform; and he did. The loving wife rejoiced in the success of her effort, and was wont to recall her first and last visit to the dram shop with a peculiar but melancholy pleasure.

There are different stages of alcoholic derangement, and the hopefulness of reform, and the ability to meet it, is somewhat in proportion to these. The first is a state of excitement, where the drink has had simply a mirth-producing effect, and he who is thus wrought upon feels that the world is jolly; that he can bid dull care be gone, and sing the hours away, regardless of any serious obligation or claim. Thousands drain the contents of the cup just for this reason, because it brings to them a blessed forgetfulness of what is imposed upon them in the various relations in life; and their straitened means and inefficient natures make them shrink from the necessary contest. Their duties to themselves and their families, their creditors and their country, are so many impelling motives to the indulgence of that which will hush these clamors, and send them into a world where none of these things are.

The last stage involves the loss of the mental and moral faculties so completely, that all the bright visions of happiness, which made life so radiant at the beginning, all pass away, and the person reels and falls under the general benumbing influence, without consideration, or appreciation of anything. This is the climax of the drunkard's condition. But there is yet an intermediate grade, where, perhaps, most of the crimes associated with intemperance come in. There is a point prior to the extreme mental and moral degradation of the last stage, when these faculties of being are not paralyzed or suspended, but are, nevertheless, so confused and bewildered, that they are not awake to actual results and conditions, and not beyond the power of action, and therefore are ready for the committal of any deed. Here comes in the overwhelming conviction that alcohol is a terrible enemy to the best interests of society; inasmuch as, by its influence, there remaineth no more fitness in man for the right performance of anything. We have seen, in the general physiological influence upon the human system, what detriment it works upon all the organs of the body, and how, by the operation of fixed laws, it extends itself to the mind, the social affections, and the moral sensibilities. But let us trace its inevitable workings more minutely, and observe the changes wrought by its introduction into the stomach. That organ, in its healthy state, as the first representation indicates, is slightly reddish, tinged with yellow, and the blood-vessels are invisible. Alcohol is taken, and these become enlarged and distended, though the stimulant be taken but moderately. Taken in larger quantities, "the inner coat of the stomach becomes corroded with small ulcers, which are covered with white crusts, with the margin of the ulcers elevated and ragged." Still later, when the man gives himself up to days and nights of habitual indulgence, there "is seen a high degree of inflammation extending over the surface, changing its color to deep red, and in some points exhibiting a livid appearance." From

EXTERNAL SYMPTOMS.

DIAGRAMS OF THE STOMACH IN VARIOUS CONDITIONS.

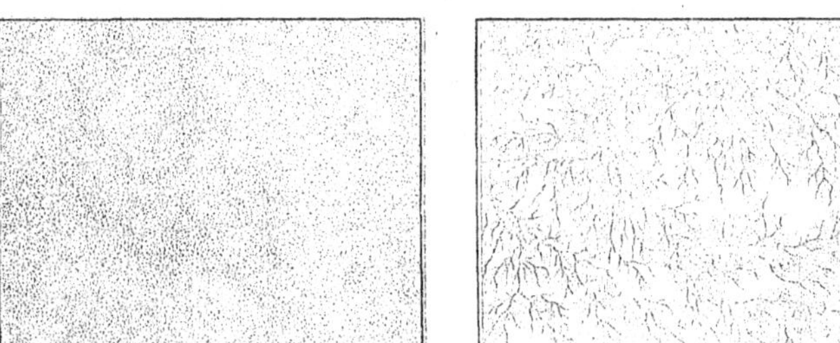

HEALTHFUL

MODERATE DRINKING

DRUNKARDS

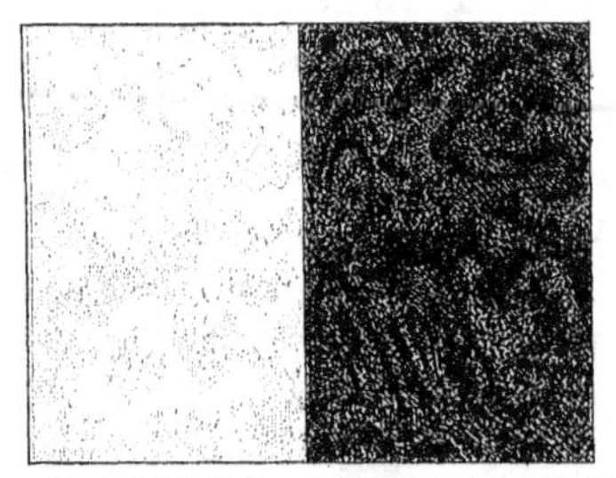

ULCEROUS

DELIRIUM TREMENS

this it goes on to the last fearful scenes, when delirium comes in to draw a veil over everything, and there is a dark-brown, flaky substance over the stomach, beneath which is traced an inflammation that seems but little less than an incipient state of mortification. "But there is still another principle," says Thomas Sewell, medical professor in Columbia College, "on which the use of alcohol predisposes the drunkard to disease and death." Not only is it the fearful cause of this wretched condition of the stomach, "it acts on the *blood*, impairs its vitality, deprives it of its red color, and thereby renders it unfit to stimulate the heart and other organs through which it circulates; unfit, also, to supply the materials for the different secretions, and to renovate the different tissues of the body, as well as to sustain the energy of the brain — offices which it can perform only while it retains the vermilion color and other arterial properties. The blood of the drunkard is several shades darker in its color than that of temperate persons, and also coagulates less readily and firmly, and is loaded with serum — appearances which indicate that it has exchanged its arterial properties for those of venous blood. This is the cause of the livid complexion of the inebriate, which so strongly marks him in the advanced stages of intemperance. Here, too, all the functions of his body are sluggish, irregular, and the whole system loses its tone and energy. If alcohol, when taken into the system, exhausts the vital principle of the solids, it destroys the vital principle of the blood also, and, if taken in large quantities, produces death; in which case the blood, as in death produced by lightning, by opium, or by violent and long-continued exertion, does not coagulate.

The inebriate having, by the habitual use of intoxicating drinks, exhausted, to a greater or less extent, the principle of excitability in the solids, the power of reaction, and the blood having become incapable of performing its offices also, he is alike predisposed to every disease, and rendered liable to the inroads of every invading foe. So far, therefore, from protecting the system against disease, intemperance ever constitutes one of its strongest predisposing causes. Superadded to this, whenever disease lays its grasp upon the drunkard, the powers of life being already enfeebled by the stimulus of alcohol, he sinks unexpectedly in the contest. Indeed, inebriation so enfeebles the powers of life, so modifies the character of disease, and so changes the operation of medical agents, that unless the young physician has studied thoroughly the constitution of the drunkard, he has but partially learned his profession, and is not fit for a practitioner of the present age."

True as the latter statement may be, it is, nevertheless, a most humiliating confession that the degeneracy of the times in this respect calls for so much of training and effort to meet the demands of its various aspects. We cannot deny that the individual and collective influences of this wide-spread traffic are sad and mighty ; that it is as though a vast army were all the while marching on to the other world, composed of those who thought, when they enlisted, they could regulate their part in the campaign to suit themselves, but found, all too late, they were deceived, and were under the dominion of a tyrant that would not let them go.

The vast majority of those who come under the power of rum and brandy are hopelessly beyond retreat. Deceived, deluded, and enslaved, such are held fast under bonds of iniquity. All the strongest principles of man's nature — fear, shame, ambition, and love — are powerless to restrain the slave of alcohol. All the terrors of human and divine law, and the love of an infinite redemption, are alike unavailing.

"If a bottle of brandy," said an inebriate, "stood at one hand, and the pit of hell yawned at the other, and I knew that I should be pushed in as soon as I took one glass, I could not refrain." There is nothing upon earth that produces such demoniac frenzy, nothing that makes one so utterly dead to every sentiment of humanity, so perfectly reckless of his destiny, for weal or for woe, in this world and the next. Dr. Jewett, in a tract entitled "Bound, and How," thus remarks: "'Why,' it is asked, 'does not the man know that he is thus sure to destroy his life, and that soon?' 'Certainly.' 'And does he not know, too, that he is afflicting terribly a most excellent family?' 'Yes.' 'And wasting his estate?' 'Yes.' 'And sacrificing a once enviable reputation?' 'Yes.' 'Why, then, does he not stop drinking?' 'Go and ask him; and if you can, by kind words and treatment, gain his confidence so that he will talk freely with you in relation to the matter, he will tell you he *cannot.* He used to declare that in his case there was no danger. 'I can drink,' he once said, 'or let it alone, as I choose.' He uses no such language now. Others may; but for him, he has received a terrible education. Perhaps it has come too late; but he now fully understands the power of his enemy, and the strength of the chain with which he has suffered himself to be bound. He has probably tested its strength a score, it may be a hundred times, striving to break it with the full purpose of his will, but as often he has failed; and now, perhaps, he has reached the last stage. It is one of despair. He now drowns reflection by drink, secures what relief he can from the torture of a disorganized nervous system by deep draughts of the poison, and awaits what to him seems the inevitable plunge."

The history of one such is essentially the history of all. From the moderate and occasional use of the lighter spirits he goes on to the frequent and inordinate use of the stronger, until, almost unconsciously, he is beyond recall. Says the author just cited, "At the conclusion of a lecture delivered in one of our Western States, a few years since, on this subject, a gentleman requested me to accompany him to his office. He was, as I learned, a physician in extensive practice, and a professor in a medical college. I complied with his request. On entering the office, he asked me to be seated, and, closing the door, took a seat near, and directly in front, and facing me. His eyes filled with tears, and every feature of his countenance, which was a noble one, was agitated with emotion, as he thus addressed me: 'Dr. Jewett, I am one of the unfortunate ones whose cases you have been considering this evening; and I have reason to fear that it is now too late for me to make any successful effort to break the chain which binds me.' 'Indeed,' said I, 'let us hope not. Have you made the effort, doctor?' 'Yes; and so far I have failed,' was his sad reply. He added, 'I have again and again resolved, with all the strength of my nature, that I would never drink another glass of intoxicating liquors, and yet I have drank again within twenty-four hours.' 'Why did you drink, doctor, after having resolved and promised yourself you would not?' I asked. Now I beg my readers to understand that I did not ask that question for information. I knew quite well why he drank again; but I wished to learn how he, a man of science, a teacher of medicine, would express the facts of the case. It was in substance as follows: 'Usually,' said he, 'when I have formed a resolution to abstain in future, it has been at the close of unusually hard drinking, when the folly, shame, and peril of the thing have come very vividly before my mind; and then I have said, and with emphasis, "This thing ends here. Not another glass, on any consideration, or under any circumstances. But I did not properly estimate the change that would come over me as the liquor, during the night, should be eliminated, or cast out of my system. In the morning I would be nerveless and wretched, and the first impulse would be to supply the system with the coveted article. But I had resolved that I would not, and so would keep about until the hour of breakfast. I would take a little food, perhaps, and a cup of coffee; but it did not meet the demands of my nervous system. I would feel a deadly *sinking* at the pit of the stomach; my hands were tremulous, as was, in fact, my whole body; I could not control or use my mind to any purpose, or scarcely my body; and my misery, increasing every hour and moment, would at last reach a point where it would seem quite impossible to endure it longer. It would seem, in fact, as if I was sinking into the very pit of hell; and in sheer desperation I have rushed to the nearest place of supply, and swallowed again the accursed thing that has brought all this upon me.' And he added, with an expression of despair in that noble countenance which I shall not soon forget, 'So I expect it will be, in the future, until I drop into the grave, as thousands of poor fellows have done before me.'"

And this is the inevitable tendency. From it there is no escape. There are but few who intend to come to this when they begin. They mistake the weakness of their own fallen nature, or the strength and power of that with which they have to do, or both, and enter the dangerous arena before they are aware of it. It not only takes the simple, uneducated, and poverty-stricken class, and makes them more so, but it embraces in its relentless grasp the higher — the refined, educated, wealthy, and most promising of young and old in the best circles. The most favored and intelligent fall into the snare with others less gifted, and it writes the same unmistakable characters upon all. There are no hieroglyphics here. The world knows the drunkard wherever he be. His looks tell it, his words betray it, and his steps reveal it to every passer-by, as plainly as though it were stamped in so many letters on his forehead. He is himself a walking sign, a perpetual monument to the enslaving power of strong drink. It would seem that the very sight of such men would be enough to warn the young against the folly of even tasting a drink that is producing such terrible consequences. There is nothing like the indifference that is manifested here, in the history of any other malady with which the world is conversant. Men will take every possible precaution, shrink from contact with an infectious disease, that lasts but a little, and may never prove mortal, and yet these same persons will pour down the brandy, when they know full well its debasing effect and deathly working, and see the living testimony to the truth all about them. They will look upon the most unprecedented acts of cruelty and injustice, and attempt to excuse and palliate the crimes, because those concerned were laboring under a temporary loss of sense by reason of too much alcohol. After Wilkes Booth had matured his plan to take the life of President Lincoln, there was still a depth in his graceless soul from whence came a shuddering at the guilt and horror of his premeditated scheme. He could not summon sufficient courage to strike the dreadful blow, and he rushed into a saloon, and cried, "Brandy! brandy!" Not until that irritating genius had effaced every shadow of a good impulse from his being, did he dare to aim the fatal ball at the defenceless head of one of the best men that ever filled the executive chair of the American nation.

It makes the brain wild, and sends it, a whirling, reel-

DELIRIUM TREMENS.

ing, giddy thing, beyond the bounds of reason, where it is subject to no law, and not a fit instrument for action in anything or anywhere ; and finally the culmination is reached in that most wretched of all conditions — delirium tremens. Probably there is nothing in all the world that brings to the spirit of man so full a realization of the horrors of the "bottomless pit," as that which comes in experiences like these. Abandoned of all that is good, and consigned, as it were, into the hands of him who only seeketh to destroy, he finds him laughing at his helplessness and mocking at his fear. Satan has no more powerful ally in the accomplishment of his work than brandy ; and when that has done all that it can do, he is satisfied, for the destructive work is complete. He lets loose his emissaries around the bed of such a one, and there is no escape from the hellish torture which well nigh rends soul and body. He gives them no welcome picture for the eyes to feast upon ; he lets them hear no sounds but the doleful skrieks of despair, or feel any change but the thickening of the darkness, and the fiercer burst of the storm.

"The room is full of devils," said one in this condition. "They are in my hair — pull them out ! They are laughing and grinning at me from the wall — send them away ! " And with the beaded perspiration on his brow, quivering and shrinking, he sought to screen himself from their gaze by hiding under the bed-clothes. But the foul spirit was there ; and starting and shrinking he exclaimed, "I'm rushing through the streets of hell — see them laugh on both sides of me ! What looks of scorn ! What derision ! I must leave it ; " and the hands of strong men only restrained the attempt to leap forth — to spring forward anywhere, so as only to be saved from the impending doom. There was no relief, whichever way he turned. "I am treading on millions of worms !

serpents are hissing and writhing under my feet — O, lift me up! O, take me away!" And so, with such an outlook, amid these fearful sights and sounds, he grappled long with these tormenting, taunting foes.

Strange, beyond all comprehension, that with a knowledge of these results any one will clutch the glass that binds him to such a fate; that he will throw himself into the embrace of all this fiendish maliciousness, and drink on, with the awful doom staring him in the face. Brandy writes a *cannot* upon every movement of the will; and one might as well undertake to escape from death, when the inexorable mandate has gone forth at the divine bidding, as to free himself from the utter helplessness of being, which an advanced stage of drunkenness induces.

"A few years since, a man of splendid abilities, when temporarily released from the power of the destroyer, gave to the world a touching and graphic sketch of his purposes and views in the following lines: —

'I've thrown the bowl aside;
For me no more shall flow
Its ruddy stream, its sparkling tide,
How bright soe'er it glow;
I've seen extended wide
Its devastating sway;
Seen reason yield its power to guide, —
I've cast the bowl away.'

He, however, miscalculated his strength, and, notwithstanding these just views and excellent purposes, he sleeps in the grave of the drunkard. So true is it, that when once the passion is excited, the appetite formed, however hard and long one may seek to subdue and put it away, it is at best but the lulling of the demon to a temporary sleep, and it is ready to spring forth and overpower him at the slightest provocation. There is no power of intellect, no brilliancy of attainment, no energy of character, or strength of purpose, that counts much of anything in this warfare. If the battle has been waging long, there is but little chance for anything but permanent defeat. Now and then the shouts of victory are heard over the rise of some low-fallen one ; but they are rare. Those who begin the mad career are almost sure to step down and still downward, until they reach the lowest depth. They may slide slowly, — perhaps almost imperceptibly at the first, — but the momentum is still constantly increasing, until at last, in the wanton recklessness of his thirst, he shrieks, In hell they never want for rum ; haste, drive me down,

> "Where rum is free; where revellers reign,
> And I can wear the drunkard's crown."

CHAPTER IX.

WHERE IS IT FOUND?

ALCOHOLIC MISERY CANNOT BE PAINTED. — LOVE OF GAIN THE PROPELLING MOTIVE. — LORD CHESTERFIELD'S REMARK. — RUM SELLER'S TREATMENT OF AN OLD MAN. — THE COUNTRY TAVERN. — HOMES AND HAUNTS OF THE DRUNKARD. — FIVE POINTS. — GROCERS' NETS. — FREE LUNCH HOUSES. — FIRST-CLASS HOTELS. — CLUB-ROOMS. — EUROPEAN AND MODERN STYLE. — POWER OF EXAMPLE.

THERE have been many discoveries made in the world by the perseverance and ingenuity of man, that have sent a thrill of joy and a tide of blessing over all the people; but could the full significance of the discovery have been comprehended when the process of distillation was first evoked, it might have been written, in letters of blood and characters of fire, from one end of heaven's broad arch to the other, "Woe unto the world because of this." It was bad enough that sin planted the image of woe around the habitations of men at the beginning, but this made it go deeper and rise higher; caused it to assume vastly greater proportions, and take on an aspect of fiercer malignity, than it otherwise would have done.

There are no calculations that can sum up the amount of human misery that has come to the world through the medium of this alcoholic agent. The delineations of pen and pencil have shadowed it forth in every conceivable light, but there is that remaining which can never be shadowed forth — never be written — that spends itself in the silent recesses of burdened, aching hearts — in sighs and tears that are not seen, except to an eye that is omniscient. We have seen what it can and will do. We have studied its nature and its effects, observed the different grades of its presentation, and followed the different stages of their action; and now the questions before us are, Who is responsible? Where is it found? And how is it that the habit of drinking is so universal?

In the first place, a love of gain is the absorbing passion of men. Whatever opens the way to this will be eagerly pursued. Questionable though the means may be, there are usually argumentative opiates enough to soothe the restless conscience, and keep it comfortably quiet, when its disturbing forces come in competition with the coveted acquisition. In the early history of the rum traffic, before its manufacture had come to be considered a degrading business, there was required no such education of this sort to bring him up to the work; but in these days of enlightened conviction, when the whole thing is pronounced morally wrong, it requires more daring in a man to stand up and declare that he will put gold in his coffers, though it be at the expense of everything that others hold dear. But the passion impels the daring, and there are not wanting men everywhere, who are ready to invest their capital and devote their energies to the manufacture of that which, though profitable, is ruinous to every interest of the world. They satisfy themselves by saying, "It will be had. If I do not furnish it, others will, and society is no worse for what I am doing;" — and so the work goes on, the facilities are multiplied, the supply is increased, and it is bottled, barrelled, and circulated everywhere. Verily the manufacturer is responsible for this.

Close these fountains that are feeding the streams which are wearing their polluting channels into the heart of society, and doubtless their proprietors would cry out for their gains as strongly as the drunkard would plead for his dram. The vast enginery of distillation is kept in motion in this way. As long as the propelling power of avarice is the distinguishing characteristic of men, so long it will continue, more or less.

Not until there is a mighty moral revolution that shall elevate the standard of public sentiment higher than it ever yet has been, will the actors in this part of the drama be roused to consider what they are doing. Just so long as it is made to flow out among the people, just so long will they gather it up, and all the long catalogue of woes that follow in its train will be swelling all the while.

Lord Chesterfield calls these manufacturers of spirituous liquors "*artists in human slaughter;*" and John Wesley declares these traffickers to be "*poisoners-general.* They murder by wholesale," he says; "neither does their eye pity or spare. And what is their gain? Is it not the blood of these men? Who would envy their large estates and their sumptuous palaces? A curse is in the midst of them. The curse of God is on their gardens, their walks, their groves; a fire that burns to the nethermost hell. Blood, blood, is theirs; the foundation, the floor, the walls, the roof is stained with blood."

This greed for gain is exemplified among all those who are interested in disseminating the drink in whatever form. Hard by the manufactory is the public house, and, indeed, in every town, village, and hamlet of the land, these institutions are opened, in every variety of style, professedly to meet the wants of the people, but primarily to get money; and in order to insure the last consideration, a bar is thought to be an indispensable requisite. If addressed on the importance of discontinuing this part of their business, because of the demoralizing influence in the community in which they live, the men who conduct them exclaim, "As well shut up my house as to close my bar. It would not pay;" and so there is hardly a place anywhere in the most retired sections but what affords the poison to anybody that will call for it. Those who sell justify themselves on the ground that they do not ask the people to come and buy; that they only keep a supply to meet a demand, and if men will take and drink more than is good for them, the consequences belong to them. Why should they share the responsibility?

It was a remark of Oliver Goldsmith's, that he "never saw a city or village yet whose miseries were not in proportion to the number of its public houses." The crowd who loiter about these places illustrate very forcibly the miserable tendency of the whole thing. They advertise the lowest condition of society; for it is here the idler, the lounger of every description, are wont to meet, and here congregate all those elements of disturbance which decent travellers feel like shunning.

The boys in the place are apt to gather around, and witness what is going on, and if they happen to escape the snare of the drunkard, they become familiar with every kind of vulgarity and profanity. The rum seller himself, if he had any mercy in his nature at the beginning, soon loses everything of the sort, and spurns the man from the door that he has helped to make brutish.

A gentleman who was travelling put up at a public house in a country place, and thus relates a scene which came under his observation at the time: "While warming ourselves by the fire in the bar-room one Saturday night, we observed the bar-keeper dealing out liquor to a venerable man, who, with tremulous hands, put the intoxicating cup to his lips. He seemed intelligent, was well dressed, and had the appearance of being a respectable man, abating his intemperance. We learned afterwards that such was his character at home, and that he lived in an adjoining town, and was waiting for a conveyance to take him to the point of his destination. At midnight the man became noisy, to the annoyance of the inmates, by reason of the liquor he had received at the bar; whereupon the bar-keeper, with characteristic benevolence, turned him out of doors to spend the rest of a most piercing cold night in the street. The next morning we heard the bar-keeper boasting, with a fiend-like exultation, how he had disposed of 'the noisy old devil.' We told him it was cruel to feed a man with rum until he had deprived him of his senses, and then turn him out to perish because he did not act as a rational man. The fire had scarcely been kindled in the morning, before the old man, shivering with cold, came back into the bar-room, where he was again received as a good customer. He formed one of the bar-room company all the Sabbath, alternately snoring in a chair and drinking, and acting like a maniac. About ten o'clock Sunday night — being saturated with rum — his hospitable landlord again turned him out into the street; and it was an intensely cold night. About an hour after he was out, a man came in, who said he had seen the old fellow sitting on the ground, and had taken him up and thrust him into a tailor's shop. But for this act of kindness he would have frozen to death in a very short time; and here," continues the traveller, "is a specimen of the tender mercies of the rum seller." When the contents of the pocket have been dropped into their till, there is no more object for them to gain. They will fill the cup and stir it well just as long as a man is capable of handing out the change, and has enough wherewith to do it, apparently thinking not, or caring, what the effect may be upon those he is robbing to enrich himself. With a complacent folding of the hands, they pride themselves upon the respectability of their position, and are content with the basis of their fortune. Says a writer, "I was once walking through a beautiful country village, in company with a farmer who had all his life resided in the neighborhood. The rural scenery around was very beautiful, with here and there touches of the romantic; presently we came to a very respectable looking public house by the road-side. The landlady, a widow, stood at the door, and, recognizing my companion, nodded to him, and he returned the saluation. The landlady was a fine, portly-looking dame, with black silk dress, and gold chain hanging down to the waist, and altogether in keeping with the house. I remarked to my companion, 'That certainly is a very respectable looking public house, and a very courteous and respectable landlady, too.' My companion replied, 'You are quite correct; that public house is the most respectably conducted house in this neighborhood, and that landlady is a most respectable woman; but I wish to tell you something about the house. Thirty years ago that house was licensed for the sale of intoxicating liquor, and, year after year, that license has been renewed. Now, during those thirty years, how many victims, think you, have perished in consequence of the drink obtained in that house?' Not liking to hazard a guess, he said, 'Well, then, I will tell you. In the course of those thirty years, to my certain knowledge, thirty victims have perished most miserably in consequence of liquor obtained at that house. Some of them were opulent farmers, belonging to this neighhood, and others were gentlemen of independent fortunes. Some of them, before their death, were reduced almost to penury, and most of them died young, or in the prime of life. Two or three of them were carried out of that house insensible, and died in their homes shortly afterwards, and others died of fever, or of delirium tremens, brought on by debauch at that house."

These are the so-called respectable dram shops; and, if these are so prolific in sowing the seeds of discord and sorrow, what shall we say of the countless places of lower standing, in the more densely crowded towns and villages, apart from rural surroundings? There are some places where they pride themselves in not selling to drunkards, but here there is no such restraint. It is dealt out indiscriminately to the lowest, and, indeed, that class constitutes by far the largest part of their patronage. They are generally in the suburbs, and dingy bottles are the sign in the window. It is here at these places that we see the saddest sights, and observe the worst phases of intemperance — here, where it is carried so far that poverty and wretchedness tell their direst tales in connection with it. The poor who will have whiskey go to these shops — those who have no pride or self-respect to maintain, who are past caring for what anybody may say or think. There are plenty of those who are ready to minister to the wants of such, for money. Would any one read the sequel to all this, let him go to the homes and haunts of those who tarry long at these places. They are usually out — down and apart from others — for respectable people have no sympathy with such extreme degradation, and so they generally congregate in a community by themselves, and it becomes a notorious quarter, where everything is in keeping, and no well-meaning person ever cares to intrude. "Their houses," it is said, "are generally known by the broken door-yard fence; the fallen gate; the windows stuffed with old hats and rags; the clapboards dangling in the air; the barns held up by props, and stripped of their boards, which have been used for fuel; a half-starved horse standing in the street; and several ragged children, who, without hats or shoes, spend their days in dragging brush-wood from the neighboring forests, or in begging pennies from door to door, to buy their mother a loaf of bread. The interior is like unto it. There is no neatness or comfort there; no bed but one of straw, laid on knotted ropes; here a show of a table, and there a broken chair; a half dozen broken plates, rusty knives and forks, and iron spoons; a mug for cider, and a bottle for rum, and, whatever else fails, these must be replenished. The last thing will be pawned to secure the last drop. 'I have known them,' said a philanthropist who visited these places, 'to sell the feathers from their bed, pound by pound, in order to secure the accustomed dram.' Neither carpet nor plastering is in such homes. If it is winter, the snow will lie upon the bed, and the mother and her children will be seen huddling over a few embers, as their only refuge. Night comes, but no sound of a father's voice, with comfortable food to cheer and gladden. Children cry themselves to sleep. The mother sits and watches until the moon goes down, and distant footsteps are heard, and horrid oaths are vented at not finding the door, causing her heart to quail; and a monster in human shape, but the father of her children, bursts upon her, and perhaps drives her out in the cold and dreary night, even in a pitiless storm, compelling her to leave her babes to his neglect or cruelty. Perhaps the mother herself, driven by despair and desperation, becomes a victim to the same habit, and adds the last bitter ingredient to the dregs of home misery. Thus sowing the wind, they reap the whirlwind, and what is transmitted to the children prepares the next generation for a kindred harvest of woe."

Perhaps a more notable example than *the Five Points*, in the city of New York, cannot be adduced to illustrate what a place and people may become when given over to the full dominion of intemperance in its lowest form. For years, the prominent feature in the case was an old brewery, that threw its doors wide open to all the surrounding population; and, if all the foul spirits of the nether world had congregated there, it could scarcely have been worse. A more ragged, dirty, miserable, beggarly set never walked the earth than was seen there. Ignorance, vice, and every species of crime stalked defiantly through all the region. The dilapidated buildings hardly covered their inmates. The very air was laden with shrieks, wails, and oaths. A respectable person could not pass through the quarter without having his every sense shocked beyond measure. Whiskey was the one consideration. It showed itself in every place and every thing. Many shunned it as a place where human life was not safe. If any, urged by a feeling of philanthropy, were moved to do anything to ameliorate the condition of the wretched inhabitants, they felt that they took their lives in their hand when they attempted to do it. As long as the Old Brewery stood, this state of things continued. It did its work as a minister of death for a long time. When, by the persistent efforts of the wise and good, these doors were closed, there came a change over the spirit of the place; and the atmosphere, so heavily charged with the fumes of the distillery and the poisonous breath of so many drunkards, became purer, and a more healthful condition of things began to prevail. Who is responsible for all this? The inspired penman says, "Woe unto him that giveth his neighbor drink."

Here is the worst aspect of the case — the darkest side of the picture. These are the deepest depths into which intemperance can plunge its victims; but it may be there is yet a phase of the question that has a sadder

THE FIVE POINTS.

hue than even this. These persons, in the main, are from the lowest grades of humanity, at the best. While it is true that drink has a tendency to bring and keep them there, it is also true that this wide-spread visible desolation is apparent more particularly among those who are naturally ignorant, vicious, and unprincipled. As persons of kindred tastes, habits, and customs are apt to attach themselves together, so these people are wont to associate themselves in a community, where their propensities are least liable to be checked or disturbed. In the most favoring circumstances, their moral instincts would be but feeble, and their higher apprehensions narrow and slow; but, while this does not excuse them for going so much lower than they need to, it may stamp the fact with significance that their doom will not be as dreadful, nor their guilt as great, as those who fall from greater heights, with more of obligation upon them, and more light and knowledge around them.

We have said before that the primary and visible effects of alcohol were the same in all cases; that the high and low, the rich and poor, are alike in this matter; and yet there is a system of caste here, where the lines are as rigidly drawn as anywhere else. There is a class above these, who love the sparkling stimulant just as well, perhaps, but who would not demean themselves so much as to hang about these low places; and various are the artifices resorted to, to meet the wants of this company. They have, it may be, a sufficient moral sense of the fitness of things to make them hesitate to go boldly and openly forward in their indulgence; and those who are ready to help them may still have some appreciation and fear of the public sentiment against their efforts; so they have a thousand ingenious and secret devisings — a new and significant alphabet, that their followers learn, but which common people are not supposed to understand. This not only meets the wants of those we are referring to, but it has become a fruitful means of beguiling the unwary, and catching them, spider-like, in the net, where they are kept beyond the possibility of recovery. The great question with the dealer is, "How can I increase the demand for my liquor, so that I may receive the profits arising from a larger sale?" Acting from this incentive, he tries every sort of plan, and, having undertaken it, every baser passion of his nature is lent to the work. There are a great many ways of doing the thing in these modern days — a great many novel arrangements got up to suit the occasion, that show, at least, the activity of mind, and its wonderful power of adaptation to circumstances. In order to realize a grand pecuniary consideration, it has become a branch business with many of various trades and callings, and it is *amusing*, not to say *outrageous*, to see the endless forms of deceit that are manufactured to cover and beguile. Grocers have opened side doors, and printed on them in large letters, "Sample Room." What more natural than to suppose such a corner requisite for their legitimate trade? What could be less likely to excite suspicion under the circumstances, or who would think of questioning the motives of the frequent visitors there? There is always a way for the hidden things of darkness to come to light, and so it has come to be known that there are thousands of just such places as these, where the *samples* are only exhibitions of spirits, that are ready to be dealt out to men who would thus conceal their shame. Proprietors of country stores roll barrels into their cellars, and, by some mysterious telegraphic communication, it is known among a certain class that it is not molasses, or sugar, or any such thing. They for whom it is provided understand it all; and there is no corner of that store that is so well patronized, for the convenience of a sly back entrance is appreciated.

To accomplish the object in the least objectionable way, there are bottles of multiform size and appearance, prepared with counterfeit labels, which profess to be the mildest form of an attractive and popular beverage that can be offered to the public; and this class shelter themselves under this style, secretly exulting in the thought that they are realizing their ambition, and blinding their friends. In the cities, there are prominent rooms on fashionable streets that hold out the sign, "Free Lunch." Does it mean that some philanthropist, mindful of the wants and ways of men, has gone systematically to work, and fitted up rooms in the gayest and most fascinating manner; setting out tables, and furnishing them temptingly and elaborately; placing about them a score of the most beautiful and winning young ladies he could command, to do the attendant honors; hiring a band of music to minister to the festivities of the dance, — does he do all this, and then say to the young men of the city, "I did this all for you; it is *free:* come in, and take your fill of pleasure"? Does it mean all this? Ah, no! It has a far different meaning from this. We will not call them philanthropists, but there are men who do all this — make all this display — in order to hide the main feature of their peculiar institution. Out of sight is a well-filled bar, which is the centre about which all these other things are made to revolve. All the gathered fascinations and attractions are as so many baits to allure men into the net that is spread for them. Thus consummate art plies the work of death, and virtue, reputation, and every good are sacrificed at these worse than Moloch shrines.

But there are yet some who have not been reached. The élite of the higher and more aristocratic circles are yet untouched. They might scorn the idea of being seen at any of those places we have mentioned, and so special provision has been made for them. The all-embracing arms of moneyed ambition would not leave them out of its grasp. The luxurious appliances of their own tables may perhaps serve for the satisfaction of their own every-day wants, but when they travel their round of pleasure, they must stop at magnificent hotels, on broad avenues, where the lavish hand of wealth has piled up luxury in a thousand dainty forms. These structures stand as so many monuments of what art and wealth can do, when used and applied by the skill, energy, industry, and peculiar ability of the people's architects. The palace-like arrangements of these institutions are remarkable, but there is one thing in which the lordly presiders are not quite at their ease. If they would please their customers altogether, and make their vast scheme an entire success, they must have a bar, and where shall they put it? The tone of public sentiment is so far against it they dare not give it a conspicuous position; so they go far back to the remotest corner, or perchance hide it beneath in the more quiet basement. They give it the elegant adornments befitting the character and reputation of such a house, and the aristocratic man can walk in and quaff his glass in all the et cetera of style. There is no danger that he will encounter the man of low degree, for the sparkling liquids that shimmer and shine in the vessels of fanciful mould have too much of gold in their price to admit of this. There he will not come in contact with the lounging idler and the reeling peasantry, for the marble floors and the gilded ceiling of those spacious rooms were never designed for such as these. The polite and the affluent drinker alone must enter here. The poison is poison still, but it is served in daintier

NEW YORK DANCING SALOON.

glasses; and the reality of the difference is, it is made to do its work in more genteel style. The social wants of this class have created another demand — given rise to an institution of another character, but which has associated with it the degenerating influences of drink, and that is the "club-room." There was a time in the history of England when its metropolitan city boasted of a brighter galaxy of poets and literary men than was ever before known. Never was so much of talent gathered together in one place as then and there. Never was genius more ably and brilliantly represented. These men were attracted to each other. Their common interest in literary pursuits induced a congeniality of spirit that brought them often into each other's society. They were invited to dine in company; and their gay sallies of wit, their pointed sarcasms and brilliant repartees, their learned discussions and lofty utterances, are matters of history unto this day. They formed themselves into a club, provided themselves with rooms, whither they repaired at certain intervals, and made them places of frequent resort. Some of these profoundly gifted men carried champagne into these circles, and it engendered a free-and-easy sort of life, that attracted the social and good-natured, who wanted a good time in a refined way. By reason of the learning and culture associated with it, the club came to hold a high rank, and possess a high reputation among the literati for its dignified exclusiveness. It was a place where social life put on its best dress. In the ever-increasing intercourse of this and that country, we have come into possession of the customs of that people and that time. The American people are not slow to appreciate and appropriate what they deem advantageous to their life, and the fascination which time and distance have thrown about this institution has invested it with a peculiar charm for them. What though they dispense with the characteristic original feature, there is still enough to it to form the basis of something that will compensate for the slower and more restricted enjoyments which the prosy and practical condition of the domestic circle enjoins.

The man of business, who is poring all day long over columns of perplexing figures and harassing ledgers, is glad, at the close of the day, to relax every nerve, and find himself in a social atmosphere, where every sense of his being is ministered unto, without any effort on his part to keep up the excitement. The truest and best moral action will send such a man home into the bosom of his family to find it there; but, lamentable as it is, there are thousands who will not do it, and so these voluntary organized clubs are formed, and furnished with everything that genial, cordial, and generous natures can bring to make them attractive. It may not be strictly after the European pattern, but it is a place where they can eat, smoke, sing, dance, and be hilarious generally — a place where they do forget their manhood, and degenerate into all sorts of lewd and gross immoralities. Young men going from the country into places of business in the city, for the sake of a more extended knowledge of the world, are often attracted to these places, where everything is so seductive, and they seldom come out unscorched by the unnatural condition of things within. Drink has a conversational, mirth-provoking tendency; and the laughing, jesting crowd come to think they have found the jolliest place in all the world, and they go again and again, until the stamp of intemperance is written legibly upon them.

It is true there are different grades in these things. They range all the way from the affluent surroundings of the most wealthy to those of far humbler pretension;

but, in them all, strong drink is working a general demoralization, and only that continually. It is to be doubted if there be a worse school for morals in our land than this; and the results of the object-teaching in these institutions, and the startling revelations in connection, are such as would make mothers, wives, and sisters blush and weep, if they knew them.

In countless other ways, and in channels we know not of, the streams are being fed that flow out, winding their course by all the hills and through all the vales of the social system. Some may exult in their power to carry on their nefarious traffic, and keep it hid from the gaze of the world, but they are yet to be confronted with the results of what they have done. The hearts they have blighted, the hopes they have crushed, the characters they have ruined, the reputations they have blasted, the fortunes they have destroyed, are all so many witnesses against them. It matters not so much where the work began, — whether among the seductive influences of the club or lunch room, or amid lower or less pretentious surroundings, — it is ultimately the same; and he who manufactures and he who aids in the circulation are alike responsible for the wreck and the ruin so widely spread.

All classes of our people drink. It is becoming sadly universal. Why is it? May it not be because there is such a systematic effort to meet the peculiar wants of each individual class in its own peculiar way? It is true the lower class are influenced a good deal by the higher. It is a great stimulant to the courage of the poor and doubting man that his master above him does the same thing that he does. If he had any feeling that it was wrong, it wonderfully lessens that compunction; for he drinks it to drown care and sorrow, and that man has no need to do it. And here again comes in the question of responsibility. Those who, by the power of their example, mislead others, and thus confirm them in a habit they know to be ruinous, have a fearful account to settle at some time. It may possibly be they may know how far they can go themselves, and how soon they must stop, to keep their own barks from floundering in the deep waters; but the humbler craft may not be able to come near that point safely.

It has been said, "If the 'moderate drinker' would abandon his cups, within twelve years drunkenness would be all but annihilated. We should only behold here and there a solitary victim, holding out in virtue of a strong constitution, a sad memorial of the drunkenness of a by-gone day."

What a blessed day for the American people, if all this active and complicated machinery of evil could be laid aside in glorious disuse! A longer stride towards millennial glory could not be taken. Nothing that could be done would clothe the earth with more of her primeval loveliness than this; nothing that would so effectually raise mankind to the heights for which they were destined, and give a grander and more speedy fulfilment to the prophecies of coming good. May it not be that the swelling tides which are filling the good with so much apprehension are to be checked, and it shall be written of them and upon them, "Thus far shalt thou go, and no farther"?

CHAPTER X.

PROBABILITY OF REFORM.

HOPE A DIM STAR. — THE YOUNG LADY'S VICTIM. — INDIVIDUAL REFORM. — GOUGH. — J. HAWKINS. — CONFESSION OF A CONDEMNED CRIMINAL. — FATHER OF THE REV. NEWMAN HALL. — HOPELESSNESS OF THE WORK. — CONFESSION OF CHARLES LAMB. — SALVATION NOT IN RECLAIMING THE DRUNKARD, BUT IN SAVING YOUTH FROM BEGINNING.

It is hardly to be supposed there will be any very extended and thorough work of reformation in a public way, as long as the manufacture and sale of ardent spirit are allowed to retain their present position. As long as it is paraded at every corner, associated with almost every pursuit, and intervoven with all the social customs of the times, where is the probability that it will fall into disuse, and the immense flood of evil that comes from it be stayed in its course? We talk of the radiant *star of hope*, but nowhere does it shine so dimly as here; nowhere else is it obscured by clouds so thick and dense. Good men and women are praying that the darkness may be dispelled; that through the pierced gloom there may come a ray of light that may be the earnest of a brighter day that is yet to dawn; that speedily the moral world may be illuminated, and mankind elevated from this low condition to a higher and better life. To look at it in the light of a wide-spread public reformation, there is a mighty work to be done. All the aggregated effort of all the present existing societies has failed to do it yet. They have worked wisely and well, but it needs more than human hand to pluck up the roots that have spread themselves in every direction over every part of our American soil. There needs to be a higher moral sentiment. There is a work demanded on the hearts and souls of men. They need to be swayed by an irresistible force — a something superior to their low appetites and passions, that shall renovate and endow them with power of will to rend asunder the links of that chain which will surely crush them in its tightening folds unless they do. Hope cannot promise much as long as the usages of society continue what they are. Just as long as the favorites of wealth and the devotees of fashion will persist in keeping wines and spirits upon their tables, just so long is there danger that those who surround them will be poisoned, and carry the infectious taint with them wherever they go. Neither will this danger be averted as long as young ladies will offer and urge a glass of wine upon their friends at the social party or the congratulatory call. Could these things be abolished altogether, it would be a long step on the march of progress. It would be striking a blow at the root, in very many cases, and there would be less occasion for the poet to sing

> "Man's inhumanity to man
> Makes countless thousands mourn."

"A young man, of no ordinary promise, unhappily contracted habits of intemperance. His excesses spread anguish and shame through a large and most respectable circle. The earnest and kind remonstrance of friends, however, at length led him to desist; and, feeling that for him to drink was to die, he came to a solemn resolution that he would abstain entirely for the rest of his days. Not long after he was invited to dine, with other young persons, at the house of a friend." Says the one who tells the story, with emphatic utternace, "Did I say *friend?* Pardon me; he could hardly be a friend who would deliberately place on the table before one so lately lost, now so marvellously redeemed, the treacherous instrument of his downfall. But so it was. The wine was in their feasts. He withstood the fascination, however, until a young lady, whom he desired to please, challenged him to drink. He refused. With banter and ridicule she soon cheated him out of all his noble purposes, and her challenge was accepted. He no sooner drank than he felt the demon was still alive, and that from temporary sleep he was now waking with tenfold strength. 'Now,' said he to a friend who sat next to him, 'now I have tasted again, and I drink till I die.' The awful pledge was kept. Not ten days had passed before that ill-fated youth fell under the horrors of delirium tremens, and was borne to a grave of shame and dark despair." "And who," says the writer of the sad tale, "would envy the emotions with which that young lady, if not wholly dead to duty and to pity, retraced her part in a scene of gayety, which smiled only to betray?" Sad as it is, the young ladies themselves are falling under the power of these pernicious habits, and it is confidently asserted, on reliable authority, that there are many in the highest circles so given to indulgence in this direction that they actually come under the condemnation of the drunkard. Startling as the fact may appear, it is declared that "nearly two thousand of the applicants for admission to the inebriate asylum at Binghamton have been *rich men's daughters;* and it is a truth equally astounding, that these favored ones of fortune will travel in foreign countries, and be seen in such condition as to need some one to steady their faltering steps through the streets. Dash every trace of the stimulating beverage from the tables of the rich, and it is believed that this most forbidding form of intemperance would cease to exist. By a well-known principle, reformation works downward. The lower are always imitating the higher, and an influence emanating from above would gradually be felt upon those below.

But, deferring the considerations of public reformation mostly to another place, we propose to have mainly to do with individual reformation in the present chapter; to behold the difficulties and probabilities of this, when once a man is under the full dominion of the habit, and to see how, in the practical illustration, if it be not utterly impossible, it approximates closely to it. There are notable instances of men who have been rescued from the lowest pit, and have become shining lights — a marvel to themselves and everybody else; but who does not know that they stand upon ground that is ever after quaking under their feet?

Gough was one of these; but it was long he lived in utter dread and distrust of himself, lest his strength of will and firmness of purpose should not be sufficient in the day of his temptation. He was afraid of himself; and who shall tell the horror of this trembling apprehension as it haunts a man in all his walks and ways? A continual watching and battling is necessary all the time, even after it seems the giant has been effectually slain; and in the first bitterness of the contest there are no words to paint the torturing helplessness of the condition. John Hawkins thus tells the story of his life when he first made an attempt to free himself from the bonds which had enslaved him so long. At the age of twenty-two he was a confirmed drunkard. "He wandered far off from his friends, to the West, where he suffered every evil from poverty, vice, and degradation; lived years in Baltimore, without providing food or clothing for his family — a living death to them." "My wife," he says, "would sit up for me until midnight, and watch to see whether I came home drunk or sober. Often have I fallen prostrate in the hall, and my little daughter would cover me with a blanket until the morning light. In June, 1840, I drank and suffered awfully — I can't tell how much I suffered in *mind* — in *body* everything, but in mind more. I drank dreadfully the first two weeks in June — bought by the gallon, and drank, drank, and was about taking my life — was drunk all the time. On the 14th, I was a wonder to myself; astonished I had any mind left; and yet, in the goodness of God, it seemed uncommonly clear. I lay in bed long after my wife and daughter were up, and my conscience drove me to madness. I hated the darkness of the night, and when light came I hated the light. I hated myself — my existence. I asked myself, 'Can I refrain? is it possible?' I felt there was not a being to take me by the hand, and say, *You can.* I felt that I had made myself friendless; that I was without help or light — an outcast; and for a time the overwhelming conviction maddened me. I had a pint of whiskey, and thought I would drink; and yet I knew it was life or death with me as I decided. I had always loved my daughter, and I felt that if I had a friend on the earth at all, it was she. As she came into the room, she said, 'Father, don't send me after any more whiskey to-day.' I was tormented before, but this was an unexpected torture. I commanded her to leave the chamber, and she went away with her eyes filled with tears. I covered myself in the bed to hide myself away from the sight or sound of a living thing, but more especially from my own loathsome self. I then thought of my past life, my degradation, misery of my friends, and felt bad enough. Hearing a noise in the room, I looked out and saw my daughter again present. Calling her to me, I said, 'I am not angry with you, and I shall not drink any more.' As we mingled our tears together, I arose and went to the cupboard, looked at the enemy, and thought, Is it possible I can be restored? and then turned my back upon it. Several times, while dressing, I looked at the bottle, but thought I should be lost if I yielded. No one could be worse off than I was, no more degraded, no more a slave to appetite. Soon after, I went to the Society for Drunkards, and there I found all my old bottle companions. I told no one, not even my family, that I was going. I felt that I had taken the first steps in the way of reform, but I was by no means persuaded that I could keep on in the way. There I met those with whom I had fished, caroused, and got drunk. In that condition we had stuck together like brothers; and now they laughed, clapped, and shouted, 'Here is Hawkins, the regulator, the *old bruiser*.' But there was no response in me for all this. I was too sober and solemn for that. The pledge was read for my accommodation. They did not say anything, but I knew they were looking over my shoulder to see if I really would write my name. I never had such feelings before. It was a great battle. I once fought the battle at North Point, and helped to run away, too; but now there was no such alternative. I found the society had a large pitcher of water, drank toasts, and told experiences; and there I laid my plan, for I did not intend to be a drone. Alcohol had promised me everything, but I had found it to be a great deceiver, and there was no way but to wage eternal war against it, and I determined to do it. At eleven o'clock I went home. Before, when I had staid out late, I had gone to my home thoroughly intoxicated, and my wife was watching for the same result, and was planning some measure that would free her from the increasing wretchedness. My yard is covered with brick,

SIGNING THE PLEDGE.

and as I went over this, she listened, as she afterwards told me, to determine whether the gate door opened drunk or sober; for she had learned to distinguish the peculiarity of sound that marked the condition. She was standing in the middle of the room as I entered, and, convinced that soberness was in the ascendant, she greeted me with a smile, that I involuntarily returned. 'I had put my name to the Temperance Pledge, never to drink again as long as I live,' said I. We both wept until our weeping awoke our daughter, and then we cried all together; and there was no sorrow in those tears but those wrung out by the fear of relapse. I tell you this," he says, "that you may know how happy the reformation of a drunkard makes his family. I slept none that night; my thoughts were better than sleep. Next morning, I went to see my aged mother — her who had been praying twenty years for her drunken son; and as I told her, she exclaimed, with unutterable joy in her face, 'It is enough; I am now ready to die.'"

If such be the joy of a single soul — of a single household — at the first dawnings of hope, what a loud-sounding anthem would it be that should celebrate the restoration of the larger number that are sighing and waiting for the same blessed redemption! What a glad era it would be for our domestic prosperity, could these scenes be multiplied all over the land!

A young man was convicted of murder, and while confined in jail, under sentence of death, he wrote a letter to warn others against a similar fate. The act had been committed while under the influence of strong drink, but the law held him responsible; and his story is but a repetition of the fact that it takes away reason, and goads on to madness and destruction continually. He writes, "O that I could only portray the horrors springing from the *first glass!* You would shun it as you would the road in which Death, in his most hideous form, was lurking. Would to God I had died before I knew the love or passion strong drink can bring to its poor, deluded victims; for then I would have had kind friends to weep and think kindly of me, as, in solemn silence, they gazed into my tomb.

"O, young man! by all that you hold dear, shun the cup — *the fatal cup!* You may think you are able to take a drink and leave it alone when you wish; let me entreat you, don't try the experiment, for when it gets hold it rarely ever lets go. It not only destroys *you*, but friends must suffer also. Think well before you touch the cup. Don't say, 'I can take a drink and leave off;' the chances are against you.

"Would to God that one year ago I could have seen strong drink as it really is, stripped of all the ornaments thrown over it by those engaged in the traffic! — could have seen it as a swift and sure road that was to lead to my unhappy condition in a felon's cell, with the prospect of a shameful death!

"My hands are ironed, irons are on my limbs, and I am chained to the floor; and whiskey has done it all. I have lost friends, character, home, all that makes life dear, by not saying, No! when asked to drink. I could have said it. God gave me understanding; I *knew* right from wrong; but I flattered myself I could go so far, and then rein up: now I am lost. Don't believe in moderate drinking; there is too much danger in it. There is no drunkard living but thought he could leave off when he wished. Say you that, 'Many drink, and do not what I have done?' *All true — but none do as I did but what drink — not one.* All say at first, "Whiskey shall not be my master; I am too much of a man for that.' How soon they find out that he who said, 'Wine is a mocker, strong drink is raging, and he that is deceived thereby is not wise,' knew more about it than they! It will hold one in fetters that are well nigh impossible to wrench off. There is no other way in which the reformation of these advanced drinkers can be secured but by abstaining altogether. A *little* will keep the flame forever burning, and it is so hard to come to the conclusion — *not a drop* — when habit cries out so strongly for the indulgence!"

The father of the Rev. Newman Hall was an intemperate man. The narrative of his experience has come before the world, under the title "The Rescued Brand." He was an infidel and a drunkard, but was won over to the true faith and to a life of soberness when he seemed almost beyond hope.

It is such a striking and illustrious example of a true reformation, and withal illustrates the difficulties attending it so clearly, we give a sketch of his life, as presented by his son: "When a young man, at Maidstone, his business pursuits placed him in circumstances of great temptation. Lively, amiable, generous, a genial companion, enjoying a sprightly joke, and singing a merry song, his society was much sought after. Social enjoyments were invariably connected with the free use of intoxicating liquors. He was thus led astray, and 'erred through strong drink.' Of his companions he informs us, 'In the town where I reside were twelve young men, who were accustomed, early in life, to meet together for indulgence in drinking, and all manner of excess. In the course of time some of them engaged in business; but their habits of sin were so entwined with their very existence that they became bankrupts. Eight of them died under the age of forty, without a hope beyond the grave; three others were reduced to the most abject poverty. Two of these had formerly moved in very respectable circles, but they are now in the most miserable state of poverty, wretchedness, and disgrace.'

"Of this party he was a sort of *ringleader*, taking the head of the table at convivial meetings, and sitting up whole nights drinking, and inducing others to do the same — never going to bed sober. He was an infidel, a disciple of Tom Paine, both in principle and practice, a blasphemer of the word of God, yet a good-natured man, who would do anybody a kindness. At length he went to reside at a distance, where, for a time, he refrained from dissipation, was married, and everything seemed prosperous around him; but, instead of being thankful to God for his mercy, and watching against his besetting sin, he gave way to his old propensity. One dark night, in the neighborhood of Stourbridge, he had been drinking. The road he took went over a canal; he missed the bridge, and rolled down the bank to the edge of the water. And here he seemed to have arrived at the end of his wicked course; but God, who is rich in mercy, had caused a stone to lie directly in his path, and thus spared him; one turn more, and he would have plunged into hell. His senses returned for a moment; and, seeing the water beneath him, he crawled back again into the road; there he was picked up, and lodged in a public house for the night. This was considered merely as a lucky escape, and he continued to pursue his career of sin as ardently as before. There were then no Total Abstinence Societies to shield him. When every one drank, was it to be expected he would abstain? The advice generally given was, 'Use, but not abuse.' Yet with his peculiar temperament and habits, one glass would so rouse his appetite that self-control was gone, and he rushed forward to the abyss which, when perfectly sober, he abhorred.

"One of these sad relapses occurred on the occasion of

a young minister visiting at his house, and taking brandy and water at luncheon. Thinking there could be no harm in following such an example, he filled his own glass, and was again overcome. After a course of drinking for some days, having come to his senses, he began to reason with himself on his guilt and folly; and, in an angry, passionate manner, he muttered, 'O, it's no use for me to repent — my sins are too great to be forgiven.' He had no sooner uttered these words, than a voice seemed to say, with strong emphasis, 'If thou wilt forsake thy sins, they shall be forgiven.' The poor man started at what he believed to be a real sound, and hastily turned round; but seeing no one, he said to himself, 'Surely I have been drinking until I am going mad.' He fell on his knees, and, half-suffocated by his feelings, he cried, 'O God, be merciful to me a sinner!' At this very time, special prayer was being offered on his behalf by his wife and others. The poor wretch was broken-hearted; and now his besetting sin appeared more horrible than ever; but it must be conquered, or he must perish. Then commenced a contest more terrible than that of conflicting armies; the soul was at stake; an impetuous torrent was to be turned in an opposite course. He now began to search the Bible, which he had once despised. Here he saw that crimson and scarlet sins could be blotted out; that the grace of God was all-sufficient. He refrained from intemperance, commenced family prayer, and hope again revived. But his deadly foe still pursued him, and he was again overcome. Now, his disgrace and sinfulness appeared worse than ever, and with melancholy feeling, he cried out, in anguish of spirit, that he was doomed to eternal misery, and it was useless to try to avert his fate. His cruel enemy took this opportunity to suggest to his mind that he had so disgraced himself that it would be better to get rid of his life at once. The razor was in his hand; but the Spirit of the Lord interposed, and the weapon fell to the ground. He would sometimes refrain for days and weeks, and then again he was as bad as ever. All hope seemed now to be gone; and especially, when, one day, after having been brought into great weakness through intemperance, death seemed to be very near. Not a moment was to be lost; he cast himself once more at the footstool of his long-insulted Creator, and, with an intensity of agony, cried out, 'Hear, O Lord, and have mercy upon me: Lord, be thou my helper.' He sank down exhausted; he could say no more, but that prayer was heard.

"A physician was consulted as to the possibility of medicine being rendered effectual to cure his intemperance. The poor man would have suffered the amputation of all his limbs, could so severe a method have rid him of his deadly habit. The physician declared that if he would strictly adhere to his prescription, not only the practice, but the very inclination for strong drink would subside in a few months. The remedy was a preparation of steel; and eagerly did he begin to devour the antidote to his misery. Every bottle was taken with an earnest prayer to God for his blessing to accompany it. In a private box, opened after his decease, a small parcel was found, on which was written, 'The mercy of God unspeakable to J. V. H.' It contained a phial bottle in which was a little sediment, and the following affecting document: 'This phial is one (of upward of three hundred) of those out of which J. V. H. drank a preparation of steel, in the year 1816. It is preserved, like the pot of manna, to show the way in which the Lord delivered his servant out of the wilderness — out of a horrible pit — out of his besetting sin. O, praised be the Lord.' When this prescription was first taken, wine and spirits were given up. But it was found that beer was sufficient to excite the morbid propensity. After several failures from this cause, beer, also, was relinquished. Then it was, and not until then, that the cure was complete; and from that day to the day of his death, being a period of forty-two years, not so much as a spoonful of spirituous liquors, or wine of any description, ever passed the surface of that man's tongue."

In him reformation did its full work eventually, and he became an earnest and efficient worker in every good cause; but no one but the man himself can tell the price at which it was purchased. Once, while ill of typhus fever, the physician proposed wine as an essential remedy for his restoration; but he rejected the idea, and declared he "would rather die."

An accident led to his decease in his eighty-seventh year. A slight operation was followed by erysipelas. Again wine was recommended. Mr. Hall, who had been lying in a state of great weakness, apparently unaware of what was said, emphatically groaned out, "Never! never!" A few days before his departure he said to his son, "Newman, if you preach a funeral sermon for me, your text must be, 'Is not this a brand plucked out of the fire'?"

There is nothing but divine power, in connection with total abstinence, that can bring up these lowly-fallen ones to the true level of virtuous manhood again. It requires the most powerful considerations that can be brought to bear upon a man's heart and conscience to make him turn backward, when he has once reached the foot of the hill. The almost superhuman effort that is involved in climbing up again, makes the poor man feel that it is easier to go with the current of his passions, and keep on sliding; and the probability is, that he will continue his drams, if it be but to bury the accusations that taunt him in every sane moment. We know of a young man who would awake after a night's revellings with the bitter cry "I wish I was in heaven!" So utterly powerless did he feel himself to be in overcoming his propensity, that he regarded everything unsafe until he could be freed from the body, and beyond the reach of temptation. Perhaps he overlooked the important consideration that there is no salvation for these wilfully perverted ones. The consciousness of being fettered was upon him, and the torment and friction of this induced the despairing cry. He was promising, talented, the pride of his parents, and might greatly have adorned the ministerial profession for which he was designed, had he not yielded, as so many do, to the solicitations of boon companions. It is to be hoped he began the work of reform before it was too late; but none such can stand where they might have stood had they remained strangers to the degrading process. It burns out all the freshness and vigor of a man's character, and when he would come up, it requires the constant appropriation of all his energies to keep himself on the right track. If he could have this same strength and energy to spend in blessing others, the cultivation of the moral vineyard would be very different from what it is now. Charles Lamb, in his "Essays of Elia" has given the "Confessions of a Drunkard," in which he vividly depicts the meaning of reform as applied to the individual soul. This brilliant English essayist was in the habit of taking a great deal of wine at his table, and it was not uncommon for him to doze away his after-dinner hours under its stupefying influence.

"Kindly, upright, and witty," he was a pleasant companion for a large and gay circle. His amusing sallies and humorous jokes always commanded attention, and this, with his general culture, made him universally popular. But here was his failing — he could not pass by the door of a country tavern in his walks but he must enter for a draught. It is said that often, while he was walking with the youthful and accomplished daughter of Sheridan Knowles, she was often left outside the haunts of gin, while he could gratify his insatiable thirst — a thirst more powerful than love, and more beguiling than affection. Not until young ladies cease to smile upon such as these will the star of hope be in the ascendant, and the matter of reform assume the importance it demands.

The result of the convictions of this famed writer we give in his own emphatic language.

"Dehortations from the use of strong liquors have been the favorite topic of sober declaimers in all ages, and have been received with abundance of applause by water-drinking critics. But with the patient himself, the man that is to be cured, unfortunately, their sound has seldom prevailed. Yet the evil is acknowledged, the remedy simple. *Abstain.* No force can oblige a man to raise the glass to his head against his will. 'Tis as easy as not to steal — not to tell lies. Alas! the hand to pilfer, and the tongue to bear false witness, have no constitutional tendency. These are actions indifferent to them. At the first instance of the reformed will, they can be brought off without a murmur. The itching finger is but a figure of speech, and the tongue of the liar can with the same natural delight give forth useful truths, with which it has been accustomed to scatter their pernicious contraries. But when a man has commenced sot — O pause, thou surly moralist, thou person of strong nerves and a strong head, whose liver is happily untouched, and ere thy gorge riseth at the *name* which I have written, first learn what the thing is; how much of compassion, how much of human allowance, thou mayst virtuously mingle with thy disapprobation. Trample not on the ruins of a man. Exact not, under so terrible a penalty as infamy, a resuscitation from a state of death almost as real as that from which Lazarus rose not but by a miracle. Begin a reformation, and custom will make it easy.

"But what if the beginning be dreadful, the first steps not like climbing a mountain, but like going through fire? What if the whole system must undergo a change violent as that which we conceive of the mutation of form in some insects? What if a process comparable to flaying alive be to be gone through? Is the weakness that sinks under such struggles to be confounded with the pertinacity which clings to other vices, which have induced no constitutional necessity, no engagement of the whole victim, body and soul?

"I have known one in that state, when he had tried to abstain but for one evening, — though the poisonous potion had long ceased to bring back its first enchantment, though he was sure it would rather deepen his gloom than brighten it, — in the violence of the struggle, and the necessity he has felt of getting rid of the present sensation at any rate, — I have known him to scream out, to cry aloud, for the anguish and pain of the strife within him. Why should I hesitate to declare that the man of whom I speak is myself? I have no puling apology to make to mankind. I see them all, in one way or another, deviating from the pure reason. It is to my own nature alone I am accountable for the woe that I have brought upon it. I believe that there are constitutions, robust heads and iron insides, whom scarce any excesses can hurt; whom brandy (I have seen them drink it like wine), at all events, whom wine, taken in ever so plentiful a manner, can do no worse injury to, than just to muddle their faculties, perhaps never very pellucid. On them this discourse is wasted. They would but laugh at a weak brother, who, trying his strength with them, and coming off foiled from the contest, would fain persuade them that such agonistic exercises are dangerous. It is to a very different description of persons that I speak. It is to the weak, the nervous, to those who feel the want of some artificial aid to raise their spirits in society to what is no more than the ordinary pitch of all around them without it. This is the secret of our drinking. Such must fly the convivial board in the first instance, if they do not mean to sell themselves for the term of life. Twelve years ago I had completed my six and twentieth year. I had lived from the period of leaving school to that time pretty much in solitude. My companions were chiefly books, or, at most, one or two living ones of my own book-loving and sober stamp. I rose early, went to bed betimes; and the faculties which God had given me, I have reason to think, did not rust in me unused. About that time I fell in with some companions of a different order. They were men of boisterous spirits, sitters-up a-nights, disputants, drunken, yet seemed to have something noble about them. We dealt about the wit, or what passed for it, after midnight, jovially. Of the quality called fancy, I certainly possessed a larger share than my companions. Encouraged by their applause, I set up for a professed joker! I, who of all men am least fitted for such an occupation, having, in addition to the greatest difficulty which I experienced at all times of finding words to express my meaning, a natural nervous impediment in my speech! Reader, if you are gifted with nerves like mine, aspire to any character but that of a wit. When you find a tickling relish upon your tongue, disposing you to that sort of conversation, especially if you find a preternatural flow of ideas settling in upon you at the sight of a bottle and fresh glasses, avoid giving way to it, as you would fly your greatest destruction. If you cannot crush the power of fancy, or that within you which you mistake for such, divert it, give it some other play. Write an essay, pen a character or description, — but not, as I do now, with tears trickling down your cheeks.

"To be an object of compassion to friends, of derision to foes; to be suspected by strangers, stared at by fools; to be esteemed dull when you cannot be witty; to be applauded for witty when you know that you have been dull; to be called upon for the extemporaneous exercise of that faculty which no premeditation can give; to be spurred on to efforts which end in contempt; to be set on to provoke mirth, which procures the procurer hatred; to give pleasure, and be paid with squinting malice; to swallow draughts of life-destroying wine, which are to be distilled into airy breath to tickle vain auditors; to mortgage miserable morrows for nights of madness; to waste whole seas of time upon those who pay it back in little inconsiderable drops of grudging applause, — are the wages of buffoonery and death.

"Time, which has a sure stroke at dissolving all connections which have no solider fastening than this liquid cement, more kind to me than my own taste or penetration, at length opened my eyes to the supposed qualities of my first friends. No traces of them is left but in the vices which they introduced, and the habits they infixed. In them my friends survive still, and exercise ample retribution for any supposed infidelity that I may have been guilty of towards them.

"My next more immediate companions were, and are, persons of such intrinsic and felt worth, that, though accidentally their acquaintance has proved pernicious to me, I do not know that if the thing were to do over again, I should have the courage to eschew the mischief at the price of forfeiting the benefit. I came to them reeking from the steams of my late overheated notions of companionship; and the slightest fuel which they unconsciously afforded was sufficient to feed my old fires into a propensity. They were no drinkers, but one from professional habits, and another from a custom derived from his father, smoked tobacco. The devil could not have devised a more subtle trap to retake a backsliding penitent. The transition from gulping down draughts of liquid fire, to puffing out innocuous blasts of dry smoke, was so like cheating him. But he is too hard for us, when we hope to commute. He beats us at barter; and when we think to set off a new failing against an old infirmity, 'tis odds but he puts the trick upon us for two to one.

"That (comparatively) white devil of tobacco brought with him, in the end, seven worse than himself. It were impertinent to carry the reader through all the processes by which, from smoking at first with malt liquor, I took my degrees through thin wines, through stronger wine and water, through small punch, to those juggling compositions, which, under the name of mixed liquors, slur a great deal of brandy, or other poison, under less and less water continually, until they come next to none, and so to none at all. But it is hateful to disclose the secrets of my Tartarus.

"Persons not accustomed to examine the motives of their actions, to reckon up the countless nails that rivet the chains of habit, or perhaps being bound by none so obdurate as those I have confessed to, may recoil from this as an overcharged picture. But what short of such a bondage is it, which in spite of protesting friends, a weeping wife, and a reprobating world, chains down many a poor fellow, of no original indisposition to goodness, to his pipe and his pot?

"I have seen a print, after Correggio, in which three female figures are ministering to a man who sits fast bound at the root of a tree. Sensuality is soothing him,

Evil Habit is nailing him to a branch, and Repugnance, at the same instant of time, is applying a snake to his side. In his face is feeble delight, the recollection of past, rather than perception of present pleasures; languid enjoyment of evil, with utter imbecility to good; a Sybaritic effeminacy, a submission to bondage; the springs of the will gone down like a broken clock, the sin and the suffering co-instantaneous, or the latter forerunning the former, remorse preceding action, — all this represented in one point of time. When I saw this, I admired the wonderful skill of the painter. But when I went away, I wept, because I thought of my own condition. Of *that* there is no hope that it will ever change. The waters have gone over me. But out of the black depths, could I be heard, I would cry out to all those who have but set a foot in the perilous flood. Could the youth, to whom the flavor of his first wine is delicious as the opening scenes of life, as the entering upon some newly-discovered paradise, look into my desolation, and be made to understand what a dreary thing it is, when a man shall feel himself going down a precipice with open eyes and a passive will; to see his destruction, and have no power to stop it, and yet to feel it all the way emanating from himself; to perceive all goodness emptied out of him, and yet not to be able to forget a time when it was otherwise; to bear about the piteous spectacle of his own self-ruins; — could he see my fevered eye, feverish with last night's drinking, and feverishly looking for this night's repetition of the folly; could he feel the body of the death out of which I cry each hour with feebler and feebler outcry to be delivered, — it were enough to make him dash the sparkling beverage to the earth in all the pride of its mantling temptation; to make him

'Clasp his teeth, and not undo 'em,
To suffer wet *Damnation* to run thro' 'em.'

"Yea! but (methinks I hear somebody object) if sobriety be that fine thing you would have us to understand, if the comforts of a cool brain are to be preferred to that state of heated excitement which you describe and deplore, what hinders, in your own instance, that you do not return to those habits from which you would induce others never to swerve? If the blessing be worth preserving, is it not worth recovering?

"*Recovering!* O, if a wish could transport me back to those days of youth, when a draught from the next clear spring could slake any heats which summer suns and youthful exercise had power to stir up in the blood, how gladly would I return to the pure element, the drink of children, and of child-like, holy hermit. In my dreams I can sometimes fancy the cool refreshment purling over my burning tongue. But my waking stomach rejects it. That which refreshes innocence only makes me sick and faint. But is there no middle way betwixt total abstinence and the excess which kills you? For your sake, reader, and that you may never attain to my experience, with pain I must utter the dreadful truth, that there is none — none that I can find. In my stage of habit (I speak not of habits less confirmed, for some of them I believe the advice to be most prudential) in the stage which I have reached, to stop short of that measure which is sufficient to draw on torpor and sleep, the benumbing, apoplectic sleep of the drunkard is to have taken none at all.

"The pain of the self-denial is all one. And what that is, I had rather the reader should believe on my credit, than know from his own trial. He will come to know it whenever he shall arrive at that state, in which, paradoxical as it may appear, reason shall only visit him through intoxication; for it is a fearful truth that the intellectual faculties, by repeated acts of intemperance, may be driven from their orderly sphere of action, their clear daylight ministries, until they shall be brought at last to depend, for the faint manifestation of their departing energies, upon the returning periods of the fatal madness to which they owe their devastation. The drinking man is never less himself than during his sober intervals. Evil is so far his good.*

"Behold me, then, in the robust period of life, reduced to imbecility and decay. Hear me count my gains, and the profits I have derived from the midnight cup. Twelve years ago I was possessed of a healthy frame of mind and body. I was never strong, but I think my constitution (for a weak one) was as happily exempt from the tendency to any malady as it was possible to be. I scarcely knew what it was to ail in anything. Now, except when I am losing myself in a sea of drink, I am never free from those uneasy sensations in head and stomach which are so much worse to bear than any definite pains or aches. At that time I was seldom in bed after six in the morning, summer or winter. I awoke refreshed, and seldom without some merry thoughts in my head, or some piece of a song to welcome the new-born day. Now, the first feeling which besets me, after stretching out the hours of recumbence to their last possible extent, is a forecast of the wearisome day that lies before me, with a secret wish that I could have lain on still, or never awaked. Life itself—my waking life,—has much of the confusion, the trouble, and obscure perplexity of an ill dream. In the daytime I stumble upon dark mountains. Business, which, though

* "When poor Mr. —— painted his last picture, with a pencil in one trembling hand and a glass of brandy and water in the other, his fingers owed the comparative steadiness with which they were enabled to go through their task, in an imperfect manner, to a temporary firmness derived from a repetition of practices, the general effect of which had shaken both them and him so terribly.

never particularly adapted to my nature, yet as something of necessity to be gone through, and therefore best undertaken with cheerfulness, I used to enter upon with some degree of alacrity, now wearies, affrights, perplexes me. I fancy all sorts of discouragements, and I am ready to give up an occupation which gives me bread, from a harassing conceit of incapacity. The slightest commission given me by a friend, or any small duty which I have to perform for myself, — as giving orders to a tradesman, &c., — haunts me as a labor impossible to be got through. So much the springs of action are broken.

"The same cowardice attends me in all my intercourse with mankind. I dare not promise that a friend's honor, or his cause would be safe in my keeping, if I were put to the expense of any manly resolution in defending it. So much the springs of moral action are deadened within me. My favorite occupations in times past now cease to entertain. I can do nothing readily. Application, for ever so short a time, kills me. This poor abstract of my condition was penned at long intervals, with scarcely any attempt at connection of thought, which is now so difficult to me. The noble passages which formerly delighted me in history or poetic fiction, now only draw a few weak tears, allied to dotage. My broken and dispirited nature seems to sink before anything great and admirable. I perpetually catch myself in tears, for any cause, or none. It is inexpressible how much this infirmity adds to a sense of shame, and a general feeling of deterioration. These are some of the instances, concerning which I can say with truth, that it was not always so with me. Shall I lift up the veil of my weakness any further? or is this disclosure sufficient?

"I am a poor, nameless egotist, who have no vanity to consult by these confessions. I know not whether I shall be laughed at, or heard seriously. Such as they are, I commend them to the reader's attention, if he finds his own case any way touched. I have told him what I am come to. Let him stop in time."

A more melancholy, heart-rending confession of the influences of drink upon the whole man could scarcely be given than is found in this recital. The love of it is as though the poisonous fangs of a viper had been fastened upon the whole system, disfiguring and paralyzing it beyond all cure.

It is true that now and then one is freed from this terrible power of the enemy, and restored to society and friends again; but we see what it costs. If those in the higher walks of life, who are surrounded with every advantage, and have every inducement to cast off their shackles, and take their rightful and enviable position among the worthy, the educated, and refined, — if these find it so hard to begin and continue the work of reform with themselves, what shall we say of those in the lower conditions of society, who have but little motive and little encouragement to undertake the herculean task? There are multitudes of such now who will go on their way unchecked; persons that are weak and irresolute by nature; those who have been ambitionless and inefficient always, and have made themselves more so by their habits. There is but little hope that these will ever exercise the requisite energy and decision to meet the emergency of reform. If the fallen pillars of Temperance are to be raised again to their true position, it belongs to the youth of the present day to begin the work. Those who have already formed the habit of drinking cannot be relied upon at all to aid in the enterprise. They may make an occasional spasmodic effort, but the chances are, that they will prove a hinderance, and not a help. Our hope of reformation lies not so much in reclaiming the drunkard, as in saving those who have never tasted.

CHAPTER XI.

Blighting Effects upon Society.

CELESTIAL INQUIRER. — CLAIMS OF THE LIQUOR FIEND. — INTEMPERANCE PRODUCES POVERTY. — INCIDENT WITH A BOSTON LECTURER. — FRUITFUL SOURCE OF PAUPERISM. — THE "SOCIAL EVIL" STIMULATES THE MURDEROUS PROPENSITY. — PROMPTS TO SUICIDE. — OPPOSES RELIGIOUS INSTRUCTION. — INDUCES PROFANITY. — THE ENEMY OF THE MISSIONARY. — THE INDIAN'S PROTEST. — APPEAL TO THE CHURCH.

"Where are they lost,
If of such incubi we count the cost?
Jails, hospitals, madhouses — they know well;
And poorhouses o'ercrowded — they can tell."

THE imagination of a modern writer has met a visitant from the heights above who thus accosted him: "Stranger! inhabitant of the earth! what mean those dark, unsightly dens which I see scattered so frequently in the dells and corners of the earth, that send forth vapor, and fire, and smoke, and stench? I see the busy multitude wending their way thither from every point, laden with the fruits of the earth, which were evidently designed by the beneficent Creator for the sustenance of man, and casting their burdens, unhesitatingly, into the fiery crater. Again I have looked to see if anything was borne away from these receptacles from which I might infer that the fruits of the earth had been worked over, and better adapted to the wants of man. But, though long I've looked with painful eyes, I've looked in vain. But I see issuing from every one of them, through dark, leaden pipes, certain fiery streams. These flow out into numerous reservoirs; and then, in innumerable smaller streams, they are conveyed to your cities, and towns, and villages, and all over your vast prairies, over your hills, and through your valleys, to almost every habitation of man. I see the multitude everywhere eager for its approach, and opening their houses, and their mouths even, to receive the fiery fluid. I see the aged and the young, the decrepit and the healthy, the male and the female, the high and the low, the rich and the poor, plunging, with desperate strides, into the stream, and gorging themselves therefrom. I see parents laving their children with it, and, ever and anon, pouring it down their necks; and the delicate female, even, receiving it to her lips; but the effects which I perceive inevitably to follow upon coming in contact with these streams, perplex and trouble me much." And so they go on, in alternate inquiry and reply, until, having surveyed the whole ground, the airy visitor pronounces the whole thing as "the work of the devil, — Satan's greatest masterpiece, — his metamorphosis, by which brutes are made of the best material, — by means of which, more than by any other instrumentality, he keeps up his dark dominion over men;" and he blesses God "that there are no railways, or steam-power by which these fatal streams can be conducted, or electro-magnetic telegraph, by which the art of making them can be conveyed to his own beautiful and happy world." But it needeth not the clear vision of a celestial being to discover the sad workings and fearful ravages of this mighty agent. It is too apparent to the view of ordinary mortals to be questioned at all. Even a cursory glance reveals all that the pure-eyed stranger saw. The deplorable effects upon individuals, and society at large, waken corresponding emotions in the hearts of all the good, and they mourn over the fact that their fellow-men will lend their support to means that are so dire in their consequences. But what are those consequences? Hear what liquor — the foul fiend — hath been made to say: "Hear, all ye people of the world! Hear! I claim the right to load the bodies of men with a slow, lingering disease, so that after ten years of suffering they shall die some horrible and disgraceful death, at the rate of one hundred thousand a year. I claim the right to injure the minds of men, so as to send twelve thousand raving maniacs to the lunatic asylum, and twelve thousand more to the asylum for idiots. I claim the right to so madden the people with ungovernable frenzy, as to make six hundred kill themselves, but, before they die, to kill, with heartless ferocity, four hundred victims, and make six hundred more perish with fierce and wild delirium. I claim the right, during these ten years these people are drinking themselves to death, to send one hundred thousand of them to the hospitals with disease, to make them squander their money and their property, and the money and property of their families, and waste their time and shorten their lives, amounting to three million years of life and industry. I claim the right, during the same ten years, to cause the people to commit a vast number of heinous crimes and offences, so as to keep twenty thousand in the state prisons of the land, and to cause two hundred thousand petty crimes and misdemeanors against the peace and good order of society, and make them harsh and cruel to their once loved wives and helpless babes. I claim the right to make five hundred thousand paupers and beggars, so as to crush out their dignity and self-respect, and blight their hopes forever. I claim the right to destroy with midnight flames a vast amount of property, by land and by sea. I claim the right to tax the honest and temperate people of the country, without their consent, to pay for all these woes and calamities, to the amount of two hundred million dollars a year. I claim the right to refuse to pay more than one twentieth of the taxes which the laws of the land have assessed as my share, and the right to force honest people to pay them for me. I claim to be above the law and beyond the law. I claim the right to dwarf the intellect and corrupt the morals of the people, and corrupt the hearts of the lawgivers, and corrupt those whom the people elect to enforce the laws. And I not only claim these rights, but in the name of wickedness, my birthright, and depravity, my acquired knowledge, and passion, my strength, and covetousness, the grand aim of my life, I will exercise these rights, law or no law, for I have usurped the authority to rule and ruin the earth."

Would that these extravagant claims were but a fiction of the imagination — the over-heated fancies of loud and enthusiastic declaimers ; but society appends ample testimony to their rigid enforcement. On every page of its history the sad truth is confirmed. Statistics declare, in startling tones, that it is all true ; and what is more, it is written everywhere, in legible characters, upon the broad surface of suffering humanity. Society is what homes and hearts make it. Its general tone and character are according to the condition of these. If the streams which issue from thence be limpid and clear, in corresponding degree will society mirror forth the same likeness. On the contrary, it shadows the darker picture, and reproduces all the tints in ever-widening effect.

Society is cursed by the *poverty* which the love of strong drink engenders. Aside from the more strongly marked forms of this evil, there is another aspect, which involves a vast amount of suffering ; and that is found in the well-to-do families, who in every respect would be favorably situated but for harboring the demon of intemperance. The Hon. Edward Everett once said, "A wealthy drunkard may have self-control enough to manage his property, and honesty enough to keep out of jail. He may fill what is called a genteel position in society, and yet he may be the very tyrant of his household; never pleased, never soothed, never gratified, when the utmost has been done by everybody to gratify him; often turbulent and outrageous, sometimes cruel; the terror of those he is bound to protect, the shame of those who would love him if they could. A creature of this sort does not take refuge in a poorhouse, or drive his family to it; but the coarsest and hardest crust broken within its walls is a dainty, compared with the luxuries of his cheerless table."

There may be an honest dread of being ranked with the inmates of the poorhouse; but the poverty outside these institutions that come by the way of intemperate habits is greater, in the amount of suffering which it occasions, than that which is seen in those. "To the victims of drunkenness, whom it has conducted to this sad refuge, one bitter ingredient in the cup is spared. The sense of honest shame, and the struggle of a commendable pride, are at length over. They can sink no lower, and may possibly become reconciled to their hard lot." But in these other cases it is different. They conceal their woes, their self-denials, from the world as long as may be, and too often broken hearts end the sad scenes. There is the seen and the unseen — the public and the private. The want and the woe that begin in the bosom of the family flow out over the whole social area. How much richer would society be to-day but for the treasure that drink has robbed it of! The money that is used by the accursed passion of the inebriate, and the tipplings of the moderate drinker, togetherwith the amount necessary to check the natural outgrowth of all this, would cover society with a richer mantle than it ever yet has known, if it could be used for its adornment. We have seen how the lovers of drink will spend the last cent of their earnings for the gratification of their ruling passion, regardless of the piteous cries and pleas of those nearest to them; and of course such as these utterly ignore the claims of society upon them, and so the many suffer privation through them. Says a gentleman lecturer, "We were addressing a Band of Hope in Boston on one of the coldest evenings of last winter. During the progress of the meeting, a drunkard entered the hall and took a seat near the door. He was a young man, about thirty-two years of age, and he listened with deep attention to the remarks. At the close of the exercises, when the congregation had passed out, so that he could approach the desk, he advanced and grasped the speaker's hand, while the tears rolled down his cheeks, and his whole frame shook with convulsive sobs, saying, in a sepulchral tone that was truly startling, '*I am a drunkard beyond recovery.*' Observing his high, intellectual forehead, that indicated marked native intelligence and manhood, we answered, 'You look as if you might be saved, and as if you were worth saving.' He replied only, in a tone that was still more affecting, 'I am a drunkard beyond recovery.' And to prove that his reformation was impossible, on account of the terrific power of his appetite, he flung open the ragged coat that was buttoned around him, disclosing that he had neither shirt nor vest. 'I sold my shirt for rum to-day,' said he. Then lifting up his right foot, to show that he was destitute of stockings, he added, 'I sold my stockings for rum today; and this is the way I have obtained my rum,' he continued, 'ever since last August, when I returned from the army. I beg a coat of one kind man, and then pawn it for rum; then a vest, and then a shirt, go in the same way, their places being soon supplied by begging other garments.' "

And this is but a specimen item in that poverty-stricken list, which are worse than so many dead weights upon society. Nor is this material loss the only feature of the case. There is a moral indigence that is worse than even this. To have all that heart and intellect can give, in their unfettered, unclouded state, is to make society rich in itself. It is the mainspring in the machinery which turns out wealth; and to be deprived of all this by an unnatural process is to reverse the whole order, and give poverty full license to desolate and waste at its will.

The poverty of this higher realm is worse than all others, and the blight upon society induced by it is tenfold more to be dreaded than the withdrawal of that which pecuniary possessions involve. True, they are more or less blended, for the cultivation and development of the moral and intellectual resources which tend to the elevation and enrichment of society are due, in a good degree, to the pecuniary forces of application. The failure of both creates one vast system of pauperism.

It is estimated that in the United Kingdom of Great Britain, one in twenty of the entire population are paupers, and that intemperance is the direct or indirect cause of nine tenths of the whole. Our own country furnishes facts of equal significance. The report of the secretary of state to the legislature of New York in 1863 showed the whole number of paupers to be two hundred and sixty-one thousand two hundred and fifty-two, or one in fifteen of all the inhabitants of the state; and seven eighths of these were reduced to their beggarly condition through the influence of intoxicating drink. Similar reports from nearly all our states show corresponding calculations at the present time. Two hundred thousand children, it is said, are annually sent to the poorhouse, and two millions of children in the United States are not in attendance upon any school, chiefly because of the wasting blight of this system. Their parents have been lodged with or before them, and society is compelled to bear the burden of their support, although it has ceased to care for them, only as gospel benevolence prompts to their rescue.

Vice and crime, too, find their instigator in the same dreadful practice. Social self-interest enters its protest against the continuance of a system which is at war with every true interest of the state. It is for the interest of society that sobriety should prevail; that there should be no vice or crime, no pauperism, no lunacy, or avoidable disease; that there shall be domestic comfort and general education; that the rates and taxes, and the demands on private charity, should be reduced to the minimum consistent with the contingencies of life; and against the whole and every part of this enlightened interest the liquor traffic wages incessant war. But for this, the so-called "*Social Evil*" would never multiply itself so fearfully as it is now doing in every part of our land, prostituting all the nobility of woman's nature to the basest shrines on earth. From whence cometh all this? Associated, it may be, with those who degrade themselves with drink, they lose their moral sense, and become insensible to the charms of virtue. One who has observed these things says of them, "The social glass blunts their own moral perceptions, and throws them off their guard, and thus they become an easy prey to the wiles of the seducer. Thousands of them come from their sweet country households, in all their health and beauty, blooming as the heather upon their native hills, or the roses that adorn the walls of their cottage homes. Led astray through the terrible agency of strong drink, they flock to our large towns, and there commence their sad career. To drown the pangs of conscience, the bitterness of remorse, and the deep sense of shame, they fly to strong drink, and thus become confirmed in vice. In a very short time, a few months in some, a few years in others, their bloom and beauty fade, and they become either bloated and blaspheming monsters, with every womanly attribute eradicted, or poor, emaciated, and diseased outcasts, homeless and hopeless." No sadder sight can meet the gaze of man or angel than is seen in this part of the picture.

Almost all the murders that are committed in the land are executed under the demoniac influence of rum, and hence the efforts on the part of so many criminals and their friends to rid themselves of the penalty of the law, because they knew not what they were doing, as if the putting themselves in that position did not merit the righteous condemnation of some stern law also. There are few who are so reckless and hard-hearted by nature as to nerve themselves to the deliberate performance of an act that would knowingly sever the thread of life, and send a soul out of the world, while they forever after were to be haunted by the conviction that they were to be confronted with a trial in the future with such a witness against them. No; take the cup of alcoholic mixtures from the hands of men, and the three hundred murders that stain our annual records would be substituted by an untarnished blank, or left to the recital of something else far less painful in its character. The cells of our prisons and jails echo to the moans of captives who would never have been found there, had they been in the sane condition they might have been. An eminent judge of New York, who lived to be upwards of eighty years old, declared in a public assembly, that "the greater portion of the trials for murder, for assaults and batteries, that were brought into court since his entrance on the practice of law, originated in drunkenness." Another one also declared, in addressing a jury, "If it were not for this drinking, you and I would have nothing to do."

In a document, published by the legislature of the above-named state, there is seen the following paragraph: —

"There can be no doubt that, of all the proximate sources of crime, the use of intoxicating liquors is the most prolific and the most deadly. Of other causes it may be said that they slay their thousands; of this it may be acknowledged that it slays its tens of thousands."

According to the computation of those interested in making the observations, there are four hundred who put an end to their own life every year, by reason of this same thing; so many who terminate their earthly career, and rush unbidden into the presence of their Creator, with no account to render but that they were weary of the existence their own course had embittered. At best, intemperance is but the prime minister of death. To it is to be attributed a large amount of the yearly mortality. The pestilential diseases that sweep across the country at certain seasons are a thousand times worse for it. The system that is poisoned by drink cannot and does not resist disease. Of these it may be said, "They do not live out half their days." Multitudes of these drop out of the social ranks, and are buried out of sight, when otherwise their lives would be prolonged, and they might be a blessing to the world. Our lunatic asylums are crowded with those who rave in the darkness of everlasting night, because the burning fluid has quenched the light of reason, and thrown them upon society — helpless imbeciles. Were the punishment to cease with the first transgressor, there might be some consolation in that; but the stare of thousands of idiotic

POLICE COURT.

children declares it to be visited upon the generation to come. The avenues to the souls of such have been wantonly closed, and they, too, make their silent appeal to benevolent humanity for protection, instruction, and support.

Dr. Story, of Chicago, in writing upon "alcohol and its effects," estimates the annual cost of the idiocy of drunkenness — counting the loss that comes through a want of intelligence and industry — at forty-two millions of dollars. However much may be done to ameliorate the condition of these, they must remain, in great measure, an incubus upon society as long as they live.

Then a home must be provided for the inebriate himself, and the public must be taxed, or Charity must bring her offerings by thousands, that a restraint might be put upon those who have no power to restrain themselves, and are therefore dangerous to the well-being of society; and so there is hardly an end to the capital which is called into requisition because of intemperance. Besides, it damages every good institution seriously. The Sabbath is not what it would be but for this. The order and quiet which should prevail upon this day are often broken in upon by the noisy revelries of those who are given to the cup, and have no regard for anything, human or divine. No law of earth or heaven intimidates them. Even isolated country places, where Nature invites to reflection, are not exempt from the shoutings and rude conduct of the drunken loafer; and, worse than this, the evil has crept into the very bosom of the church, and some are sheltered in its embrace whose example does a ruinous work for those outside, to say nothing of the unhappy influence upon them, and those with whom they are so sacredly connected. Temperance is one of the cardinal virtues of the gospel, and if there is a place upon earth where it should shine with untarnished lustre, where it should be preserved in all its Heaven-appointed purity, that place is the church. That should be the beacon-light on the hill, to allure and guide the steps of every wanderer on the wilds, and within its sacred enclosure there should be nothing to cast a shadow. The church is planted for the elevation of society, and whatever is true and ennobling within it, is due largely to the workings of this mighty instrumentality; but it has to cope with a giant evil.

An English writer, in speaking of the religious advancement of his people, in connection with this subject, says, "We stud our land with churches and chapels; we employ thousands of clergymen to preach to the people, and hundreds of missionaries to visit them at their homes; thousands of Bibles and tracts are distributed to them gratuitously every year, and thousands of Sunday schools are established for the religious education of the young; yet, notwithstanding all these appliances, licentiousness and ungodliness abound in our midst, and the noblest aspirations of humanity receive some mysterious check, and instead of finding expression in a pure and godlike life, they are kept under, and vice and drunkenness are pursued. Now, how are we to account for this sad state of things? It is because the ministers of morality and religion are opposed by the ministers of vice and immorality, and buildings dedicated to the worship of God are opposed, and vastly outnumbered, by temples set apart to the worship of Bacchus."

There is no fitness or inclination to appreciate sacred things when reason and conscience are altogether perverted from their legitimate use; when everything before the mind is only impure and unholy, and they have resigned themselves, soul and body, to the dominion of an evil spirit, to be controlled by it. Hence the fearful amount of profanity in society. If one has any reverence for the name of the Most High, he cannot walk through the streets of a city, or scarcely a lane in the country, without having his moral sensibilities shocked beyond measure, because of the oaths and imprecations that come to his ears; and he is constrained to say within himself, Verily intemperance is blighting our fair heritage. And who are these? They are not always among the low. A large proportion of these are *young men*, "the bone and sinew of the republic, the hope of the church and the state, and many of them connected with the best families in the land. Many of these have been taken from the bar, the medical profession, the pulpit, from mercantile and mechanical walks, where they might have been eminently useful;" and they have turned their backs upon all the interesting relations of life, and all the sacred connections of society, with a determined bent, as it seems, to defeat the end of their creation. To see how the wasting influence spreads, we have but to observe the testimony of those who have gone out to foreign lands, professedly to carry light to those who have it not, and see how their work is made tenfold harder, because men will manufacture and circulate everywhere the wretched poison. Says the English author already cited, in speaking of the counteracting influence that intemperance opposes at home, —

"The drink system is no less obstructive to missionary operations abroad. Missionary societies are the glory of the age in which we live, and one of its most striking characteristics; and we cannot also but greatly admire those noble, self-denying men, who, spurning fatigue and hardship, and fearless of danger, forsake home, country, and kindred, in order to carry into remote and barbarous climes the blessings of civilization and Christianity. But, alas! here we find cause for sad reflection and tears. The ship which carries the missionary to his field of toil and danger also, alas! carries with it an agent that shall prove more deadly, destructive, and debasing to the savage than even their senseless idolatry. That agent is *fire-water*. Thus do we more than undo all that the missionary accomplishes. We carry to the heathen the gospel in the right hand, and the whiskey bottle in the left; and to every convert made to the former, a thousand are made to the latter. When we mark how Europeans have contaminated the natives of the Pacific islands, of the American wilds, and even of India, with the abominable vices and loathsome diseases of Britain, we may surmise that, had we never touched their shores, but left them entirely to their ignorance and their idols, they would not have been in a worse condition than they are now. Indeed, how can we expect them to receive readily the gospel at our hands, when they know that day by day we are inflicting upon them disease and misery?"

While we fully believe that Christianity is a power that is destined to triumph, and that it is slowly but surely working its way among the children of superstition and sin, we cannot hide ourselves from the fact that it is not what it might be, were there no untoward obstacles in the way. A missionary of Upper Canada, at Owen Sound, says, —

"Indians — men that I love and value as brethren — have told me, with low and melancholy voices, of the devastation of this thing. A friend, a few weeks ago, told me of an effort he once made to induce a chief of a tribe of the Mohawk nation to allow a friend of his, a missionary, to come and dwell among them.

"'What you preach? *Preach Christ?*'

"'Yes.'

"'Don't want Christ — no Christ!'

"My friend persevered. At length the chief got

warm, and, towering to his full height, with a volcanic fire in his eye, broke out, —

"'Once we were powerful; we were a great nation; our young men were many; our lodges were full of children; our enemies feared us; *but Christ came, and brought the fire-water.* Now we are very poor; we are weak; nobody fears us; our lodges are empty; our hunting-grounds are deserted; our council-fires are gone out. We don't want Christ. Go!'"

From India, Persia, and the islands of the sea, it is all the same. They bear universal testimony to the corrupting power of the unhallowed stimulant.

Rev. Mr. Ellis, of the Sandwich Islands, writes, —

"Since the introduction of Christianity to these islands by the missionaries, there is no means which the enemies of morals and religion have employed more extensively and perseveringly, for the purpose of counteracting the influence of Christian instruction and corrupting and degrading the people, than the importation of spirituous liquors; and no means of evil have been employed with more injurious effects."

In connection with this thought is coupled the assertion and the appeal, which should not be without its effect, —

"Had the Christian church, in all its different denominations, waged war from the commencement; had she, at the origin of the movement, made it a great religious question; had she then put forth all her power, and used all her appliances, in this direction, — we should not now have been weeping over the wholesale destruction and debasement of our people; nor would that church herself have had to deplore her empty fanes and desolate altars, and the increasing indifference of the people to receive instruction at the hands of her appointed ministers. But 'it is never too late to mend.'

Let the church of Christ, in all her different departments, take up this great question, and identify herself with it, nailing under the banner of the cross the banner of teetotalism, and, with both waving above her, she will march onward to certain victory over licentiousness, inebriety, and 'the legions of Sin.'"

No one can look at even this outline sketch, and not see how the social system is suffering from the deadly incubus of drink. No pestilence that has ever swept through the country is to be compared to it. That is but temporary. The winds of heaven, the heats of summer, or the frosts of winter, may modify the procuring cause of these things; but none of them touch those blighting agencies of which we speak. Its devastations are worse than those of war. Its contests may be long and bloody, and we may turn from the immense sacrifice of human life with horror; but there comes a time when the sword is sheathed, and Peace proclaims a jubilee. But Intemperance is always marshalling her ranks, and filling up her armies — always slaughtering her thousands, and keeping up the din and roar of her battling legions. Society is bleeding, groaning, suffering, because of it. To stay this moral blight is the question of the day. No grander movement could claim the attention of men, and earth and heaven wait the result.

CHAPTER XII.

National Loss.

THEORY OF SOUND. — WHAT CONSTITUTES NATIONAL LIFE. — "BANK FOR LOSINGS." — PRODUCTIVE LABOR OF THE NATION LESSENED BY A DRINKING HABIT. — MOTIVES OF POLITICAL ECONOMY. — THE GRAIN-DESTROYING CURSE. — OBSTRUCTS TRADE AND COMMERCE. — IMPAIRS THE ARMY AND NAVY. — CURTAILS THE POWER OF LITERARY INSTITUTIONS. — AN IMAGINARY PICTURE.

THERE is a theory among men that anything once started never ceases its action; that sound, once wakened, goes on and on in endless vibration, as if it were a chain, whose ever-added links went on to infinity. If this be true in the natural world, something quite like unto it is true in the moral world. There are circles of influence that are ever widening, ever deepening, until they reach the farther shore of man's being and nature, and are lost in the larger ocean of aggregated existence, but still go on agitating and affecting things and conditions to their remotest bounds. The little thing that we saw nursed in the bosom of the family has become a threatening giant in our midst. We have followed it from the individual through family and social life, and now we come to the outer circle of visible results as the American people — the nation.

But what is the nation?

It is "the union of many homes, the people of which possess the same general characteristics, and have many interests in common, the whole being united under one government. It has also its laws, its great national institutions, its literature, its commercial relations with other lands, and a history of its own, pregnant with instruction. A nation, as an individual, should have noble purposes to accomplish, and a destiny to fulfil. This includes the protection of the people, the development of their resources, and, through the union in council of their greatest intellects, the blessings of education, and of all the loftier forms of civilized life. A nation, in fact, ought to be a blending and union of all the noblest traits that adorn our species. There is an ideal of a perfect nation, as well as of a perfect individual, and the world is struggling to attain it. The revolutions and changes going on among the nations are so many steps in this direction, and all, for the most part, so many expressions of those longings for that perfection of society of which, ever and anon, we have inspiring glimpses.

"Now, it is the prevailing opinion — an opinion based upon stern, grim facts, educed by careful inquiry, and confirmed by extensive observation — that intemperance is the great curse of this country, in comparison with which all other evils combined are as nothing; so that, were this one vice eradicated, we should attain to a state of unprecedented prosperity and greatness. It is acknowledged, even by our statesmen, that intemperance is the incubus which oppresses the national life, and that to roll this away would be to set the nation free in a glorious path of progress."

What hope can we have for the vigor and prosperity of the national life, if the streams which feed it have corrupt and deadly elements? Every individual is a part of this great organism, and is responsible, to a certain extent, for what it is. Down through these and the family, the social and state relations, there is coming that which will add to, or detract from, national glory and interest. It is in these several departments that the material is furnished that is to mould the character and destiny of the higher life; and in proportion to the strength and efficiency manifested here will be the development and application of the national resources which are to contribute to its wealth. We have seen how extensively the drinking system prevails in all the lower grades of life and action, and it requires no long-drawn conclusion to forecast the stamp of the higher. "The child is father to the man," said a would-be philosopher; so the blending and inter-blending of these public relations write the character of the former upon the latter. The nation cannot, will not, be what it ought, and what it might be, if all that ministers to its growth is withheld, or feebly supported.

In this connection, we are reminded of what Theodore Cuyler calls the "National Brandy Bank for Losings." It furnishes a key to the solution of many problems that are written with reference to our financial condition. It shows what becomes of the money that ought to go for the building up of the nation. Writing from the place where he resides, he says, —

"On the chief thoroughfare of this city, I often pass a stately savings bank, built of freestone, and I see groups of working people going in to deposit their hard-earned money. Some are mechanics; some are Irish domestics; some are poor widows laying by a few dollars for their fatherless children. But on the same street the Tempter has opened more than one *Bank for Losings.* In some parts of the city there is one nearly on every corner. In almost every rural hamlet, too, there is a similar institution. New York contains six thousand of them. In each of these Banks for Losings is a counter, on which old men and young, and even some wretched women, lay down their deposits in either paper or coin. The only *interest* that is paid on the deposits is in redness of eyes, foulness of breath, and remorse of conscience. Every one who makes a deposit *gains a loss.* One man goes into the bank with a full pocket, and comes out empty. Another goes in with a good character, and comes out with the word *drunk* written on his bloated face. I have even seen a mechanic enter in a bran new coat, and coming away again as if the mice had been nibbling at his elbows. I have known a young clerk to leave his *situation* behind him in one of these Banks of Losings. Several prosperous tradesmen have lost all their business there. Church members have been known to reel out from these seductive haunts, trying to walk straight, but *backsliding* at every step. If the cashiers of these institutions were honest, they would post on their doors some such notice as this: —

"BANK FOR LOSINGS.

"Open at all hours. Nothing taken in but good money. Nothing paid out but disgrace, and disease, and degradation, and death. An extra dividend of *delirium tremens* will be given to old depositors. A free pass to Perdition given to those who pay well at the counter. Also, tickets to Greenwood and other cemeteries, entitling the holder to a *Drunkard's Grave!* All the children of depositors sent, without charge, to the orphan asylum, or the almshouse."

It is because these banking institutions cost the national government so much, that we are impoverished, and come short of those rightful accumulated gains which should make us richer and better. These "dividends" and "deposits" are all in the wrong way — misnomers all. The destructive and obstructive influences occasioned thereby are almost beyond conception.

A whole nation is sometimes afflicted with famine, and this dispensation of Providence excites the sympathies of people, and stirs their benevolence in a most wonderful manner; but this, at its worst, can only touch the body, while this other ruins the soul, and is therefore more to be dreaded than any mere physical want, however great that may be. To think that men are voluntarily at work diminishing the strength of the national life, and dwarfing its very existence, is a most serious consideration. Let us look at some of the carefully prepared statistics that show how this is being done.

In the first place, it diminishes the productive labor of the nation. It is well known that those addicted to intemperance are not fitted for the discharge of their ordinary duties in any direction. Large numbers of them are given to perpetual idleness, never accomplishing anything. They are the most abject kind of hangers-on — leeches that draw out the life-blood of the nation continually. It is estimated that one seventh of all the people in the whole republic are actually within the ranks of the intemperate; that there are three hundred and thirty thousand men who are directly engaged in making and vending the destructive beverage, whose industry is thrown into the same channel, and who furnish this paradox to the world — the more industrious they are, the less remuneration does the nation receive at their hands. Calling the whole thing a waste, as we must, we see how great a proportion of industry is perverted from the nation's use, and made to subserve only its detriment. Add to this the capital invested in buildings, and the loss to industry from drunkards, criminals, and paupers; and the expense of police, of courts of justice, of prisons and poorhouses; and the wholesale and all unlicensed dealers, numbering over twenty-one thousand, — and we have the loss of the labor of five hun-

hundred thousand persons, which, at five hundred dollars a year, as an average, amounts to two hundred and fifty millions of dollars. This does not include the loss of time of the seven hundred and fifty thousand drunkards. Half the time of these, at the rate of two dollars a day, amounts to two hundred and twenty-five millions a year. Nor does this take into account the imbecile thousands who are supported at the public expense besides.

The quantity of liquors made annually now, in their various departments, is estimated to be about five hundred and forty million gallons, — "enough," it is said, "to float a respectable navy." Many of those who are engaged in this traffic, directly or indirectly, become rich; and is not the nation benefited through them? How is it? Dr. Story asserts that "it takes about ten years, on an average, to make a fortune in the liquor business; and if they are so destructive to human health as to destroy, annually, one hundred thousand lives, as has been demonstrated, and since those who fall victims to drunkenness die twenty years before their time, it follows that every time one hundred thousand fortunes are made, twenty million years of human life are wasted, which is equal to sacrificing two hundred years of human life and industry, in order that one man shall amass a fortune.

Only one hundred thousand men make fortunes out of the business, while thirty-one million nine hundred thousand lose by the traffic, as they have to pay more for the necessaries and comforts of life than they would if it were suppressed. Thus we see that three hundred and twenty men lose, in order that one man may make. Is that fair? Is that economy? But supposing all who engaged in the liquor traffic, directly and indirectly, made more money than they could in any other way, to the full number of one million men, while all the rest of the people were losers, — is *that* fair? Is it right to tax thirty-one people in order to enrich one person, and that one no better than the rest? Would it be fair to tax four persons to enrich us? What has become of the good old democratic maxim, 'the greatest good of the greatest number?'"

The total result he sums up as follows: "Suppose that a day's labor is worth one dollar and board, and that there are three hundred working days in a year; then the one million people engaged in the liquor business would be worth three hundred million dollars a year. And the two million years of life and health (and therefore industry) that are annually destroyed would be worth six hundred million dollars, or a total of nine hundred million dollars. So that the whole thing is at variance with the first principles of political economy. It detracts so much from the truest and best interests of the nation. A gentleman of Massachusetts, in speaking upon this point, says, 'The capitals, materials, and labor, converted into ardent spirit, becomes a *total loss to the world*, and the community is taxed to make up the loss. Though the producer obtains his exchange, the manufacturer his reward, and the retailer his profit, the *consumer loses the whole*. Place the mind on this point, with all the intenseness of minute discovery, and show me the benefit which the consumer has derived from his purchase. If some benefit is not and cannot be derived, then it must be a *total loss*, involving all the capital, labor, and profit which the purchase costs. It is loss to the world, and doubly so to the *consumer;* for with this loss his physical and mental powers are impaired — the very capital he had invested for future use. Had the devouring element consumed the purchase, and spared the purchaser, his loss would have been comparatively small.

When labor and the resources of the country are applied in advancing the great objects for which man was created, and civil and political communities formed, and mature, and elevate, and purify the mind of man, and perfect all his powers, they become beneficial instruments for the public good. The more deeply this principle becomes fixed in the minds of men, the greater will be the demand upon these investments for carrying on the great purposes of improving the world, till man arrives at the highest elevation of which he is susceptible, in his present state of existence. The argument for the manufacture and sale of ardent spirits, derived from the fact that these employments afford occupation for multitudes, when viewed in its bearings on political economy, are unsound. What one gains another loses. Even if the government derive a revenue from the manufacture or sale, it changes not the case; the consumer loses the whole. The government can never be benefited by a traffic the result of which is a total loss to every one of the entire amount of the article which is the object of the traffic.'"

Some idea of the extent of the business is to be gained from the fact, that during the last fiscal year the amount of tax collected by the United States government on liquors was over fifty-two million dollars. Is the nation so much the richer? Poverty rises in the background, and utters an emphatic *No!* What a bartering of the more precious things are involved! What a story of mental, and moral, and pecuniary waste is back of it all!

Think, too, how the fruits and grains of the earth, that were meant for the actual sustenance and comfort of man, are appropriated. Englishmen complain bitterly of this. There was a time in the history of Ireland when the rage for drink was such, "that the inhabitants of that country converted their grain into spirit to such an extent as not to leave themselves sufficient for food to sustain life. Famine and privation were the result; and to prevent a recurrence of this state of things, the legislature passed an act to check the practice of free distillation. When famine again desolated that ill-fated land, in 1847 and 1848, and the greatest distress and privation were experienced by the poor, it was distinctly proved that there was an ample supply of grain to meet the necessities of the people; but, instead of being brought into the market to be disposed of for food, it was locked up in the granaries of breweries and distilleries, to be wantonly destroyed in the manufacture of intoxicating liquor. As a terrible result, half a million of people perished from starvation." If it be not true in its extreme renderings, as applied to our own country, it is, nevertheless, an almost incredible appropriation. Without staggering the mind with overwhelming totalities, take a single instance of a single branch, and that beer. There are three thousand breweries in the United States, that consume annually twenty-three million bushels of barley. Of course, this is multiplied, again and again, in other departments, so that a vast amount of the productions of the earth goes to swell the tide of human misery, instead of allowing it to accomplish its original design. That which should minister to the process of nutrition, in a natural way, is converted into that which poisons and blasts; reducing where it should strengthen, and tearing down where it should build up. All the great industries of the nation are related to each other, and are more or less dependent on one another. Trade and commerce are not what they would be were they unobstructed by this gigantic power. In various ways it is brought to bear upon the multiform schemes which tend to establish the laws that have it for their end to place these things upon a permanent and reliable basis.

A sober judgment, a cool and calm comprehension, and a broad and clear understanding, are all requisite to appreciate and carry out these things successfully. We have said it too many times to need the repetition of the truth here, that all this is lost in the condition of the intemperate man.

There are, then, the loss and disaster occasioned by the direct mismanagement and inefficiency of those upon whom devolves the care of that upon which the issue depends. How many valuable cargoes have been lost, and how many vessels with their entire crews have been buried beneath the waves of the ocean, simply because intemperance was at the helm! The army and navy have been sadly demoralized by reason of it. It was declared the greatest possible hinderance to the discipline of soldiers, by all the most thoughtful and sober-minded generals. Concerted plans of action, which demanded prompt and decisive measures, were often overthrown and rendered useless for this one reason, and when society looked for the return of her disbanded soldiery its solicitude spent itself mainly upon this one feature. "Drunkenness is *the* vice of the army," it hath been said. Away from all the gentle and restraining influences of home, and its watchful guardians, the tendency is to rioting and excess; and the natural indulgence of those feelings seems to be in one direction — that of drink and its consequent vices; and in this way, what is provided for the salvation of the country goes to further its ruin. Our educational institutions are the pride and glory of our land, and yet they do not occupy that position, or exert so wide and all-controlling an influence as they might, if their standard of temperance was as high as it ought to be. We look upon them as strong and mighty bulwarks, as moral safeguards, as so many stepping-stones up the ladder of national greatness; and so they are, in a very good degree ; but who does not know that the perfection of all these would be greatly enhanced by certain conditions — conditions which involve the uplifting and training of a mass of now degraded minds ? We know of many who have fallen out of these institutions by the way, and the consequences of their fall cannot be measured except by those ever-widening circles that we have seen to touch a remote boundary.

Bribery and corruption have not escaped the highest political action of states, and there are many stories of disgrace and defeat that are whispered about in private circles, or, perhaps, are chronicled among the historical literature of the day, that show with painful certainty the fact, that there is no stream left uncontaminated by this all-pervading taint.

But where are the words to follow up and trace out all these windings ? We are proud of our nation. The heathen Romans never despaired of a man who was proud of their republic. We hesitate not to acknowledge a pride in ours, and with that emotion there is mingled a profound regard for its honor ; but who or what threaten to assail it with fiercer hate and more disastrous consequences than this same demon of intemperance ? Facts are appalling, statistics overwhelming.

" President Everett computes that the use of alcoholic beverages has cost the United States, directly, in ten years twelve hundred million dollars ; has burned, or utterly destroyed, five million dollars more of property ; has destroyed three hundred thousand lives; sent one hundred and fifty thousand to our prisons, and one hundred thousand children to the poorhouses ; caused fifteen hundred murders, two thousand suicides, and has bequeathed to the country one million of orphan children. . . . . It is plain enough that this tremendous drain upon the nation's increase and substance, and the deepening degradation, year by year, of our industrial strength, cannot long continue without fatally undermining prosperity, the public credit, and political freedom. Measurably, the government is already passing under the control of two hundred thousand liquor dealers' besotted customers. Numbers of chief cities have been, and still are, held in what is little better than a state of siege by the rum power. State and city elections, not a few, are conspiracies against the republic, made possible by strong drink. Different departments of national and municipal authority have become foul with dishonor through intemperate and debauched officials. Not unlike the ancient fabled Laocoon, our country is in the constricting coils of the mighty serpent of the still, and we must bruise its head, or it will kill us and our children."

Imagine, now, what it would be to have all this reversed; to have these coils loosened, these fetters broken, and all the links sundered that bind us to the huge monster; to have all the vast enginery of individual, social, political, and national being move on with all the beauty and harmony that clear-headed reason could devise; to have all the moral and intellectual machinery of the land work on without any great disturbing friction; to have all the spiritual efforts for the renovation of the race pass on to full fruition by an unimpeded power; in short, to have everything free from the slimy trail of the foe. Who can picture what the American nation would be under such an administration? Is there no remedy? Are there no glimmerings of hope that this will ever be? It cometh not but by a mighty work; and whoso shall aid in perpetuating it will do something in ushering in the good time that all the good are hoping for.

CHAPTER XIII.

WHAT IS THE REMEDY?

NO "HAPPY VALLEY" BUT IN FANCY. — MORAL SUASION. — SIGNING THE PLEDGE. — SELF-RESPECT NEVER REGAINED. — GOUGH'S CONFESSION. — TOTAL ABSTINENCE THE ONLY TRUE REMEDY. — THE COURT CLERK. — TESTIMONY OF AN ENGLISH GENTLEMAN. — ANECDOTE OF FARRAGUT. — BIBLE PRINCIPLES. — HOMES FOR INEBRIATES. — VIEWS OF MR. POMEROY. — FROM THE PATIENT'S STANDPOINT. — CHAPLAIN'S STATEMENT. — LAW INTERFERENCE.

IT is pleasant to stand and gaze at a beautiful picture, when every figure and every scene upon the canvas make silent but eloquent appeal to the senses, in a way that ministers to the gratification of the whole being. It might be pleasing to our exacting desires for happiness, if we could always dwell amid beautiful sights, and be regaled with delightful sounds; but earth, in its best conditions now, affords no such "happy valley" to invite the children of men to a calm repose. Such places exist only in the regions of fancy, and there is no basis for any such hopeful anticipation, except as the mind soars aloft into the realm of the spiritual, and finds in the everlasting beyond a fulfilment of the promise that this ideal beauty and perfection are to be realized at some time and somewhere, in certain cases and under certain conditions. This side the immortal boundary the pictures of life are darkly shaded. In the shifting kaleidoscope with which we have to do, they are ever assuming new forms, and awakening new sensations. We would gladly escape from the view of many of them; but as we cannot, the question is, How shall we touch and retouch, so as to make the colors brighter and the forms fairer?

The picture of human life upon which we have been dwelling is sad and forbidding indeed. To see the creations of the divine Artist disfigured and discolored in such reckless manner as scarcely to leave a trace of the original beauty and workmanship, is a sorry sight indeed. The piteous, fallen spectacles of humanity that have passed before us in one long, melancholy procession, have served to confirm the idea that *total depravity* is written upon the hearts and ways of men. It almost inspires a feeling akin to that which impelled the monks and hermits of old to retire into the caves and deserts, that in these mountain fastnesses and retired places they might escape the contamination of the world, and a knowledge of what passed within it. This, however, betrays weakness, inasmuch as it implies a want of moral inertia, and an indisposition to grapple with the temptations of life, and be one of the laboring host to aid in the reformation of those who have gone astray. This work, in connection with the subject before us, is vast, urgent, and complicated. What can be done to save this host of drinking men? What arguments can be brought to bear upon them?

It is hardly to be supposed that the inventive genius of man can bring forward anything new, though he be urged by the strongest and highest motives of philanthropy. The hope lies in the persistent use of the same means and the same incentives that good people have been using for a long time. Some think that moral suasion ought to be sufficient to reclaim the drunkard; that if he is reasoned with rightly on the duty of abstaining from his self-indulgent habits, and warned of the inevitable consequences that will result therefrom, it will do as much good as anything. But, at the beginning, does he not know all this just as well as the one who tells him? Is he not perfectly sensible that it works all that his friend tells him, and more too? Said the author of the "Temperance Tales," "I believe moral suasion alone, as a means of ridding the world of drunkenness, would prove about as effectual as a bulrush for the stoppage of the Bosphorus. In spite of the expectations of the most sanguine suasionists, unless opposed by some more powerful barriers, this river of rum and ruin will flow on to eternity.

"The moral suasionist of modern times," he continues, "though not always inspired, presumes to accomplish, without the aid of law, more than was achieved, in the days of the apostles, by the power of the law and gospel combined." The most eloquent appeals that could possibly be made to bear upon one have been applied to individuals without any effect whatever. If there were any power in words, the pathetic, soul-melting, conscience-softening entreaties that have come from loving lips would have saved many a poor fellow from the curse of the drunkard. No! it is not in words to save one that has yielded himself to the power of this slavish habit. Some regard the "Pledge" as a certain means of reformation, and imagine that if you can once induce a man to put his name upon paper, he is on a firm platform ever after. At a certain stage, and with certain characters, there is hope that they will feel the force of the obligation, and honor the contract they have bound themselves to fulfil. While we give the "Temperance Pledge" honorable mention, and yield to its claims as a reformatory power in many instances, we yet have comparatively small faith that it will accomplish much for the salvation of the advanced drinker. The utter defiance of all law and order against all their convictions in these cases, the ignoring of all the most sacred pledges of love and affection in all their other relations, show what effect it is likely to have. Such a one might sign the pledge in a sober moment, when the pressure of persuasion is upon him; but these momentary resolves are swept away at the first breath of temptation, or the first sight of a boon companion. Does not a man give the most solemn pledge of his life, when he leads the being of his choice to the sacred altar, and declares that he will cherish and protect her as long as he lives, in all the days of good and evil that may come to them; and yet, what power hath this pledge when the demon of drink hath taken possession of him? If he will not regard this, what reason that he will honor that, when all his feelings, affections, and sensibilities are blunted and deadened, if not destroyed? There are some happy exceptions, it is true. It has been the first stepping-stone to honor and integrity in a good many instances, and therefore we gladly place it among those agencies that are to help on the blessed reform.

A few years ago, when the temperance reformation assumed a popular form, and so many reformed drunkards took the stand to plead the cause, the pledge had a prominent place. When John Hawkins was making his first speech, and telling the story of his degradation and restoration, a man from the gallery cried out in a tremulous voice, "Can I be saved, too?" 'Yes!" said the speaker, "come down and sign the pledge;" and amid the plaudits of the assembled multitude, he went and enrolled his name with those who promised to break away from an enticing and ruinous habit. Others, stimulated by example, followed on, and many, it is believed, were true to their engagement; but the best of these reformed ones never feel safe. Gough knew all the different phases of drunkenness and reformation; but hear what he said years after he had signed the pledge. It was a declaration during one of his lectures. "I am now fifty-three years old; and as I look back upon the past, as I mingle with the wise, the good, the pure, and the true, as I shake hands with such men as have grasped my hands to-night, I feel intense disgust and abhorrence of the days which that man spoke of as being happy. I would give my right hand to-night if I could forget them; if I could tear out from my memory the remembrance of the dark, black, damning days of degradation. But some say, 'You have recovered.' No! we can never recover from the effects of such a life. What a man sows, that shall he reap. Little things show whether such men recover or not. One little thing I may say, personally, if you please. I have tried to bring up some children, not my own — and two of them are on the platform to-night. One of the hinderances to my speech is, that they are there, and hear what I say. Last summer. I heard one of those girls say to my wife, 'Aunt Mary, is it not strange that uncle John should have got drunk?' I felt ashamed of myself; and is that not some penalty for a man to pay all the days of his life? I do feel ashamed; I feel as if I could hide myself in the earth; I felt to-night, when I took hold of hands that had never been stained with the intoxicating cup, as if I could lie down and let them set their feet upon me. There is not a man so well known to the public so utterly lonesome and isolated as I am. Did you ever hear of my ever being at a party? Never. I have not attended two for twenty-five years. Did you ever hear of my ever calling upon great men? No! and when I invite them, I do it with so much timidity that I do not much expect them to accept the invitation. I have asked some of the gentlemen here to-night to come and see me, but I do not believe they ever will. If a man invites me to a dinner party, I find an excuse. I never go to see people, because I stained the pages of my life's book. Though I may turn over ten thousand stainless pages, the stains on the other pages will remain."

So true is it that the sad effects of intemperance can never be fully wiped out. The most perfect and reliable cures have yet an element of uncertainty about them. We have become more and more convinced, with the turning of every leaf in this tragic history, that there is no safety, and no remedy, but in one thing, and that is *total abstinence.* If young men would take this as their motto, when they go out into the world, write it upon every finger of their hands, and live up to it in all their ways, it would do more to inaugurate a glorious reformation than all the brilliant theories of the moralizer, backed up by the most remarkable gifts of persuasion. If they would never begin to taste, and sip, and dally with the accursed thing, they would be all right, and never need to be hedged about with the thousand devices of temperance nurseries, that seek to keep them within proper bounds. We have yet to confront the manufacturer on his own ground; but while the thing exists, and is likely to, while it is made and sold everywhere, and so many are tempted by it, we shall have to dwell upon ways and means to check and avoid its influence as far as possible. Whatever other methods may be presented, however varied may be the advantages of any other system, there is but one rule of universal application — but one thing that meets the necessities of every condition, from the moderate tippler to the confirmed inebriate; and that is the last consideration we have named — the *entire* abstinence from everything that intoxicates. There is nothing but the entire removal of it from all sight and smell that will answer, in a majority of cases. We have seen how the habit grows upon one, how the thirst becomes so insatiable in its cravings as to brook no control, and in what way it bears the victim downward as by a swift and irresistible current. We believe there are thousands who are addicted to the use of the cup, who would lift up their heads and rejoice could they know that another drop of the deadly stimulant would never again pass before them; and yet they have not the moral courage to resist it.

At one time, the prohibitory law was up for consideration in a certain court. The clerk was a man given to drinking, and all the time through the debate he sat in fearful suspense lest the restraints which he deemed necessary would not be imposed. On the morning of the decision he entreated one of the judges to spare the law. Said he, "Sir, you know I am addicted to drinking; but you do not know — no living person can know — how I have struggled to break off this habit. Sometimes I have succeeded, and then these accursed liquor bars, like so many man-traps, have effected my fall. For this reason I have labored for the prohibitory law. Your decision is, with me, a matter of life and death." When the decision was handed him to record, he felt it to be like signing his own death-warrant. Hope failed him, despair seized him; amid the horrors of delirium tremens, when four men could not hold him, he sank away; and in less than four days was no more. Is there anything but abstinence that can save such as these? and how shall that be realized, unless the thing is put altogether beyond their reach, where there is no possibility of their laying hands upon it? It is urged that this is an extreme measure — and so it may be; but extreme cases demand extreme measures, and nothing short will meet the emergency. No half-way work will do here. Is there hope of a drinking man, when he says he will leave off gradually — that he will take only a little as he needs it? Do not his "needs" extravagantly multiply in his own estimation, until it takes an almost incredible supply to meet them?

There are a great many weak natures that are altogether incapable of bringing themselves up to any very strong powers of resistance; neither can they be brought so as to be kept up by any external influence, while within range of the peculiar temptation. They are good-hearted and generous, and in all respects would be a desirable acquisition to society but for this one thing. There is hope that such might be restored to their position and their privilege, if once abstinence was placed upon the throne, and they were made to feel its power. There are some among good people who seem to think this condition too rigid; that it costs too much; and that, perhaps, after all, a man is not any better off for so much severity. Not long since an English gentleman — member of Parliament — testified, before one hundred and fifty medical gentlemen at a public breakfast, that there was nothing like this total abstinence to promote his health and efficiency. "I myself," he says, "a long time ago, for the sake of influencing some men, who, I saw, were rapidly going down hill to destruction, determined to put myself in the position to give them unsuspected advice. I said, I will abstain for a month, and see how it answers with me; and finding it did answer, I went on for another month, and then for another. At the expiration of fifteen years subsequently, I thought it my duty to testify that, during the whole of that period I had enjoyed the best health, good spirits, and a great capacity for work; and now, seventeen years later, and after thirty-two years of abstinence from intoxicating drink, I confirm the same to you all. I testify before all this company, that scarcely any man can have had more uniform vigorous health than I have had; and for which I am deeply thankful, during the whole of the period I have named; and I have been a tolerably hard worker too; and I verily believe that I have been able to do more than I should have been able to do, if I had not been a total abstainer." The folly of those who believe it a special preparation for a special work, is a thousand times demonstrated by actual trial.

Secretary Seward used to tell the following story: —

"Everybody admired Farragut's heroism in clinging to the topmast to direct a battle; but there was another particular of that contest that no less forcibly illustrates his heroic character. 'Admiral,' said one of his officers, the night before the battle, 'won't you consent to give Jack a glass of grog in the morning; not enough to make him drunk, but enough to make him fight cheerfully?' 'Well,' replied the admiral, 'I have been to sea considerably, and have seen a battle or two, but I never found that I wanted rum to enable me to do my duty. I will order two cups of coffee to each man at two o'clock, and at eight o'clock I will pipe all hands to breakfast in Mobile Bay.' And he did give Jack the coffee; and then he went up to the mast-head and did it."

Some argue against total abstinence with the show of being wonderfully devoted to the interest of the country, and so declare that all this fanaticism of abstinence, if carried out, would impoverish the nation, by cutting off an immense revenue.

We fancy this would be more than met by the wealth that would pour in from a thousand other channels, as a consequence of the more intelligent and efficient system of labor that would prevail. Brain is by far the best propelling force of the country. It matters not what its hidden resources may be, if there be no discriminating power to develop and apply, and any one who has observed the deterioration of mental and physical energy under alcoholic sway knows full well that there is a vast expenditure in the wrong direction; that there is an almost incalculable waste of the material that would otherwise enrich. We would that it might be put to the test; that for a term of years the whole range of intoxicating drinks might be swept from the land, and all the department of industry be filled with men who could act out their own natural impulses and energies; and we would not fear for the results from this stand-point.

Torn from every other support, there are those who will flee to the Bible, and interpret it so as to favor their prejudices. To them it is of wonderful significance that Timothy was advised to take a "*little wine.*" They jump to the conclusion at once that Paul was not in favor of the "*total;*" and so they take license for indefinite indulgence, and feel very comfortable under the conviction that they have a mighty apostle to uphold them. Now, it is the easiest thing in the world for the unbiassed mind to discover that the spirit and teachings of the sacred Scriptures are all in harmony with this matter of abstinence.

"In regard to the assumption," says one, "that whatever is not expressly enjoined in the Bible is opposed to its spirit and aims, we must remember that it is not a book of *details.* It does not lay down special precepts to guide us in *all* those multitudinous circumstances under which mankind may be placed. Why, the world itself would not hold such a book, and to master it we should have to attain to the years of Methuselah.

"The Bible, in the main, is a book of broad and grand *principles*, easily applied to the circumstances of life. These principles are but few in number, easy to understand and remember. And what the sincere Christian should inquire is this: Is the temperance enterprise in harmony with these principles, or opposed to them? If the former, our duty is plain and unmistakable. If the latter, our duty is equally plain and unmistakable. When the Parliament of Tahiti consulted the queen respecting the admission of intoxicating drinks, she said, 'Let the *principles* contained in the New Testament be the foundation of all your proceedings;' and immediately they enacted a law against trading with any vessel that brought *ardent spirits.* It was not so much any isolated text, as the *principles* of the book generally, that guided their determination. They saw that love to God and man is the grand principle of the book, and that this love enjoins us to do nothing which would prove the means, directly or indirectly, of making a brother stumble, offend, or become weak, or fall into sin."

Well would it be if this Christian nation would emulate the example of these sea-girt islanders. Whichever way we turn, we cannot hide ourselves from the conviction that total abstinence is the only safety for man at the beginning, and the only cure for the drunkard. The public have recognized this latter fact in providing Homes for Inebriates, the special object of which is to remove them from all possibility of obtaining their wonted drink. They are regarded and treated as diseased persons, and probably there is no disease on earth that is so difficult to effect a radical cure as this. These institutions start with the position that alcohol is a poison; that systems charged with it are desperately poisoned, and in order to be saved, must be subjected to a thoroughly renovating process; and this is slow or more rapid according to the time the destructive elements have been at work. They also regard the inebriate as under the conditions of a certain kind of insanity, and therefore one part of their treatment lies in the diversion of mind from the one delusion; and so the same entertainments and amusements are provided in the one case as the other. There are several institutions of this character in various parts of the country; one at Chicago, Ill., one in Maryland, the "Washingtonian Home" of Boston, Mass., and one in Kings County, N. Y.; but as the one at Binghamton, N. Y., is the oldest, we confine ourselves to that, as a specimen of the characteristic working of the whole. It is said of him who founded it, "If he had possessed scientific ability and rectitude of purpose equal to his energy and persistence, he would have been acknowledged one of the great benefactors of his race, to be ranked with Howard, and Wilberforce, and Clarkson."

In order to have a clearer comprehension of the object, system, and results of these peculiar asylums, we quote from a pamphlet published under the direction of the superintendent at this place, by J. N. Pomeroy, Esq.

"This asylum was the first of its kind in the world. Others have since been established; but still there is in the public mind a complete ignorance in respect to its real objects and methods, a most profound misunderstanding as to what it professes to do, what it can do, and how it does its work. Doubtless nearly every patient who comes here shares in this ignorance. I have talked with several who pronounced the whole thing a failure and a delusion, because it does not accomplish what it never professed to perform, and what it would be impossible to perform without the help of Omnipotence. Many persons expect that the curative process is to change human nature; is to eradicate appetites and passions which were implanted in man by the Creator, and form a part of his very being; or to so transform the body that it may in future escape the dire effects of indulgence in alcoholic stimulants. Beyond a question, most persons without the institution, and most patients at their arrival, have a vague and confused notion, either that all appetite and desire for stimulants will be utterly destroyed, or that their physical systems will, in some manner, be so fortified that the moderate use of intoxicating drinks may thereafter be indulged in with impunity; and these patients and their friends are doubtless often disappointed or disgusted because such wonderful results are not accomplished. At the very opposite pole of opinion, there is another class of individuals who are equally wrong, both in their premises and their conclusions. Very many persons, generally those who are profoundly ignorant of mental and physiological phenomena, deny that the word *cure* is at all appropriate to the inebriate. They assert that, as the alcoholic habit is purely voluntary, it must be abandoned solely by an act of the will, and that it may always be thus overcome, no matter how closely it may have bound its willing victim.

"The temperance movement fails to accomplish the reclamation of very few confirmed drunkards, for the simple reason that it ignores all those radical changes, physical and mental, wrought by the alcoholic habit, and calls upon the drunkard, whose body is disorganized and whose will is weakened and almost destroyed, to achieve unassisted that which needs all the helps of the best medical science, and of the most complete sanitary discipline. As well might societies be formed for the suppression of insanity, which should content themselves with urging upon the insane to disregard and throw off their morbid delusions by the mere unaided efforts of their own will.

"What is meant by an inebriate, and what by his cure? Without now stopping to inquire into the effects of alcohol in all possible cases, — without now troubling ourselves with the vexed question whether it is at all times, under all circumstances, and with all individuals, injurious, — it is enough to say that there are persons whose original physical constitution and temperament are such that alcohol, once used, becomes to them a necessity; the brain and nerves, by virtue of some primary tendency, welcome the intruding force, and require the repeated stimulant, until at last they demand it with a vehemence which admits of no denial. The alcoholic habit is thus fixed, and the whole system must be wound up each day by increased doses of the poison, before either the mind or the body can perform their usual functions. Such persons are inebriates, and are none the less so because the use of alcohol may never be pushed by them so far as to produce complete intoxication.

"If a person once discovers that alcohol, at stated and regular times, has become a necessity to him, — if the leaving off from the accustomed amount, although that may be small, requires a struggle, — he may be absolutely certain that the primary constitutional tendency towards complete inebriety or alcoholism exists in him, and that he is in the most imminent danger. If the habit has once been thus formed, — if the stimulant has thus become a regular necessity, no matter how small may be the amount used, — it is as certain as death that that amount will be, and must be, steadily increased, until at last it obtains a complete mastery over body, mind, and soul.

"I know that we have all heard accounts of some extraordinary persons, some aged uncles or grandfathers, or other veterans, who, during a long life, took their stated number of glasses each day, never increasing or diminishing the amount consumed, and were none the worse. Such stories may be true, but they are opposed to all the deductions of medical science; they are opposed to an almost universal experience; in fact, they are to be regarded only as those few and solitary exceptions which bring into a stronger and clearer relief the terrible uniformity of the rule. I repeat, if the alcoholic habit is once fixed upon a man, the quantity of the stimulant required by him will steadily, and often with amazing rapidity, increase. Those who have formed this habit — no matter in what stage of its development they may be — are inebriates. There are thousands and tens of thousands who accurately answer to this description. They are not secluded from society; they are found in every profession and business; they engage in all the activities of our national life. The end of all is not the same. Many fall mortal victims of the poison, and die destroyed by alcohol as directly and truly as a soldier does by the bullet. Others linger through a longer life, with health impaired, with families shamed, with friends alienated, with powers weakened, with opportunities lost, until the end comes, and their career is acknowledged by all to have been a failure.

"Now, what is the cure? It is certainly not the total destruction of all appetite for stimulants, nor the eradication of the original constitutional tendency which I have described, for either of these would be simply impossible to all except the Creator himself. Nor is it any such physical change as will enable a person to resist the morbid effects of the poison, and will permit the use of alcohol in future with impunity; for such a re-organization of the body is clearly beyond the reach of medical science. There is no Medea's caldron from which the inebriate may emerge, and enjoy a perpetual youth of self-gratification. The cure consists solely in the destruction of the habit by absolute cessation, and in producing once more such a condition of body and mind in the patient that complete abstinence from the stimulant may become possible to him in the future. The very fact that the habit has once been formed shows that abstinence is necessary; for it demonstrates the existence in the person of that original constitutional tendency, which no appliances can remove, and which, yielded to, becomes as fatal as the plague or the leprosy. We may concede that others can drink from time to time without danger of excess, and with no perceptible injury, because, for some reason or other, their systems, their brains and nerves, do not fully respond to the effects of the poison. But the man in whom the fatal alcoholic tendency exists, and who has once yielded to it, and has become the slave of its terrible tyranny, cannot expect to be made any stronger to resist its destructive effects than he was at the very outset. If he can be placed back again into his primary condition, into that state of body and mind which existed before the first use of alcohol, he must be content; all the cure possible for him has been wrought."

After thus speaking of the object of the Asylum and its theory of cure, he says, —

"It must be confessed at once that the results do not come fully up to the lofty conception. We find, in fact, that, of all the persons who resort thither, some are not benefited in the least; some receive a partial or temporary good; while others still are permanently cured. How large a percentage of the whole number the latter class forms, it is of course impossible for me to say; but it is certainly very considerable — at least, fifty per cent."

There are three classes who are found within these institutions — those who have keenly felt the sad effects of the wretched habit, and are really and earnestly desirous of being, in some way, freed from its terrible power; then there are those who enter these folds to be exempt from the immediate physical consequences of excessive indulgence; and, lastly, those who have been placed there by their friends, and who have not sufficient desire to reform in themselves to make them willing to yield to the sanitary restraints. For this latter class, it is affirmed, but little can be done. In order to illustrate the power of the social element in the matter, we give an extract from the remarks of one who had himself graduated from this same institution: —

"Since intemperance is thus clearly a social sin, it seems to me that its cure is best sought by social means. It would be found impossible, I am convinced, to take each inebriate separately, and work his cure. The attempt, if made, would prove a failure. The patient would only brood over his sin and sufferings, grow morbidly conscious that the whole world despised him, fret and despond under restraint, and return to his evil habits, in order to seek relief from oppressive thoughts, as soon as the period of his probation or imprisonment was over. For this reason, the old methods of sending a young man on a voyage to China, of rusticating him in a retired farm-house, and other varied contrivances for freeing him from temptation by shutting him up with only his thoughts for companions, have proved to be failures. These plans all lacked the social element, and could not be successful without it. Man is so constituted that he needs companionship in all that he does. It is one of the oldest axioms of revelation that 'it is not good for man to be alone.' As an upright and pure citizen, he needs the support of those who will work with him in things 'lovely and of good report.' Much more, as a wavering, weak inebriate, does he need the countenance and sustaining example of those who are endeavoring to accomplish for themselves the task that he has undertaken. To my mind, — and I speak from experience, and not as a theorist, — this is one of the strongest arguments in favor of the establishment and hearty support of asylums for the cure of inebriates. I hold society responsible for the fall of most of those who are drunkards, and therefore bound to do all it can for their restoration. Until lately, it has been content to tempt young men to the indulgence or creation of an appetite for intoxicating liquors. When it had succeeded in arousing the thirst for liquor, it turned its back upon the maddened inebriate as an outcast; throwing him into prison when his body became helpless, or burying him in the Potter's Field when the natural result of ruin and death were accomplished.

"Let us be thankful that we have reached a day when the people begin to see the error of their ways, and are learning to take part of the drunkard's sin on their own shoulders. This feeling of responsibility is sufficient to arouse and quicken the public mind in the matter of saving and reforming the inebriate. But when, in addition, it becomes evident that this reformation has a social side, the best way in which the public can work for this end is made apparent. To be successful, the cure must be sought by means of asylums, where a number of patients are gathered together. Take the subject in its practical bearings. After a long course of indulgence in drink, a man finds that his will power is almost destroyed. He has made solemn promises, and broken them; has signed pledges, and violated them before the ink was scarcely dry; has tried change of location, and found the experiment unavailing. A friend advises him to go to an inebriate asylum. He hesitates, from natural shame of exhibiting himself in such a character, but at last consents. On his journey he fancies himself scorned and despised when he arrives at his destination, or given over to the companionship of the wrecks and dregs of humanity. But how is it in fact? As he enters his new home, he finds himself greeted by intelligent, refined, and robust gentlemen, gathered from all the walks of life. They are swift to make him realize that they all stand on the same footing, and that there is no one in the asylum who has the right to hold him in contempt. One after another details his experience as they become acquainted, and all tell him of what they are doing for themselves and one another. As soon as he is in a state to realize this fact, he is a new man. His moral sensibilities are awakened, and he begins to realize that there is hope for him in the future. What others are doing and have done he also can do for himself. Here are men, some of them the first in the land, who will never despise him, and he begins to believe that there may be others in the world whose hearts will be as kind. Henceforward, for him, 'there is no such word as *fail*.' Brooding thoughts are exchanged for healthy companionship, and doubts and fears for high resolves. As the result of this social influence, the work of reformation grows easier every day. From one and another he hears the story of those who have gone forth from the institution, and taken their places again in the busy world. They fill high positions in the professions, and places of trust in the business circles, and are living proofs of what can be done for the inebriate. When his own will has become strong enough to be trusted, he goes out into the battle with his eye on those whose story he knows, and who know his story, assured of their support and respect in the struggle that is to follow. This source of strength will always be with him; and it will grow and spread, until society at large will become eager to grasp the reformed inebriate by the hand, and restore him at once to his forfeited place, as having earned it by right of a hard battle crowned with victory.

"It will be seen that I am strongly in favor of institutions which have a large number of patients. The social effect is better. From a multitude of companions each person can choose those who are best suited to his habits and modes of thought. Besides, the presence of numbers increases self-confidence. It implies a practical belief in reformation, and a determination to shake off the bondage of vice. The presence of a dozen patients would appear merely experimental; the presence of a hundred has the appearance of settled convictions. Again, I speak from experience, recalling the good effect of the companionship of ninety inebriates, representing all sections and all classes, in my own case. They appealed at once to the social side of my nature, making me realize that there was yet a place that I might fill, and work for me to do. Their presence strengthened and upheld me in the dark hours of doubt that will come to all who are warring against an enemy within themselves. Without their help, the will would have to war alone against a foe whose wiles are legion."

With regard to the time necessary, Samuel W. Bush, the chaplain of the asylum, says, —

"It accords with my observation that the longer any one who is in such a condition as to be compelled to come here remains, the better it is for him. Six months, at least, are required to secure signal and permanent benefit. One year would, in many cases, be better. Of course there are many exceptional cases. After a life of wild and reckless dissipation, in which evil habits and modes of thought have become ingrained in his very nature, and with a constitution greatly impaired, it is not the work of a day to supersede all this by the use of means which will give health to the body, clearness and strength to the mind, and vigor to the moral and religious sensibilities, and the establishment of correct habits of thought and action. These being secured, the patient leaves the asylum, the grace of God accompanying him, a truly restored and renovated man.

"The value and necessity of an institution like this is not doubtful. *All* are benefited, without an exception, while within its walls; and more than half, it is believed, on data on which reliance can be placed, are permanently reformed. The most eminent of the medical faculty concur in the opinion that intemperance is a disease. However this may be, it is certain that it has a vampire hold on the unfortunate victim, from which to release himself he finds his own efforts powerless, and which is surely and rapidly spreading destruction throughout his whole nature. He therefore needs the aid of a physician, skilled in the maladies of both body and mind; a place — an asylum — where, free from temptation, and with ample time for reflection, in conjunction with his own efforts, he can allow the medical, hygienic, and moral treatment to work out its legitimate results."

This institution is not altogether a place to which the rich may flee to hide themselves, — those who are able to pay for all they have, — but it is largely of charitable working. The report for a recent year stands thus: —

20	per cent. are at the rate of	$20.00 per week.
20	" " " "	15.00 " "
30	" " " "	5.00 to 10.00 per week.
30	" are free.	
100		

While in all this we see how difficult it is to overcome the fearful habit of intemperance, it is not yet quite impossible

> "That men may rise on stepping-stones
> Of their dead selves to higher things."

Considering, however, the extreme risk that men run in the matter, it were safer and wiser not to bring themselves to this living death, where they are obliged to take these painful steps backward to regain a lost manhood. But back of all this individual obligation there is something more to be done. These remedial measures may do a good work as far as they go, but there needs an axe at the root of the tree. These roots are spread far and wide, and they need somebody to wield the axe long and well to make it effectual. Just as long as the law will lend its giant forces towards upholding and sustaining the spreading branches of this mighty thing, it will continue to curse the land. Multitudes will gather under and about it, and, lounging in the shadow thereof, they will idle their time away, waste their energies, and cripple the best interests of society and the nation, to say nothing of their own personal wreck and ruin.

If there were anything else that was capable of doing so much for mankind as total abstinence can do, the whole land would be wild with determination to procure it at whatever cost. There is nothing that allures the individual more strongly with promises of health, wealth, honor, peace, and every kind of happiness than this — nothing that prepares him better to become an ornament and support to society, and a blessing to the world generally. Would that the flag of total abstinence was waving over all the land, and all the people were safe within its folds! Surely that would be one kind of millennium.

CHAPTER XIV.

Temperance Workers.

GREAT PRINCIPLES IMMORTAL. — DR. BACON ON SLOW IDEAS. — THE FIRST PLEDGE. — THE EARLY AGITATION. — DR. JUSTIN EDWARDS. — THE FEARLESS PREACHER. — HON. THEODORE FRELINGHUYSEN. — DR. JEWETT. — REV. THOMAS P. HUNT. — REV. JOHN PIERPONT. — JUDGE CROSBY. — "THE NOTT CONTROVERSY." — FATHER MATHEW. — FATHER TAYLOR. — WASHINGTONIANS. — JOHN B. GOUGH.

We have affirmed our belief in the idea, that *great principles will eventually triumph;* that they will be sure to come out right in the end, although subject to a thousand untoward influences in the progression, and assailed by the malignant hates and envies of men. In this we are met by the taunting voices of many, saying, Where is the promise of this? Is it better now than it was in earlier times when there was less said or thought about it? On the contrary, is not intemperance stalking abroad more defiantly through all the land, raising its hydra head more threateningly than ever? In reply, we confess that its form is terrible, and its dominion from one end of the earth to the other; that in all the high and low places of our country there is great disturbance by reason of it, and yet there is a great difference in the way it is regarded now from what it was in the earlier history of our people. Intoxicating drinks are not so universally tolerated now as they once were. In thousands of places where they were once deemed essential, they are now ruled out as unworthy and un-Christian. It argues not against the work of reform that it has made no greater progress. Great reformations are always slow. It is not a quick work to uproot the rank and noxious weeds from the fruitful soil of the human heart. It is very much like trying to get rid of a crop of Canada thistles. There is no help in this latter case but to eject them, roots and all; and it takes time to do it. Dr. Leonard Bacon once said, while speaking of the progress of the temperance idea, "The most interesting aspect in which the temperance reformation presents itself to my mind, is as an illustration of the slow, but sure and certain, progress of one idea — of a simple, but great and just idea. That idea, when it was first announced, was announced in its legitimate connection with Christianity. It came from the bosom of the church of God; it came from the head of Christianity. It was argued and proved with texts from the gospel of our Lord Jesus Christ and the Epistles of the apostles. We wondered — those of us who composed it at that early period — wondered that there should be so much resistance to it, and we ascribed it to the power of selfishness; for we saw in every direction great interests, great commercial ambition, and powerful political interests, united against the progress of this idea. And yet, I apprehend, we ascribed too much of this resistance to the power of selfishness and interest. We ought to have remembered, more distinctly, perhaps, that great ideas, simple and commanding as they are, make but too slow progress to dominion over the minds of nations and individuals. You may convince an individual of the truth of an idea in conversation with him alone; but he does not stay convinced. The sympathy between his mind and that of the vast multitude is too strong, and it is with your argument as it fared with Cato when he read Plato on the immortality of the soul; he was convinced, and believed; but when he had shut the book, he could not remember the force of reasoning in the argument. It is therefore in this way, on this principle, that truth, simple and commanding as it may be, makes but slow progress towards dominion over communities and nations." If it be that it is slowly permeating society, that it is silently perfecting itself in the convictions of men, there is hope that the day of practical results is coming. There are a host of honorable worthies who have given themselves to this work with untiring energy and zeal. They have lent the full force of their commanding talents to aid in the mighty enterprise, and many of them have gone up to receive the reward of their labors in a higher sphere. We have not space to give to each and all that consideration which their merits respectively demand; but we propose to give sketches of some of the leading spirits of different periods, and the manner in which they addressed themselves to the existing evil. Heaven never moves the world to a great work but what it supplies agencies to meet the demand. When great occasions call for superior intellects, they are always forthcoming. They rise up, perchance, from some obscure corner, where they have been held in a course of unconscious training for their special work, and surprise all by their peculiar fitness.

It is often found, in tracing things back to their sources, that great matters have originated in a small way, through acts that have borne no significance to their after consequences. It is like throwing the stone into the water, and the narrow circle grows wider and wider still, unto the end. One Micajah Pendleton, of Virginia, is said to have drawn up the first temperance pledge of which we have any knowledge. That was in the year 1800, and was designed in a special manner for his own household, and was on the total abstinence basis. As this came to be known, other families imitated his example, until it became quite an extensive home institution in the state. Eight years later, the first real temperance organization was effected at Moreau, Saratoga Co., N. Y., under the guardianship of Dr. B. J. Clark and Rev. Lebbeus Armstrong, and forty-seven male members signed the pledge. One article of their constitution provided that no member should drink "rum, gin, whiskey, wine, or any distilled spirits," and a fine of twenty-five cents was imposed upon every one who should be guilty of violating the pledge. There was no movement of general interest, however, until 1811, when Dr. Rush, of Philadelphia, came before the General Assembly of the Presbyterian church, in session there at the time, and urged the necessity of inaugurating some scheme that should have a tendency to awaken the public mind to the wide-spread and increasing ravages of intemperance. But these were only the faint streaks of dawn before the day.

In 1825, the Rev. Dr. Justin Edwards, that mighty and fearless worker in every good cause, took his stand, in battle array, against the foe, and produced a strong impression on the public mind by his well-directed efforts. Possessing a remarkably clear and discriminating mind, having a strong and commanding utterance, there were few men of that day or this who could rivet the attention of a congregation, either in the pulpit or the more public convention, more strongly than he. He seemed to be raised up by Providence to act a special part at this particular stage of the great reform. His denunciatory language and powerful arguments appealed to the hearts and consciences of men, and they heard and trembled. At this period both ministers and people looked upon the infant reformation as something to be kept outside the church. To have it cradled in her bosom was more than they could bear. "Talk temperance as much as you please," they said, "in your temperance meetings; but bring it not into the pulpit on the Sabbath." Faithfulness and boldness in this matter turned many a minister from his place of settlement; and, if it was nothing more, a single sermon might so offend some of the best families, so called, — some wealthy brewer, distiller, or, perhaps, wholesale dealer, — that they would withdraw their patronage and friendship, and make it as uncomfortable as possible for the well-meaning brother. But once convinced of his duty, Dr. Edwards was not the man to hesitate or parley. He felt bound to come out and openly remonstrate against the prevalent delusion, and thus he spoke: "Shall the fires which make this poison, burn on the Sabbath? Shall Jehovah be insulted by the appearance in the sanctuary of men who use it, and yet the Sabbath not be occupied by light and love to abolish the use? Shall it cause the word of the Lord, even from the pulpit, to fall as upon a rock, and yet the pulpit be dumb? or speak only on week days, when those who traffic in it have so much to do in furnishing the poison, that they have no time, and less inclination, to hear? If Satan can cause this to be believed, and those who manufacture, sell, and use the weapons of his warfare, and multiply the trophies of his victory, not hear of their sins on the Sabbath, when God speaks to the conscience; or be instructed from the pulpit, his mercy seat, by the tears and blood of a Saviour, to flee from coming damnation, — the adversary will keep his stronghold; church members will garrison it, and provision it, and fight for him. From the communion table he will muster recruits, and find officers in those who distribute the elements to fight his battles, and people, with increasing numbers, his dark domains to the end of time. If we may not, in this warfare, on the Lord's day, when he himself goes forth to the battle, and commands upon the field; if we may not use his weapons, forged in heaven, and from the high places of his erection pour them down, thick, heavy, and hot, upon the enemy, we may fight until we die, and he will esteem our iron as straw, and our brass as rotten wood; our darts he will count as stubble, and laugh at the glittering of our spear."

Another minister, of unrecorded name, was greatly distressed on the question of duty. There were those among the members of his church whose business it was to sell the vile stuff, and others who were using it in their families, and all seemed given over to the fell influence of the soul-destroying curse. He knew it was most hazardous to allude to the evil on the Sabbath. He expected, if he did, some of his best people would leave the house; but he said, "Sink or swim, live or die, I cannot go on so. I must do my duty, and leave the event with God." He did it, and boldly called the selling of ardent spirit as a beverage a crime, and the using of intoxicating drink a sin against the body and against the soul. Men felt that they were in a house on fire, and there was no escape into the open air. Women felt there was no religion in it, and they would not hear such preaching. The next morning, some wholesale dealers and consumers, heavy tax-payers, met on the sidewalk, and said one to another, "We will bear this no longer; let us drive him off." A dry wag, listening to their complaints and threats, said, "That's right, brothers;" and, alluding to several noted for their infidelity, profanity, and Sabbath-breaking, "Go and get those," he continued, "and get a vote to drive him out." They started back, for they were professors of religion, and good men. They saw where they were, and where their minister stood, and how he had done his duty. Some gave up their traffic, all were quiet, and never more had that man any difficulty in doing his duty.

Dr. Lyman Beecher thundered forth his anathemas, and made such language as the following ring in the ears of every one engaged in the traffic: —

"Can we lawfully amass property by a course of trade which fills the land with beggars, and widows, and orphans, and crimes; which peoples the graveyard with premature mortality, and the world of woe with the victims of despair? Could all the forms of evil produced in the land by intemperance come upon us in one horrid array, it would appall the nation, and put an end to the traffic in ardent spirits. If, in every dwelling built by blood, the stone from the wall should utter all the cries which the bloody traffic extorts, and the beam out of the timber should echo them back, who would build such a house? What if in every part of the dwelling, from the cellar upward, through all the halls and chambers, babblings and contentions, and voices and groans, and shrieks and wailings, were heard day and night? What if the cold blood oozed out, and stood in drops upon the walls, and, by preternatural art, all the ghastly skulls and bones of the victims destroyed by intemperance should stand upon the walls, in horrid sculpture, within and without the building? who would rear such a building? What if, at eventide and at midnight, the airy forms of intemperance were dimly seen haunting the distilleries and stores where they received their bane — following the track of the ship engaged in the commerce — walking the waves — flitting athwart the deck — sitting upon the rigging, and sending up from the hold within, and from the waves without, groans and loud laments and wailings! Who would attend such stores? Who would labor in such distilleries? Who would navigate such ships? O! were the sky over our heads one great whispering gallery, bringing down about us all the lamentation and woe which intemperance creates, and the firm earth one sonorous medium of sound, bringing up around us from beneath, the wailings of the damned, whom the commerce in ardent spirits had sent thither, — these tremendous realities, assailing our sense, would invigorate our conscience, and give decision to our purpose of reformation. But these evils are as real as if the stone did cry out of the wall, and the beam answered it; as real as if, day and night, wailings were heard in every part of the dwelling, and blood and skeletons were seen upon every wall; as real as if the ghostly forms of departed victims flitted about the ship as she passed over the billows, and showed themselves nightly about stores and distilleries, and with unearthly voices screamed in our ears their loud lament. They are as real as if the sky over our heads collected and brought down about us all the notes of sorrow in the land; and the firm earth should open a passage for the wailings of despair to come up from beneath."

Hon. Theodore Frelinghuysen was another man of resolute will and determined purpose, who gave his combined efforts to the matter of total abstinence, not allowing *wine* — as some were pleading for in his time, because they felt they were called upon to cut off the "right hand" and the "right foot," also. "The great principle," said he, "contended for, is the moral expediency of this pure standard. Let it be granted that men may lawfully drink wine; that in Palestine, where grapes hung upon the boughs in the greatest profusion, men did drink wine; that our Saviour himself drank wine, and sanctioned it by his example; yet how different are the circumstances in which we find ourselves at this day! Then there was no such thing as ardent spirits, by which men were brutalized and destroyed, both body and soul; and it might not have been necessary then to abstain from that which in our day we look upon as a temptation and a snare, leading men directly to intemperance. But now the case presents itself to us in this light. A great moral power, which may be exercised to promote the welfare of our fellow-men, is offered to us in this total abstinence principle. In a spirit of benignant feeling towards our race, we adopt it."

Dr. Jewett was long a faithful and earnest advocate — a popular lecturer — and by his own personal efforts did much to promote the cause in various parts of the country. In his story of "Forty Years' Fight with the Drink Demon," he relates the incidents and adventures of this long conflict, and also speaks of many of those who were associated with him in the great enterprise. Among these was Rev. Thomas P. Hunt, of Pennsylvania, of whom it is said, he gave the whole subject a more thoughtful and candid consideration than almost any other living man. Those who knew him recollect the deformed figure, and also remember the expression of his keen eye, the peculiar tones of his impressive voice, which lent a charm and power to whatever he said. A friend says of him, by the time he had related an incident, "all eyes were riveted upon that little crooked man, with the large mouth and the lightning eyes, and all ears were open to hear instruction from him." Such was the effect of the following, with which he commenced his narrative on a certain evening: —

"Ladies and Gentlemen: I last evening delivered a discourse at Washington Factory Village, in the town of Coventry. As I was quite at leisure during the afternoon preceding the lecture, I proposed to walk out for a little exercise. A friend suggested that I might do some service to the people of the village, perhaps, by calling on Mr. Capwell, the keeper of the hotel, and having a talk with him. He was represented to me as a very clever sort of a man, good-natured, not at all inclined to be abusive, and it was thought my words might be of service to him. I called upon him; introduced myself as the person who was to speak on temperance in the evening, and found him disposed to listen to me with patience and candor. I told him I had been informed that he was the possessor of considerable real estate in the village, and assured him that whatever should have the effect to lessen the intelligence of the people, and to lower the standard of public morals, as I was quite sure his traffic would do, though he might not intend it, would most certainly diminish the value of his real estate, as it would render the village a less desirable place of residence. And I suggested to him that, in the long run, he would lose more by this depreciation of property, than he would gain, directly, by his traffic. He was listening to me with evident interest, and I could not but hope I was making a favorable impression on his mind, when, all at once, a side door opened, and a little bit of a woman rushed into the room so swiftly that her cap-border was turned back on her head by the current of air she created, and in a very excited manner, and with a very shrill voice, she exclaimed, 'I *do* wish that people would mind their own business.'

"Taken quite aback for the moment by this startling introduction and speech, I replied, 'Well, madam, and so do I! I agree with you, exactly, madam. That is an *excellent* sentiment of yours. I approve of it everywhere and always. I am a temperance lecturer, madam, and you see now, that while I am persuading this gentleman, your husband, very likely, madam, to abandon the sale of liquors, which make men drunk, I was laboring right along in the line of my business. You see I agree with you entirely. That is an excellent sentiment of yours. One reason why I labor to persuade men to leave off drinking, is because the use of liquor does, notoriously, lead men to neglect their business. For instance, here is a carpenter. He has a fine shop and good tools. He is himself a good workman, and has not only apprentices to aid him, but also skilled workmen. He ought to do a large business, but he does not. What is the trouble? The public know that he is a free drinker, and that he has, frequently, in the midst of an important job, gone off on a spree, and the work has stopped in consequence. Business men don't like to intrust to him important jobs on that account. Now, don't you see, if I could induce that clever carpenter to leave off his drinking, he would thereafter *mind his own business*. You see I agree with you exactly, madam.' Just here she turned upon her heel and rushed out of the room, not even stopping to bid me good afternoon. I felt aggrieved at it. I naturally like the ladies, and love to be in agreement with them always when I can. And when, as in this case, I take great pains to prove that I am in accord with them, I like to have the fact appreciated, and to be treated with courtesy."

In 1838, at a state convention held in Boston, Mass., it was resolved that an effort should be made to secure, from the legislature of the state, at its next session, a law prohibiting the traffic, and Rev. John Pierpont was commissioned to present a petition to that honorable body, in which occurs this emphatic and eloquent paragraph: —

"If I be willingly accessory to my brother's death, by a pistol or cord, the law holds me guilty; but guiltless if I mix his death-drink in a cup. The halter is my reward if I bring him his death in a bowl of hemlock; if in a glass of spirits, I am rewarded with his purse. Yet who would not rather die, who would not rather see his child die, by hemlock than rum? The law raises me a gallows if I set fire to my neighbor's house, though not a soul perish in the flames. But I may throw a torch into his household — I may lead his children through a fire more consuming than Moloch's — I may make his whole family a burnt-offering upon the altar of Mammon, and the same law holds its shield between me and harm.

"It has installed me in my office, and it comes in to protect alike the priest, 'the altar, and the God.' For the *victims* it has no sympathies. For them it provides neither ransom nor avenger. But there is an *Avenger*. While these sacrifices are smoking on their thousand altars, through the length and breadth of our land, the Ruler of the nations is bringing upon us the penalties of his laws, in the consequences of breaking them. Even now, He who renders to every land, as to every man, according to its works, is showing us that He is as strict to visit with suffering those who violate his organic and moral laws, as he is ready to accumulate good upon those who observe them. The fields of our great country, which He has charged with the elements of plenty, — which are, every year, waiting to be bountiful, — which He waters, 'that they may bud and bring forth, and give seed to the sower, and bread to the eater,' are becoming like the field of the slothful man of old. They are 'overgrown with thorns; nettles are covering the face thereof; and the stone walls thereof are broken down.' The hand and the mind of the cultivator are struck with the palsy of intemperance. A great portion of the bread-corn, which the land, grateful for even niggardly culture, pours into the husbandman's bosom, is snatched from his children's mouths for the craving maw of the distillery; and when that which God gave as the supporter of life has been converted into its destroyer, the vessels that waft the destruction to the nations on the Baltic, the Mediterranean, and the Black Seas, bring back from those nations, and at their own price, the very bread of which we have first robbed ourselves, in order that we may ruin them."

The law was enacted, and Judge Crosby, agent of the Massachusetts Temperance Union, sent out a circular, which embodied an urgent appeal to the friends of temperance everywhere to sustain the majesty of law, and work for the general good of the cause. After suggesting some methods, he concludes by saying, "Remember that deliverance from the evils of the rum traffic and use is too great a blessing to be obtained without great labor. Would you have angels' joy? Do angels' work: visit the sick — feed the hungry — clothe the naked — bind up the broken heart — and wipe away the tear of the drunkard's wife; and will not the laborer have his hire?"

In 1846 occurred what was called the "Nott controversy." Dr. Nott, President of Union College, entered the field as a temperance lecturer, and by the power of his commanding eloquence and distinguished scholarship, he drew large and appreciative audiences, and exerted a wide influence. But, notwithstanding his finished productions, many took exception to the whole thing, because of an inclination which was manifest to favor the use of wines, as largely exempt from alcoholic influence. Total abstinence had come to be a thing of meaning among the people, and it was feared that such authority would be so perverted as to produce bad practical results. Eminent men took issue against him, and the contest was warm; but it was finally settled by the bold statement of the venerable president, which left no doubt as to where he stood: "I hold to the utter abandonment of the use, as a beverage, of distilled or fermented liquors of every sort, especially of wines, whether good or bad, having much or little alcohol in them;" and this is the language with which he addressed the venders: —

"Brethren, inn-keepers, grocers; whose business it has been to sell to drinkers the drunkard's drink, has it never occurred to your minds that the liquors dispensed were destined, though unseen by you, to blanch some glow of health, to wither some blossom of hope, to disturb some asylum of peace, to pollute some sanctuary of innocence, or plant gratuitous, perhaps enduring misery in some bosom of joy? Have you never in imagination followed the wretched inebriate, whose glass you have poured out, or whose jug or bottle you have filled, — have you never, in imagination, followed him to his unblessed and comfortless abode? Have you never mentally witnessed the faded cheek and tearful eye of his broken-hearted wife — never witnessed the wistful look and stifled cry of his terror-stricken children, waiting at nightfall his dreaded return, and marked the thrill of horror which the approaching sound of his footsteps sent across their bosoms? Have you never, in thought, marked his rude entrance, his ferocious look, his savage yell, and that demoniacal frenzy under the influence of which — father, husband, as he was — he drove both wife and children forth, exposed to the wintry blast and the peltings of the pitiless storm, or, denying them even this refuge, how he has smitten them both to the earth beneath his murderous arm?

"And ye, men of fortune, manufacturers, importers, wholesale dealers, will you not, for the sake of the young and the old, the rich, the poor, the happy, the miserable, — in one word, for the sake of our common humanity, in all the states and forms in which it is presented, — will you not shut up your distilleries, countermand your orders, and announce the Heaven-approved resolution never hereafter to do aught to swell the issue of these waters of woe and death with which this young republic is already flooded? Have you never thought, as you rolled out and delivered to the purchaser his cask, how many mothers must mourn, how many wives must suffer, how many children must supplicate, how many men of virtue must be corrupted, men of honor debased, and of intelligence demented, by partaking of that fatal poison? These are evils which God registers in his book of remembrance, and which the day of judgment will bring to light; for at home and abroad, in the city and the country, in the solitude and by the wayside, it is not blessings, but curses, that the venders of intoxicating liquors dispense to their customers."

The reformation received a new impetus in 1849 by the arrival of Father Mathew from Ireland. He had been a zealous laborer among his own countrymen, inducing thousands to sign the pledge, and encouraging them in every way to hold on in the good way. His fame had spread to these shores, and much was hoped for, especially among those of his own nationality, by his peculiar force and tact. They flocked about him, and listened to him as they would not listen to any other on the blessings of temperance, and the importance of taking a decided stand for it. On one occasion, an old man kept drawing nearer to his side, until within reach of his hand, when Father Mathew placed it upon his head in blessing. The astonished subject looked up and stammered forth, —

"And here ye are a blessing a hot-headed *Orange*-man!" alluding to a political distinction of his own country.

"I don't care if you are a *lemon*-man," said the fervid apostle, "if you will sign the pledge and keep it."

He went through the country, awakening an interest in the grand work wherever he journeyed. At all points the people did him honor as the champion of a good cause. At Washington he was invited to a seat within the bar of the House, and several handsome tributes were paid to his worth by some of the first men in the country. General Cass said, —

"This is but a complimentary notice to a distinguished man just arrived among us, and well does he merit it. He is a stranger to us personally, but he has won a world-wide renown. He comes among us upon a mission of benevolence, not unlike Howard, whose name and deeds rank high in the annals of philanthropy, and who sought to carry hope and comfort into the darkest cells, and to alleviate the moral and physical condition of their unhappy tenants. He comes to break the bonds of the captive, and to set the prisoner free; to redeem the lost; to confirm the wavering; and to aid in saving all from the dangers and temptations of intemperance. It is a noble mission, and nobly is he fulfilling it."

Societies sprang into existence that were made to bear his name, and multitudes ascribed their salvation, from a temporal foe at least, to his efforts.

L. M. Sargent was a young man of collegiate education, who prepared himself for the legal profession, but, inheriting sufficient pecuniary resources to enable him to rise independent of that, and having decided literary taste, he took the pen in defence of the popular cause, and by his books and tracts he disseminated widely the spirit of resistance against the nation's enemy.

"Father Taylor" was another warrior in the ranks. Dr. Jewett says of him, —

"I have a very distinct recollection of his speech at a temperance soiree, got up by the ladies of Charlestown, Mass. All matters connected with it had been happily arranged, and "Father Taylor" was in one of his best moods. After presenting to the assembled throng some startling views of the terrible system on which the ladies were then waging a pretty vigorous war, he closed by one of those bursts of eloquence which it would seem impossible to forget. Scores, perhaps hundreds, now living in sight of the granite shaft, will remember the occasion, and, if they shall peruse these pages, will bear witness to the accuracy of the report I am about to make of his words, after the lapse of almost thirty years: —

"'And here it is yet, the accursed system, to plague and torture us, although we have exposed its villanies until it would seem that Satan himself ought to be ashamed to have any connection with it. I am not sure but he is, but some of his servants have more brass and less shame than their master. Yes, here it is yet; and over there, too, in the great city, — the Athens of America, where the church spires, as they point upward, are almost as thick as the masts of the shipping along the wharves, — all the machinery of the drunkard-making, soul-destroying business is in perfect running order, from the low grog holes on the dock — kept open to ruin my poor sailor boys — to the great black establishments in Still House Square, which are pouring out the elements of death, even on God's holy day, and sending up a smoke as from the pit forever and ever! And your wives and daughters, even as they walk to their churches on Sunday, brush the very skirts of their silk dresses against the mouths of open grog shops that gape by the way. And your poorhouses are full, and your courts and prisons are filled with the victims of this infernal rum traffic; and your homes are full of sorrow, and the hearts of your wives and mothers; and yet the system is tolerated. Yes, and when we ask some men what is to be done about it, they tell you you can't stop it! No, you can't stop it! And yet' (darting across the platform, and pointing in the direction of the monument, he exclaimed, in a voice that pierced one's ears like the blare of a trumpet), 'there's Bunker Hill, and you say you can't stop it! And up yonder are Lexington and Concord, where your fathers fought for the right, and bled and died. And you look on those monuments and boast of the heroism of your fathers, and then tell us we must submit to be taxed and tortured by this rum business, and we can't stop it! No! And yet' (drawing himself up to his full height, and expanding his naturally broad chest as though the words he would utter had blocked up the usual avenues of speech, and were about to force their way out by an explosion, he exclaimed, in a sort of whispered scream), 'your fathers — your patriotic fathers — could make a cup of tea for his Britannic majesty out of a whole cargo, and you can't cork up a gin-jug! Ha!'"

Such was "Father Taylor," the sailor preacher. "His name and fame had reached distant states and cities, and distinguished scholars and statesmen would, when in Boston on the Sabbath, find their way to the Mariners' chapel, to listen to the man of the sea, who got his diploma before the mast, whose theology was about as variable as the wind and the weather, and yet whose earnestness and native eloquence had power to captivate and hold in rapt attention, often for a full hour, the most gifted and highly cultivated in the land, while bringing tears to the eyes of bronzed and hard men, as he cheered the desponding, startled the thoughtless and indifferent, and awakened in the breasts of many of the charmed circle before him aspirations for a higher and better life."

In what was called the Washingtonian movement there came a new and novel feature to the work. Drunkards from the lowest depths of degradation lifted themselves up, and went on to the stage with their thrilling narratives of how they fell and rose again, and it created a sensation almost without a parallel. Under the influence of that movement, thousands signed the pledge, and were saved to themselves, their families, and their country. All along down through the pathway of the years, there have not been wanting faithful workers in this part of the vineyard. They are a noble host, and their names would make a long list. They live in the memories and hearts of men, and whatever they have done for the good of their race will meet its appropriate reward.

THE WASHINGTONIANS.

There is one more name, without which our galaxy would not be complete — John B. Gough. He still lives, and the world knows him, and what he has done. The power of his resistless eloquence to touch the heart and sway the multitude is seen and felt by all who have heard him. Words cannot describe it, but, as a specimen of his early efforts, we give the following paragraph in closing: —

"What fills the almshouses and jails? What brings yon trembling wretch upon the gallows? It is drink. And we might call upon those in the tomb to break forth. Ye mouldering victims! wipe the grave dust crumbling from your brow; stalk forth, in your tattered shrouds and bony whiteness, to testify against the drink! Come, come forth from the gallows, you spirit-maddened man-slayer! give up your bloody knife, and stalk forth to testify against it! Crawl from the slimy ooze, ye drowned drunkards, and with suffocation's blue and livid lips speak out against the drink! Unroll the record of the past, and let the recording angel read out the murder indictments written in God's book of remembrance! Ay, let the past be unfolded, and the shrieks of victims wailing be borne down upon the night blast! Snap your burning chains, ye denizens of the pit, and come up sheeted in the fire, dripping with the flames of hell, and with your trumpet tongues testify against the damnation of the drink!"

Of those who began this work, some are living to-day, and I should like to stand now and see the mighty enterprise as it rises before them. They worked hard; they lifted the first turf, prepared the way in which to lay the corner-stone; they laid it amid persecution and storms. They worked under the surface, and men almost forgot that there were busy hands laying the solid foundation far down beneath. By and by they got the foundation above the surface, and then commenced another storm of persecution. Now we see the superstructure, pillar after pillar, tower after tower, column after column, with the capitals emblazoned, "Love, truth, sympathy, and good-will to all men." Old men gaze upon it as it grows up before them. They will not live to see it completed, but they see in faith the crowning cope-stone set upon it. Meek-eyed women weep as it grows in beauty; children strew the pathway of workmen with flowers. We do not see its beauty yet; we do not see the magnificence of the superstructure yet, because it is in process of erection. Scaffolding, ropes, ladders, workmen ascending and descending, mar the beauty of the building; but by and by, when the hosts who have labored shall come up over a thousand battle-fields, waving with bright grain, never again to be crushed in the distillery; through vineyards under trellised vines, with grapes hanging with all their purple glory, never again to be pressed into that which can debase and degrade mankind; when they shall come through orchards, under trees hanging thick with golden, pulpy fruit, never to be turned into that which can injure and debase; when they shall come up to the last distillery, and destroy it; to the last stream of liquid death, and dry it up; to the last weeping wife, and wipe her tears gently away; to the last little child, and lift him up to stand where God wills that mankind should stand; to the last drunkard, and nerve him to burst the burning fetters, and make a glorious accompaniment to the song of freedom by the clanking of his broken chain — then, ah, then! will the cope-stone be set upon it, the scaffolding will fall with a crash, and the building will start in its wondrous beauty before an astonished world.

CHAPTER XV.

Temperance Societies.

UNITED ACTION, FIRST NATIONAL TEMPERANCE CONVENTION. — VIEW OF DR. HITCHCOCK. — MEETING AT FANEUIL HALL. — REV. JOHN MARSH. — WORLD'S TEMPERANCE CONVENTION AT LONDON. — TEMPERANCE AND LIFE INSURANCE. — SONS OF TEMPERANCE. — GOOD TEMPLARS. — THEIR ORIGIN. — FATHER BRISTOL. — TEMPLARS OF HONOR AND TEMPERANCE. — EXTRACT FROM TEMPLARS' MANUAL. — RECHABITES. — GOOD SAMARITANS. — IS TEMPERANCE A FAILURE ?

"Union is strength." A general cannot fight his battles without an army of disciplined soldiers. They must be organized, equipped, and labor with some concerted plan of action, or failure will be written upon every attempt. So these able and efficient workers in the temperance movement thought, and they went to work to marshal their forces and decide upon some definite plan of action, some systematic method of procedure. A high purpose urged them onward. Their eyes were fixed upon a grand consummation — upon the time when victory should perch on their banners, and the world should be free from the dominion of intemperance. It nerved them to mighty efforts. Such results were worthy of united and persistent action, and by such only could they be obtained. It was no sectional consideration. The whole land was suffering, and the plan must embrace the uttermost border. Most of those who were deeply interested were men engaged in preaching the everlasting gospel, and their hearts were absorbed in the work; but how could the Heaven-appointed truths with which they had to do, have any power over the hearts and consciences of men while they were hardened and seared under the stupefying potions of an ever-active poison? A way must be paved whereon truth must do its legitimate work, or their labors were fruitless. Thus they reasoned, and upon this they acted. From the commencement of the agitation there had been a steady progression of the ideas and principles of reform. The opinions and efforts of these men had been like leaven, silently working its way into society, and showing its influence everywhere. The rapidity of action may be seen in the fact, that in six years from the first inauguration of effort, it was estimated there were, in different parts of our country, over four thousand temperance societies, with over half a million of members; fifteen hundred distilleries had ceased their operations, and four thousand merchants had ceased to continue their unholy traffic in the unwholesome beverage. It was also supposed that a million and a half of persons had abstained from the use of ardent spirits, and that twenty thousand families were in ease and comfort who otherwise would have been cursed with poverty and wretchedness. This greatly cheered and encouraged those who were interested in the matter, and agencies were multiplied, new conditions of working added; so that the year following that which made the above calculations, the statistics had nearly doubled, and the interest had extended not only through the land, but also to our ships on the ocean; and those who were wont to set sail with this in their cargo, now knew it no more.

It would swell the present volume far beyond our intention, to follow out, minutely, the different societies, with their varied forms, that have been springing up, here and there, all along down the pathway of years. Their name is Legion. While we give our attention to a few of the more prominent, and seek to trace out the advance of the public mind in these, we yet commend the many for their works of mercy and labors of love, all of which shall be counted in the summing up of those things which are to redeem, as we hope, our fair heritage from the curse that has so long been upon it. The first National Temperance Convention was held at Philadelphia, on the 24th of May, 1833, in the Hall of Independence. There were present at that meeting four hundred delegates, from twenty-one states. It was pronounced the largest assembly that ever convened together for any moral purpose, in this or any other country. The presiding officers were strong men. Their "object was, by the diffusion of information, and the exertion of a kind moral influence, to extend the principles and blessings of temperance throughout the world." To us, who occupy the present high plane of temperance reform, it seems strange to observe the action on this occasion; but it is to be remembered that the stalwart conditions of manhood are not to be looked for in infancy. It was a promising little thing, but it was not grown up. They had a long and animating discussion upon "a resolution which expressed the sentiment that the traffic in ardent spirits, to be used as a beverage, is *morally wrong*, and ought to be universally abandoned." It was finally passed; and says a writer of the time, "Had the convention done nothing else but, after examination, expressed their opinion on this point, they had done a deed which would have marked them as benefactors to their country."

Such they were, and as such are they regarded to this day. Their ideas became the basis of reform; but gradually the lines were drawn closer, and the conditions made more rigid, until in 1836, when the American Temperance Union was formed on the principle of total abstinence, and was destined to become the leading organization of the land. The pledge of the Union was as follows: "We, the undersigned, do agree that we will not use intoxicating liquors as a beverage, nor traffic in them; that we will not provide them as an article of entertainment, or for persons in our employment, and that in all suitable ways we will discountenance their use throughout the community." The sweeping nature of this created much opposition. Some doubted the propriety of having anything to do with the exclusion of fermented drinks; some believed that wine and beer were essential to a certain class; especially was the latter useful to our foreign population; and others dreaded the agitation and conflict in various ways. About this time, Dr. Hitchcock, of Amherst College, came out with a declaration that was of no uncertain sound. "I have watched," he says, "the reformation of some dozens of inebriates, and have been compelled to witness the relapse of many who had run well for a time; and I say, without any fear of contradiction, that the greatest obstacle to the reformation of drunkards is the habitual use of wine, beer, cider, and cordials by the respectable members of the community; as in very many, I believe in most, cases, intemperate habits are formed, the love of alcoholic drinks induced, by the habitual use of these lighter beverages. I rejoice to say, that a very great majority of the several hundreds of clergymen of my acquaintance are decided friends of the temperance cause, and, both by preaching and practice, inculcate total abstinence from all that can intoxicate, as a beverage."

In this way, and under such patronage, did the idea gain strength, and obtain practical lodgment in the minds of the people; and from the parent societies there went forth innumerable local branches that contributed to the vigor and development of the whole. In 1840, the famous Washingtonian Society came into existence, having for its prime movers a few from the lowest ranks of intemperance. These banded together, and bound themselves to the work of reform. They told their determination to others, and it went, like an electric current, into the very heart of society. Everywhere drunkards began to think of the possibility of doing likewise. Immense meetings were called and addressed by these reclaimed ones. We have before spoken of John Hawkins, and of his wonderful restoration. A large meeting was held at Faneuil Hall, Boston — so large that the ancient building was not capable of their accommodation; and there he made a speech which contained these words: "When I compare the past with the present, my days of intemperance with my present peace and sobriety, my past degradation with my present position in this hall — the Cradle of Liberty — I am overwhelmed. It seems to be holy ground. I never expected to see this hall. I had heard of it in boyhood. It was here that Otis and the elder Adams argued the principles of independence; and we now meet here to declare ourselves free and independent; to make a second declaration, not quite so lengthy as the old one, but it promises life, liberty, and the pursuit of happiness. Our forefathers pledged their lives, and fortunes, and sacred honors. We, too, will pledge our honor, and our life, but our fortunes have gone for rum. Poor though we drunkards are, and miserable, even in the gutter, we will pledge our lives to maintain sobriety." Numbers flocked to sign the pledge, and a City Society was at once formed, which, at the latter part of the year, had sent out two hundred and seventeen delegates, to one hundred and sixty towns, in five different states, on errands of love. Baltimore was the centre from whence these influences radiated. The Rev. John Marsh, who was for thirty years corresponding secretary of the American

Temperance Union, thus writes with reference to this period: "I was induced to go to Baltimore to attend the first anniversary of the Washington Temperance Society, and there saw one thousand men stand in a line as reformed men, and moved in procession with thousands more about the city. It was a most interesting spectacle, as their wives and children stood on the sidewalks, many of them weeping for joy as they beheld their husbands and fathers marching onward in sobriety and moral dignity. In proof of the genuineness of the work, it was ascertained that the whiskey inspections for the city were reduced, in six months, forty thousand five hundred and eighty-two gallons, — a decrease of twenty-five per cent., — and that great peace and quietness everywhere prevailed. These extraordinary movements at Baltimore and elsewhere, among our drunken population, filled all hearts with joy at our sixth anniversary, and at the third National Convention at Saratoga Springs. In the annual report which I presented in May, I condensed, as far as possible, the wonderful events which had transpired, and which will be contemplated, when these generations have passed away, as almost incredible; but never to be surrendered as wild enthusiasm and profitless hallucination. Never, probably, was there a large body of men, of high intelgence and business character, so melted into gratitude, joy, and love, as were the attendants on that National Convention at Saratoga Springs, in the month of August, at the relation of their experience by several of the reformed, and the relation of numerous most affecting incidents by others. As chairman of the business committee, I found no difficulty in framing suitable resolutions for the occasion; and where there was such a prevalence of love and gratitude, the presiding officer had no occasion for force to control the meeting. It was a sort of millennium to thousands who had hoped and prayed that sin and sorrow from intoxicating drinks might be done away. "Never before," said a venerable member, "did five hundred and sixty men assemble, and continue days as a deliberative body, without one unkind look or action." It is thought that, under these reformatory influences, one hundred and fifty thousand decidedly intemperate men took the pledge, and abandoned their cups.

Dr. Beard, one of our noted countrymen, — a scholar and a philanthropist, — was travelling about this time in foreign countries. He had previously caught the spirit of the new crusade, and he carried it with him, and was instrumental in kindling the flame of feeling against intemperance wherever he went. This, in conjunction with American interest, culminated in the idea of a World's Temperance Convention, where, from all quarters of the globe, the advocates of the cause might gather together, and by united wisdom and consultation speed on the work so gloriously begun. It was decided that London should be the theatre of action in the important matter. A voyage to Europe was not so common a thing as now, and only thirty-one among all our states were found ready to go; but these were a host in themselves — strong, vigorous, and ready for the work. The single state of New York furnished eight of these, and Massachusetts the same number. "In England there were high-raised expectations from this gathering of the friends of reform." "As a mere matter of curiosity," said the Teetotal Times, a temperance organ of that place, "there will be much to interest. Who does not wish to see the founders of great systems, the originators of wise plans, the first apostles of important truths? We pray that the spirit of wisdom and charity may shed its choicest influences on the assembly, and that its deliberations may prove instrumental, through the divine blessing, in accomplishing a vast amount of good."

"The convention sat five days, listening to able papers which were prepared for the occasion; to discussions of important resolutions; to reports of different countries, and to projects of reform, and greater extension of the temperance cause. Says the indefatigable secretary already quoted, "While in England, I spent not a little time and strength in kindling up a civil war. I saw there the beer-and-brandy-god wringing out the life-blood from thousands and tens of thousands of her sons. And yet it was England's greatest benefactor! Everywhere the god was praised, as bringing vast revenues to the crown; as the life of the army and of the navy; as the source and spring of all mental energy and social happiness. The licensed victuallers of London alone paid the government eleven millions annually. So I proposed, in my speech at Exeter Hall, that, as London was full of statues to distinguished benefactors, a statue should be erected in Hyde Park to England's greatest friend, the beer-and-brandy-god, higher than any statue ever conceived; and, to carry it out as it should be, I would have, on one side, carved by the most eminent sculptors, groups of miserable drunkards, raving in delirium tremens, tearing the hair of their wives, beating their children; and on another side I would have paupers, lunatics, and criminals, in chains and on the gallows through strong drink; on another, parents pressing into the horrid temple, and leading their children up to their god, to drink early of his cup. But not ridicule, it was found, could move England in her self-complacency. There must be war — exterminating war. 'Down with the tyrant!' I cried; so we found it in America; and as I said this, I was received with shouts and applause. The public press responded, and said, 'These Americans have put some new thoughts into our minds. We confess we are converts to their views; and we are greatly mistaken in the signs of the times, if the late interviews which the teetotalers have had with the Americans have not produced similar results in the minds of others. Hence a crusade against the traffic has already commenced.' "

Thus were things made to act and react in the great work. Men clasped hands from across the sea, and pledged themselves to labor for the redemption of a sin-cursed people. In 1850 there arose an agitation of the subject in connection with life insurance companies. The attention of the American mind was enlisted by the statement of an English fact, to the effect that "the number of deaths in the Temperance Insurance Company were less than half of that insured in all other companies of the kingdom; while they suffered no losses from intemperance." It therefore took upon itself this form: "Should a temperance man join in a company with a hard-drinking man, or even a moderate drinker, much more an intemperate man, his money might for years be going to the families of such, while his family, through his long continuance in life from temperance, would have no benefit." The more the subject was contemplated, the more were all impressed with the importance of a company on the abstinence principle. The very existence of such an institution, it was thought, would be a powerful auxiliary to the cause of temperance in general, besides operating as a restraint upon the individuals immediately concerned. Strong men indorsed the scheme, and, after much deliberation, it was decided to make the attempt. A constitution was adopted, and a capital of one hundred thousand dollars fixed upon, in one thousand shares of one hundred dollars each, on which ten dollars were to be paid at the beginning. Officers were chosen, and all things bade fair for a successful opening; but, alas! public sentiment was not sufficiently advanced to afford the requisite basis. One who was interested in it says, "Other cities wished for the location; moneyed men in New York were already stockholders in institutions which might be injured by this; a spirit of rivalry and jealousy sprang up; temperance men might be good moral reformers, but no managers of moneyed institutions; and so, from a failure to get the stock taken, it died out, when, it is even now believed, it might have become one of our greatest insurance companies, and have been of incalculable importance to the cause of temperance."

The subject is again revived, and efforts are being made at the present time to secure the achievement of this important result. In addition to the various temperance societies that have sprung up in almost every town and state in the Union, there are various *orders* of equally wide dominion, having for their ostensible object the suppression of the evils of intemperance in every prevailing form. Some of these are secret organizations, and, consequently, the working of the internal machinery is concealed from public view. The tree is known by its fruits, is an inspired statement; and every one has this principle before him to determine his judgment upon their action.

The "Sons of Temperance" was one of the first institutions of the kind, and was organized in 1842, and now numbers thirty-seven grand and about two thousand subordinate divisions, located in the different states and territories, and extending over the borders into other dominions. This order has secret pass-words for admittance to their meetings, and the members are required to make weekly payments, which constitute a fund towards the relief of their suffering brethren, or whatever the general interest of the association may demand. At their twenty-eighth annual session, which was held in

Chicago last year, the committee on the state of the order thus spoke: "In relation to political action, its necessity and duty should be impressed on every member of our order. We are bound to vote temperance as strongly as we are bound to practise it. But of the mode of doing it, every member must be left free to decide for himself. It must be wholly left to each man's judgment and conscience. The state of our Order, and its success in the future, depend not so much on what is done within us, as upon what is done outside divisions. We shall be, and ought to be, judged by our work. Many things are to be done; the inebriate is to be reclaimed, the pledge is to be circulated, the press is to be sustained, the lecture field to be supplied, the young are to be trained to temperance in the cadet section and the Sunday school, the ballot is to be invoked, prohibitory legislation is to be secured and sustained, not only in our states and provinces, but by national action, where that is requisite; to do all this, that agency must be used that does its work the best. The future of our order is, therefore, in our own hands, and dependent upon ourselves." There are "Sons," and "Daughters," and "Cadets" of Temperance; the latter being a youthful band, who, after the requisite training, are to be received to the fostering care of the parent society. Their underlying principle is total abstinence.

Another strong organization is the "Good Templars," which originated in 1851, and now numbers forty-five grand and about six thousand subordinate lodges. It has become a mighty power in the United States, reaching in some way almost every town, village, and county in the land. The total membership of the last report was nearly four hundred thousand. This, too, is a secret agency. An effort has been made to trace it to its origin, but without any satisfactory result. A history of the order has been issued by J. Newton Pierce, of Pennsylvania, a prominent official of the ranks, and whatever we give we state upon his authority. "No record," he says, "is now to be found in the printed literature of our country that gives any account of its origin." It has seemed as if tradition and memory were to be the only sources from which we could possibly derive any information relative to the inception of the Order and the first meeting held. "The following paragraph," he says, "lately going the rounds of the temperance papers, adds but little certain knowledge upon the subject; nor is it correct in point of fact, as it is number twenty-two (!) on the record and on its charter;" but it shows "the early struggles to popularize a temperance order that has since spread itself so rapidly and widely over our fair land, that its name is in every hamlet, its light in nearly every borough, and a Grand Lodge in almost every state.

"Probably the oldest Good Templars' Lodge in the world is the Senaca Chief, in New York. One after another, it saw its sisters sink in despair and die; but the old veteran Chief had no thought of dying, and to-day, erect and vigorous, it gives a kindly smile and encouraging word to the great army that has sprung up around it. Its history is one of extensive notice. The members, each for himself and herself, made a solemn resolve, and wrote it on the innermost tablet of the heart, that, while life should last, the lodge-room should be lighted every week, the fire burning, and the door open to the inebriate. Week after week, a few devoted members met in that room. There was but little business to be done, save to put their hands into their pockets, and pay the rent; but little encouragement in the future. But never wearying, never despairing, that little band kept vigilant guard over the precious principles and secrets that to-day are implanted in the breasts of over half a million Good Templars." This last estimate, it will be seen, is a little higher than the official report; but there is no question but that the numerical strength of the order is rapidly increasing. Mr. Pierce thus relates his interview with Dr. R. C. Dunham, of Seneca Falls, one of those earliest interested in the project. He was seeking to trace out things to their source, and called upon him for information. "We found this veteran in the temperance cause at home. He accompanied us to the hall of their lodge, and there, upon one of its walls, we saw the original charter of 'Seneca Chief Lodge, No. 22, I. O. of G. T,' granted by Garry Chambers, G. W. C. T., January 6, 1853. And there he recounted how, night after night, they met in that room, during those trying years from 1855 to 1864, when the lodges all around them, and all over the state, were going down. When their Grand Lodge ceased to exist, for several years they made up their own pass-word; for they knew not to whom to send to obtain it. And yet, during all that time, they never had a thought of giving up. That time-worn and yet beautiful silk banner, the early pride of their lodge, was never allowed to trail in the dust, or to become a by-word and a mockery. That beautiful figure upon it, extending charity to fallen man, is yet bright and vivid, and, as ever, emblematic of the motto above it, of 'Faith, Hope, and Charity.' The name of Nathaniel Curtis, a reformed Washingtonian, is associated with the early history of the society. 'To have conceived this order, as it now exists,' says their faithful historian, 'would have required a mind of no ordinary calibre. It might not be necessary to have the most scientific training, or the highest literary culture; it might not be essential to have the most refined poetical taste, or mathematical acumen; but it must be a mind pre-eminently practical, capable of grasping the realities of life, and moulding them in such form as to make them practical for good. Our Order was not like a ship which starts not on her voyage until every part is fully perfected, and all needed supplies fully stored away. It was first started by a spirit of injured pride and dissatisfaction, by a young mind that had no comprehension of the magnitude of the work, nor of the moral machinery necessary for its success. Not until it passed from his hands, and was conducted by an older and wiser head, did it grow. Then was it found necessary to modify, amend, and add to its proportions, to make it effective and self-sustaining.'

"The 'Ritual' was afterwards put into the hands of Rev. Dr. Bristol, and, through his influence and working, the Order assumed a permanency and character before unknown. His faith was strong in the foundation of Good Templar principles, and that they must succeed in the overthrow of the rum power, and the establishment of prohibition. He deplored the disposition of some dissatisfied spirits, who will ever waste time in picking at the ritual and private work, instead of working for temperance with the best means at hand. 'It were much better,' says he, 'to put up with the few errors we have, than to rush into others we know not of, and work diligently and earnestly for the cause with the means placed in our hands. Man is not perfect, and never can make so perfect a ritual but that some fine-grained literary casuist may pick at what he may think he can prove to be an error or defect here or there.' He further says that the ritual and the degrees 'were designed to furnish temperance work, temperance literature, and temperance instruction, for the evening, for all lodges, uniformly, everywhere. It was to be the work of the evening, and thus would become the binding chain that would unite them in one grand army.'

"'Templars of Honor and Temperance' is an organization that was established in 1845, and now embraces twenty Grand Temples, with subordinates in nearly every state in the Union. It was intended as a higher temperance and fraternal organization, with advancement by degrees, as the members should be proved worthy. From their own 'Manual' we transcribe words which shall introduce the reader to their inner sanctum, and disclose the pillars on which their structure rests. The badge of a Templar 'is not only a symbol of innocence and purity, but of obedience to a vow. Long years ago, when truth and error were in close conflict, and the light of Christian principle was dawning upon the dark mountains of Europe, a small but chosen band of Knights Templars won the admiration of Christendom by their valiant deeds of noble daring. They were bound together as brothers by vows of obedience, purity, and charity, and consecrated to the defence of the Holy Temple and the devout pilgrims who pursued their way thither, or knelt at its sacred shrine. Above them, in the bloody conflict, had waved the banner of the cross; and when the contest was won, and it floated in triumph from the walls and towers of Jerusalem, they ceased not their duties, but became the protectors of the oppressed and the scourge of the oppressor. They were few in number, but dauntless in heart; for they knew that "Truth is mighty, and must prevail." We are Templars of Honor and Temperance. Our vow is one of abstinence and fraternity, our enemy is alcohol, our war one of extermination. To be successful, we must be united. Each one must add his strength to that of his brethren. We must not despise that which the feeblest can do. Each snow-flake is a constituent part of that mantle with which winter enshrouds the regions of the poles; each rain-drop quickens the mighty pulse of being. You must each labor for the other and the cause in honor and in truth; you must labor for humanity. Crime stalks without, linked with poverty and bloated with disease. Time, health, and money are squandered; bread is turned to poison, homes are laid waste, and every sacred thing is dishonored.

"'Fidelity to your vow will make you a true and loving, pure and faithful, knight-errant to the human race. Your Templar's vow is registered in heaven. None but brave men dare take such vows. The open enemy and stealthy foe await you. You have a shield and spear, and a God above. Stand forth, therefore, the champion of eternal principles, and you shall become pillars in our beautiful temple. You have approved our creed, and been admitted to our temple. You know how dark is the world, and how miserable the condition of those who tarry long at the wine, and mingle strong drink. You have seen the darkness disappear at the approach of light. Read our emblems. The five-pointed star symbols to us the first temperance movement. Its light struggled with the dark clouds of ignorance. Its rays are dim, for it symbols a feeble effort. It may have been brilliant to those who first beheld it; but its light penetrated not the deep caverns where the demon held his revels, and forged chains for his first victims. It served only to show the degradation to which the drunkard had fallen, and discover the infamy he had drawn around himself and those who should have looked to him for counsel, example, and support. It showed the road to the drunkard's doom; but it illumined no path that would lead him back to the quiet bowers of domestic bliss, and the fair fields of social confidence. The star of brighter rays, with its six points, reminds us of the Washingtonians. Their efforts were noble, and deserve the admiration and homage of every heart. Raised by the hand of God from the lowest deep of drunkenness, they proved that their manhood was not gone; that even the drunkard was a man, an immortal man; that he had the same aspirations, the same feelings, the same hopes and fears, as other men, down deep in his heart; that in his soul were the same longings for happiness and purity; that with him, in all his degradation, his better nature at times would assert his birthright, tell him of his immortality, and plead with angel eloquence for his redemption. He was saved. This was a new era in this godlike reform; it was a stand-point, brilliant with the light of hope, upon which the Christian philanthropist could place himself, and, by faith, view the redemption of every inebriate from the thraldom of intemperance. The star enclosed in the typical triangle is the emblem of the Sons of Temperance, that noble band of brothers, who rallied to continue what the Washingtonians had begun. An organized band, it sought to win the inebriate from his cups to a higher life. Its divisions multiplied all over the land; its tri-colored triangle was borne aloft in every state. Its plan was simple; its aim was noble. Its heart desired to accomplish all; but its arm was too feeble for the task. The temple, brilliant with the light of its nine-pointed star, is a symbol of our noble order. It brought the experience of the past and the wisdom of the present to perfect its organization. It is the result of consolidated mind, warmed by the fire of glowing hearts. By its ritual, embodying eternal truths; its ceremonies, as beautiful and chaste as matured imaginations can conceive; its signs, and grips, and secret tokens, — it lays hold of the strongest elements of success and perpetuity, and gathers around its altar hearts that never quail, and hands that never falter in its life-long crusade against intemperance and wrong.

Gaze upon that altar. It has deep significance to him who can read the lessons it imparts. It rests on the rock of Temperance, out of which gush crystal streams. Its sides are emblazoned with the emblems of truth, love, purity, and fidelity. On its top you see the Holy Bible, the blest book of God. From its pages come our principles and our duties. From Mount Sinai to the Mount of Beatitudes, it is resplendent with the truths our Order inculcates; and from Olivet to the holy city measured by John, gleams the light of hope to us. Here, too, is the triangle, enclosing the triple triangle, the emblem of our Order. Love, purity, and fidelity gleam upon its outer bars. The bars of the inner triangle are bright with our duties to God, to our brothers, and ourselves. Obedience to Him who hath created us with powers to enjoy the bliss of living, and with minds that can contemplate the magnificent grandeur of the universe, and apprehend the melody of its sublime and harmonious movements; love to Him whose daily care preserves us from death, and crowns us with immortality; worship to Him whose holiness is perfect, whose wisdom is infinite, whose power is omnipotent, whose love is boundless, whose purity is spotless, and whose fidelity is unchanging; justice to our fellows, for it is their right; forgiveness, for we do err; fraternity, for they are our brethren; sustenance to ourselves, for Nature demands it; protection, for our weakness requires it; education, for our immortality desires it. Above these stands a lamp. Its ever-burning light is an emblem of the warmth of that divine love which illumines our path with the light of truth. The group with clasped hands, open brows, and honest hearts represent fraternity, honor, and sincerity. Our union is complete. Each one is bound to all, and all are pledged to each one. Our brotherhood is perpetual. Our temples rise upon its solid basis in beautiful proportions. Each upright pillar supports its dome. May it remain firm as the pillars of the globe, and beautiful as the arch of heaven!'

"Order strikes at the root of the great upas tree. It contends that the only remedy for the evils of intemperance is prohibition of the manufacture of and traffic in alcoholic beverages, sustained and upheld by correct public sentiment. To accomplish this consummation so devoutly to be wished for, may require your life-long assistance. We ask for none to enter here who do not heartily agree to co-operate with us — not for a season only, but for life! Death is the only release from the vow you here must take. It is no idle purpose in which you must engage. No empty titles or honors will be conferred upon you. Devotion to temperance, morality, and truth must win the meed of praise. Suffering humanity demands your constant labor. Self must no longer control the will, and be the leading purpose of life. Time, talent, and money must be sacrificed for the good of your fellow-men. In a world of perishing mortals you must stand forth as undaunted and firm as those heroes who have fought and conquered for the right; you must endure, unmoved and unwearied, the trial of affliction and persecution, and trust in God for ultimate success."

The "Independent Order of Rechabites" were introduced into this country from England in 1842, and spread rapidly through the United States, numbering at one time over one hundred thousand; but they afterwards declined, and became nearly extinct. A few years since they re-organized, and they are again in active operation, and have quite a large membership. "Good Samaritans" are still another order. They were organized in the city of New York, in 1847. It is a benefit society, and they have their working forces distributed in nearly every state of the Union. It is their object to reach the lower stratum of the drinking population of the cities, to go out into the narrow lanes and by-ways, and take up the wounded and fallen when others have passed them by. The true Samaritan spirit is shown forth in this enterprise, and much good has been accomplished.

From these centres there are yet other radiating points that unite in the one grand concentration of clearing the world from the vile impurities of intemperance. Children have their "Cold Water Armies," and their "Bands of Hope," and it would seem that the world's regeneration in this matter ought to be close at hand. With all these appliances brought to bear upon the people, their conversion to the principles and practice of temperance should be sure and decided; and still the streams of alcohol are permitted to flow, and men fill their glasses and drink until they are no longer manly, and keep falling when they ought to rise and assert the dignity of their God-given nature. Are all these noble, philanthropic efforts, then, to be called a failure? Have all these good men preached and labored in vain — this host of worthies wrought to no purpose? At the fifteenth anniversary of the American Temperance Society, in 1851, Dr. Cleveland, speaking of progress, said, —

"When two trains meet, travelling at the rate of twenty-five miles an hour, we seem to be going fifty when we are going but twenty-five. The croakers say we are now going backwards. The question is, whether the croakers are right, who say we have done nothing, or the temperance workers, who think we have done much for which to be thankful. I think we have mowed a pretty handsome swath. I am willing to admit, there is as much rum drunk now as there was twenty-five years ago; yet it must be remembered, that twenty-five years ago there were but twelve millions of people in the land, whereas now there are twenty-five. If we have reformed no one, we may have kept our twelve millions from falling into the sin and ruin of drunkenness." Says another, "To speak positively, a mighty work has been accomplished, and few are the men who will not acknowledge it. If we had only gained the liberty of drinking or not drinking, as we pleased; of having or not having the drink on our tables, as we pleased; of giving workmen drink or not giving, as we pleased, — we should have accomplished a great work. But we have gained a vast and most important knowledge of the subject of Intemperance; the nature, cause, and cure of drunkenness; the nature of the alcoholic poisons, and subject of adulteration. We have firmly established the great principles of temperance; we have driven liquor from our farms, our manufactories, our firesides, our sideboards, our shipping, our navy; from our Christian and ministerial families, our pulpits and Christian churches, and all missionary stations, and from among those who would evangelize the world. Here, under God, are the triumphs of temperance."

It would be cheering to record far grander results, but if all that has been done is only in the line of preparation, who does not see that victory is more certain in the coming battle, because of the vast forces in training, and the burnishing of these mighty weapons? The machinery of the universe is silent and unseen at many points of its working, and sometimes there are apparent dis-harmony and confusion, that fill the mind of short-sighted mortals with dismay and alarm, lest the world get out of tune altogether, and there be no more good in it; but time always straightens out the seeming crookedness, and men and nature smile again. So it will doubtless be with this moral aspect. It may be dark for a time, but it shall have a glorious triumph in the end.

CHAPTER XVI.

Adulteration of Liquors.

FASHION AND PURITY. — THE COLORADO SALOON KEEPER. — FOURCROY, THE FRENCH CHEMIST. — PROFESSOR LEE'S STATEMENT. — ASSERTION OF DR. STORY. — STRYCHNINE. — STRAMONIUM. — THE DEAD FISHERMEN. — THE IRISH TOPERS. — COCCULUS. — CONFISCATION AT BOSTON. — ANALYTICAL OBSERVATIONS OF DR. COX. — PURCHASE OF NEW YORK PHYSICIANS, — "GUIDE" RECEIPTS. — THE DRUGGIST'S BRANDY. — RUM. — GIN. — BEER.

When Fashion popularized the drinking of spirituous liquors, in the times of our forefathers, it was comparatively a pure beverage — pure of its kind. Drunkenness may not have had that peculiarly aggravating character that it bears at the present day. It is true that alcohol, in its best condition, is nothing less than a poison to the human system; and we have seen how deleterious are its influences through its physiological action upon mind and body; but there are poisons more rapid and destructive than even this, and the avariciousness of men has freely mingled them in the cup which they have given their brother man to taste. As if it were not enough that it would bring misery and death of itself, they have gone to work to intensify it, so as to make the effect more disastrous and the result more sure. In what other department of trade would corresponding iniquity be tolerated? It may be there are scales upon the eyes of the world, and they see not, neither do they know, the tricks and frauds that are practised in secret places, that shams may take the place of realities. Villany likes concealment, and so it works in by-places, down, back, and away, where honesty and integrity would not think of going; and there, with barred doors and guarded entrances, with hushed voices and stealthy tread, they carry on their nefarious doings. In some way or other sin will always be found out, and so it has come to be known what these deliberate schemes for man-poisoning are, and how and by whom they are accomplished. A man may be driven in his desperation to counterfeit money, that he may be relieved of his distress and perplexity, and close confinement and hard labor in prison are considered none too good for him. Public opinion frowns, and law executes its stern threats; but he may follow a more infamous trade, and counterfeit that which has to do with the most precious of all human interests, and still he goes on, while men wonder and the law is dumb. In the first case, the man may have been under the power of stern necessity, that goaded him on to the performance of an action that his better nature revolted against; but in the latter, it is more often a calculating policy that would make the piles of wealth accumulate higher and faster. It is an effort to obtain money without returning an equivalent; to grow rich without having it cost little or nothing. They know that men will have a drink that has some stimulating quality; that it is this element which the drinking man demands, and brings the effect he seeks, and therefore anything whatever that will tend to produce the requisite condition is used. If the temporary excitement is gained, no matter how it is done, or what the after consequences, he glories in the success of his mixture.

A Colorado saloon keeper said of a rough crowd, "I couldn't get their whiskey strong enough to suit them; so, after trying every way, I at last made a mixture of oak poison and butternut. I called it the 'sheep-herder's delight,' and it became a popular drink. The first Pike to whom I gave it became frantic with delight; the next took two drinks, and turned a double somerset in front of the house; and the third was a peddler, who, after considerable indulgence, stole his own pack and hid it in the woods." In the low phraseology of a certain class, anything to get the "drunk."

It is the intoxicating constituent in strong drinks that is specially objectionable on the ground of temperance, and this is extracted from substances through evaporation and condensation; it is a product of *fermentation.* The great French chemist, Fourcroy, says, "The formation of alcohol takes place at the expense of the *destruction of a vegetable principle;* thus spirituous fermentation is a commencement of the destruction of principles *formed* by vegetation. The acid, or acetous fermentation is the second natural movement which contributes to reduce vegetable compounds to more simple states of composition. Wine, in turning sour, absorbs air; so that a certain portion of the oxygen of the atmosphere appears to be necessary to the formation of the acetous acid. Finally, after vegetable liquors, or their solid parts moistened, have passed to the *acid state*, their decomposition continuing, under favorable circumstances (viz., a warm temperature, exposure to the air, and the contact of water), leads them into putrefaction, which terminates in volatilizing most of the principles under the form of gas. Water, carbonic acid, carbonated, and even sulphurated hydrogen gas, volatile oil in vapor, and sometimes even azotic gas and ammonia, are evolved; and after this there remains nothing but a brown or black residuum, known by the name of mould. Though all the circumstances of putrefaction are not yet described, or even known, we have discovered that they are confined to the conversion of *complex substances* into substances *less compound;* that Nature restores to new combinations the materials which she had but lent, as it were, to vegetables and animals; and that she thus accomplishes the perpetual circle of compositions and decompositions, which attests her power and demonstrates her fecundity, while it announces equal grandeur and simplicity in the course of her operations."

Thus, by a process through which man has made the fruits and grains of the earth to pass, has that been distilled which has deepened the curse upon man more than any one thing in the world. "*Nature* never forms spirituous liquors; she rots the grape upon the branch, but it is art which converts the juice into (alcoholic) wine." Chemical combinations, in her hands, are safe and healthful. Man alone perverts, and wrests from the natural conditions the distillation of death. The proportion is seen in the declared fact that "there is more food in one bushel of barley than there is in twelve thousand gallons of the best beer."

But, notwithstanding all that can be said of these things, — that there is no nutrition, nothing whatever that is desirable, in these liquid combinations, — men will go on imbibing them extravagantly; and as they will indulge, men will minister to their indulgence; and if the most natural materials are not sufficient, they will manufacture others, and it is all right if the people are deceived and satisfied. A thoughtful person will very readily see there are not fruits and grains enough to meet the vast demand for spirits in our country, if they were all poured into the distilling granaries for that purpose. It is computed there are not less than three hundred firms engaged in the debasing traffic of poison-mixing, which they palm off for the choicest brands of the genuine article. From four of these manufactories, nearly two million gallons are sent out annually on their death-dealing mission, having this only recommendation —it enriches promptly, and kills swiftly.

Professor Lee, of New York, says, —

"A cheap Madeira is made here by extracting the oils from common whiskey, and by passing it through carbon. There are immense establishments in this city where the whiskey is thus turned into wine. In some of those devoted to this branch of business, the whiskey is rolled in in the evening, but the wine goes out in the broad daylight, ready to defy the closest inspection. A grocer, after he had abandoned the nefarious traffic, assured me that he had often purchased whiskey one day of a country merchant, and before he had left town the same whiskey was sent back to him turned into wine, at a profit of from four hundred to five hundred per cent."

It becomes a matter of interest, to those who are thus imposed upon, to know the extent of the imposition, and its peculiar characteristics — to know something of the ingredients of that with which they grace their tables and treat their friends. What, then, are the materials so widely used in the adulteration of liquors? With Dr. Story as authority, we say, —

"There is one set of ingredients used to adulterate the alcohol itself, another set used to give it the color, and others to give age and bead, and all to deceive. If you wanted," he continues, "to convert one gallon of new corn whiskey into four gallons of old peach brandy, you would use one set of ingredients; into old Jamaica rum, another set; into best Holland gin, another set; and if you wanted to convert it into ten gallons of old Port wine, you would use still another set of ingredients, though the one used in the place of alcohol might be the same in all cases. The coloring and flavoring would be different, though the intoxicating ingredient would be the same. Among the things used, strychnine is one of the most prominent. It is said that one drug store in London sold more of this article to one liquor manufacturing establishment last year than was required by all the medical men in their profession. It is so very strong that it takes but little, added to a bushel of corn, to make an extra gallon of whiskey, and therefore it is extensively used. Three cents' worth of this commodity, with a gallon of water, adds to the distiller's fortune with great rapidity. In 1857, the legislature of Ohio passed a law forbidding the use of this and other poisons, under a penalty of imprisonment in the penitentiary, at hard labor, not more than five or less than one year; but men are shrewd in their attempts to evade the law, and the work went on secretly, as it had done before. The love of gain is stronger than all other considerations, and therefore the conclusion of men is, We will try it a little longer and see."

Stramonium is another popular poison. It is extracted from a poisonous weed, sometimes called jimson-weed, and is very common in country places, and, on account of its cheapness, is extensively used by those who manufacture and retail what they call *spirits*. Such a one buys whiskey, one fourth of which is already composed of strychnine, and proceeds to form a new composition by adding this latter ingredient; but, as this is likely to create unpleasant sensations in the stomach, he adds a little opium to counteract the effect, and a little potash to modify the taste and smell, all of which can be done at the cost of a few cents. It is said, "Two fishermen, in a little town on the Ohio River, bought a pint of whiskey, and went up the river to fish. That afternoon they were both found, on the bank of the river, dead. The bottle was empty. When the retailer heard they were dead, he immediately emptied that keg of whiskey into the ditch. As the proof was destroyed, of course he was not found guilty. In all probability he, through mistake, put more stramonium into the strychnine whiskey than he intended, or perhaps forgot to add the requisite amount of water. The fishermen are dead, and who is to blame?" After having passed through these two processes, a third retailer takes it, and by the addition of another powerful poison — belladonna — he increases the quantity of liquid that is to enrich him by a large percentage, and injure his customers correspondingly.

Every one knows of the deadly nightshade, and how it grows in great profusion in shady places, around the corners of fences, and by the side of walls, with berries of purplish hue and sweetish taste, and children are warned against touching it in any way, as leaf, stem, berries, root, and all are full of poison. It is this same thing that enters into the retailer's compound. "About two cents' worth will make a gallon of liquor, which sells in the market, at wholesale, for a dollar and a half." One gallon of whiskey, by the time it has passed through this third stage, becomes four times as much, yielding a retail profit of six or seven dollars to the gallon, which of course is a brilliant temptation.

Dr. Cox, a distinguished chemist in Ohio, was directed by the legislature of that state to analyze and examine the liquors of their market. For two years and more, he gave his attention to the matter; but opposing influences were made to bear so strongly that his report was never made public. But many facts have come to light through his personal statements. As the result of his inspections, he declares that "over ninety per cent." of all that he examined — and his examinations were quite extensive — "were adulterated with the most pernicious and poisonous ingredients. I called at a grocery store one day," he says, "where liquor was being sold. A couple of Irishmen came in while I was there, and called for some whiskey. The first one drank, and the moment he drank the tears flowed freely, while he, at the same time, caught his breath, like one suffocating or strangling. When he could speak, he said to his companion, 'Och, Michael, by the powers, but this is warming to the stomach, sure!' Michael drank, and went through like contortions, with the remark, 'Troth, an' wouldn't it be foin on a cowld frosty mornin', Timothy?' After they had drank, I asked the proprietor to pour me out a little in a tumbler. I went to my office, got my instruments, and examined it. I found it seventeen per cent. alcoholic spirits, when it should have been fifty; and the difference in percentage was made up by sulphuric acid, red pepper, pellitory, caustic potash, brucine, and one of the salts of nux vomica. One pint of such liquor, at one time, would kill the strongest man. I had the manufacturer indicted; but by such villany he had become wealthy, and I never have, owing to some defect in the law, been able to bring that case to a final issue."

Cocculus is another thing that is used, more especially in beer, as a substitute for malt or hops. It is an East Indian plant, and in its native country the people use it as a stupefying potion, throwing it into the water when they would catch fish, so as to make them their easy prey. When given to dogs, it has been known to produce convulsions and death, in the quantity of five or ten grains. It is used extensively in Europe and America, although at the former place it is forbidden by law, under heavy penalties. A kind of tobacco, known as "dog-leg," is also used in large quantities. This is very cheap, and consequently it is used very freely. Its tendency is to produce nausea, and hence this condition is neutralized by adding a little opium or stramonium.

During the war, one of our regiments took possession of a whiskey saloon. Several of the soldiers became drunk over one cask; and when it was drained, one of their number smashed the head of it, and found about fifteen or twenty pounds of this kind of tobacco, well soaked, that looked as if it might have been there a twelvemonth or more. These two last ingredients are more extensively used in the adulteration of colored liquors. In other cases, it is subject to chemical decomposition, so as to extract the coloring matter, the same as strychnine.

There recently appeared in the Boston Journal the following account of the quality of the liquors seized and confiscated, as offered for sale in violation of law: —

"Since June, 1872, whenever the strong arm of the law has descended upon the stocks of dealers in liquors in this commonwealth, the captured material has been first carried to the nearest storehouse of the state police, where it has remained for several weeks, until it is either returned to the owners or confiscated by order of the courts. If confiscated, it is then delivered to the state commissioner, who has all the liquors from a great many seizures assembled together for examination and analysis, in Boston, preparatory to disposing of them. These collections of *trash* are quite remarkable, representing, as they do, the alcoholic beverages of all kinds, taken just as they are sold in every part of the state. Packages of almost every conceivable kind may be seen among them, as the seizures include hogsheads, barrels, kegs, demijohns, jugs, bottles, decanters, tin cans, tubs, measures and pails of wood and metal, kitchen utensils, pitchers, crockery vessels, &c., in great numbers. And the marks on these packages are also various and ingenious. Whiskey is sometimes labelled as "Extract of Lemon," "Vanilla Syrup," or "Tincture of Energy," and it may be designated by a single letter or number. Occasionally, some proprietor comes out boldly, and marks a favorite drink with such refreshing names as "Green Mountain Tonic," or "Sandy's very best."

The liquors themselves are generally very bad. They are most commonly *extended* with "French spirit," water, sweetening and coloring matters; but a very considerable proportion of them is made from spirits flavored with dangerous "oils" and extracts, in imitation of brandy and other liquors. Many curious cases might be cited in confirmation of this; but the occasional seizures, by the officers, of the pure "oils" in two-quart jugs, with written and printed directions for making them into brandy, whiskey, gin, and so forth, or of the mixtures in process of manufacture, are certainly an unmistakable indication of the increasing activity in this miserable business of making liquors for immediate use. The following extracts from a circular recently taken, with some of the "oils," from a small dealer in one of the neighboring towns, are copied by way of illustration. This circular is headed "Hints to Liquor Dealers;" and, among other items, we find that "full instructions accompany each package;" so you can make the liquors in a few minutes.

French brandy oil, sufficient to make forty gallons brandy, ... $5 00
Otard brandy oil, *very fine*, sufficient to make twenty gallons brandy, ... 5 00
Bourbon whiskey oil, sufficient to make forty gallons Bourbon whiskey, ... 5 00
Holland gin oil, sufficient to make forty gallons Holland gin, ... 5 00
Goods sent, securely packed, free from observation.
A sample case, containing three oils of above list, a copy of "Secrets Liquor Trade and Bar Tender's Guide," sent for 12 00

Another good illustration is found in a small card of directions, printed in French. This is entirely a different thing from the circular quoted above, and it is headed "Extract Fine Liqueur de Paris, manufacturée par la Société Philanthropique Francaise, W——, Mass." Then follow directions for making an excellent family beverage, that will not cost more than one dollar per gallon, and which surpasses any other liquor, costing at least four dollars a gallon, in purity and flavor. Some of the confiscated liquors are not very skilfully compounded, and the common spices of the kitchen, with raisins, fruits, onions, and tobacco, are found in them. Occasionally, a whole barrel of unmixed "French spirit" (alcohol and water, without flavor), is seized from some retail dealer, who never has occasion to sell anything of this kind unflavored. Pure brandies and wines are very seldom seized, and they are generally so much changed that the original wholesale dealers would not recognize them.

It is asserted that the greatest profit arises from the adulteration of *wine*, and that probably the greatest amount of injury is done in this connection. "Give me six hours' notice of what wines you like," said a French merchant, "and you shall have it out of those two barrels." "To brighten, color, clear, and make astringent wines, alum, Brazil wood, gypsum, oak sawdust, husks of filbert, and *lead* are employed; and for the purpose of communicating particular flavor to insipid wines, bitter almond, cherry, laurel water. In the Isle of Sheppy, many persons are employed in picking up *copperas* stones from the sea-beach, which, being taken to a manufactory, copperas is extracted, and then shipped to Oporto, to be sold to the wine-dresser and wine merchant, and by them is mixed with the port wine to give it a peculiar astringent quality. One writer, who knew whereof he affirmed, said, "We know very well that the Spaniard would not touch the wine he manufactures for us, and the Portuguese would spit out our port like so much poison." Dr. Cox, the chemist already quoted, makes this statement as more or less true of all the port wine that came under his analytical observation during the special period his attention was given to the subject: "As a basis, either water, cider, vinegar, or a mixture of water and sulphuric acid, with the juice of elder-berries, privet berries, beet-root juice, and logwood, with alum, technically called sulphate of alumina, and potassa, sugar to cover the pernicious mixture, and sometimes I found one or two per cent. of Jamaica rum, or neutral spirits, added."

Of sherry, madeira, muscadel, &c., he says they are all, or at least all that he has inspected, either mixed, or have, as a basis, water, cider, wort made of pale malt, of a mixture of sulphuric acid and water to the acidity of weak vinegar, with brown sugar, honey, orris-root, and neutral spirits to give it alcoholic percentage; and this, he adds, was the character of two samples of wine — port and sherry — that he inspected, which were sent from a store, the proprietors of which are honorable and high-minded gentlemen, who had paid a high price for their liquors, got them out of a custom-house in an Eastern city, with an assurance that they were genuine and imported, and yet there was not one drop or symptom of wine in either of them, — the one having its warming, stimulating influence from sulphuric acid, and one per cent. Jamaica rum; and the sherry having six per cent. alcoholic spirits imparted to it by neutral spirits, with sulphuric acid, bitter almonds, brown sugar, and honey. These mixtures are all flavored with various oils, mixed to suit the flavors of the different wines. One of these is a poison so intense in its nature, that one fourth of a drop has been known to kill a rabbit, and one drop a dog.

A New York physician bought a bottle of what was called genuine champagne, of the importers, and on subjecting it to chemical tests, it was found to contain a quarter of an ounce of sugar of lead. On the arrival of a cargo of wines in New York, it is at once purchased, and perhaps poured into vats, where these various substances are mingled with it, and it is again sent forth not only doubled and quadrupled in quantity, but its whole character completely changed. Europe and our own country are alike engaged in the same baneful traffic. The Edinburgh Medical Journal gives the following incident: "The family of a baronet in Roxburgshire, together with several visitors, were taken seriously ill during dinner, or soon after it. The symptoms in all were sickness, vomiting, and diarrhœa. In the course of the night all were affected with a sense of heat in the stomach, throat, and mouth; and in the morning the lips became incrusted, and the skin cracked and peeled off. On analyzing some of the matter thrown off, the two hundred and fiftieth part of a grain of arsenic was discovered, and in the remains of a bottle of champagne two ounces of wine gave one grain and a quarter of sulphate of arsenic." It is evident that these things cannot be imbibed with safety. They are poisons, and act as such upon the human system.

Passing from wine to the stronger liquids, we find the "Vintner's Guide" affording the following receipt for improving the flavors of brandy: "A quarter of an ounce of English saffron, and half an ounce of mace, steeped in a pint of brandy for ten days, shaking once or twice a day; then strain it through linen cloth, and add one ounce of terra japonica, finely pounded, and three ounces of spirits of nitre; put it into ten gallons of brandy, adding, at the same time, ten pounds of prunes, bruised." Then, to give it all the qualities of the old, that it may have the popular recommendation of *age*, "add thirty drops of aqua ammonia to one gallon of new brandy, shaking it well, that it may combine with the acid, on which the taste and other qualities of the new liquor depend." With reference to brandy, Dr. Cox says, "I have inspected brands, of various kinds and qualities, fresh from the custom-house, with the inspector's certficate, which accompanied them, and was assured that they were freshly imported, and yet the chemical tests gave me corn whiskey, with abundance of fusel oil, or the oil of corn, as a basis, with sulphuric acid, nitric ether, prussic acid, copper, chloroform, quinia, pepper, tannin or tannic acid, with sometimes a very small percentage of brandy, and frequently not a drop."

A gentleman of veracity, in Cincinnati, too, a druggist, that he might have a pure liquor as a medical article, and that kind of purity that he could recommend to his customers, went to New York and purchased two half pipes of splendid Leignette brandy — one pale, the other dark. When passing, one day, he called me in to see his beautiful pure brandy, just from New York. I stopped, looked at it, smelled it; but, before tasting it, happening to have some blue litmus paper in my pocket, I introduced a small piece; it came out as red as scarlet. I then called for a polished spatula, put it into a tumbler containing, perhaps, half a gill, and waited on it, perhaps, fifteen minutes, at the expiration of which the liquor was black as ink. The spatula corroded, and when dried, a thick coating of rust, which, when wiped off, left a copper coat almost as thick as if it had been plated. I charged him on the spot, under the penalty of the law, not to sell a drop of it; took samples of it to my office, and the following is the result of my analysis: First sample — dark, 55 per cent. alcoholic spirits by volume, and 41 per cent. by weight; specific gravity, 0.945. The tests indicate sulphuric acid, nitric acid, nitric ether, prussic acid, quinia, pepper, and an abundance of fusel oil, base common whiskey — not a drop of brandy. Second sample — pale, 54 per cent. alcoholic spirits by volume, 40 per cent. by weight; specific gravity, 0.955.

They were purchased on four months' time. The purchaser immediately notified the New York merchant of the character and quality of the goods, and directed him to send for them; but instead of doing that, he waited until the notes became due, and brought the suit into the Court of Common Pleas at Cincinnati. The chemist analyzed the liquors in the presence of the court and jury, showed them satisfactorily that they were the pernicious, poisonous, and villanous liquors that he had represented them to be, and the defendant gained his case triumphantly, and the merchant vanished before a state warrant could be got out, otherwise he would have had ample time to learn an honest trade in one of the institutions of Ohio.

It may be that rum is not quite so extensively adulterated as some of the other spirits. It is supposed to be originally a simple distillation of the sugar-cane; but a very inferior article is often purchased, and by the addition of ale, "porter, shrub, extract of orris-root, cherry, laurel-water, extract of grains of paradise or capsicum," it is made to put on the airs of fine old Jamaica, and sold correspondingly.

Gin is more fearfully complicated. In this may be found "oil of vitriol, oil of cassia, oil of turpentine, oil of caraway, oil of juniper, oil of almond, sulphuric ether, extract of capsicum, extract of grains of paradise, extract of orris-root, extract of angelica-root, water, sugar," to say nothing of the introduction of lead, that often finds its way in with the host of other things. The poisoning process goes on through all the malt liquors, with perhaps a more complicated list of wretched ingredients. No less than twenty-eight or thirty different articles are specified that go to make up beer, and some of them are the rankest poisons, and mixed in a way that shows such an accumulation of filth as would shock the man of lowest taste, could he see it, much more the fastidious.

It is related that some dissipated men and women were drinking ale and porter in a dram shop, in Hull, England, not long ago. "The landlord had occasion to leave the shop, when one of the women, seeing on the counter a pitcher full of what she supposed to be porter, drank a good draught, replacing the pitcher. In a very short time she was seized with nausea and griping pains, and fell down on the floor in a state of hopeless stupor and intoxication. In this state she was conveyed to the hospital, when, the contents of the stomach being evacuated, she was rescued from being poisoned, although it was several days before she was able to be removed. The matter ejected was found to be a strong solution of cocculus indicus. The man acknowledged that the drug had been used by him to bring up his ales to a strength to suit his customers. This was a noted house for *genuine ales and bitter beer.*"

It is not necessary to multiply these instances. Enough has been said to show any one that it is scarcely possible to indulge in any of the alcoholic drinks of the present day without taking into his system the rankest poisons the world can furnish. It is sufficient to make the most inveterate drunkard pause, and consider what he is doing. It certainly should make the moderate drinker stop, and ask himself the question, if he can deliberately consent to poison the fountain of his being in this way. Surely, he who begins just to sip a little, or take an occasional glass for the sake of a jolly time with his friends, should ponder long and well if he can afford to do it.

CHAPTER XVII.

LICENSE AND PROHIBITION.

GOOD AND EVIL AT WAR WITH EACH OTHER. — THE TWO LEADING PRINCIPLES. — FOR WHAT DO WE GRANT LICENSE. — MINER BEFORE THE MASSACHUSETTS LEGISLATURE. — A HUNDRED DIFFERENT LAWS. — DECLARATION OF DR. HUMPHREY. — CONSTABLE'S REPORT. — STATE BOARD OF CHARITIES. — WHAT ALBERT BARNES SAYS. — PROHIBITION THE ONLY THING. — PROTECTIVE POWER. — ENGLAND'S POSITION. — NEAL DOW FATHER OF PROHIBITION. — TESTIMONY AS TO RESULTS. — CALL TO ACTION.

THE powers of good and evil in the world are always antagonistic. Those who are arrayed upon the one side are always in opposition to those on the other. They who would see the cause of right prosper, and mankind take their true position in the scale of being, are always seeking by every condition of law and order to bring it about. The less careful ones are more intent upon procuring measures that shall sanction self-indulgence, and throw no restraint upon their *liberty*, which they declare to be their special gift from Heaven to do with as they please. In this manner are arrayed the friends and the enemies of temperance. The former are bringing all their influence to bear upon the suppression of that which all history and experience proves to be the greatest evil that can possibly exist in any land. They labor themselves, and multiply agencies of every description and character, to hasten a consummation they so devoutly wish would come. They look abroad upon the wide-spread misery and woe, and every glance confirms them in their determination to wage war upon that which inflicts so much of sorrow upon the human race. They plead — they petition the authorities of state and nation to send forth their commanding tones, and put the final touch to what they have begun. On the contrary, the enemies of the cause are incessantly at work to defeat the whole. The millennium has not yet come, and evil is strong in the land, and there are times when apparently it is in the ascendency, and wicked men exult that their schemes override all others. The true man says, Banish the infernal drink that is devastating society, and drowning myriads as if with an overflowing flood; shut up the places that are as so many schools of vice, and let those who sustain them be evermore forbidden by the stern mandate of law, and those who work at the fountain be made to stay their unrighteous proceedings by a similar omnipotent decree. The other class say, Away with your sanctimonious folly, and let us have a little cheer for this humdrum life; let us eat, drink, and be merry, and once in a while forget the cares and sorrows of our pathway; and so it is acting and counteracting all the while, and the time and manner of its ending is yet an unsolved problem. The two great leading principles of action with the friends and foes of temperance are license and prohibition. The cursory glance we give these will not admit of minute and specific details of their origin and working, but only some of the advantages and objections urged, and their general character.

There are thousands engaged in the miserable traffic, who nevertheless pronounce the business in itself an unmitigated evil. It is profitable, and therefore they quiet their consciences by saying, that as long as others are permitted to do it freely, they might just as well. The consequences will be no worse to individuals or society for our selling, for it will be had, and it might just as well be had of us as any one. These and those who patronize them say, It is an evil, we know, but let it be regulated and shielded by a license law. They like to sit under the shadow of some such institution, for it has a wonderfully cooling effect upon their overheated and panting natures. They can sit down and deal out the contents of the whiskey keg or the beer barrel with the utmost complacency, for the state has given them authority to do it, and not every one has been thought worthy of the signal honor; for this is one of the pleas of the license men, that it makes it *respectable* — as if anything could write *respectability* upon that which has evident woe in it from the very beginning to the end thereof. At least, it so far comforts its votaries, that it makes them feel they are doing a legitimate and honorable work. There may be restraints and regulations to keep them in check; but what care they for these, while the law upholds them in their main object. They are the ones singled out from among the people, as being peculiarly fitted to engage in that occupation. So far from considering it a mark of honor and respect to be thus delegated, it is a wonder that such a one does not stop short in his career, and shudder at his prospect. Let him ask himself the question, For what am I granted license? and then listen to the reply: —

"We grant license the taxes twofold to increase,
To destroy or defame the whole neighborhood's peace;
To fan up the flame in the inebriate's breast;
To deprive him of reason, and rob him of rest;
To wound and degrade him on honor's bright roll;
To ruin and kill him, both body and soul;
To freeze and to starve his affectionate wife;
To afflict her, and ruin her whole prospect in life;
To beggar his children, and leave them forlorn;
To receive from the cold world but pity or scorn;
To affect courts of justice, and rule their decision;
To degrade, and pollute, and keep them in derision;
To rule or to ruin the affairs of the city;
To pour rum broadcast without mercy or pity;

To bribe legislators; to ruin the state;
To increase state prisoners, and leave them to fate;
To soil the legislative department of the nation;
To befoul and pervert each condition or station;
To fasten on government a stain and a blot;
To give credence to rumor — Our ruler's a sot;
To ruin church members, in life and in death,
To deprive them of reason, religion, and breath;
To leave them to the fates in eternity given,
To the law — No drunkard shall enter God's heaven."

Is it an honor to be commissioned to do all this? Can conscience take a "license," and go deliberately forward in this work? It is said, it *regulates* an evil. But why not come up to the full measure of the standard of right, and seek to banish that which is acknowledged an evil, instead of retaining it, and trying to curb and prune it, to make it more respectable and tolerable. Plainly, if it is licensed, an evil is fostered, and if one evil, then a host of kindred evils also might claim protection; and where is there a limit to this high carnival of iniquity? There is no fairness in allowing a few men to do all this mighty work.

Rather spread it, lest the terrible reward be as a crushing millstone grinding the few to powder. In an argument before the Massachusetts legislature in 1867, on this question, by A. A. Miner, he says, "The business itself is not one that will invite men of high character to enter into it. Whatever your course may be on this subject, the liquor sellers of Massachusetts, so long as you cherish the character which the state now enjoys, will be men of moderate moral attainments. Why, gentlemen, though an eminent representative of the traffic, standing here the other day, admitted that he wanted a law to make his business respectable, I allege that the thing is impossible. Massachusetts cannot enact a law that will make the selling of liquors, as beverages, respectable. If the angel Gabriel should come down to earth, and sell liquors as beverages, he would not lift the business up to heaven, but the business would drag the angel down to hell. If I were to define a license law, stringent or otherwise, I should say it was a legal means of making drunkards."

To those who say, I have a license, and therefore I can and will sell, the Rev. John Pierpont replies, in a most sarcastic manner, "You have a license—and that is your plea; I adjure you to keep it; lock it among your choicest jewels; guard it as the apple of your eye; and when you die, and are laid in your coffin, be sure that the precious document is placed between your cold and clammy fingers, so that when you are called upon to confront your victims before God, you may be ready to file in your plea of justification, and boldly to lay down your license on the bar of the Judge. Yes, my friend, keep it; you will then want your license signed by the county commissioners, and indorsed by the selectmen."

The very conditions of the license law show its weakness. One of these forbids selling to a man already intoxicated. A man may drink until he ceases to be himself, and then he has only to refrain until he reaches a certain commendable stage of soberness, before he can begin and act the same over again. Is that making the probability of his becoming a drunkard any the less? "A minor may not drink without the consent of his father." Has not a father who would give such *consent* forfeited all right to dictate to a child what he shall or shall not do? What power can give him a moral right to allow that he knows will be his certain destruction? "It must not be sold to intemperate men, when forbidden by their wives." Did the law-makers stop to think, how much better it would be for those wives if they had gone farther back, and laid their restrictions where they belonged, instead of leaving them to bear the torrents of abuse which such action would pour upon them? "It shall not be sold to be drank upon the premises." This protects the rum seller, and shields him from all the sad consequences of his doings, and carries them all into the sanctuary of home, to torture and afflict innocent families that are ever mourning the fruits of license. Some who found it hard to give up their pet institution, thought they were bringing things up to a higher plane when they suggested that large sums be demanded for license, so that the rich only would come into the trade, and all the "low groggeries" be closed; as if the matter was to be greatly dignified by letting wealth and standing take the best people and make them respectable drunkards. O the folly of men when their own wishes and interests are at stake!

"The life of a nation is too short," says one, "for the art of suppressing the liquor traffic by *license*. For over two hundred years our fathers tried to perfect a 'stringent license law,' and died without the sight. Their despair may well be crowned when they behold the bungling workmanship of the wise men of to-day." During all these years, more than a hundred different laws were passed with reference to licensing and regulating this branch of trade; and says this same person, "An attentive perusal of them would constitute a complete demonstration of the inherent weakness of all such legislation." Dr. Humphrey, of Amherst College, said, in 1833, —

"It is plain to me, as the sun in a clear summer sky, that the license laws of our country constitute one of the main pillars on which the stupendous fabric of intemperance now rests." In the same year Frelinghuysen declared, "If men will engage in this destructive traffic, — if they will stoop to degrade their reason, and reap the wages of iniquity, — let them no longer have the *law-book* as a pillow, nor quiet conscience by the opiate of a *court license.*"

For some years previous to 1865, a prohibitory law had been in force in Massachusetts; but at this date there was a determined effort among its enemies to abolish it in favor of the license system. The Secretary of the Temperance Alliance for that year says, "Strange as it may appear, a minister of the gospel volunteered to carry a license law through the legislature, thus rendering the services of rum sellers themselves unnecessary, so far as this favorite law of theirs is concerned. With a champion from the church and pulpit, whose sacerdotal robes would contribute to the dignity of his singular mission, the liquor dealers of Massachusetts could ask no more." The effort was a long and strong one, but it failed, at the time; but owing to certain conditions of party policy, it triumphed, and in November, 1867, the law was declared, not to take effect until the spring of the following year, however. A few months' experience under the new administration was convincing proof to all that a great mistake had been made; that license was miserable in principle, and a failure in action. The practical fact that it was of regulative tendency was nowhere apparent. The commitments to prison for the same length of time were more than doubled. "It may well be doubted," says one, "whether intemperance would have increased with more rapid strides, if no legislative regulation of the sale of intoxicating liquors had ever been made." The law opened and legalized about twenty-five hundred open bars in the various cities and towns, besides over a thousand other places where it was supposed they would not sell by the glass. In January, 1869, the constable of the commonwealth reported to the legislature thus: "The rapid increase of crime and violence during the past year over former years is without precedent in the history of criminal experience. The state prison and houses of correction never held within their limits such numbers as at the present time; while the wheels of justice are almost clogged with the trial of constantly accumulating criminal business, and the district attorneys of Suffolk find it almost impossible to clear their criminal docket from month to month, notwithstanding the courts in this county are in almost perpetual session. Is it unfair to suggest that the open bar and inviting sale of intoxicating liquors, licensed and unlicensed, in every street, is, to a considerable extent, chargeable and responsible for this state of things?" The Board of State Charities for the same period says, also, —

"While in our cities there is an undeniable increase in intoxication, and consequent crime, the change is more noticeable in the smaller towns, and the effect in general is so palpable that public opinion seems already frowning upon the unseemly order of things, and demanding a return to the safer regime of prohibition, with reasonable penalties, and a faithful attempt to execute the law. Poverty and vice are what the poor man buys with his poisoned liquor; sickness, beastliness, laziness, and pollution are what the state gives in exchange for the license money which the dram seller filches from the lean purse of the day-laborer and the half-grown lad, and hands over, sullied with shame, to the high-salaried official who receives it. But the treasury reaps little from this revolting tribute; for along with the licensed shops and bars twice as many that are unlicensed ply their trade, and debauch the poor without enriching anybody but the dram seller. These are the practical results of a license system in Massachusetts. The increase of intemperance, which the reaction of last year against the strictness of prohibition has greatly promoted, interferes at once with our industrial interests, fosters pauperism and disease, and swells the list of criminals. That intemperance has increased will appear from the prison statistics, soon to be submitted; that crime and vice have also increased, will be shown by the same impartial test, as well as confirmed by the observation of all who have attended to that subject, and noticed what has been going on in the past year. If it is desired to secure in the best manner the repression of crime and pauperism, the increase of production, the decrease of taxation, and a general prosperity of the community, so far as this question of intemperance is concerned, it is clearly best that Massachusetts should return to the policy which prohibits the sale of intoxicating drinks, except for mechanical or medical purposes." Some idea of the traffic may be obtained from the fact that the direct rum tax for 1868 was *three million dollars.*

"An evil always becomes worse by being sustained by the laws of the land," says Albert Barnes. "It is much to have the sanction of law, and the moral force of law, in favor of any course of human conduct. In the estimation of many persons, to make a thing *legal* is to make it morally *right;* and an employment which is legal is pursued by them with few rebukes of conscience, and with little disturbance from any reference to a higher than human authority. Moreover, this fact does much to deter others from opposing the evil, and from endeavoring to turn the public indignation against it. It is an unwelcome thing for a good man ever to set himself against the laws of the land, and to denounce that as *wrong* which they affirm to be *right.* It is a virtue to be law-loving and law-abiding; and it is a principle which every good citizen cherishes, to do what he can to give additional force to the authority of law, and not to lend the sanction of his name to that which would weaken its moral power.

"Hence such men are often slow and reluctant in attacking that which is an undoubted evil, for the attack seems to be made upon the legal fabric as such, and to do just so much to weaken the authority of law. The good are deterred from opposing it, for they do not wish to seem to be arrayed against the laws. The bad are confirmed in their course, for they feel that they are sustained by the laws of the land; and for them that is enough. They can claim, too, some popular sympathy when they are denounced for doing that which is *legal.* They can pursue their course in spite of all that others can do. Thus the evil grows in strength by all the boldness given to them by the sanction of the laws, and by all the reluctance of the friends of reform to denounce that as *wrong* which the law affirms to be right." The same principle holds true in the attempt to regulate it, and therefore there seems no alternative but to prohibit it. It may be said that prohibition will not accomplish the desired result; that law itself cannot restrain the appetites and passions of men, and that somehow, in some way, they will find the means for their personal indulgence. Doubtless they will; but if a man is to take a journey, he cannot reach the end as quickly by going long distances round, climbing over hedges, and dodging various obstacles, as though he went straight forward in an unobstructed pathway. Neither can a man go to his own destruction as fast under prohibition as under license. This has been fully demonstrated. The people of Massachusetts were glad to return to the former, after the reign of the latter for a twelvemonth.

Of course there are always individual exceptions to every rule. There will always be those who will violate any law, however wise and necessary that law may be; but this argues nothing against the wisdom, justness, and efficiency of the law. If it be found to be advantageous to the public good generally, that it ministers to the comfort, peace, and prosperity of people, it is sufficient to secure its maintenance. There are those who scoff at legal prohibition as an invasion of their just rights and liberties. They affirm they have been in the business when the protecting arm of the law was about them, and the people have no right to rise up and withdraw it, saying unto them, Thou shalt not! But where would society be, if universal sufferance were given to all the desires and imaginations of men. It is bad enough with all the checks and restraints that can be brought to bear upon it; but remove all these, and the inhabitants of earth would be ripe for another deluge. Manifestly, intemperance is a great moral and social evil, and unless some effectual barrier is placed in its way, there will be no limit to its spread. What but coercion will answer? Certainly men will never put it away of themselves. The rigid enforcement of a prohibitory law will doubtless do more than anything else to stay the rushing tide. If this could be made to thunder in the ears of the manufacturer until he should close his doors and cease to convert into poison the good things of earth, there would be hope for the rest.

But these men deny the right of society even to whisper of such a thing. Have they not a right to choose their own business, and to conduct it in whatever form they please? No! not if it is plainly detrimental to the public good. "It is the main prerogative of a civil government to prohibit just such things as this. *Protection* is its end and business — the protection of the possessions, the rights, the industry, and the virtue of a community from the invasions of the lawless and the mischievous. Hence the main function of a government is *prohibition*. Its office is to supervise the complicated and often clashing operations of self-love among the associated thousands of whom society is composed, and restrain its injurious workings. We need a civil government, simply because in the social state we are exposed to injury from the evil-minded. Its end is protection; and its power to protect lies in this very power to prohibit whatever conflicts with social order and private rights. Turn, now, to our statute law, and you will find this the real meaning of each enactment. More or less obviously, each statute is a *protective prohibition.* It pre-supposes some lawful interest endangered, some laudable pursuit molested, some social or individual right invaded; and the statute is the arm of the social body stretched forth to protect the violated right by prohibiting the invasion."

Strong drink has always been considered a great and sore evil. Those who sell it and those who drink it are unanimous in the one verdict when they speak out the honest convictions of their hearts. Because these convictions have no weight in their practical life, it is pretty good reason there is needed some kind of enforcement from outside to operate as a compelling power. The public good far transcends private interest and convenience. The law is for the greatest good of the greatest number, and therefore it is for the individual to yield when his plans would subvert the broader foundations. Everywhere the good are looking to this one principle as their only hope. One of England's philanthropists speaks thus at the present time: "As electors and citizens, we are always willing to aid any measure that really proposes to *restrict* the present ruinous system; but it is not for us to take the initiative, seeing that this would be to compromise with the enemy, and to divert us from the great *end* before us, viz., 'The *total* prohibition of the liquor traffic.' All amendment schemes we leave to others; our object is not to amend, but to annihilate. All that tends in this direction in amendment schemes we will accept as instalments only. Our *ultimatum* is the destruction of the liquor traffic, *root and branch.*" Nothing short of this should satisfy the American people. As long as they parley with the enemy it will remain within their borders, the same formidable, ever-threatening giant. They need to throw the stone straight into its forehead, if they would behold its prostrate form, with its bold, defiant air, forever laid low. If it could be banished from our land, it would be the greatest victory that was ever achieved for man upon the earth. There might then be proclaimed a "year of jubilee," and it would be an occasion at which the angels themselves might like to minister. It were idle to waste words upon the glory of such a time. Imagination paints it, and the conceptions of mind revel in all that is bright and fair; but it is the *heart* especially that exults in the transcendent blessing, for it would be like bathing in a clear stream, when the foulest of waters have long been pouring over one.

There are men who call everything a *failure* that does not suit their ideas; so there are many who declaim loudly against the working of the prohibition principle. They see no great difference — men sell, and men drink, and where is the good? The eyes of these men, and their ears too, need to be subjected to some kind of operation that shall enable them to discern a little more clearly of the signs of the times. Prohibition was born, cradled, nurtured, and has grown up in Maine, and Neal Dow, the father of the child, thinks it is anything but a failure. He looks upon it as about the fairest creation that was ever presented to mankind, and he makes no hesitation in saying, wherever he goes, that it corresponds more nearly with his ideal than anything he has ever known. Its practical influence is in every way desirable. In 1872 the governor of the state said, "In some places liquor is sold secretly in violation of the law, as many other offences are committed against the statutes, and the peace and good order of society; but in large districts of the state the liquor traffic is nearly or quite unknown, where formerly it was carried on like any other trade." The Hon. W. P. Frye, member of Congress from the Lewiston district, and ex-attorney-general of the state, also says, "I can, and do, from my own personal observation, unhesitatingly affirm that the consumption of intoxicating liquors in Maine is not to-day one fourth as great as it was twenty years ago; that in the country portions of the state the sale and use have almost entirely ceased; that the law itself, under a vigorous enforcement of its provisions, has created a temperance sentiment which is marvellous, and to which opposition is powerless. In my opinion, our remarkable temperance reform of to-day is the legitimate child of the law." Any amount of similar testimony might be adduced, were it necessary. Everywhere in the land, where it has been tested, it is with the same result. Certain localities may perhaps give it distinct phases and coloring, but there is one united voice in its favor among those who appreciate the good order of society, and are interested in the lifting up and advancement of the race. The figures which show the diminution of crime, the decrease of taxation, and all those things, are an eloquent appeal for its universal adoption. They stand an unanswerable argument in its favor. Then —

"Up for the conflict! let your battle peal
Ring in the air, as rings the clash of steel
When, rank to rank, contending armies meet,
Trampling the dead beneath their bloody feet.
Up! you are bidden to a nobler strife —
Not to *destroy*, but *rescue* human life;
No added drop in misery's cup to press,
But minister relief to wretchedness;
To give the long-lost father to his boy;
To cause the widow's heart to sing for joy;
Bid Plenty laugh where hungry Famine scowls,
And pour the sunlight o'er the tempest's howls;
Bring to the soul that to despair is given,
A new-found joy — a holy hope of heaven.

CHAPTER XVIII.

Legislative Action.

TREE OF LIBERTY. — ANCIENT EMPIRES. — SUPPRESSION. — ORIGIN OF THE MAINE LAW. — MASSACHUSETTS LEGISLATION. — CONNECTICUT AND NEW HAMPSHIRE. — NEW YORK. — SPEECH OF HENRY WARD BEECHER. — OPPOSITION AT TAMMANY HALL. — LOCAL OPTION. — CIVIL DAMAGE. — MEMORIAL TO CONGRESS. — THE PLEADER'S WORDS. — THE GREAT TEMPERANCE MOVEMENT.

Americans have long boasted of their overshadowing tree of liberty, and have pointed with pride to the unexampled growth and prosperity of the people embraced within its encircling branches. It is fair and goodly; but the goodliest thing will not retain its goodness without care; it will not preserve its vigor and freshness without it is watched, cherished, and cultivated. There is no question but that intemperance is a worm at the root of this tree, threatening its vitality, and, through this, its very existence. Say not it is too firmly established, that it has defied the storms of too many winters, and braved the blasts of too many tempests, to be easily uprooted. We grant that it is strong; but we know, too, that the influences at work are mighty also, and that, unless they are stayed, there is danger. The great empires of antiquity rose to splendid heights, and they fell. Why? Because the destructive agencies within themselves were allowed to have full sway. It may be we have a broader basis of intelligence, and that our free institutions are a sort of safety-valve for the nation; but how long would these remain unimpaired, if the intemperate habits of the people were permitted to go on unchecked and unrestrained? The safety of our nation actually demands consideration on this subject, and not only this, there is imperative need for prompt and decisive action.

The most dangerous foes to any government are those within its own borders. If the people are loyal and true, and determined to preserve the honor and integrity of their nation at whatever cost, they will present a united front to whatever foreign ally that may oppose them, with hope of success; but let them become demoralized among themselves, lose their discipline and valor, and there is danger that the subjects of such a government will not be true to her best interests in the time of its necessity. What a proud empire was Greece, and how much she had to be proud of! Her days of classical story were brilliant. Were the trophies of genius ever piled higher than there? Did mind ever sparkle and shine with greater lustre than among her philosophers and sages? Was not Athens world-renowned for the perfection of the arts and sciences and the graces and accomplishments of her people? But all this did not save it. It fell, not so much by the force of the Roman arms, as by her own effeminate indulgence. The pageantry and pomp of the seven-hilled city was once a wonder to the world; but the tumult of the multitude has long since died away, and its mighty ruins alone remain to tell the story of its former greatness and magnificence to the passing traveller. It is true, the Goths and the Vandals came down upon her plains, and set fire to her cities; but a reckless ruler, and a careless and besotted people, wantonly fed the flames that consumed their glory, instead of rising to repel the invading foe. Wine and extravagance had taken the heart out of the nation, and unnerved the otherwise powerful arm, and its doom was sealed. Proud Babylon was another ancient city, flourishing and famous, and history tells how drunkenness and revelry made it easy for the Medes and Persians to become its conquerors, and appropriate its vast possessions. "Had it not been for the debauchery of her king and princes, and the general effeminacy of her people, she might long have reared her lofty brow among the nations, with her hanging gardens and fair palaces, the admiration and delight of all beholders." And so it has been, and so it will be. A worm at the root may destroy the loftiest proportions, and lay that low which seems as the cedars of Lebanon in strength.

It is not impossible that our own fair land may come under the withering stroke at some future day, unless the destructive ravages of the foe be stayed in their course. If intemperance be allowed to grow unchecked, we are not exempt from the fate of other nations. Its own legitimate results are the same everywhere. But we believe the American people will not abandon their heritage to such a doom. If they take not warning from the example of other nations, their own inherent energy in the cause of truth and right will impel them to the use of means for their country's salvation. All through our wide dominions there is a voice that is an increasing volume of sound against the inroads of this mighty evil. *Suppression* is the cry, and the best measure for its accomplishment is the question. It is hopeful. It is a gigantic enterprise, and it requires a vast deal of machinery to keep it moving. Then let none despair, though it move slowly. The people are being educated up to the work, and in due time we may hope for glorious results.

There has been a great deal of legislation upon it in the different states, and various forms and measures resorted to, with the hope that some cure might be found for the terrible malady that is upon so many of our people. As every one knows, Maine was the first to wake up to the consciousness that something decisive must be done in the work of reform, and Hon. Neal Dow was the man to instigate and help forward the mighty enterprise. He was a man eminently fitted for the position. Already a public man, and enjoying the confidence and esteem of the people, it was not difficult to rally them when he lifted up the banner of temperance, and called them to his side. Of course, those who love to drink and those who like to sell will always wage unrelenting war with those who seek to take from them what they consider their own peculiar right and privilege. So it was there. But the strong man gained his cause. The prohibitory form in its beginning was less stringent than now. The agitation commenced in 1846; but it was not until 1851 the law took such shape as really to affect the evil. Under the management of the practical and efficient leader, the bars and shops were closed that before had been inviting every one to enter and take as they pleased; and the change which was soon apparent in the community not only awakened joy in the immediate vicinity, but operated as a grand inspiration to the men of other states, who went and did likewise. The results far surpassed the most sanguine expectations of its friends. Mr. Dow was mayor of Portland, and there he brought all his personal and political influence to bear upon the cause, and for a time all went well. But underneath the surface there was a volcanic element at work, until finally it burst upon society, and did its scorching work. Every possible pretext was resorted to by a certain class as an excuse for disturbance. At length they banded together at a midnight hour, and made a raid upon a quantity of liquor in possession of the municipal authorities, and in the excitement which followed, one of the men lost his life. From this time there was fearful disorder among these disaffected ones, and it continued to increase until the following election, when there was a contest of almost unparalleled fierceness between those who wanted the law and its non-supporters. The temperance vote was really stronger than before; but owing to unusual and peculiar combinations, they were lost, and the legislature and governor were after the pattern of the rum-loving people. Five years the law had been giving out its blessings; but now the thing was reversed. License took the place of prohibition, and in every city, town, and village there was the open bar, the gay saloon, and the less inviting shop. Liquor was flowing everywhere in the state, and so alarming were the consequences, "the philanthropist, patriot, and Christian sprang to the rescue;" nor did they cease their labors until the law again triumphed for the right, and they were planted more immovably than ever on the prohibitory platform. From this time they became an abiding power in the land.

Other states tried the same with varying results. Some have been found strong enough to enact the law, and yet have been wanting in moral force to insure its application, and consequently have failed to reap the good of it. Massachusetts took it to herself in 1852. Alternate success and defeat have been its history ever since; but, in the main, the friends of temperance have held the ground. "What is right never fails," says one, "though the ignorant and sordid may reject it for a time. Wrong always has failed, and in spite of the 'archangel ruined,' it always will." This thought animated the host of temperance workers, and nerved them for action in every hour of seeming repulse. As a specimen of the efficiency of the law, the United States revenue tax on sales of liquor was reduced in one district in Boston, by the vigilance of the state constable, acting in obedience to the prohibitory statute, from twenty-four thousand dollars a month to six thousand dollars for the same time. Under the temporary victory of the liquor sellers, it was raised almost immediately to nearly the original sum — a very evident fact in favor of the law of prohibition. In two years it closed hundreds of dram shops, and shut up more than twenty-five hundred bars in the city of Boston alone; and in less than a year paid almost two hundred and fifty thousand dollars into the treasury of the state, realized from fines, and value of liquors seized and sold.

The people of New England continued to knock at the doors of their respective legislative halls, and one after another of the representatives of the different states were commissioned to petition for this beneficent law.

It went into operation in Connecticut in 1854, under the administration of Governor Dutton, a wise and eminent statesman, who held it — to use his own words — "as a rod over the heads of those who would otherwise cause intemperance to spread." New Hampshire came under its dominion a year later, and the estimation in which it is held there is seen in the statement of one of her leading men, Judge Upton, who says of it, "It has been matured by the ablest jurists in the state and not a man known in the political history of the same ever recorded his name against it. It has stood the test of judicial investigation, and has proved its power. Its effectiveness will disarm its opponents and perpetuate its existence."

When the bill came up for discussion in New York, that state became the theatre of great excitement. On its presentation to the legislature, every possible thing in the line of opposition was brought in its way; and in the Senate, also, every available obstruction was placed in its path; but still it passed, and received the signature of the governor; and when it was known, a burst of gladness was heard from every side. The news spread rapidly, and never was a law more gladly heralded than that among an anxious and waiting people. A congratulatory meeting was held in the city of New York, and the vast assembly seemed determined never again to submit to alcoholic dominion. Spirited speeches were made, and general enthusiasm prevailed. Henry Ward Beecher, in speaking of it, said, "This was the most important meeting that had been gathered in New York for many a day. The whole state would be looking towards it. They would ask, What does the city of New York think about that Maine Law? What is the pulse there? and what do they intend to do about it? We had, at last, procured common and statutory law to this effect, that making and selling intoxicating drinks, for purposes of diet, was now declared, by the voice of the people (what he regarded as common law), and by the voice of their representatives (which was statutory law), to be a crime. We might be baffled and balked a great while before we could make all the teeth of this law meet, with a good subject between them; we might have to deal with men who could come, and disappear, as spirits do; but there was one thing they could not reverse; after years of discussion, the people in this Empire State had declared, that the making and selling of intoxicating drinks, for such purposes, was a crime. The principle was born; and there was nothing born on the face of this earth that carried such joy as the birth of a moral principle. They could never get that back again; they might as well try to crowd the last year's chicken into the shell. Till now, we had been working zigzag before this Sebastopol; but we could not be long taking it. Efforts would be made to destroy the law in the courts; but what the courts decided to be wrong could be rectified; we were in for the battle, and would have perseverance and ingenuity until the law succeeded. The voice which the state sent up to the city was, "Will you abide by the prohibitory law?" The response he would send back was this: "We are watching and waiting; we are like the men at Waterloo, lying close to the ground, until they should hear the old hero cry, 'Up, Guards, and at them.'"

This meeting was followed by another of a different character at Tammany Hall, where the liquor dealers and their sympathizers assembled, and in violent language denounced the law as unconstitutional and fanatical. For a time, the mayor of the city — Mr. Wood — seemed disposed to recognize the dignity of law, and give his authority to its enforcement; but he was finally overruled by injudicious advisers, and the law was practically a dead letter. Not so was it in every place. There were those who stood boldly up, and said, "The law is a law now," and wherever it was violated it was the duty of officials to recognize the violation, and act accordingly. Shortly after, however, the matter was brought before the Court of Appeals, and the whole declared unconstitutional. An effort was made to introduce a prohibitory bill, but it was rejected, and the legislature adjourned, leaving the state without any law that would touch the nefarious traffic. Thus was enthusiasm speedily turned into mourning. After a while the license system was adopted, though with restrictions that made it a little more hopeful for those who were waiting for the redemption of the people from the bondage of rum. Those who drank and those who sold found quite a margin for their comfort in it, for, in good measure, the thing was legalized and protected by the state. Notwithstanding all the effort that was put forth, — and it was by no means small, — the "Excise Law" remained on the statute-books of the state. Remonstrance was useless. The "Local-Option" bill was adopted, but the veto of the governor put an end to that. In 1873, another effort was made to secure the passage of a prohibitory bill; but this, too, proved abortive in the end, and the problem is yet before the people.

Several states have adopted the "Civil Damage" system — a law which had its origin in Massachusetts, and makes rum sellers responsible for damages. It is considered "a wise and righteous provision to attach to a law of prohibition; but attached to a license law, as in Illinois, it is simply a provision to license men to sell rum, if they will put themselves under three thousand dollar bonds to pay all damages; which is just as wrong as it would be to license men to do any other evil, if they will pay damages." Michigan and Iowa have been able to secure legislative action in favor of prohibition, but most of the states are still struggling towards this goal of their ambition. Pennsylvania is under "Local Option," and Delaware, West Virginia, and Illinois have the "Civil Damage" features; all of which do something to check a bad cause, but fail to realize the ideal of what the true friends of temperance wish to see, and hope, eventually, to accomplish. In all the Western States, and far on to the Pacific coast, the public sentiment is thoroughly aroused. All the various temperance societies are working to secure legislative interference in such way as shall effectually suppress the growing evil. But state legislation is not enough in the matter. A national evil requires national consideration, and therefore the wise and thoughtful among the friends of temperance resolved that something be done to make it a national as well as a local issue. Looking at it in connection with the public economy and welfare, it assumed an importance second to none other, and therefore the following "Memorial" was presented to the United States Senate and House of Representatives. This was done through the action of the National Temperance Society, the last year, and was approved and indorsed by the various organizations and societies that were enlisted in the cause of temperance.

"Your memorialists, citizens of the United States, respectfully represent, that the use of intoxicating liquors as a beverage is a prolific source of pauperism and crime, resulting, directly or indirectly, in the destruction of the happiness of many thousands of your constituents; that the manufacture, importation, and sale of such liquors, to be used as a beverage, is inimical to the public welfare; that, in the pecuniary aspect, the amount of revenue derived to the government from intoxicating liquors is much more than counterbalanced by the taxation which their use as a beverage occasions, together with the loss of wealth-producing capacity on the part of those who use them; that it is the proper function of government, after the divine model, not to legalize iniquity for the sake of gain, but to restrain and prohibit that which tends to the demoralization of the people, and to promote the general welfare. We therefore respectfully ask you to authorize the appointment by the President, by and with the advice and consent of the Senate, of a Commission of Inquiry of five or more competent persons, to serve without salary for one year, more or less, whose duty it shall be to investigate: First. The subject of prohibitory legislation, and its effects upon intemperance during the period (over twenty years) covered by such legislation, in

Maine, Massachusetts, and other states of the Union; Second. To inquire and take testimony as to the results of the legalized liquor traffic, in states wherein it prevails, upon the general condition, the moral, social, intellectual, and material well-being, of the people; and, Third. To recommend what additional legislation, if any, would be beneficial, on the part of Congress, to prevent, in the sphere of national authority, the traffic in intoxicating liquors as a beverage. We ask that the Commissioners be appointed solely with reference to personal fitness for the duties with which they will be intrusted, irrespective of political or partisan consideration; and that they be authorized to employ a clerk, with reasonable compensation, and to have such expenses as are incidental to their investigations defrayed. We are well assured that the full and impartial investigation for which we ask, with your official authority and co-operation, concerning this vital subject, will be most welcome at the present time to a large, influential, and intelligent portion of citizens in all parts of the country.

"WILLIAM E. DODGE, *President.*

"J. M. STEARNS, *Corresponding Secretary.*"

This was done with the hope that a more comprehensive and reliable statistical information would be brought before the people generally, which should be to them as accurate and convincing proof of the alarming extent of the evil, and also of the wisdom and efficiency of the measures already in existence and in process of operation. Said he who stood up to plead in its behalf, "I believe the hour is at hand when we must take a forward step in dealing with this problem; when, if we would not go backward, we must wisely take a step forward. Look about in the different states of this Union, and you will find, in almost all of them, this question has thrust itself forward. It cannot be, it will not be, it ought not to be put down; and we bring it here because here are the headquarters; here, too, is the responsibility just as direct on your shoulders as representatives of the nation, as in your respective states the responsibility is direct as citizens thereof." The matter was fully discussed on the floor of Congress, and what shall be the result remains for the future to disclose. When the American people as a nation shall rise in their strength, and proclaim prohibition through the length and breadth of the land, and moral principle shall be sufficiently strong to prove a propelling force in its application, there will dawn a brighter day than has yet been known in all their history. Nothing that can be done would so elevate and ennoble the mass of the people as this. Nothing but "total abstinence for the individual and prohibition for the state," can save us from the withering blight of intemperance. The contest is open, and the war is being waged; and who will enlist? It is a better and more hopeful work than animated the crusaders of old, and made them willing to peril their lives by a long and doubtful pilgrimage. As a partial and forcible reply to the question we have asked, we subjoin the following from the pen of Dr. Holland on

THE GREAT TEMPERANCE MOVEMENT.

For years and years, and weary, suffering years, multiplied into decades, have the women of America waited to see that traffic destroyed which annually sends sixty thousand of their sons, brothers, fathers, and husbands into the drunkard's grave. They have been impoverished, disgraced, tortured in mind and body, beaten, murdered. Under the impulse of maddening liquors the hands that were pledged before Heaven to provide for and protect them have withdrawn from them the means of life, or smitten them in the dust. Sons whom they have nursed upon their bosoms with tenderest love and countless prayers, have grown into beasts, of whom they are afraid, or have sunk into helpless and pitiful slavery. They have been compelled to cover their eyes with shame in the presence of fathers whom it would have been bliss for them to hold in honor. They have been compelled to bear children to men whose habits had unfitted them for parentage — children not only tainted by disease, but endowed with debased appetites. They have seen themselves and their precious families thrust into social degradation, and cut off forever from all desirable life by the vice of the men they loved. What the women of this country have suffered from drunkenness, no mind, however sympathetic, can measure, and no pen, however graphic, can describe. It has been the unfathomable black gulf into which infatuated multitudes of men have thrown their fortunes, their health, and their industry, and out of which have come only — in fire and stench — dishonor, disease, crime, misery, despair, and death. It is the abomination of abominations, the curse of curses, the hell of hells!

For weary, despairing years, they have waited to see the reform that should protect them from further harm. They have listened to lectures, they have signed pledges, they have encouraged temperance societies, they have asked for and secured legislation, and all to no practical good end. The politicians have played them false; the officers of the law are unfaithful; the government revenue thrives on the thriftiness of their curse; multitudes of the clergy are not only apathetic in their pulpits, but self-indulgent in their social habits; newspapers do not help, but rather hinder them; the liquor interest, armed with the money that should have bought them prosperity, organizes against them; fashion opposes them; a million fierce appetites are arrayed against them, and, losing all faith in men, what can they do? There is but one thing for them to do. There is but one direction in which they can look, and that upward! The women's temperance movement, begun and carried on by prayer, is as natural in its birth and growth as the oak that springs from the acorn. If God and the godlike element in women cannot help, there is no help. If the pulpit, the press, the politicians, the reformers, the law, cannot bring reform, who is there left to do it but God and the women? We bow to this movement with reverence. We do not stop to question methods; we do not pause to query about permanent results. We simply say to the glorious women engaged in this marvellous crusade, "May God help and prosper you, and give you the desire of your hearts in the fruit of your labors."

It becomes men to be either humbly helpful or dumb. We who have dallied with this question; we who have dispassionately drawn the line between temperance and total abstinence; we who have deplored drunkenness, with wine-glasses in our hands; we who have consented to involve a great moral reform with politics; we who have been politically afraid of the power of the brutal element associated with the liquor traffic; we who have split hairs in our discussions of public policy; we who have given social sanction to habits that in the great cities have made drunkards of even the women themselves, and led their sons and ours into a dissolute life; we who have shown either our unwillingness or our impotence to save the country from the gulf that yawns before it,—can only step aside with shamefaced humility while the great crusade goes on, or heartily give to it our approval and our aid.

This is not a crusade of professional agitators, clamoring for an abstract right, but an enterprise of suffering, pure and devoted women, laboring for the overthrow of a concrete wrong. It is no pleasant, holiday business in which these women are engaged, but one of self-denying hardship, pregnant in every part with a sense of duty. Is is the offspring of a grand religious impulse which gives to our time its one superb touch of heroism, and redeems it from its political debasement and the degradation of its materialism. It is a shame to manhood that it is necessary; it is a glory to womanhood that it is possible.

If the experience of the last century has demonstrated anything, it is that total abstinence is the only ground on which any well-wisher of society can stand. The liquor traffic has been bolstered up for years, and is strong to-day, simply through influence which is deemed respectable. It must be made infamous by the combination of all the respectable elements of society against it. It must cease to be respectable to drink at all. It must cease to be respectable to rent a building in which liquors are sold. There is no practicable middle ground. So long as men drink temperately, men will drink intemperately, whether it ought to be otherwise or not; and it is with reference to the development of a healthy public opinion on this subject that we particularly rejoice in the woman's crusade. Our own vision is so blinded and perverted that we can only see the deformity of the monster which oppresses us through woman's eyes, uplifted in prayer, tearful in shame and suffering, or bright in triumph, as the strongholds of her life-long enemy fall before her.

GENERAL REMARKS.

Here and there in the history of the past, we are led to see the workings of some great reform, and as the historian leads us on through all the intricate windings that must needs be compassed before the grand result can be reached, we are convinced that nothing worthy,—nothing far-reaching and substantial can be wrought out except through much toil and pains-taking. The most valuable things of earth can be had only by delving for them. The richest veins of metals lie where man must dig long and patiently, if he would make them available for practical use. Glistening pearls lie embedded in the ocean sands, and the diver must subject himself to peculiar danger and hardship, if he would make their rare brilliancy minister to human gratification; and the gold and the pearl, after they are brought to light, must needs go through a process of one kind and another before they are fitted to meet the demands of those who require them. It seems to be a universal law—one that heaven has instituted—that labor and toil shall be the price of every thing good. The thoughtful mind will perceive the wisdom of the plan, and see how it tends to the highest good of men, and the development of the truest and most efficient character. This same principle that holds good in the natural world is also true in the moral. Almost all the revolutionary movements that have affected the moral condition of mankind, have been characterized by slow and laborious working, that at times have made their strongest supporters grow faint lest they fail of the ultimate good they had in view. Truth and error have always been at war with each other, and the good is only evoked through conflict. That mighty reformation of Luther's time cost a great deal. There were prisons, and judgments of various kinds, before those who were bent upon realizing the lofty ideal that a heaven-directed imagination had given them to see. Nothing could intimidate those heroic souls, that were bound to do and dare for the sublime purpose of freeing human souls from the shackles of priestly superstition, and opening the door through which all might pass to the land of religious freedom. That, like a beautiful Canaan, was ever beckoning them onward. The promise of what might be enjoyed there was always an incentive to vigorous action, and thus allured, they counted not their lives dear to them, if so be the goal could be won. The victory was gained, and it sent a wave of blessing through all the earth, vivifying, by a thousand crystal streamlets, the moral vineyard every where. We exult to-day in what was wrought out so painfully. We are higher in the scale of being now, for every weary step of those determined, earnest workers.

Let us not fail to understand and appreciate the way in which the most and the best of life's blessings come to us. They are associated with toil and sacrifice. Somebody must work long and hard to make them available in practical life. There must be delving and digging somewhere to bring out and beautify the gems that are encrusted with much of crude material that make the process slow and discouraging at times. Thoughts like these take possession of the mind, as we stand and look out upon the present agitation which is swaying the friends of temperance, and moving them to a work of reform.

It may, and doubtless will be, a long and stern conflict; and those who go forth to do battle need to be well panoplied, and to gird themselves for resolute action, and be prepared for all sorts of patient endurance. The Crusaders of old faltered not in their march, though upon every print of the foot they left their life-blood as a mark. Before them was a holy shrine, and that shrine was in the hands of profane men, as they thought, and at all hazards it must be rescued and preserved. A far more sacred object is before the Temperance Crusaders of to-day. There are thousands of shrines in human hearts that are polluted and endangered, and the question is, Can they be saved? Let the small host who have risen up to start on the mighty enterprise, be made still stronger. Without distinction of rank or sex, the ranks should be increased, for the end sought is of universal interest, and any one who enlists in the service can work with the confident assurance that every thing done in this direction is a part of that blessed reformation which the world greatly needs, and which, could it be obtained, would be like bathing us all in sunshine. The magnitude of the work should by no means appall. It will cost a great deal, but it is worth the cost. If the veterans fall before the goal is won, let others take their places and march on to the front. If the standard-bearers grow feeble and faint, let the more youthful and stronger ones seize the banner and carry it forward to victory, amid the shouts and rejoicings of a grateful people.

19

A

FULL DESCRIPTION

OF THE

ORIGIN AND PROGRESS

OF THE

NEW PLAN OF LABOR BY THE WOMEN

UP TO THE PRESENT TIME.

By T. A. H. BROWN,

REPORTER FOR THE CINCINNATI GAZETTE, WHO WAS CONSTANTLY IN THE FIELD.

INTRODUCTION.

BY DIO LEWIS.

EARLY IMPRESSED WITH THE POWER OF PRAYER. — THREE HUNDRED AND FORTY LECTURES ON THE SUBJECT. — THE FIRST INSTANCES WHERE THIS POWER WAS TRIED UPON GROG SHOPS. — DIXON, ILL., AND BATTLE CREEK, MICH., DRIVE OUT THE DRAM SELLERS. — HOW THE MOVEMENT WAS SMOTHERED IN MANCHESTER, N. H. — THE MOVEMENT ANALYZED. — A PRAYER MEETING FROM BEGINNING TO END. — DIFFERENCE IN PRAYERS. — THE PLAN WHICH LARGE CITIES SHOULD ADOPT.

THE present wide-spread interest in the Woman's Temperance Movement has suggested the preparation of the following facts in its history.

When I was a boy, my father's habitual intemperance kept our humble home in a deep shadow. My mother was obliged to earn with her own hands the food for her five children, and then to cook it; she was obliged to earn the material for our clothing, and then to cut and make it; she was general provider, cook, housekeeper, nurse, — in brief, she was everything to her family. In addition to all this, she was not unfrequently the victim of abuse and personal violence. But, a high-spirited woman, she refused to entertain the idea of separation, and bore all her sorrows with Christian fortitude. But sometimes the trouble was more than she could bear, when she would burst into tears, and, leaving us, would climb up into the garret of our house

DIO. LEWIS
DR. JEWETT
GOUGH
MRS RUNYAN
MOTHER STEWART

to pray. We youngsters used to listen and hear her cry out in anguish, "O Lord, how long, how long, how long! O God, help me, help me, help me!" Then she would be still for a while; and when she came down to us again, we noticed that although her eyes were red, her face shone like an angel's. The day was never so dark at our house that my precious mother could not go up into the attic, open the cloud, and let in the light of heaven.

I grew up with an exalted conception of the power of a woman's prayer. Even now, at the distance of more than forty years from those dark days, I never think of any great evil or criminal, that my mind does not immediately busy itself with the thought, that, through woman's prayer, all this might be cured.

About twenty years ago, I prepared with great interest an Address upon the Power of Woman's Prayer in Grog Shops. During these twenty years I have delivered that Address more than three hundred and forty times, and have constantly cherished a firm confidence that the time would come when through woman's prayer the dram shops of our country would be closed.

About nineteen years ago the plan was tried in a small village in New York, with good results. About fifteen years ago, while lecturing in the west, on the subject of Physical Education, I proposed, at Dixon, Ill., to the Rev. Mr. Harsha and other clergymen in Dixon, to deliver my Address on the subject of the Power of Woman's Prayer in Grog Shops, if, on a certain Sunday evening, they would all forego their regular exercises, and attend in the large hall. They expressed some doubt about the propriety of temperance lectures on the Sabbath day; but when I explained the general spirit and drift of my address, they consented. The hall was crowded, and at the close of the meeting a committee of three women was elected to prepare an appeal from the women of Dixon to the dealers in intoxicating drinks there, and a committee of fifty women to circulate that appeal among the dram sellers. The next morning the visiting committee held a meeting, heard the appeal read, liked it, adopted it, and immediately started out with it and several pledges which had been prepared meantime. They went from saloon to saloon, pleading, singing, praying. In one week their task was finished; thirty-nine dram shops were closed, and the papers announced that not even a glass of lager beer could be purchased in town.

I left Dixon soon after, and went on my way, discussing and urging the cause of physical training for the young of our country, in which I was then, and, indeed, have ever since been, deeply interested. It is not improbable, if this movement had been pushed, and town after town enlisted in the good work, that the great revolution now going forward in the country might have been developed at that time; but I was then so deeply impressed with the vital importance of the educational work I had undertaken, that I thought even the temperance reform one of secondary importance. However, a few months later, the Woman's Temperance Movement was inaugurated at Battle Creek, Mich. The Rev. Charles Jones, Congregational minister of that city, now residing at Saxonville, Mass., and, indeed, all the clergymen of that city, including the Episcopal, responded to my suggestion for a union Sabbath evening temperance meeting in the large hall, dismissing the regular religious exercises in the churches, and bringing their congregations with them to the hall.

The same steps were taken; a committee of five women to draft an appeal, and a committee of a hundred women to circulate it, with the prepared pledges, were elected at the close of the meeting; and before noon of the following day, the committee of visitation, marching two by two, and extending more than two blocks, halted in front of the hotel where I was stopping, to show me a large sign with the word "Saloon," which four of them were carrying, the first trophy. Within two weeks the fifty dram shops in town had been closed, with the exception of one, a large drinking, billiard, and gambling institution, which held out for three weeks longer.

But even this marvellous success did not induce me to turn aside from the cause of physical education, and engage in the Woman's Temperance Movement.

Soon after that time, I went to Boston to establish the Normal Institute of Physical Education, to train teachers of the new gymnastics. For years I continued, body and soul, in that work; and then came that part of my history devoted to the establishment of the educational institution at Lexington, where I hoped to illustrate the possibilities in the physical training of young women during the period of their school life.

During the four years given to the Lexington work, and up to the time that those magnificent buildings were destroyed by fire, I scarcely thought of anything outside.

I removed again to Boston, six years ago, with the intention of devoting the residue of my life to writing and lecturing upon the subject of education. In one of my books published shortly after, through the Harpers under the title of "Our Girls," I recurred to the Woman's Temperance Movement, and published in that work the details of the attempts made years before to close dram shops through the pleading, songs, and prayers of women. I then seriously resolved to attempt the inauguration of a Woman's Temperance Movement in New England, and selected Manchester, N. H., for the first trial. I spent a week in that city in preparation.

Nearly all of the clergymen were interested, and many leading citizens promised to occupy seats on the platform. Mr. Clark, United States senator, presided. The meeting was held in Smythe's Hall, was immense in numbers, and not only was conducted in accordance with the programme, but was altogether one of the most magnificent meetings I have ever attended. At the close of the meeting we attempted to organize the regular committees; but the crowd was so great that it was thought better to adjourn, to meet the next morning at ten o'clock, to complete the business arrangements. The meeting next morning was full and enthusiastic; the committees were appointed, and everything looked most auspicious. I had thus far been so conspicuous in the work, and was so anxious withal that it should be a Woman's Movement, that I thought it wise to leave Manchester and our good cause in the hands of the committee of two hundred women. I returned to Boston, and waited for reports from Manchester. The women had a large meeting the next morning; were advised by the men not to go at once to the dram shops with the appeal and pledges which had been prepared, but to circulate petitions through the city, and gather the names of all the women and girls over fifteen years of age, which should be published and circulated among the dram shops before the visits of the women began. This task occupied two weeks; the names were published, making quite a large pamphlet. These pamphlets were circulated among the dram sellers, and in four weeks the women called a meeting with the intention of starting out in the regular work of visiting the dram shops, but the meeting was a small one, and lacked enthusiasm; great variety of opinion was expressed in reference to the propriety and wisdom of this and that, and the Woman's Temperance Movement in Manchester was abandoned, though all cherished the belief that much good had been done by way of elevating public sentiment.

At Nashua, N. H., Natick, Mass., and at other points in New England, I made attempts to establish the work, but was everywhere more or less disappointed with a lack of unanimity and enthusiasm among clergymen. Since that time I have continued, as the public knows, to lecture on the subject of education, and have published several volumes on the subject, which have had a wide circulation.

Last December, while lecturing in Southern Ohio before the Lyceums upon the Higher Education of Our Girls, I devoted some spare evenings to the discussion of the Woman's Temperance Movement. The first meeting was held in Hillsboro', the second in Washington, Fayette Co.; the whole world knows the rest of the story.

I cannot give the story of the Woman's Temperance Movement without giving my own relations with it. Omitting this, it would seem to have been a series of accidents, of inexplicable happenings. I trust the reader will excuse so much that is merely personal.

The Woman's Temperance Movement is one of the most profoundly religious revolutions the world has ever seen. It is very simple; a prayer-meeting from beginning to end. What seems a series of stages in the work is nothing but a change of place for the prayer meeting. First it is in the closet, then in the vestry of the church, then in the saloon; but it is nothing more nor less than a prayer meeting from beginning to end. And I notice that many clergymen and religious papers speak of it as illustrating the power of prayer, and as a triumphant response to Professor Tyndall's proposition. I am happy and grateful in the belief that this view is just; but I must take pains to say that I have not observed that prayer has served in this cause, unless it is of one peculiar kind. I have heard men pray, during the last few months, for the suppression of dram shops. I do not believe that their prayers have added to the success of the Woman's Temperance Movement. Their prayers have been mostly from the base of their brains. Let me illustrate. Not long since, in Ohio, I heard a man pray in a gathering about a saloon. I recall distinctly certain sentences in his prayer, but I shall not be able to give you his manner; I can only say that his fists were closed, and he shook his head while he was praying. He cried in a loud voice, "And now, Almighty God, wilt thou soften his hard heart; wilt thou, with thy own right arm, break his obdurate will," &c. Of course that prayer was not meant for God's ear; it was designed for the chap inside of the saloon; but an eternity of such prayers, uttered by all the men on the globe, would not close one dram shop.

Shortly after the man's prayer was finished, an ignorant girl prayed, and her prayer was the sort which has accomplished this great temperance revolution. I recall some of the sentences which were uttered in a voice sweet and tender beyond my power of description. She said, "Father, we thank thee that we can do this; and if thou dost not give us the answers we ask, we are thankful all just the same. Dear Father, we thank thee that we are permitted to do this work of love; we feel ourselves coming nearer and nearer to thee. Dear Father, we thank thee for this sweet privilege with all our hearts. Dear Father, the distance between thee and the best of us is so great, and the distance between the best of us and the worst of us so small, that if thou canst be patient, loving, and forgiving towards the best of us, we shall find it easy to be patient, loving, and forgiving towards the worst of our fellows. Dear Father, fill our hearts with love; in all our thoughts, in all our words, may we breathe only the spirit of Jesus."

Thus, when it is claimed by Christians that the success of the Woman's Temperance Movement is in answer to prayer, it must never be forgotten that the kind of prayer which has been followed by the great blessing is that uttered by this Ohio girl. This gives the key-note of the great campaign.

That the Woman's Temperance Movement is successful in villages and small towns no one doubts; but there is very considerable doubt about its success in large cities. For myself, I have not a shadow of doubt that it will prove successful in the large cities, under the following management: —

First. Let each church organize a daily prayer meeting. From this prayer meeting let committees of two or three women be sent out at once, and constantly to visit the owners of real estate where drams are sold, and the private homes of those who keep the saloons. They will plead with these persons to sign the pledge that they will do so no more. These small committees will report every day at the prayer meetings, and within a week ten or fifteen of these small committees will have visited as many persons as they can undertake to labor with.

Second. After one or two weeks, these church prayer meetings will send out committees of five women, to visit the dram sellers at their places of business, to quietly plead with them, and before they leave, kneel in a corner of the bar-room for a few moments of silent prayer.

Third. After one or two weeks of this labor, the women will generally conclude to send out larger parties, say of thirty to fifty, to hold religious exercises in some of the larger drinking places, with a distinct understanding that when a disturbance is threatened, they immediately resolve themselves into the smaller committees of the second method, and do not gather again in large companies perhaps for that day, certainly not until they see an opportunity to work more effectively in large bodies.

God is in the cities quite as much as in the country; the women of the cities are as intelligent and as sorrowful over the curse of dram shops as their sisters in the country; and if they manage in the way I have suggested, will as certainly succeed as the women of small towns.

Very respectfully,

DIO LEWIS.

CHAPTER XIX.

ORIGIN OF THE WOMAN'S MOVEMENT. — THE NEW LAW FOR THE SUPPRESSION OF INTEMPERANCE. — DIO LEWIS'S PLAN AT HILLSBORO'. — WASHINGTON COURT-HOUSE THE NEXT PLACE. — HOW SLATER WAS SQUELCHED. — THE FIRST TABERNACLE. — SIEGE OF CHARLIE BECK, ETC.

Seven cities of ancient Greece contended for the honor of being Homer's birthplace, and so there are several places that claim to have given to the world the "Woman's Temperance Movement." The controversy, however, narrows down to two small towns in Southern Ohio, the names of which have already become familiar to the whole country. Before the remarkable scenes which closed the year 1873, Hillsboro' and Washington Court-House were obscure hamlets, content with being the honored seats of their respective counties — Highland and Fayette. The movement was begun first in Hillsboro', but attained the most strength in Washington, from which it came to be known as the "Washington Court-House plan."

Hillsboro' is one of those old aristocratic and somewhat conservative towns which are sometimes found in the middle southern states, like a relic of a past generation, and a standing reproof against the push and hurry of the average western city. It has about three thousand five hundred inhabitants, many of whom are descended from the old Virginia stock, and inherit the bibulous customs of the old-style gentleman. So many of the men were accustomed to their daily stimulant, that the public mind was anything but sensitive on the temperance question, and saloon keepers were wont to ply their calling unmolested by law. Where liquor drinking was looked upon with some allowance, liquor selling was not deemed a disgrace. It seemed, therefore, one of the most improbable things in the range of possibilities that Hillsboro' should lead off in as radical a movement for temperance reform as the world has ever seen. But it was destined so to be.

On the evening of December 22, 1873, Dio Lewis, a Boston physician and lyceum lecturer, delivered in Music Hall a lecture on "Our Girls." He had been engaged during the autumn previous, by the Lecture Association, to fill one place in the winter course of lectures, merely for the entertainment of the people. At the close of his address, he announced that he would speak to as many as chose to come and hear him, on the following night, on the subject of temperance. He gave some hints of a plan which he proposed for a campaign in the interest of society. The audience, by a rising vote, requested him to remain and speak.

On the following night a large and enthusiastic audience assembled in the same place, to hear the proposed plan elaborated. Dr. Lewis delivered a stirring address on the general subject of temperance, after which he told, at some length, how a band of women in a New England manufacturing village had driven rum from their midst by a crusade of prayer and song. It was one of those dull, dead places, where the boys worked in the mills, and the men got drunk for a business. There were six saloons in the town, and one night a company of these boys were enticed into one of them, and made drunk. When they were taken home their mothers and sisters were horrified. They saw that unless something was done, their brothers and sons would soon be as worthless as their husbands. One of these women was the speaker's mother, the wife of a drunken husband. Next day she collected a band of the mothers, wives, and sisters of the place, and they went to the church. There they poured out their hearts in prayer, and, kneeling about the altar in a circle, joined hands, and solemnly promised God and each other never to give up until every dram shop in town was closed.

Next day they went in a band to the saloon of the man who had made the boys drunk, and prayed and pleaded with him until he pledged himself never to sell intoxicating liquor again. Then they went to the other places, and after a while all but one promised they would quit if the rest would. The obstinate liquor seller for a time treated them with sarcastic politeness, thinking it was a feminine freak that would soon wear out. He ordered his "Boston rocker," and pillows for his head and feet, and, there being no other chairs in the room, urged the ladies to take seats, go on with their praying, and make themselves at home, while he took a nap. His business kept him up late at night, and made him sleepy. Then while they prayed and sang he snored; but they knew all the time that he was awfully wide awake. At length there was a rustling of paper. The saloonist opened one eye a little, and the ladies were taking out lunches! When it came night, and they went home, "Charlie" urged them to come again. He was always glad to see his friends, especially the ladies. They came again, and day after day, until Charlie's urbanity had subsided into sullen silence. At length, one day he broke in upon their devotions with, —

"Hold on a minute. I want to know how long this devilish business is going to last!"

"Just so long," was the quiet reply, "as you persist in selling whiskey to our husbands and sons."

A few more days, and Charlie yielded, and all the saloons were closed. That was nineteen years ago, and never from that day to this has there been a place in that village where a glass of intoxicating liquor could be bought.

This was the doctor's plan for driving out saloons. The people of Hillsboro' could do it, if the women only had the energy, persistency, and true Christian spirit. So forcibly was the thing presented, that a motion was made to put the new idea into execution at once. It was carried by a rising vote. Secretaries were appointed, and seventy-five ladies enlisted on the spot to undertake the task. Addresses were made by the pastors of churches present, and by Colonel W. H. Trimble, all indorsing the movement, and pledging it their support. Mrs. J. H. Thompson, Mrs. P. J. Jeans, and Miss E. L. Grand-Girard were appointed a committee to write an appeal to be read to the liquor sellers by the committee of visitation. After voting to meet next morning, at ten o'clock, in the Presbyterian church, the meeting adjourned. It ought also to be stated that seventy-five men, in this meeting, put their names down as moral and pecuniary "backers" of the undertaking.

At the morning meeting the ladies put their signatures to the following solemn compact: —

"We, the ladies whose names are hereto appended, agree and resolve that, with God's help, we will stand by each other in this work, and persevere therein until it is accomplished, and see to it, as far as our influence goes, that the traffic shall never be revived."

On Christmas morning, at nine o'clock, all preliminaries being arranged, one hundred and fifteen women filed out of the church, formed a procession, and marched to the drug stores. They went with trembling limbs and anxious hearts. It was to them a strange experiment, a new idea. It seemed subversive of all the recognized rules of womanly conduct. The thought of going into a low part of the town, and entering one of those vile dens, which respectable people abhorred at a distance; of kneeling in sawdust and filth to plead with bloated and beery saloon keepers, was all overwhelming to their finer sensibilities, and shocking to their modesty. They shrank from the task, half in doubt and half in fear. But again they thought of the drunkards that were reeling home from those saloons every night, — perhaps into their families, — and of the temptations that were lying in wait for their children in the future. Their misgivings left them, and personal considerations no longer had any weight.

The drug stores were the first to receive attention. It was known that at one of these places, at least, the pestle and mortar at the door, and the rows of polished jars on the shelves, were but a disguise, under which was carried on an extensive retail liquor trade. A pledge was prepared to meet the case of all druggists, and on the morning of their first visit it was signed by two of the four drug stores — J. J. Brown and Seybert & Isamenn. Dr. W. R. Smith, the third druggist, who was also an elder in the Presbyterian church, would only sign with the proviso that he, as a physician, had a right to prescribe liquor, and sell on his own prescription. Of the fourth druggist, W. H. H. Dunn, more hereafter.

On Friday, December 26, the saloons were visited. There were eleven of them, and they presented a defiant front. Mrs. J. H. Thompson, daughter of the late Governor Allen Trimble, made the first prayer in a liquor saloon during the movement. They secured no signatures that day. Uhrig was stubborn; Ward said he was in a bad business, and meant to stop as soon as he felt able to do so; Bales was flippant and hard; the hotels couldn't do a profitable business without selling liquor; and so the ladies separated to their homes, on the evening of the first day, with no victories to boast, but with new strength and determination in their hearts.

The next morning the ladies received a communication from Dunn, in reply to the appeal of the committee of visitation. It was as follows: —

"LADIES: In compliance with my agreement, I give you this promise, — that I will carry on my business in the future as I have in the past; that is to say, that in the sale of intoxicating liquors I will comply with the law; nor will I sell to any person whose father, mother, wife, or daughter, sends me a written request not to make such sale."

This was the first defiant blast from the notorious Dunn, who was destined to give more trouble to the "crusaders," — as they came to be called, — than any other man during the whole course of the movement. Dunn is represented as a man of frank, open disposition, and a high sense of honor, which rendered the people unprepared for the violent opposition which he manifested. He was moved by no prayers, and would listen to no entreaties. For a while he made no objection to the ladies coming into his store, and carrying on their devotions; but at length, one Friday morning, they found the door locked upon them, and were thereafter inexorably excluded. But this neither detracted from their ardor nor diminished their numbers. Prayer meetings were held on the walk in front of his door, while hundreds of sympathizing listeners stood about.

It was a sight calculated to melt the stoutest heart. However bitter the cold, or piercing the wind, these women could be seen, at almost any hour of the day, kneeling on the cold flag-stones before this store. In the midst, with voice raised in earnest prayer, is the daughter of a former governor of Ohio. Surrounding her are the wives and daughters of statesmen, lawyers, bankers, physicians, and business men — representatives from nearly all the households of the place. The prayer ended, the women rise from their knees, and begin, in a low voice, some sweet and familiar hymn, that brings back to the heart of the looker-on the long-forgotten influences of childhood. Tears may be seen in the eyes of red-nosed and hard-hearted men, supposed to be long since past feeling. Passers-by lift their hats and step softly. Conversation is in subdued tones, and a sympathetic interest is depicted on every face. Then follow another subdued prayer and a song, at the close of which a fresh relay of women comes up, and the first ones retire to the residence of an honored citizen, close at hand, where a lunch is spread for their refreshment. Soon it is their turn to resume their praying and singing; and so the siege is kept up, from morning till night, and day after day, with little variation in method or incidents.

Meanwhile the saloons had not been neglected. There was one kept by Joseph Lance, and known as the "Lava Bed" — doubtless a reminiscence of the Modoc war. This was the first to yield; but as Joe had been arrested for the illegal sale of liquor, and two formidable indictments were hanging over him like a nightmare, his surrender was not considered as a clear victory. But the establishment was closed forever, and the late proprietor embarked on a more respectable career as a fish-dealer. His fish were known as "cold-water fish," and found ready sale.

Schwartz and Koch capitulated after a siege of two weeks, and shipped their liquors back to Cincinnati.

Anxious to earn an honest penny, they made an auction of the various articles which comprised the outfit of their saloons, and thus afforded the temperance ladies an opportunity of expressing their professed friendship in dollars and cents. It was an amusing sight to see the crowd of pious sisters at the sale, running up old decanters, beer mugs, tumblers, and bottles, to fabulous prices, and then lugging home the trophies with an air of joyful pride! They would not pay the saloon keepers for their stock of liquors, or loss of business, but when the whole was voluntarily abandoned, they were eager to help the men who suddenly found themselves without an occupation.

Koch was formerly a shoemaker by trade, and no sooner had he resumed his old occupation than his fair customers fairly overwhelmed him with orders for shoes. Old dealers, who found their trade thereby so much diminished, almost wished they had been saloon keepers too, so they might have passed through the profitable experience of surrendering. Schwartz bought a stock of groceries, and found a good run of patronage from the start. He now measures out molasses and vinegar in the place of brandy and gin, and has neither the fear of the Adair law nor of praying women before his eyes.

The war upon the saloons made slow but certain progress. By the 30th of January five saloons and three drug stores had yielded, and about the same number of saloons and one drug store remained. The following amusing "inside view" of one of these saloon visits appeared in a Cincinnati paper. It was given by a young blood who was there. "He and half a dozen others, who had been out of town, and did not know what was going on, had ranged themselves in the familiar semicircle before the bar and had their drinks ready and cigars prepared for the match, when the rustle of women's wear attracted their attention, and looking up they saw what they thought a crowd of a thousand ladies entering. One youth saw among them his mother and sister, another had two cousins in the invading host, and a still more unfortunate recognized his intended mother-in-law! Had the invisible prince of the pantomime touched them with his magic wand, converting all to statues, the tableau could not have been more impressive. For one full minute they stood as if turned to stone; then a slight motion was evident, and lager beer and brandy smash descended slowly to the counter, while cigars dropped unlighted from nerveless fingers. Happily, at this juncture the ladies struck up—

> "O, do not be discouraged,
> For Jesus is your friend."

It made a diversion, and the party escaped to the street, "scared out of a year's growth."

Leaving the ladies praying with the remaining saloons and the invincible Dunn, we must follow the movement to Washington Court House, where it had been raging all this time with even more force, and with much greater success. The work was inaugurated in Hillsboro' on the day before Christmas. From there Dio Lewis went to Washington, the county seat of Fayette County, where he delivered his lecture on "Our Girls" the same evening. During the course of his lecture he told his hearers he would like to see them all, Christmas morning, and talk to them a little on the subject of temperance. Quite an audience was on hand at the appointed time, and after some general arguments, the doctor startled them with his prayer plan, substantially as before stated.

ie plan was taken hold of by the ladies, as if it was

the very thing they had so long been waiting for. No time was lost. An organization was formed, petitions and pledges prepared, and the very next day the ladies, to the number of sixty, marched. They had ten saloons and three drug stores to deal with, but before they rested, the whole circuit had been made. They were treated by the astonished saloon keepers with some show of respect, until they came to the concern conducted by Peter Scheirman and his devoted spouse. They were very much enraged with the interference with their rights as American citizens under the constitution, declaration of independence, and star-spangled banner, and in broken and excited English threatened the most terrible things if the women came again. But they went again and again, without suffering any serious consequences, until at last Peter and his frau saw the matter in a different light. The band increased daily in numbers and zeal. Bad weather and ill treatment had no effect but to inspire them with new energy. In a week the procession had more than doubled in size. Composed as it was of the best Christian women of the town, it began to have a moral power which the liquor sellers, sneer or argue as they might, could not stand up against. From the first the ladies exhibited that rare discrimination and judgment in their movements which have characterized the whole campaign. Under no circumstances did they allow themselves to lose their temper. Generally they avoided all argument with stubborn saloon keepers, and asked permission before they began a prayer meeting upon the premises. It was the usual programme to enter a saloon, explain to the proprietor briefly their mission, present him with the dealer's pledge, and if he refused to sign it, some one led in prayer, a hymn was sung, and he was personally entreated to abandon his business. If all failed, these visits were renewed from day to day. Entreaties were persistently pressed upon him. His customers dwindled down to a few of the most wretched description. Perhaps a few indictments were secured against him, in case any persuasion of that kind should be needed. The saloon keeper, finding himself cut off from respectable society in the village, with an unprofitable business on his hands, and conscious that he was liable at any moment to be prosecuted for violation of the law, generally concluded, after a few days of resistance, that the easiest way out of the whole difficulty was to quit, and promise never to sell another drop.

So great was the success of the Washington ladies that, at the end of the first week, half the dram shops in the place had been closed up. The men that still held out shut their doors in the face of the ladies, and tried to escape the influence of the prayers and hymns. Offers were made to compromise or sell out. One of the so-called druggists, who had begun in trade eight years before, with a keg of sour beer and a gallon of whiskey bought on credit, and who had built up a profitable business behind jars labelled drugs, offered to give up his whole stock to the women for two thousand dollars; but his proposition was not entertained for a moment. They kept steadily on, and in four days more every saloon keeper in the corporate limits of Washington had quit the business, and every druggist signed the pledge to sell no liquor for a beverage. The siege had lasted eleven days, and in that time eleven saloons and three drug stores had capitulated. It was a remarkable victory, and none were more surprised at it than the temperance workers themselves. They were not expecting such speedy results. Old topers and gay gentlemen of leisure had suddenly found themselves without their customary stimulants or places of resort, and a howl of anguish went up from them that the good people had waited long to hear.

"Why," one old, gray-haired guzzler was overheard to say, — "why, man, you'll ruin your town with your nonsense about temperance, shutting up saloons, and all that sort of stuff. Look here," he continued, laying the dirty forefinger of his left hand impressively upon the dirty palm of his right, — "look here; half the money that comes to your town comes through the saloons; half of the people of your town live on that money. Cut off that money, and how are they going to live? Answer me that; how are they going to live? I've traded in this town now goin' on forty year, and I'm blowed if I don't trade in Wilmington from this time on — from this time on, sir. And there's pleuty more like me."

It did not enter into his calculation that Wilmington, in a few days, was to be as dry as Washington.

But the work of the women was by no means finished. Just outside the village limits two establishments were having a monopoly of the trade. Those whose appetite for stimulants could not be subdued, were subjected to the necessity of making regular excursions to these places for their daily drinks. It was felt that these must be suppressed, or the work would be incomplete. But before they were ready to make an advance upon Beck and Sullivan, a new enemy faced them in their very midst. One Slater had set up a saloon, and avowed his intention to fight the women as long as they desired. His lawyer and priest had fortified him with the doctrine that whiskey selling was a legitimate business under the laws of the state, and he would be protected in it. But no sooner had he opened his door than the women were with him; and they staid with him. Their prayers and persuasions had no effect whatever, and he grew more violent every day. His wickedness became so notorious, that he was commonly known as the "John Allen" of Washington. One day he bethought himself of the plan of freezing the women out. He allowed his fire to go out, opened the windows and doors, and wet the floor down with water until it stood in pools. It was a bitter cold January day, and the atmosphere of the place was almost unendurable. But the marshal of the village kept up a huge fire in the street; and the inward fires of zeal made them proof against the weather.

But the ladies were as fertile in devices as their wily enemy. Mr. Slater was surprised one morning to find before his door a small portable building, hastily constructed of boards, supplied with a stove and seats, and looking as though it had come to stay. The side facing his saloon was open, and yawned before him like an immense mortar, ready to be discharged and blow his frail shanty into atoms. But it was, probably, the most peaceful engine of war ever constructed. This peculiar institution came to be known as the "Tabernacle," possibly owing to its resemblance to the structure which the Israelites carried with them through the wilderness; and that name has clung to it, wherever it has appeared, throughout the whole campaign. Comfortably seated in this, the besieging party continued singing and praying during the entire day, and until late at night. But still the obstinate saloonist held out. It was then discovered that the building belonged to another party than the occupant, and the women resolved to buy the building out of his hands. But he threatened to start again within two hours in some other locality. At last, when all efforts at "moral suasion" had proved ineffective, a stronger argument was called into use. A case was made out against him under the Adair law, and he was brought to terms about the middle of January.

Again the village proper was free. But there still remained the beer hall of Charlie Beck, about half a mile out, and the wayside saloon of James Sullivan, still farther away. To these the women turned their prayerful attention. Beck was one of those good-natured, yet stubborn and excitable members of the German race, who look upon beer drinking as an essential element in man's social and moral nature, and think everybody a Puritan or fanatic who holds different views. His place looked more like a country school-house than a saloon. It stood back from the road, and was surrounded by well-arranged grounds. Carriages were furnished the ladies, free of charge, from the temperance livery stable of Collins & Bitzer, and in these the band made daily visits to Beck's. After a while Beck, who kept a sharp lookout, when he saw the ladies coming, locked his door, and fled to his residence close at hand. It was during one of these intervals that a Cincinnati reporter came reconnoitring about the place. There were no women around, but the door was locked, and the cautious Teuton had fled. After some pounding at the door, the following response was elicited from the residence close at hand: —

"Hello, mein freund; vat you vant, eh?"

The man with a nose for news explained his errand, whereupon Beck broke out with, —

"I got no vitnesses. Dem vimens dey set up a shob on me. But you don't bin a 'bitual troonkard, eh? No, you don't look like him. Val, goom in, goom in. Vat you vant — beer or vine? I dells you dem vimins is shoost awful. Py shinks, dey build a house right in de shtreet, und stay mit a man all day singin, und oder foolishness. But dey don't git in here once agin, already."

It seems that some one had been trying to entrap the

cunning beer vender, by coming to buy liquor with the intention of going away to swear to it, and thus make out a case against him under the Adair law. He was naturally, therefore, very suspicious of strangers, and was even led to look with distrust upon some of his old and faithful customers. These were trying times, and his beery brain was racked with anxiety and excitement.

"You bin a reborter? Vell, I shoust likes to see a goot man here von der Enguirer von Cincinnati. Anodder man yesterday goom mit dem vimins; I tells zem all, 'You shoust go ouat; you got no peesness here.' And den he puts his hand so, in his pusom, for a peestol, und zay, 'You tooch dem vimen, I put you vare you don't zell beer any more, already.'"

During this running fire of broken English, he kept moving from one window to the other, expecting every moment that the dreaded invaders would heave in sight.

"Dem fellers in town, dey shkinned out and left me alone," he complained bitterly. "But I'll never shtop for dem vimin. I sell vine, beer, und cigars, und I don't got any trunken men in mein house."

Accordingly, to show his contempt for the women, Beck called in his faithful adherents, together with his lawyer, and spent most of the night in a drunken powwow which went a little beyond any of his former achievements in that line. The shouts of the revellers could be heard during the night in the distant village, and in the morning a reminiscence of the entertainment was found in the form of a man dead drunk upon a manure pile near the livery stable.

This gave fresh energy to the women, and they were on the war-path early next morning. Seeing them coming in larger numbers and with more determined mien than before, Beck tore off to the town, whence he soon returned with his "gounsel, to see ven he got no more any right to his own property."

The scene grew exciting. The lawyer and reporter took up convenient positions on the fence. The ladies filled up the door, and extended away to the right. Bystanders stood in knots a few yards away, while rushing wildly about among them all was the excited Beck. Fervent prayers were offered for the blessing of God on the temperance cause generally, on that place in particular, on Beck and his household, — all who loved him, — and on the women engaged in the difficult and delicate task before them. Appropriate hymns were sung in the intervals, and the women appeared to be getting happy in about the same ratio that Beck was growing miserable, when at length, at the conclusion of one of the songs, the lawyer slid down from his perch on the fence, advanced towards the ladies, and addressed to them the following speech: —

"Now, ladies, I have a word to say before this performance goes any farther. Mr. Beck has employed me as his attorney. He cannot speak good English, and I speak for him here. He is engaged in a legitimate business, and you are trespassers on his property and rights. If this thing is carried any farther, you will be called to account in the court, and I can assure you the court will sustain the man. He has talked with you all he desires to. He does not want to put you out forcibly; that would be unmanly, and he does not wish to act rudely. But he tells you to go. As his attorney I now warn you to desist from any further annoyance."

Again the ladies sang, —

"My soul, be on thy guard;
Ten thousand foes arise," —

and a fervent prayer was immediately offered for the

lawyer and his client. It was decided to retire peaceably from the premises; but a man who owned the adjoining lot was friendly to the cause, and invited them to establish their "Tabernacle" there, where it would be almost as effective as before the very door of the saloon. Then the siege of prayer and song was resumed. Strong reflectors were placed so as to illuminate the entrance to the beer garden. Guards were constantly on hand, till late at night, and few were found bold enough to face the lanterns for a glass of beer. Beck's business was ruined, and he and his lawyer felt that something had to be done. Application was made for a temporary injunction, and after two weeks' delay it was granted. The Tabernacle disappeared, the daily visits were stopped, and peace once more reigned in the neighborhood of Charlie Beck's beer garden.

But the law proved a double-edged sword. Hitherto the temperance workers had carefully refrained from any appeal to legal force; but when they found it employed against them they no longer hesitated. The Adair law had been violated by both Beck and Sullivan scores of times every week, and it did not take long to make out strong cases against them. Sullivan yielded at once, and soon after Beck ran up the white flag, and surrendered.

At last Washington Court House was free! Not a drop of spirituous or malt liquor could be bought for miles about. It was the first great victory of the campaign, — the first demonstration of the power of women to do what men, with fifty years of legislation, had failed to accomplish. The bells of the town rang out with joy. Great excitement prevailed, and the chief business for a few days was the interchange of congratulations.

But the ladies realized that their work was not done.

The nail so well driven must be clinched. Their campaign would be but a poor success if the results were not made permanent. Accordingly they devoted their energies to the circulation of the different kind of pledges, and by continuing the daily mass meetings and prayer meetings, endeavored to mould the excited public sentiment into definite and permanent shape. The personal pledge was pushed with special industry, and nearly the whole population of the place added to the roll of names.

The following are the forms of the various pledges, which are substantially the same as those used in other towns, throughout the whole movement: —

"We, the undersigned, druggists of ——, hereby pledge ourselves, upon our honor as business men, that from this date we will under no circumstances sell or give away, or allow to be sold or given away by any of our agents or employes, any alcoholic or intoxicating liquors, wine, beer, or ale, except upon satisfactory evidence that the liquors are to be used for medicinal or mechanical purposes."

"We, the undersigned, property holders in ——, pledge ourselves, upon our honor, not to let or lease our premises (or premises for which we are agents) in this city, or permit them to be used or occupied, for the sale or dispensing in any way of spirituous liquors, wine, beer, or ale, to be used as a beverage."

"We hereby pledge ourselves, upon our honor, not to sell, furnish, or give away, or allow to be sold or given away by any agent or employe of ours, either by retail or wholesale, any spirituous liquors, wine, beer, or ale, except for medicinal or mechanical purposes."

"We, the undersigned, physicians of ——, upon our honor as professional men, promise hereby not to prescribe the use of spirituous liquors, wine, beer, or ale, only in case of absolute necessity."

"We, the undersigned, do solemnly promise that we will neither make, buy, sell, nor use as a beverage, any spirituous or malt liquors, wine, or fermented cider; and that, in all honorable ways, we will discountenance the use of the same by others."

The following is the appeal presented by the ladies to the liquor seller: —

"Knowing, as you do, the fearful effects of intoxicating drinks, we, the women of Washington, after earnest prayer and deliberation, have decided to appeal to you to desist from this ruinous traffic, that our husbands, brothers, and especially our sons, be no longer exposed to this terrible temptation, and that we may no longer see them led into those paths which go down to sin, and bring both soul and body to destruction. We appeal to the better instincts of your hearts, in the name of desolated homes, blasted hopes, ruined lives, widowed hearts, for the honor of our community, for our prosperity, for our happiness, for our good name as a town, in the name of God, who will judge you as well as ourselves, for the sake of your souls, which are to be saved or lost, we beg, we implore you, to cleanse yourselves from this heinous sin, and place yourselves in the ranks of those who are striving to elevate and ennoble themselves and their fellow-men; and to this we ask you to pledge yourselves."

The following resolution, adopted by the Hillsboro' ladies, will show what they thought of liquor on their own sideboards, or in their mince-pies and puddings: —

"Whereas it is written, 'Be ye clean that bear the vessels of the Lord,' therefore

"*Resolved*, That any woman connected with this Visiting Committee who has wine or brandy, or other alcoholic drinks, in her house, to be used for culinary purposes, be requested to dispose of the same immediately, and hereafter to discontinue and discourage such use."

Washington was destined to have one more bout with whiskey before it was finally and effectually squelched. Some of the old soakers, who began to grow exceedingly dry, opened communication with one Charles Passmore, of Cincinnati. They represented to him that there was a fine opening there for a young man with a few kegs of beer and casks of liquor. He would have no record by which they could proceed against him under the Adair law, and could enjoy an entire monopoly of the trade. Viewed from the Cincinnati stand-point, it looked absurd that a few praying women could afford any serious obstacle to a man with any backbone; and Mr. Passmore came on with his kegs. A room was secured, and the hopeful saloonist was about tapping his first barrel, when he was surprised by a call from a hundred ladies or more. The alarm-bells had been sounded, and the women were ready to march on the instant. After a few prayers and songs, the astonished Cincinnatian ventured to inquire how long they proposed to stay.

"That depends entirely upon yourself," was the reply. "We have come to stay with you till you promise never to sell another glass of liquor in this place."

"That puts a different face on the matter," thought Mr. P., and the next day the kegs were re-shipped to Cincinnati, never having been opened. Mr. Passmore followed them, and from that time Washington has enjoyed perfect immunity from saloon-keepers, and lived on the virtuous principle of total abstinence.

CHAPTER XX.

MARVELLOUS SPREAD OF THE MOVEMENT. — SUDDEN REDEMPTION OF WILMINGTON. — THE EPIDEMIC IN GREENFIELD. — THE FAMOUS SIEGE OF VAN PELT AT NEW VIENNA. — HIS WICKEDNESS AND HIS SURRENDER. — THE GLOOMY HISTORY OF MORROW A GOOD TEMPERANCE TRACT. — ABOUT SELLING CORN TO DISTILLERS. — A WAYNESVILLE PRAYER MEETING REPRODUCED. — A FORTY-NINE DAYS' SIEGE AT CORWIN.

SOME idea of the marvellous rapidity with which this movement began to spread may be had from the fact that, within two weeks from the day it was first inaugurated at Hillsboro', three or four of the leading counties in Southern Ohio were taken by storm. As fast as the news could be carried to neighboring towns, they caught the spirit, and began the crusade of prayer and song. The whole section of country seemed ripe for the movement. Dio Lewis said it was the first soil he had found where his temperance plant would grow. The public press, which had hitherto contained but meagre reports of the movement, said that it was destined to be the sensation of the day; special correspondents were despatched to the scene, and the daily reports crept up from paragraphs into columns, and from columns to pages. The outside world began to grow interested. Those who had regarded the movement as the fleeting excitement of an hour now began to see in it a bright promise of hope. And as the lovers of temperance and order grew interested, the liquor men, from distiller down to the lowest whiskey seller, grew alarmed. A contemptuous sneer was all the attention paid to the matter for a time; but as the work went on, and its strength became more apparent, the liquor dealers commenced to organize for a desperate resistance.

Wilmington is the thriving county seat of Clinton County, adjoining Fayette. On the 4th of January, ten saloons and four drug stores were driving a brisk trade in drinks that intoxicate. On the 5th, the respectable people of the town came together to talk the matter over. They had heard of the wonderful things going on in the adjoining county, and decided on the spot to adopt the same plan. Two hundred women, the most esteemed in the city, fell into the ranks, and among them were a number whose remarkable talent and energy soon gave them a reputation beyond the limits of their own town. Mrs. Runyan, Mrs. Hadley, and others will long be remembered for their faithful service at home, and missionary labors abroad. The same plan was pursued as at Washington; and so vigorously was it carried on that within four days all the druggists had signed, and at the end of ten days the news was telegraphed abroad that every saloon had surrendered, and that no liquor could be bought in the town.

The Saturday which closed the first week was a day which the people of Wilmington will not soon forget. Crowds from the country had heard of the excitement, and flocked in to see what was going on. The streets were filled. At ten o'clock the bells announced that the ladies had begun their march. They went in eight parties, numbering from twenty to thirty each. These squads relieved each other at the tap of a bell, and thus there was a band at every saloon in town during the whole day. The solemn regularity and clock-like precision which characterized their movements would have done credit to a well-drilled military brigade. The air was cold and raw, and the streets were filled with slush; but the women seemed perfectly oblivious to such trifles. Their zeal was rewarded. At night two more of the saloon keepers signed the pledge, and shipped their liquors back to Cincinnati, and on Monday and Tuesday the remainder followed their example. The same car which bore the liquors back was filled with similar freight from Washington Court House.

Ten days of hard fighting, and Wilmington was redeemed from whiskey. And from that day to the present time, there has not been even a keg of beer on tap in the city. Some confirmed soakers have, at a great outlay of time and money, gone to distant towns, and stealthily lugged home long black bottles of "tonics" and "blood purifiers," but whiskey selling as a business has ceased. A few amusing attempts have been made to smuggle into town, under cover of the darkness, a solitary half barrel of Cincinnati beer; but the attempts proved wretched failures. In one instance, the keg was dropped from the train half a mile out of town, and surreptitiously hustled off to a haystack. But the temperance folks got on the scent, and the unfortunate keg was hunted down as if it had been so many gallons of pestilence. Like the ark of the covenant, now it fell into the hands of the Philistines, and again adorned the Israelite camp. Its thirsty guardians had a weary struggle, and were not rewarded by a single drink.

Greenfield, in Highland County, was the next point struck by the epidemic. A temperance league was formed, on the following platform: —

"First, That intemperance is the great evil of the times.

"Second, That it is especially a great evil in Greenfield; and

"Third, That it can be eradicated by this method, if persistently adhered to."

One hundred and ten ladies and nearly as many men joined the first night. As in the other towns, the league was composed of the best people in the place. The first thing done was to invite all the liquor sellers to meet a committee, and thus give them an opportunity to yield gracefully in advance. Out of the fifteen dealers but one came, and he was a druggist. Next day, ninety-one women formed a solemn phalanx, and marched to the saloons. Coming at the end of a series of religious meetings, the movement in Greenfield took, from the first, a deeply religious cast. The most solemn earnestness pervaded the mass meetings at the churches, and seemed stamped upon the countenances of the women on the street. They were generally older than those engaged in the work in Washington and Wilmington, and, from the pathetic words and sad, care-worn faces of many of them, it was evident that the terrible blight of intemperance had rested heavily upon their own homes. It was early determined not to promise any patronage or threaten any prosecution for compliance or refusal, but simply to appeal to the better nature of the saloon keeper, and trust to the power of prayer to move him.

On the 22d of January, it was reported that one third of the liquor dealers had signed the pledge. Rev. A. C. Hirst, fresh from the battle at Washington, came down to exhort and encourage. Crowded mass meetings were held every evening in the churches, and reports of the day's proceedings were read. These reports of the secretary, Miss Kate Dwyer, so well reflect the spirit of love and deep devotion with which the work was carried on, that we append the following extract: —

"The law of the Lord is perfect, converting the soul; the testimony of the Lord is sure, making wise the simple. Knowing that all our wisdom would indeed be of God, and that the souls of all men are in his hands, we took up our work this morning again. It seemed that the very presence of the Lord could be felt as we walked softly towards the house of Mr. B. Devout prayers were offered, and songs were sung, then the pledge presented, but still the prayers and entreaties of God's people in his behalf were unsuccessful. As slowly and solemnly the procession proceeded from there to Mr. H.'s. He, too, heeded not the appeal. Again finding Mr. P.'s door locked, we made known the requests of our hearts to God in prayer and song from the sidewalk. From there we directed our steps to the saloon of Mr. K. He professes to sell liquor while the laws of the land give the license. God's will and laws are higher than those of man, and he can enforce them. The next place visited was Mr. C.'s drug store. He professed to be unmoved, either temporally or spiritually. The Lord looketh from heaven. He beholdeth all the sons of men ; he fashioneth their hearts alike ; he considereth all their works. Our prayer is, that God may touch that heart with the finger of his love, and cause it to melt like wax before the fire.

"In the afternoon we visited Mr. S.'s establishment. He being absent, we presented our pledge to his clerk, and held devotional exercises ; pledge unsigned. After that we went to both the saloons of Mr. C. He is also absent from town, but those in his employ refused the pledge. From there we returned to the church, trusting in God for the fruit of our day's labor. On entering we found glad tidings awaiting us — a druggist's pledge, with the signature of N. Squier. O, how great is thy goodness which thou hast laid up for them that fear thee, which thou hast wrought for them that trust in thee! Be of good courage, and He shall strengthen your heart, all ye that hope in the Lord."

On the 6th of February, after nearly a month of unceasing work, the ladies resolved to celebrate their victories in a grand thanksgiving jubilee. H. Thane Miller and W. H. Doane, of Cincinnati, and all other sympathizers, were invited to be present. Business was suspended, and the schools dismissed. The cause for the rejoicing was summed up in the following brief report, made at the opening of the meeting: —

Three drug stores signed the druggists' pledge.

Five saloons signed the dealers' pledge.

Two thousand one hundred and ninety-eight persons signed the personal pledge.

One of the unsubdued, a druggist named C. K. Clinton, found himself getting a notoriety almost equal to that of Slater or Dunn. His drug store was nothing more than a saloon in disguise. He received the ladies with uniform urbanity, but never showed the least disposition to relent. It was his custom to go down to his "den of iniquity" (as he proudly called it) in the morning, sweep out, build a good fire, arrange the chairs in order, and sit down with his paper till the "women came." That ceremony over, he was ready to go about his accustomed business in the old way. Although he never allowed himself to appear disturbed, the words of the kind-hearted and soft-spoken ladies sometimes reached a tender spot.

"I thought I had sand enough in my craw," he confessed to a friend, "to stand anything; but I'll be confounded if the prayers of these women don't somehow take hold of a fellow. It's enough to sink a wooden man."

The "sand in his craw" was not sufficient to enable him to withstand those earnest prayers much longer. He held out until his companions dropped off one by one; and when he found himself at last alone, the focus

FIRST CALL, OR LAYING SIEGE TO VAN PELT'S SALOON.

of the prayers and entreaties of the whole female community, and the sole object of daily mass meetings, he ceased his stubborn resistance, and Greenfield was added to the shining list of the emancipated. But while these things were going on at Greenfield, the eyes of the whole country began to be turned on New Vienna, a small railroad town a few miles west. The story of New Vienna is the story of Van Pelt, who was destined to play so important a part in the history of the movement in Ohio. John Calvin Van Pelt, the wickedest man in Ohio, soon became a familiar character to the public. Near the depot was a forbidding-looking one-story structure, appropriately known as the "Dead Fall," and presided over by Van Pelt, a tall, solidly built man, with a red nose and the head of a prize-fighter. He had formerly served the public in the capacity of an oyster dealer on Sixth Street, Cincinnati, at which time he became identified with the interests of the cockpit, and won considerable notoriety for his bull-dog pluck and strength of will in any undertaking in which he embarked. He possessed a sort of humor and sociability which made him a popular leader among his companions at New Vienna.

The league was formed in the usual way, and, after visiting the drug stores, the ladies directed their steps toward the "Dead Fall." Van Pelt seemed infuriated. He threatened, if they came to his saloon again, to hang, draw, and quarter them. The next day, one of his windows was decorated with flasks filled with whiskey. Across the other one was an axe, covered with blood. Over the door were suspended empty flasks, and near them a large jug, branded "Brady's Family Bitters." Over all floated a black flag. As if this array was not sufficiently dramatic, he could be seen within, brandishing a club, and defying the temperance band, at the risk of their lives, to enter.

But even these bloodthirsty demonstrations had no effect upon the ladies. Next day they went, about fifty in number, entered his saloon, and began their usual devotions. About two hundred men were outside, expecting some attempt at violence. A lady began in prayer, and was just about praying that the heart of the saloon keeper might be baptized with the Holy Ghost, when Van Pelt seized a bucket of dirty water.

"G—d d—n you," said he, "I'll baptize you!" And with this he threw the contents against the ceiling overhead, from which it came pouring down upon the kneeling ladies. They stood, however, heroically to their post, and it was not until drenched with dirty slops and beer that they retreated to the outside.

The crowd surrounding the place were enraged, and were only prevented by the intercession of the ladies from mobbing the ruffian. Inhuman as he was, the women had faith to believe they could conquer him without violence, or even law. But the fathers and husbands of those insulted were not so tender in their sentiments, and Van Pelt was arrested and sent to jail. There he languished for several days, unable to find bail. His brother, also a desperate character, did the honors at the saloon, and for a day or two allowed the women to enter, and carry on their devotional exercises. On the third day, however, he shut them out, and they again patiently went on with their prayers on the walk outside.

Meanwhile Van Pelt found bail, and was released from the calaboose. His week's imprisonment seemed only to have made him the more bitter and determined. He had the boldness to attend the meetings of the ladies in the Friends' church, and argue the case with them publicly.

"Why did the Lord put the stimulant in the corn and

grape, if it was not for the use of man? What would the farmer get for his grain, if whiskey was not made and sold?" These and like arguments, which he had carefully studied up, he hurled at the heads of the temperance people, and, with his quick wit, proved quite a formidable disputant for the logicians of the other party to encounter. At length he gave evidence of a growing weakness in the knees by repeated propositions to sell out. His first price was five hundred dollars; then he fell to three hundred, and at last to ninety-five, that being the amount expended by him in lawyers' fees, &c. On payment of this sum, he was to quit the town forever. It was a tempting inducement, and many were for taking him up. A meeting was called to consider the matter. The debate naturally ran back to the beer slops indignity.

"He may be glad he got off with his life. In any other town he would mighty quick go to try the realities of another world; but we are a peaceable people, and only ask him to go while he can go safe. We don't owe him anything," &c. This was the argument of Mr. Amberg.

"I was the one who got the most of it," said one of the ladies; "but I have forgiven him, and continue to pray that I may have no hard feelings against him; and though I maintain we don't owe him a cent, yet I am willing to make him a small present just for good will."

These two arguments illustrate very well the different spirit entertained by the men and by the women on the same subject.

On the 26th, Van Pelt proved his indisputable claim to the title of the wickedest man in Ohio. He put a cap on the climax of his wickedness. When the ladies called at his saloon, as usual, he met them at the door, and told them they might come in and pray on one condition. That was, that they allow him to make every other prayer. In amazement the women said yes, and the farce began. After some lady had concluded the first prayer, Van Pelt began a long and blasphemous harangue in the form of a prayer. It is to be regretted that no reporter was on the spot to preserve the curiosity to the world. He asked the Lord to have mercy on the women, whom he classed with the brutes, and to teach them wisdom and understanding. Woman, he said, first caused man to sin, and there was great need for prayer in their behalf. He said the Lord operated the first distillery; or, at least, made the first wine, and he (Van Pelt) was but following the Lord's example, &c., &c.

Before the services were ended he had made three long prayers of this description. The women were almost speechless with astonishment, half expecting that the hardened wretch would be struck dumb on the spot. But this was only the darkness before day. One week from that time Van Pelt had surrendered, and, like Saul of Tarsus, took up the cause he had fought so long, and became one of its most shining apostles.

The day before the surrender was dark and drizzling. All day long the women stood guard before the door, changing at intervals. In the evening meeting the secretary read out the names of all who had entered Van Pelt's place during the day. A determination was evinced to fight it out on the line already begun. Next morning the ladies met promptly at eight o'clock, and proceeded to the "Dead Fall." Van Pelt met them at the door, and told them if they would go away and come again at two o'clock he would give them his final decision. It was noised abroad that Van Pelt was going to surrender. At noon the bells were set to ringing, and boys went through the streets with hand-bells, crying,

VAN PELT'S SURRENDER.

"Everybody meet at Van Pelt's saloon at two o'clock, and hear his decision!" People closed up their places of business, and rushed from all parts of the town towards the depot. An immense crowd of men and women assembled before the scene of so many prayers and songs. Each looked at the other, and wondered what was going to come next.

After singing and prayer by the ladies, Van Pelt came to the door, and in a few remarks full of feeling, made a complete surrender of his stock and fixtures to the cause. He said he yielded not to law or force, but to the labors of love of the women. He then requested all the men, except the ministers, to retire beyond the railroad track, and called upon Rev. D. Hill and Rev. H. H. Whitter to roll out the barrels. There was one barrel of whiskey, another of cider, and a keg of beer.

Van Pelt then seized an axe, and stepping forward, held it up, crying, —

"This is the same weapon I used to terrify the ladies. I now use it to sacrifice that which I fear has ruined many souls." So saying, he stove in the heads of the barrels, and the liquors gurgled out into the gutters.

Prayer was offered, a hymn sung, and Van Pelt made a few more remarks, saying, —

"Ladies, I now promise you to never sell or drink another drop of whiskey as long as I live, and also promise to work with you in the cause with as much zeal as I have worked against you." He also remarked that he hoped the women of the United States would never cease until every drop of whiskey was emptied upon the ground, as his was.

Just then the train from Cincinnati arrived. The crowd set up a deafening cheer; a photographist caught the scene, and preserved it to posterity; the women gathered around Van Pelt, shaking his hands and congratulating him, and the glad news spread through the town, creating great excitement.

In the evening a thanksgiving meeting was held in the Christian church, and Van Pelt spoke. He was humble in his manner, and made a good impression on the audience. He had felt, he said, for some days, deep convictions that he was doing a mean business, but had used every argument he could to sustain himself — had tried to argue with the ladies, and get the best of the argument; it was not arguments, but their prayers and suffering that had touched his heart. No man or set of men would suffer and endure what the ladies had endured in this work. He referred to his saloon as a low doggery; saying, "Yes, I'll call it a low doggery, for no man can keep a high one." He had often taken the last ten cents from a man for whiskey when he knew the money had been earned by his wife or child. Every man who sells whiskey does this. Little faces thus robbed had often appealed to his heart with greater force than any words of man. He was now determined to quit this business forever, and throw his strength on the other side of the question. He thought places of innocent amusement and resort ought to be established, to entertain those who seek company at saloons. He believed this emphatically a ladies' work. He believed God had led them into this work. He wanted to encourage them to go on till the country is freed from the greatest curse of the land. He had been thinking for several days that perhaps the great God who overrules all had allowed him to go into that low business, that he might see the great iniquity, and be better able to influence others to quit the terrible business.

In another week Van Pelt was in the field as a temperance lecturer!

One of the most hopeless places, to all appearances, in Ohio, was Morrow, a small railroad town about forty miles from Cincinnati, on the Little Miami road. The wickedness of Morrow had passed into a proverb. The place seemed whiskey-ridden, and the cause of its desolation was visible at almost every turn. The correspondent of a Cincinnati paper, who visited the place soon after the temperance excitement had broken out, summed up the situation graphically as follows: —

"Population, eleven hundred; drinking places, fifteen; increase of population in ten years, two hundred persons; increase of municipal taxation, one hundred and thirty per cent.; decline in business reported at twenty-five per cent.; manufactures nothing, and no increase in the value of property; eighteen vacant dwelling-houses, and numbers of the best citizens removed. Such are the facts given me by the 'old and reliable.' Verily it was time for the law or the gospel to do something. The place has a beautiful and romantic site. They have three railroads, and expect connection soon with a trunk line to the east. On one side is the river, and on the other the beautiful hill, with hundreds of sites for palatial residences. In the neighborhood is good fishing and hunting, and all around is scenery unsurpassed in the State of Ohio. Apparently this is just the place for a favorite summer resort.

"Twenty-five years ago Morrow had aspirations. There were, and are, unsurpassed facilities for manufacturing — still unimproved. Three large hotels at that time were filled most of the summer with families and visitors from Cincinnati. The society was good; church, school, and lyceum were thoroughly organized; and, besides the manufacturing interests which were being established, the place expected to become a city of elegant retired country seats. Somehow the saloons got the start, the manufacturers took the alarm, the expected good families did not come, and many that were here moved away. If the place has improved in twenty years, that fact is not apparent to the naked eye. Still there are many good families in Morrow. They have borne the demoralization and tyranny of the whiskey power until it has become a question of life and death with them; and they have entered on this struggle in the spirit in which patriots fight for their homes, feeling that unless they conquer, they must emigrate. It is not a question of philanthropy alone, and other people's good, here, as in some places; they must conquer or die."

The immediate source of the contagion was Wilmington. Mrs. Runyan, the wife of the Methodist minister at Wilmington, and Mrs. Hadley, a soft-spoken but determined Quaker lady, came over from that place, told the ladies of Morrow how a few days of energetic work had cleared all the saloons out of Wilmington, and offered their services. They were gratefully accepted. Over fifty women of Morrow rallied around them, and the campaign began in earnest. This resolute band met at ten o'clock in the morning in the Methodist church, and started out on their mission of love, while the men remained behind to pray and consult. Lewis Fairchild, an aged warrior in the temperance cause, who had withstood the rebuffs and rotten eggs of two or three generations of rum sellers, was chairman of the league, and was always on hand with encouragement and advice.

There were some hard cases to treat among the saloonists. Looskin was going to shoot the first woman who crossed his threshold. Opes and Goepper posted up conspicuous notices, "No singing and praying women allowed here." Weingartner would sell out if they would pay him six hundred dollars for a few old chairs, tables, and empty bottles. Mrs. Krumpf, a German woman across the river, could "sprech kein English." Martin Fath, when he saw the women coming, temporarily turned his saloon into a tailor's shop, and worked away at his sewing machine for dear life. Goepper, Briesah, and Kebbel locked them out. There was little to encourage the ladies in their first two or three rounds.

One of the most discouraging cases to deal with was Henry Scheide. He was a young German of good disposition and friendly manners. He had received a good education in the Cincinnati schools, having been designed, it is said, for the ministry. Then he was a clerk in a dry goods store in the city. But the saloon business promised greater profits, and he removed to Morrow, where he established the "respectable saloon" of the place. He allowed no drunkards about him, and conducted his establishment with such skill that it became the popular resort for the young men of the town and surrounding country. Therefore it was that Scheide's was considered by the women the flowery path that led to the bad place.

The following rambling talk which Scheide confided to the bosom of a Cincinnati reporter will serve to illustrate the views of his class quite generally: —

"We'll worry 'em some, though I'm the only one that lets the ladies in. It don't bother me much; they only sing and pray, and stay about half an hour. I'll open every time they come, shutting doors on nobody. There's no rowdies come into this place. Those ladies don't understand it. They have a foolish prejudice about this business. Now I can run this establishment just as nice as a dry goods store, and I do. . . . 'O, if they'd stay all day, I'd soon stop that. This is my business, and I won't let anybody interfere with it. There's a state law against selling by the drink, but nobody pays any attention to it. We run that risk. No man but a low sneak, who has a spite against you, will drink in your house, and then go and make complaint against you. The Council won't make any order here. They're men of too much sense. I tell you a town must have a decent saloon, or it won't prosper. All the farmers nearly in the country, when they go to sell their grain or buy goods, are going where they can get a dram. They will have their beer or ale. Stop the sale here, and two thirds of our travel leaves us. Maybe, though, if no town had saloons, it might make it even; but the others will have them.

" . . . Women get along in all these towns because they have no opposition. Mayor and officers and lawyers were all with them, because it was a new thing. But here we've got some rights. Our lawyers are with us. It's politics that's really at the bottom of this thing. It's been tried here. The Methodists and temperance men are trying to get up a ticket of their own, and can't make it win."

The ladies from the first acted on the rigid principle of no compromise. They would pay no man for his liquors. The basis of negotiations must be unconditional surrender, except in cases where families were in indigent circumstances. Then, if the saloon keeper made a complete sacrifice, they would make every effort to relieve him from want, and start him in some more honest calling.

The corn question was sprung upon the morning meeting one day quite suddenly, and proved a perplexing subject to wrestle with. The saloon keepers sent a committee to say that Mr. Ludlum, an active worker in the temperance cause, was then loading a car with corn for a distillery. If the women allowed that thing to be done, they need expect no more concessions from the liquor dealers. It was like a bomb in the camp at first; but presently it was explained that Mr. Ludlum did not sell his corn to a distillery, but to commission men, over whom he had no control. If it eventually found its way into whiskey, the fault could not be laid at his door. However, if this seemed an inconsistent course, he was ready to give up the whole business of dealing in corn. Then the farmer would have to give up raising, and so on through all branches of trade. The matter was dropped as a side issue, and a ruse of the enemy to set the temperance folks by the ears.

And so the campaign went on. The women were out every day, in constantly increasing numbers. Enthusiastic mass meetings were held every night. Almost every man, woman, and child in the vicinity, not engaged in the liquor business, signed the total abstinence pledge. One after another the saloon keepers gathered their traps about them and silently stole away, until the number was reduced to three or four.

One of these was Max Goepper, a brother of the wealthy Cincinnati brewer, who kept a low place close by the depot. To this the women devoted their attention, and passengers on the Little Miami trains might see them at almost any hour, from six in the morning until ten at night, kneeling on the steps before the door with their piteous faces upturned, and pleading with the Almighty to have mercy upon that saloon keeper, and change his heart. Just within the door stood Goepper, with a cigar in his mouth and a sardonic grin on his face, winking at the train men, or at some old customer whom he saw in the crowd. In the window hung a caricature of a dead man being carried off on a bier, and underneath the inscription, "This man was prayed to death." It was a sight that brought tears to the eyes of many a traveller, at the same time that it provoked a smile.

At last, on a morning early in March, the ladies came as usual, and found only the empty shell of the old shanty. Goepper and his effects had disappeared. Scheide, who had some time before obtained an injunction* against one hundred and sixteen of the women, together with Dio Lewis and Van Pelt, forbidding them to pray near his premises, had also fled, and only two insignificant doggeries were left. The bells were rung loud and long, and the patient and persistent workers wept for joy. It was one of the most signal victories of the campaign.

A few miles farther up the Little Miami River lies Waynesville, a quiet, comfortable village of strong Quaker proclivities. Across the stream is a collection of houses grouped about the railroad station, and named Corwin, after the illustrious governor and departed statesman of Ohio. This was the scene of perhaps the most protracted siege of the whole campaign. Waynesville is the centre of a group of villages in Warren County that dot the country round about within a radius of ten miles; and for generations it has been the custom of the inhabitants of those places, and of the surrounding farmers, to bring in their jugs periodically and have them replenished. On this trade, and the little used for home consumption, two saloons in Waynesville and one in Corwin were making a very good thing of it when the temperance crusade came along. The first intimation of the coming storm was a petition largely signed by citizens, and sent in to the village Council for an ale and beer and tippling-house ordinance. The

* The history of this and other injunction cases is detailed at length in a succeeding chapter.

ordinance passed, but the ladies had heard of the moral achievements in neighboring towns, and proposed to close up the saloons without the aid of the law. At this juncture there was printed and circulated about town the following literary gem: —

NOTICE. As it has come to my hearing that there is a rumor in circulation that some of the ladies in and about Waynesville, O., are about to visit my grocery on Saturday, the 17th inst., for the purpose of holding a prayer meeting, I advise all the ladies concerned in the movement to keep clear of my grocery, and to keep within the bounds of the law, as my grocery is not a place of worship.

TIMOTHY LIDDY.

WAYNESVILLE, O., Jan. 16, 1874.

The challenge was accepted, and within a day or two the women were praying in Mr. Liddy's "grocery." The other saloon, kept by William F. Roper, also received a full share of attention. The band went daily. Sometimes they were admitted, and as often locked out, when they held their devotions on the pavement in front. But after this plan had been operating a while, with no visible results, another was adopted. The women were divided into small squads, who went in succession to the saloons, thus keeping up a constant guard. But the enemy made a flank movement, and shut out one and all. Then things began to get warm. The women stuck by their erring brethren outside of the door, and when the weather was inclement, a covered carriage was drawn up in front for their use. It happened that the two saloons were on diagonally opposite corners, while on a third corner was a vacant room, which was turned over to the use of the ladies. It was temporarily fitted up with a stove and chairs, and the ladies came by detachments day after day, as to an advance picket post, and watched the two saloons. A book was kept in which was registered the name of every man entering either place. The result was a sudden and remarkable falling off in the patronage of those heretofore prosperous establishments. One of the pickets on duty was asked how long they intended to keep up the watch.

"Until the saloons are closed up for good," was her decided reply.

"But, then, won't they open again as soon as you quit?"

"If they do, we will commence the watch again. We will keep the war up till we see the end of whiskey here."

The praying visits, however, were not wholly suspended. The following report of one of these meetings, taken on the spot, will serve to show the spirit in which such exercises were almost everywhere conducted. The band was composed largely of Quakeresses — Hicksite and Orthodox promiscuously mingled. The scene is Roper's saloon. The band having solemnly entered the room, a hand is extended to Roper, and a kindly voice inquires, "How's thee to-day, brother?" Then all kneel, and after a few moments' silence an earnest, pleading voice is raised in prayer.

"Almighty God, thou knowest the barrier in the case of this man. Thou alone knowest the key that may unlock his heart. For his own sake, for Christ's sake, wilt thou not turn him from his present course? Thou hast all things to give; he has nothing to lose. . . . Lord, show mercy to our fathers, our husbands, our brothers, our sons, who may be in danger of the blight of intemperance. Bless the homes and the hearts that are already desolated by its effects. Take thou the control of these weak efforts of ours, and direct us to glorious success."

Then in a low voice was sung:

> "Watchman, tell us of the night,
> What its signs of promise are."

And after another prayer, the hymn —

> "My faith looks up to Thee,
> Thou Lamb of Calvary."

Then from the 25th and 26th chapters of Isaiah were read the words —

"And it shall be said in that day, Lo, this is our God; we have waited for him, and he will save us. . . .

"And he shall bring down their pride, together with the spoils of their hands.

"Thou wilt keep him in perfect peace whose mind is stayed on thee, because he trusteth in thee. Trust ye in the Lord forever, for in the Lord Jehovah is everlasting strength."

The protracted siege, already referred to, was at the grocery saloon of Tom Franey, at Corwin. Franey was noted for his politeness, and when the ladies came over from Waynesville, to plead and pray with him, he several times ordered his team hitched to an omnibus to take them back. At last his suavity began to give place to coldness, and he commenced making a careful calculation of the damage done to his valuable business, with the announced intention of suing the society, or the husbands of the ladies, for the amount. But a little legal advice probably discouraged him from that undertaking, and he thereafter shut his fair visitors out. But the women never left him. Day after day, for *forty-nine consecutive days*, the siege was kept up, and they were finally rewarded with an unconditional surrender.

No longer the rural jugs and bottles came in to Waynesville for replenishment. No more drunken men and boys stagger through the streets. Quakers sing hymns; all denominations mingle freely, and the era of good fellowship prevails.

CHAPTER XXI.

REVIEW OF THE LEGAL CASES. — WERE THE WOMEN TRESPASSERS ON PRIVATE RIGHTS? — THE CELEBRATED DUNN SUIT. — THE WARNING, THE TABERNACLE, AND THE INJUNCTION. — OTHER FUTILE EFFORTS TO ENJOIN THE WOMEN. — THE SCHEIDE INJUNCTION, AND HOW IT WAS DISSOLVED. — LEGAL PROSECUTIONS AT LEBANON. — A COMPARISON OF THE LAW AND GOSPEL METHODS.

THE reader cannot have failed to observe how wholly the success of the women was due to love. They conducted the warfare on the gospel method of moral persuasion, instead of force. It was whiskey selling they were fighting against, and not the whiskey seller. Many a hardened saloon keeper, with tearful eyes, has confessed that it was about the first time he ever thought anybody cared for him, when the best Christian women of the town took him kindly by the hand, and talked to him as to a brother. If men had come about his premises, and in their bungling way attempted to drive him out of his business, he would have had his coat off for a fight in an instant. If the law had been used to suppress him, he would have united all the money and stubbornness of the liquor interests in resistance. But when a band of weak women, whom he knew as the wives and mothers of the best citizens, came, with tender words and earnest prayers, it was an enemy he hardly knew how to fight. In these trying circumstances, it was very rare that one of the band ever lost her temper; and it was this very principle of meekness and good nature that disarmed opposition and gave the women their extraordinary power.

"I tell you, my young friend," said a Hillsboro' merchant to a reporter, "the women have more power in favor of temperance, ten times over, than the men. They are free from political entanglements. They don't have to vote for anybody for office, and they ask nobody to vote for them. So they can exert their moral power without hinderance. We are hampered in business and politics; they work for the pure love of humanity. A hundred women can do more good for a moral reform than ten thousand voters. We can only make laws, but they can touch the heart. It must be a hard-hearted man who can stand in his saloon and resist the pleadings of a good old mother whose son has been ruined by liquor, when she comes with tears in her eyes and prayer on her lips. Yes, sir, if the women in each town would take hold as they have done here, Ohio could be made a temperance state in six months."

Wherever this movement was begun and carried forward to any success, it was the avowed wish of the crusaders to avoid, as far as possible, any resort to law. A lady in Greenfield summed up this idea in the following words: —

"We intend to cure this disease by a better treatment, that shall not leave a drug disease in the system. Extirpation by law would leave hatreds and jealousies in the community; but prayer and good words leave no sting behind. We don't intend to try legal remedies till prayer and good words are exhausted, and love has lost its power; and we don't intend that shall be until the whole work is accomplished."

There were extraordinary cases, however, where legal persuasion was found a very convenient and effective means of bringing incorrigible persons to terms. Again, the law was invoked, in some instances, by the whiskey sellers, and the peace-loving ladies were compelled to meet their opponents with the same weapons. Some of these cases were of such interest, and had so important a bearing on the subsequent progress of the movement, that we devote this chapter to a review of the principal ones.

It early became a question how far these women were invading the private rights of property. Saloon keepers claimed that theirs was a legitimate business, recognized by the laws of the state and of the nation, and that the praying women were violating the law of trespass, and laying themselves liable to damages. On the other hand, it was a well-known fact that the law was violated daily in almost every saloon, and there were few whiskey dealers who felt themselves legally clean enough to throw the first stone.

Dunn, the notorious Hillsboro' druggist, was one of these. In a preceding chapter we left the ladies praying on the steps before his door. Within, he and his clerk were sitting about the stove, waiting for the few whiskey customers still left him — a remnant of his once flourishing business. The front door was locked to shut out the ladies, and the back entrance was carefully watched lest he might sometimes entertain spies unawares.

At length, on the morning of the 31st of January, the following "Notice to the Ladies of Hillsboro'" was found distributed about town, and posted up in conspicuous places: —

"WHEREAS many of you, among whom are Mesdames Wm. Scott, Wm. Trimble, Sams, W. O. Collins, J. M. Boyd, A. Evans, Reece Griffith, Jonah Langley, Wm. Hoyt, Caroline Miller, Wash. Doggett, W. P. Bernard, Misses Marian Stewart, Rachel Conrad, Sallie

Stevenson, Maggie Bowles, Clara Rhodes, Annie Wilson, Grace Gardner, Jennie Harris, Emma Grand-Girard, Mollie Van Winkle, Emily Grand-Girard, Libbey Kirby, Ella Dill, Laura Rockhold, Eddy, Alice Speese, Kate Trimble, Alice Boardman and sister [fifty more names follow], who are aided by the following named gentlemen: Messrs. E. L. Ferris, H. S. Fullerton, Samuel Amen, Asa Haynes, J. J. Brown, J. S. Black, W. C. Barry, E. Carson, Joseph Glascock, Wm. Scott, Thomas Barry, S. E. Hibben & Son, T. C. Lytle, R. S. Evans, L. McKibben, R. Griffiths, J. L. Boardman, John Cowgill, Lewis Ambrose, H. Scarborough, Wm. Ambrose, Wash. Doggett, H. Swearingen, Rev. E. Grand-Girard, and many others;

"And who, although not directly participating in your daily proceedings, are, nevertheless, counselling and advising you in your unlawful proceedings by subscriptions of money, and encouragement in the commission of daily trespasses upon my property since the 24th day of December last, by reason of which my legitimate business has been obstructed, my feelings outraged, and my profession and occupation sought to be rendered odious, by reason of which I have suffered great pecuniary damage and injury. Therefore, you and each of you, together with your husbands (or such as may have them), and the persons who are thus aiding you with their money, encouragement, and advice in your unlawful proceedings, are hereby notified that I cannot, nor will not, longer submit to your daily trespasses on my property, and injury to my business.

"While I am willing to excuse your action in the past, I cannot submit to such outrages in the future. Cherishing no unkind hostility towards any one, but entertaining the highest regard for the ladies of Hillsboro', distinguished heretofore, as they have been, for their courtesy, refinement, and Christian virtues, I feel extremely reluctant to have to appeal to the law for protection against their riotous and unlawful acts.

"You are therefore hereby further notified that if such action and trespasses are repeated, I shall apply to the laws of the state for redress and damages for the injuries occasioned by reason of the practices of which I complain.

"All others aiding or encouraging you, by means of money or otherwise, are also notified that I shall hold them responsible for such advice and encouragement.

"Yours, respectfully,
"W. H. H. DUNN."

This produced a great sensation. Some thought he would prosecute; others were sure that he would not. When Mr. Dunn reached his own store that morning, he found the wives of the mayor and Methodist minister — Mrs. Doggett and Mrs. Conden — already there to talk the matter over. They argued and pleaded with him for nearly an hour; but all the satisfaction they got was the following: —

"I am doing a legitimate business, according to the laws of Ohio and all well-recognized rules of morality. I am not a Heathen Chinee, that you need to come and pray with me. I tell you again and again, in the presence of these gentlemen, that I don't want you to pray in my house, or come into it except on business. I have treated you as well as I know how, until my patience is worn out. I now tell you again to leave, and I will prosecute all who interfere with my business," &c.

At nine o'clock on the same morning, a large number of temperance people came together at the church, and by exchanging views found that they were not scared so badly, after all, by the proclamation. It was resolved to go on with the work; and in order to facilitate matters, it was decided to erect a "tabernacle," on the Washington Court House plan, already described. The consent of the mayor was obtained, and in less than an hour a score of willing hands were hammering away at the structure. When it was completed, eighty-three ladies at once took possession, and went on with their praying and singing as though there had been no interruption. This was more than the resolute Dunn could stand. The lawyer who had so zealously defended Charlie Beck against the women at Washington Court House, was called in. There was then sitting on the bench of the Probate Court one Judge Safford, a man whose term had nearly expired, and whose sympathies were anywhere but with the ladies. To him Dunn and his lawyer applied for a temporary injunction dissolving the tabernacle and the temperance party. Their success may be seen in the following order of the court:—

"You are hereby notified and warned that David Johnson and W. H. H. Dunn, plaintiffs, have this day obtained an order of temporary injunction, and a restraining order, in an action pending in the Court of Common Pleas, for the said county of Highland, wherein they are plaintiffs, and you, the above-namod persons, are defendants, and have given an undertaking according to law. This is, therefore, to command you, the said above-named defendants, each and all of you, from using for prayer, singing, exhorting, or any other purpose, a certain plank and canvas structure or shanty, erected on High Street, in Hillsboro', Ohio, in front of the drug store of said W. H. H. Dunn; and it is further ordered that you, said defendants, are ordered to remove the said structure or shanty forthwith, and each and every part of the same, whether plank or canvas, and you are each and all hereby restrained and enjoined from re-erecting or replacing the said structure, or any similar structure, in said locality or upon said street, to the annoyance of the said W. H. H. Dunn; and it is further ordered that you, the said defendants, each and all of you, are hereby enjoined and restrained from singing, praying, exhorting, or making a noise and disturbance in front of said drug store of said W. H. H. Dunn, or on the sidewalk, or on the steps thereof, or in the vicinity thereof, to his annoyance, or from trespassing in or upon his said premises, or in any manner interrupting his said business, and this you will in no wise omit under the penalty of the law.

"Witness my hand and the seal of said Court of Hillsboro', the 31st day of January, 1874.

[SEAL] "J. K. PICKERING, *Clerk.*

"A true copy: C. P. PAPE, *Sheriff.*"

There was no resistance to this injunction. In the dead of night the Tabernacle was quietly taken down, and next morning not a trace of it was visible.

Then came on the trial of the case. High legal talent was employed on both sides. The defendants retained Judge Matthews and J. H. Thompson, Esq., of Hillsboro', and M. J. Williams, of Washington Court House; and the plaintiffs, Messrs. Dunn, Beeson, Collins, and Parker. There was a long and weary contest in the Court of Common Pleas, beginning on the 17th of February, Judges S. F. Steel and T. M. Gray upon the bench. Judge Safford now appeared as an attorney to defend his action as a judge.

Dunn, through his counsel, summed up his grievances in the following petition for a permanent injunction: —

"The plaintiff, Dunn, claims that he is the lessee of a certain piece of property on High Street, of Hillsboro', which is owned by the other plaintiff, David Johnson; that he has for —— years past been engaged in a 'drug business' therein, and that he has kept an orderly and quiet house, &c.; that on or about the 24th day of December, 1873, certain defendants joined and agreed together to break up and destroy his lawful business; that they held 'temperance prayer meetings' in his house from day to day thereafter, against his will and protests, and that he was compelled to lock his door and keep it locked; that they met on the steps and sidewalk before his door, and held prayer meetings 'all day,' from day to day, and kept customers away from his place of business; and that they made a 'noise and disturbance by singing, praying, and exhorting,' to the annoyance of said Dunn, and to the depriving him of his rest and comfort; that he warned them repeatedly to desist; and that on the night of January 30, 1874, he caused handbills to be struck and circulated, warning those so engaged, that if they did not desist he would appeal to the laws of the state for protection; that on the afternoon (January 31) these men and women, avowedly for the purpose of breaking up his lawful business, erected a plank and canvas structure, or 'shanty,' on the street, before his store, about seventeen feet in front thereof, and five feet from the curbstone, open in front, and closed on three sides, &c., &c., which shanty prevented his customers from reaching the hitching-posts before his door, and obstructed the highway; that said defendants occupied said structure, and threatened to occupy it day and night, and to persecute and annoy him until they forced him to yield to their unlawful demands; that said shanty is a nuisance, decreasing the value of the property and obstructing the highway, and that the singing and praying are annoying to them and to the neighborhood, and therefore they (Johnson and Dunn) ask for an abatement and perpetual injunction."

The defendants asked for a dissolution of the injunction on the following grounds: —

1. Because the undertaking (bond) of the plaintiff was insufficient.
2. Because of the misjoinder of plaintiffs and defendants, and of actions.
3. Because of the misjoinder of nuisances, the plaintiff claiming that the shanty and the singing and praying disturbed his mind.
4. Because of the omission of W. H. H. Dunn's Christian name in the petition and injunction.
5. Because that the affidavit was made only by Dunn, and not by Johnson.
6. Because there was not sufficient damage shown to have occurred to call for an injunctive interference.
7. Because the cause of action in favor of the plaintiffs was not a joint but a several cause.

8. Because the order was granted without sufficient notice, &c.

9. Because the order is vague, uncertain, and void on its face, and without authority of law.

The case was argued with great skill and pertinacity on both sides. It was held by the defendants that it must be more than a fanciful annoyance to entitle one to an injunction. Could singing one of the soft old hymns, "Come, humble sinner," or, "Bring forth the royal demijohn, and let us sell it all," have destroyed Dunn's actual ease and comfort? And as for Johnson, he had been too deaf to hear thunder for thirty years.

The plaintiffs, in turn, told how an ambassador in an Oriental land was annoyed by a howling dervish, who made demands upon him, and when they were not acceded to, remained continually before the house, keeping up his religious exercises. The ambassador applied to the authorities for relief, but was told that because of the man's "sanctity" he must not be made amenable to law. "Our dervishes are Christians in good standing, but the law gives good and bad their rights alike."

Judge Safford's argument in defence of his own injunction was a failure. Three fourths of his speech was an attempt to vindicate himself before the people of Hillsboro'. Neither his defence of his injunction, nor that of himself, was deemed a success.

At last, after four days of argument, during which the most eager interest was shown by the people, the case was concluded, and Judge Steel gave his decision. The temporary injunction was dissolved, but only on a technicality, and not on the merits of the case. The decision was, that the action could not go on because the petition made no case in favor of Johnson, the owner of the property. The result was a disappointment to both parties, and to the elements which they represented throughout the state. The plaintiffs appealed the case to the District Court, where, at this writing, it is still pending.

After Dunn had succeeded in getting a temporary injunction on the women, efforts were made in scores of towns, where the movement was now in progress, to check their operations in the same way. But the courts were generally in sympathy with the ladies. Judge after judge was applied to in vain. It was only in Morrow that any further serious hinderance was experienced by the temperance people in the way of restraining orders of courts. This case, and the decision in it, are of such interest, that we give at length the main features.

On the 17th of February, Henry Scheide (he who kept the "respectable saloon" at Morrow), went before Judge Gilmore, of Eaton, with the following petition: —

"The said Henry Scheide, plaintiff, prays that each and every one of the said defendants, individually, jointly, and collectively, be restrained, prohibited, and enjoined from molesting, disturbing, or hindering the said Henry Scheide in the prosecuting and conducting his said business, upon any pretence or pretext whatever, and invading, or meeting in or about his premises, to obstruct his said business; and also prays judgment against all of said defendants for the sum of one thousand dollars, and prays for all other proper relief in the premises."

The said defendants were, —

Mrs. E. R. Grim,
Frank Forshnell,
Geo. W. Davis,
John Hanford,
Oscar T. Hanford,
B. F. Wilson,
Mrs. H. J. Coffeen,
Josiah Fairchild,
Porter Corson,
Jas. H. Jeffery,
W. P. Hanford,
J. T. Welch,

and one hundred and four other ladies and gentlemen, among whom were Dio Lewis and Van Pelt.

The trial came off at Lebanon the 28th of February. It was before Judge Smith, of the Circuit Court, and was conducted on the part of the women by Ex-Lieutenant Governor McBurney, Gen. Durbin Ward, Messrs. Brabosee and Van Harlingin, of Lebanon, and Cunningham, of Morrow; and on the part of the plaintiff by O'Neil, of Lebanon, and Wallace and Mayor Scantlin, of Morrow. It was a great day in Lebanon. The whole town of Morrow had come over and emptied itself upon the unfortunate village. A public dinner was given by the Lebanon ladies to their persecuted guests. Forty of the defendants marched to the court-house in solemn procession. Every inch of space in the building was packed full, even to the sacred precincts behind the bar, and on the bench.

It is not necessary to review the arguments. The decision of Judge Smith, however, has a permanent interest, and we herewith reproduce the principal points. The ground on which the case was decided, it will be seen, was that the plaintiff had no right to ask legal protection for a manifestly illegal business.

"On the 17th day of February a temporary injunction was allowed in this case by Judge Gilmore, restraining the defendants as prayed for in the petition. This court is now asked to dissolve that injunction, for the reasons set forth in the motions which have been filed, and which, briefly stated, are the following:—

"1. That Judge Gilmore, when in another county, and while this court was in session, had no legal authority to grant it.

"2. Because the statements of the petition do not warrant a court of equity in granting the relief asked for, as it is apparent therefrom that he has an adequate remedy at law, and that the grievances complained of, or their continuance, have not, and cannot work a great or irreparable injury to the plaintiff.

"3. Because the allegations of the petition are untrue.

"To support these, a very large number of affidavits have been filed in court here by the defendants, and some (additional to those on which the temporary injunction was allowed) have been produced by the plaintiff, to maintain the allegations of this petition."

After noticing the first two points at length, the judge decides on the third point of the case as follows: —

"But there is another ground, which, in my judgment, effectually disposes of this motion. That is the third, viz.: That the allegations of the petition are not true. He alleges that he kept a house where he conducted business according to law. From the nature of the case, the character of this business in this respect is directly in issue, and from the proof it is perfectly clear to my mind that instead of this it was a place where intoxicating liquors were habitually sold, in violation of the laws of the state, and where gambling was constantly being carried on.

"Such a place as this our statute expressly declares to be a public nuisance, and which being shown in a proper case would have to be ordered by the court to be shut up. Now, the doctrine is perfectly well settled that a nuisance, either public or private, may be abated even by force, so no breach of the peace is committed. Surely, then, the means used here, with the view of abating this nuisance, were not unlawful or in derogation of the rights of the plaintiff; for, as the keeper of such an establishment, the maintainer of a public nuisance, and a gambling-house, he can have no standing in a court of equity, when he asks to be protected in his unlawful and criminal business. The injunction will be dissolved at plaintiff's costs."

Thus the women triumphed in the only injunction case of the crusade that was decided on its merits.

There was great rejoicing at Morrow. A correspondent, writing from there under the inspiration of the good news, gives the following graphic description of the scene: —

"As I write the band is playing and marching through our streets, followed by an immense throng of men, women, and children, shouting and rejoicing. Every church bell, school bell, &c., in town is ringing, and two or three locomotives are creating a terrible noise, whistling and ringing their bells. In fact, the entire town is wild with excitement. Hundreds of country people, hearing the noise of the bells and general tumult, are flocking to town from all quarters, many thinking the village was in flames. An immense meeting is now in progress at the Presbyterian church, in addition to the immense throng upon our streets. Speeches are being made, and cheer upon cheer is rending the air. Morrow never had such an awakening, everybody being happy except the lawyers who defended Scheide, and four or five saloon patrons."

It was too much for Scheide. He shut up his establishment, and left the town; and thus ends the history of the "only respectable saloon in Morrow."

In connection with these legal prosecutions against the women, it may be interesting to note one of the few instances where the saloonists were made to suffer by the law. As will be seen by reference to the statutes of the state, published in the following chapter, no saloon could carry on a paying business and comply strictly with the law. But there never has been, in any community, a public sentiment strong enough to enforce these laws, and the result was, saloon keepers, before this temperance revival, had come to look upon them as a dead letter.

About the time the "moral suasion" plan of Dio Lewis was put into operation so successfully in Hillsboro', Washington, and Wilmington, Lebanon resolved to suppress the evil by legal force. It is interesting to compare the results of the two methods. Lebanon is one of the staid, virtuous old towns of Ohio, cut off from railroads and their attendant evils, and boasting four thousand inhabitants, nine churches, and (until recently) three saloons. The temperance fires have been kept burning there from the earliest times, and years ago the village corporation passed ordinances forbidding the sale of ale and beer, and prohibiting the keeping open of tippling-houses. A few cases were tried when the ordinances were new, but they gradually fell into disuse and were forgotten. But there came, early in the winter of 1873, a deep religious awakening, and, following close upon it, a revival of public sentiment on the subject of temperance. Some one thought of the rusty old ordinances, and it was determined to bring them out and see how they would work.

John Braden, Henry Glady, and Nathan Woods were the three members of the liquor selling fraternity. They were shrewd men to deal with, and though every one knew they were selling daily, in violation of the law, it was not so easy a matter to make a good case against them. Foreseeing difficulties of this kind, the young Congregational minister, Rev. E. B. Burrows, who was a leader in the movement, quietly slipped down to Cincinnati and employed the services of a detective. The stranger came to town, seemed a jolly good fellow, loafed round the saloons, taking a daily drink at each place, and when the prosecution came on he was ready to swear that he had drank for fifteen consecutive days at the defendants' bars.

The first cases were against Braden & Glady, who were partners, and John Glady, who run a separate establishment alone. The immediate cause of the suit was a quarrel between Glady and one of his customers and chronic loafers. The latter, to gratify his personal feelings, commenced a prosecution for violation of the village ordinance. Ferd. Van Harlingin, a recently reformed drunkard, who had once been a brilliant lawyer, took up the cause and prosecuted it with all his might. The arrests were made quietly, but the suits soon began to attract the public attention. The temperance people stepped in, and the opposition arrayed all their forces. When the trial came off in the court-house, the roughs made an attempt to collect in numbers and bully the case through, in the manner such suits were generally disposed of. But they were met by a counteracting influence. The wealth, influence, and respectability of the place turned out in such force that the court-room was filled to overflowing. The trials began early in January, and lasted a week. The saloon keepers were beaten, and got the full extent of the law. The firm Braden & Glady were fined ninety dollars, and ten days each in the calaboose, and John Glady two hundred and eighty dollars, and ten days in the calaboose.

When the baffled saloonists were languishing in their cells, their views began to moderate. They concluded they would compromise. A proposition was made by Mr. Glady (who virtually controlled both concerns), to sell his real estate and quit the business and the place providing the fines and remainder of the imprisonment be remitted. The compromise was accepted, and but one saloon was left in Lebanon — that of Nate Woods. A suit was soon brought against him, and he was sentenced to one hundred and twenty dollars fine, and seven days in the jug. He served out his term, paid his fines and costs, and returned to his business, but only to sell by the quantity, according to law.

This system of selling according to law, — i. e., not to be

drank on the premises,—which came to be adopted by frightened saloon keepers in many places, during the progress of the movement, is a unique and somewhat amusing one. A shelf full of two-ounce bottles is kept all ready filled, and when a customer wants a single drink one of these bottles is sold him. The thirsty party then retires around a corner, into an alley, or anywhere off the premises, and takes his refreshment. If he has some friends to treat, a number of small bottles are bought and distributed among the party. These bottles are generally thrown away, and it was said that the small boys at Lebanon derived quite a revenue from picking them up and disposing of them at the drug stores.

It will readily be seen that this excellent law, which has so long lain unobserved on the statute books of the state, would, if enforced, do away with the whole system of treating,—that absurd and pernicious American practice,—and thereby restrict the amount of drinking by at least one half. It would clear bar-rooms of those wretched specimens of our race who hang around, expecting an invitation to drink. It would suppress that pot-house sociability by which politicians buy their way into office. It would save thousands of young men from forming an appetite for liquor, by drinking because their companions do, whether they want it or not. It would shut up, within a week, two thirds of all the saloons in Ohio. In short, it would confine the whole business of drinking to the bottle-at-home plan.

But is it possible to enforce this law? and, if possible, is it expedient? Before this temperance excitement began, there was scarcely a community in Ohio that contained moral force enough to confront the liquor men with this legal weapon; now, there are hundreds of places where the law can be carried into speedy execution the moment there is a necessity for it. So much the woman's movement has accomplished, at least. But it is one of the fundamental principles on which the women are working, that legal arguments shall only be resorted to when all others have failed. The gentle method of love generally does the work much more effectually, and leaves behind it no heart-burning and hatred. Yet, when the present excitement has subsided, as it eventually must, this wise provision of a past generation of legislators will be found very convenient in making permanent the victories of prayer and song.

CHAPTER XXII.

A CHAPTER OF TEMPERANCE LAWS. — THE CELEBRATED ADAIR AND BAXTER LAWS. — OTHER MUNICIPAL AND STATE LEGISLATION. — THE "McCONNELSVILLE ORDINANCE." — HOW FAR THE LAWS HAVE FAILED IN EXECUTION, AND THE REASONS THEREFOR. — LITIGATION UNDER THE ADAIR LAW. — DAMAGES SELDOM RECOVERED IN THE CITIES, BUT OFTEN IN THE COUNTRY DISTRICTS.

THERE has been no lack of legislation on the subject of temperance for the past twenty years. The statute books of the various states contain laws wisely framed and properly enacted, which they know little, and care still less, about. What the result of this legislation has been, it is not necessary here to discuss. License, prohibition, restriction, — every form of law has been tried; but Intemperance stalks forward, apparently unchecked. No fault can be found with the laws; the difficulty lies back of them. People are beginning to realize that what is wanted now is agitation, and not legislation. The machinery of law may be skilfully constructed and then set to work, but unless it have the motive-power of a strong and healthy popular sentiment, it will not grind out a temperance commonwealth, or make the individual more virtuous.

Allusion has been so frequently made to the statutes of the state on the subject of temperance, that it may be well, before proceeding farther, to give a summary of some of the principal liquor laws now existing.

In 1857, when the new constitution of Ohio was presented to the people for adoption or rejection, an additional section was submitted, for the purpose of obtaining an expression of the electors on the subject of license and prohibition, by a separate ballot. This section was in the following words: —

> "No license to traffic in intoxicating liquors shall hereafter be granted in this state; but the General Assembly may, by law, provide against the evils resulting therefrom."

The vote of the people on this question resulted as follows: License to sell — No, 113,239; yes, 104,255; majority for no license, 8,984. It thus became a constitutional provision that the legislature was incompetent to license the sale of intoxicating liquors for the next twenty years. Popular sentiment, at that time, was strong upon the temperance question, and the proposition to license was voted down by this large majority, notwithstanding the recent influx of foreigners.

The first legislature which assembled under this new constitution passed a bill (May 1, 1854 — Swan & Critchfield, vol. ii., p. 1431), which has been the basis of all subsequent legislation in Ohio. The provisions of that statute were briefly as follows: —

Section 1. The sale of intoxicating liquors, to be drank on the premises where sold, or in any adjoining room, or place of resort, connected with such building, was prohibited.

Sect. 2. It shall be unlawful for any person, by agent or otherwise, to sell intoxicating liquors to minors, unless upon the written order of their parents or guardians, or family physician.

Sect. 3. This section prohibits the sale of liquors to any person intoxicated, or who is in the habit of becoming intoxicated.

Sect. 4. All places where liquors are sold in violation of this act shall be declared public nuisances, and abated as such, and the keeper thereof punished as hereinafter provided.

Sect. 5. Any person who shall, by the sale of liquors, cause the intoxication of any other person, shall be compelled to pay a reasonable compensation to any one who shall take charge of such intoxicated person, and one dollar per day additional for every day he shall be kept; which sums may be recovered by any court having jurisdiction.

Sect. 6. It shall be unlawful for any person to get intoxicated, and every person found in a state of intoxication shall, on conviction thereof, be fined five dollars.

Sect. 7. This section provides that any wife, child, parent, guardian, employer, or other person injured in his or her means of support by such intoxication, may bring an action for damages against the person selling the liquor. (The Adair law, hereinafter given, is a substitute for this section of the statute.)

Sect. 8. Section eight provides penalties for the violation of the first, second, and third sections of this act, and was amended in 1859.

Sect. 9. The giving away of intoxicating liquors, or any other shift or device to evade the provisions of the act, shall be held unlawful selling.

Sect. 10. This provides for the collection of fines, stating who and what are liable, and was repealed by the Adair law, passed in 1870.

Sect. 11. All prosecutions under this act shall be in the name of the state, and shall be begun upon a written complaint, under oath or affirmation, before any justice of the peace, or mayor of the town, village, or city corporation within which the offence was committed, or by information or indictment.

Sect. 12 states the form of complaint in such proceedings.

Sect. 13. In these prosecutions, it shall not be necessary to state the kind of liquors sold, or to describe the place where sold; and for any violation of the fourth section, it shall not be necessary to state to whom sold; and in all cases the person or persons to whom intoxicating liquors shall be sold, in violation of this act, shall be competent as witnesses to prove such fact, or any other tending thereto.

Sect. 14 repeals all previous statutes on the same subject.

With the exception of some unimportant amendments, this was the only legislation in reference to selling and drinking intoxicating liquors in Ohio until April 18, 1870. The General Assembly then passed, by a close vote, the bill which has attracted so much attention under the name of the Adair law. Owing to its important bearings on the present woman's movement, and frequent reference made to it, we herewith append the full text of the bill : —

THE ADAIR LAW.

Be it enacted, &c., that sections seven and ten of the above-recited act be so amended as to read as follows : —

Section 7. That every husband, wife, child, parent, guardian, or employer, or other person, who shall be injured in person or property, or means of support, by any intoxicated person, or in consequence of the intoxication, habitual or otherwise, of any person, such wife, child, parent, guardian, employer, or other person, shall have a right of action in his or her own name, severally or jointly, against any person or persons who shall, by selling or giving intoxicating liquors, have caused the intoxication, in whole or in part, of such person or persons.

And the owner of, lessee, or person or persons renting or leasing any building or premises, having knowledge that intoxicating liquors are to be sold therein, in violation of the law ; or, having leased the same for other purposes, shall knowingly permit intoxicating liquors to be sold in such building or premises, that have caused the intoxication, in whole or in part, of any such person or persons, shall be liable, severally, or jointly with the persons selling or giving the intoxicating liquors aforesaid, for all damages sustained, as well as exemplary damages.

And a married woman shall have the same right to bring suits, and contest the same, and the amount recovered, as a *feme sole;* and all damages recovered by a minor under this act shall be paid either to the minor, or to his or her parent, guardian, or next friend, as the court may direct; and the unlawful sale or giving away of intoxicating liquors shall work a forfeiture of all rights of the lessee, or tenant, under any lease or contract of rent upon any premises where such unlawful sale or giving away shall take place; and all suits for damages under this act shall be by a civil action in any of the courts of this state having jurisdiction thereof.

Sect. 10. For all fines, costs, and damages assessed against any person or persons in consequence of the sale of intoxicating liquors, as provided in section seven of this act, and the act to which this is amendatory, the real estate or personal property of such person or persons, of every kind, without exception or exemption, except under the act to amend an act entitled an act to regulate judgments and executions by law, passed March 1, 1831, passed March 9, 1840, took effect March 15, 1840, shall be liable for the payment thereof; and such fines, costs, and damages shall be a lien upon such real estate until paid; and in case any person or persons shall rent or lease to another, or others, any building or premises to be used or occupied, in whole or in part, for the sale of intoxicating liquors, or shall permit the same to be so used or occupied, in whole or in part, such building or premises so leased, used, or occupied shall be held liable for, and may be leased to pay all fines, costs, and damages assessed against any person or persons occupying such building or premises.

And proceedings may be had to subject the same to the payment of any such fine and costs assessed, or judgment recovered, which remained unpaid, or any part thereof, either before or after execution shall issue against the property of the person or persons against whom such fines and costs or judgment shall have been adjudged or assessed; and when execution shall issue against the property so leased or rented, the officer shall proceed to satisfy said execution out of the building or premises so leased or occupied, as aforesaid; and in case such building or premises belong to a minor, insane person, or idiot, the guardian of such minor, insane person, or idiot, who has control of such building or premises, shall be liable to account to his or her ward for all damages on account of such use and occupation of the building or premises, and the liabilities for the fines, costs, and damages aforesaid; and all contracts whereby any building or premises shall be rented or leased, and the same shall be used or occupied, in whole or in part, for the sale of intoxicating liquors, shall be void, and the (lessee) person or persons renting or leasing said building or premises shall, on and after the selling of intoxicating liquors aforesaid, be considered and held to be in possession of said building or premises.

This bill, which went into effect July 4, 1870, made the business of keeping a saloon a precarious and unprofitable one, where the law was complied with.

SELLING TO MINORS AND DRUNKARDS.

Section 1. Be it enacted by the General Assembly of the State of Ohio, that it shall be unlawful for any person or persons to buy for or furnish to any person who is at the time intoxicated, or in the habit of getting intoxicated, or to buy for or furnish to any minor, to be drank by such minor, any intoxicating liquors whatsoever, unless given by a physician in the regular line of his practice.

Sect. 2. That for every violation of the provisions of the first section of this act, every person so offending shall, upon conviction thereof, forfeit and pay a fine of not less than ten nor more than one hundred dollars, or be imprisoned in the jail of the county for not less than ten nor more than thirty days, or both of them, at the discretion of the court, and shall pay the costs of the prosecution.

[Passed and took effect April 5, 1866.]

RIOTING AND DRUNKENNESS IN TAVERNS.

Section 1. Be it enacted by the General Assembly of the State of Ohio, that if any tavern keeper shall permit or allow any kind of rioting or revelling, intoxication or drunkenness, in his house, or on his premises, every such tavern keeper shall, for every such offence, on conviction, be fined not less than five nor more than one hundred dollars.

[Passed and took effect February 27, 1867.]

TO BE GIVEN IN CHARGE TO GRAND JURY.

Section 1. Be it enacted by the General Assembly of the State of Ohio, that the act entitled "An act to provide against the evils resulting from the sale of intoxicating liquors in the State of Ohio," passed May 1, 1854, shall be given in special charge to the grand jury by the Judges of the Court of Common Pleas of each term thereof.

[Passed and took effect March 8, 1865.]

MUNICIPAL CORPORATION ACT.

Section 199. (As amended April 18, 1870.) All cities and incorporated villages shall have the general powers hereinafter mentioned, and may provide by ordinance for the exercise of the same. . . .

Paragraph 5. To regulate, restrain, and prohibit ale, beer, and porter houses, and places of notorious or habitual resort for tippling or intemperance. . . .

[Passed May 7, 1869.]

Under the authority given in the above act, the incorporated village of McConnelsville, Ohio, passed the following prohibitory ordinance, which has been declared constitutional by the Supreme Court of Ohio, and all parties interested may make use of it to the advantage of their own localities: —

THE "McCONNELSVILLE ORDINANCE."

Section 1. Be it enacted by the Council of the incorporated village of McConnelsville, Ohio, that it shall be unlawful for any person or persons to keep within the said incorporated village of McConnelsville any house, room, shop, booth, arbor, cellar, or place of habitual resort for tippling or intemperance.

Sect. 2. Be it further ordained, that it shall be unlawful for any person or persons to keep within the said incorporated village of McConnelsville a house, shop, room, booth, arbor, cellar, or place where ale, porter, or beer is habitually sold or furnished to be drank in, upon, or about the house, shop, room, booth, arbor, cellar, or place where so sold or furnished.

Sect. 3. And be it further ordained, that for any violation of the first section of this ordinance, the person or persons so offending shall, upon conviction, forfeit and pay a fine of not less than ten dollars, or more than fifty dollars, and shall also be imprisoned in the county jail for a period not exceeding thirty days. That for every violation of the second section of this ordinance, the person or persons so offending shall, upon conviction, forfeit and pay a fine not exceeding fifty dollars, and be imprisoned in the county jail not exceeding twenty days.

Sect. 4. Be it further ordained, that all prosecutions under this ordinance shall be in the name of the incorporated village of McConnelsville, and shall be commenced under a written complaint, under oath or affirmation, before the mayor of said village; and, upon the filing of such complaint, the mayor shall issue a warrant, directed to the marshal of said village, for the arrest of the accused. The marshal shall forthwith arrest the person thus charged, and bring the accused before the mayor, who shall proceed as provided by law; and the mayor, upon the conviction of any person for the violation of any of the provisions of this ordinance, may make it a part of the sentence that the accused shall stand committed to the jail of the county until the fine and costs assessed against such person shall be paid or secured to be paid, or otherwise discharged, according to law.

Sect. 5. It shall be the duty of the marshal and assistant marshals of said village to make complaint against all persons found violating any of the provisions of this ordinance.

Sect. 6. This ordinance shall take effect on and after its second publication in the Conservative, a newspaper printed in said village of McConnelsvile, Ohio.

JAMES WATKINS, *Mayor.*

JOHN H. MURRAY, *Clerk.*

SELLING LIQUOR OR TRADING NEAR CAMP MEETINGS.

Section 1. (As amended May 1, 1861.) Be it enacted by the General Assembly of the State of Ohio, that no person shall sell, or expose for sale, give, barter, or otherwise dispose of in any way, or at any place, any spirituous or other liquors, or any articles of traffic, whatsoever, at or within the distance of four miles from the place where any religious society and assemblage of people are collected or collecting together for religious worship in any field or woodland ; provided, that nothing in this act shall affect tavern keepers exercising their calling, nor distillers, manufacturers, or others in prosecuting their regular trades at their places of business, or any person disposing of any ordinary articles of provisions, excepting spirituous liquors, at their residences ; nor any person having a written permit from the trustees or managers of any such religious society or assemblage to sell provisions for the supply of persons attending such religious worship, their horses or cattle, such persons acting in conformity to the regulations of said religious assembly and to the laws of the state.

Sect. 2. (This provides for the manner of prosecution, &c., under the above act.)

[Passed and took effect April 12, 1858.]

SELLING LIQUORS ON ELECTION DAYS.

Section 1. Be it enacted by the General Assembly of the State of Ohio, that it shall be unlawful for any person within this state to sell, barter, or give away, any spirituous, vinous, or malt liquors on the day of any election held within this state, under the constitution or laws thereof; and it is hereby made the duty of each and all persons who are authorized under or by the laws of this state, or the municipal regulations of any city, town, or village of this state, to sell or barter any spirituous, vinous, or malt liquors, to close their respective establishments on those days. Any person offending against the provisions of this act shall be fined in any sum not less than five nor more than one hundred dollars, and be imprisoned in the county jail for a period not exceeding ten days for each offence so committed; and it shall be the duty of all mayors of cities and incorporated villages within this state, on the days of election, as aforesaid, to issue a proclamation, warning the inhabitants of such city or village of the provisions of this act, and that all violations of the same will subject the offender to prompt and speedy punishment, and requiring marshals and police officers, under their respective jurisdictions, to close all houses found violating the provisions of this act, and to report forthwith all violations thereof to such mayors.

Sect 2. (This provides for the disposition of fines, &c.)

[Passed and took effect March 10, 1864.]

Laws also exist in relation to the adulteration of liquors; to provide for the appointment of guardians for habitual drunkards; and others, which are not deemed of sufficient importance for republication here. The city of Cincinnati has an ordinance making it unlawful to sell liquor on Sunday; to allow revelling, drunkenness, gaming, or disorderly conduct on the premises of any person; to sell liquor to minors, or persons intoxicated; providing a penalty of not less than ten nor more than fifty dollars for every violation of the ordinance, and making it the special duty of the mayor, chief of police, and other proper officers, to enforce such ordinance strictly.

THE INDIANA BAXTER LAW.

The Baxter law of Indiana was passed by the legislature on the 20th of February, 1873. It is one of the most unique and interesting pieces of temperance legislation ever adopted. It contains the main provisions of the Adair law in Ohio, and several additional features of importance. The effect of this law, if enforced, would be to place in the hands of every community the power to regulate the liquor traffic in its midst; and, furthermore, to make the liquor seller liable for damages.

Section 1 makes it unlawful for any person to sell or give away intoxicating liquors, to be drank on the premises, until such person has obtained a permit from the Board of County Commissioners, as hereinafter provided.

Sect. 2. Any person desiring a permit to sell intoxicating liquors, shall file in the office of the County Auditor, not less than twenty days before the session of the County Commissioners, a petition in writing, stating his ward or township, street, number, &c., which petition shall be signed by the applicant, and also by a majority of the legal voters of the ward or township where the applicant proposes to sell intoxicating liquors. Such petition shall be examined by the board, and if found to be in proper form, the Auditor shall deliver to the applicant the permit asked for.

Sect. 3. Before the granting of a permit by the Board of Commissioners, the applicant shall cause to be executed and properly acknowledged, a bond, payable to the State of Indiana, in the sum of three thousand dollars, with good freehold security thereon, of not less than two persons, to be approved by the Board, and conditioned for the payment of any and all fines, penalties, and forfeitures for the violation of any of the provisions of this act; and conditioned further, that the principals and sureties therein named shall be jointly and severally liable for all damages which may be inflicted upon any person or property by reason of such sale of intoxicating liquors. Separate suits may be brought on said bonds by the person or persons injured, but the aggregate amount recovered shall not exceed the amount of three thousand dollars. In case said bond shall be exhausted by recoveries thereon, a new bond shall be filed within ten days, and in default thereof, said permit shall be deemed to be revoked. Such bond may be sued and recovered upon in any court having civil jurisdiction in the county, except Justices' Courts.

Sect. 4. The majority of votes cast in the last preceding congressional or municipal election, shall be deemed a majority of voters whose signatures are required to such permit; and any person signing such petition, who is not a legally qualified voter, shall be fined not less than fifty dollars, nor more than one hundred dollars.

Sect. 5. No permit shall be granted for a longer or shorter time than one year. And it is further provided, that a copy of the order of the commissioners must be conspicuously posted up in the room where the liquors are sold, and any failure to comply with this provision shall work a forfeiture of the permit.

Sect. 6. It shall be unlawful for any person to sell or give liquors to any minor, or to any other person in the habit of getting intoxicated.

Sect. 7. All places where intoxicating liquors are sold in violation of this act shall be closed as public nuisances.

Sect. 8 makes the saloon keeper liable for the cost of caring for an intoxicated person.

Sect. 9 makes it unlawful for any person to get intoxicated, and provides that any one convicted of intoxication shall be required to designate the person from whom he bought the liquors.

Sect. 10 prohibits the sale of intoxicating liquors on Sunday, on Election days, on Christmas or Thankgiving day, on the Fourth of July, and on any public holiday. It also prohibits the keeping open of saloons after nine o'clock at night, and before six o'clock in the morning.

Sect. 11. Bartering or giving away liquors shall be deemed the same as selling.

Sect. 12 provides that any husband, wife, child, parent, guardian, employer, &c., shall have the right of action against the seller of the liquor causing intoxication. (This corresponds to the similar provision in the Adair law of Ohio.)

Sect. 13. In case the intoxicated person has no relative or other person to bring action against the saloon keeper for injury, it shall be the duty of the Township Trustee, having in charge the poor, to bring such action, the money thus collected to go to the benefit of the poor in that ward or township.

Sect. 14 to 16 provide for the fines and penalties under this act, and for the jurisdiction of courts.

Sect. 17. It shall be unlawful for any person to buy for, or furnish to, any person who is at the time intoxicated, or in the habit of getting intoxicated, or to any minor, to be drank by such intoxicated person or minor, any intoxicating liquor. Any person violating this section shall be fined not less than five nor more than fifty dollars.

Sect. 18. In all prosecutions under this act it shall not be necessary to state the kind of liquor sold, or to describe the place where sold, and it shall not be necessary to state to whom sold; and in all cases, the person or persons to whom intoxicating liquors are sold shall be competent witnesses to prove such facts or any tending thereto.

The remaining sections of the act indicate the form of complaint, repeal all conflicting laws, and provide that the act shall take effect as soon as passed.

Such is the substance of the temperance legislation in the two States of Ohio and Indiana. One would think that with such admirably constructed laws, the traffic in intoxicating liquors must be under perfect control. But what do we find to be the case? Until quite recently, except in isolated cases, there was scarcely a pretence of carrying any of these laws into execution. The bold front of the liquor interest presented too many terrors for private citizens to undertake prosecutions, and the officers to whom the duty was delegated, in too many instances, owed their election to the very men whom they were expected to prosecute. Moreover, if a public official undertook the execution of the law, it was rarely that he found a public sentiment strong enough to sustain him and keep him in office.

The Adair law, at this writing, has been in force nearly four years. It may interest many to know how extensive and successful the litigation under it has been. Upon the occasion of a woman obtaining a verdict of fifteen hundred dollars in Cleveland, recently, a paper in that city made the statement that that was the only instance in a large city where damages had been recovered under the law. The statement was somewhat startling, and though not strictly true, it showed that the law in the cities is practically ineffective. In Cincinnati there have only been two or three instances where the plaintiffs have recovered, and these only in small sums. Ten times that number of actions have been brought, but the result has been, almost invariably, a compromise, or a verdict for the defendants.

In the country, however, the case is quite different. Literally, thousands of suits have been brought by the wives and children of drunkards, and in a good proportion of the cases, damages, to a greater or less extent, have been recovered. The cases have been generally contested with great obstinacy, and frequently appealed to higher courts. Five or six have thus found their way to the Supreme Court of the state, which has always declared the Adair law constitutional in every particular. In regard to the last section of the law, which declares a lease to a liquor seller, selling contrary to law, invalid, it has been decided that to set aside such lease a separate suit must be brought.

In Indiana the experience has been very similar to that of Ohio. In the country districts the law has been quite readily and thoroughly enforced; in the cities it has, so far, proved a total failure. The bold and ingenious methods by which the saloon keepers have dodged the law will be found in a subsequent chapter on the work in Indiana.

CHAPTER XXIII.

THE TRIUMPHAL MARCH OF DIO LEWIS. — THE MAN AND HIS OPINIONS. — THE XENIA MASS MEETING. — INAUGURATION OF THE WORK IN SPRINGFIELD, LEBANON, MOUNT VERNON, ETC. — MOTHER STEWART, THE SPRINGFIELD LEADER. — INTERVIEWS WITH SALOON KEEPERS. — WHY THE MASS MEETING AT COLUMBUS FAILED. — THANKSGIVING JUBILEE AT WASHINGTON COURT HOUSE. — THE TRANSFORMATION OF XENIA, MOUNT VERNON, ETC. — REMARKABLE SURRENDER OF THE SHADES OF DEATH.

ON the last day of January Dio Lewis wrote from Boston to the Cincinnati papers that he could no longer deny himself a visit to the front. Soon after his lecture at Washington Court House he had returned east, little expecting that the movement he had inaugurated was destined to reach such stupendous proportions. It was an experiment that he had often tried during the last nineteen years, but he had never before met the women with the moral courage to carry it through. Southern Ohio was the first soil he had found where his temperance plant would grow; and its growth had been a marvel alike to him and to the whole world. After watching the battle for a while at a distance, he determined to enter the field and lend a helping hand "where the movement had not yet been fairly inaugurated, or where another soldier might help to turn the fortunes of the day."

Let us take a general survey of the field at this time. The excitement had penetrated every corner of Southern Ohio, and was spreading rapidly northward, and into other states. It was the prominent topic of conversation everywhere. People who ridiculed the movement at first, as a species of fanaticism, now saw it growing into a great social revolution. Nowhere had the women been vanquished, thus far, in a fair fight with whiskey. They had achieved the most astonishing victories over stubborn saloon keepers, and by their very success compelled the respect of their opponents. Just about this time the Cincinnati Gazette published statistics from about twenty-five towns, showing that one hundred and nine saloons had been closed, and twenty-two drug stores pledged to sell no intoxicating liquor.

Such was the general situation on the 9th of February, when Dio Lewis arrived in Cincinnati. Of course he was straightway "interviewed" by reporters of the city press, and appropriately written up. In person he was found to be a fine specimen of the physical man, six feet in height, with a muscular development and freshness of appearance that was a walking argument in favor of his great theory — temperance. His mental faculties were also about as well developed as his physical. He had decided views about the whole question, and was never at a loss for words or facts to sustain them. The reportorial gimlet was first applied in relation to the legal cases, an outline of which has been given in a previous chapter. The following was the result: —

"There never was a day since this movement was inaugurated that presented such a golden opportunity as that now offered to the ladies of Washington and Hillsboro'. For years these saloon men have been violating every law of God and man, and the men have treated it lightly. Now the ladies, in this holiest of causes of mere human interest, have violated some technicality; the law, the mighty law, is appealed to at once. Now let the ladies prove equal to the occasion — go two hundred strong, and kneel and pray before Dr. Dunn's store, and then submit to the law. The blood of the martyr is the seed of the church. Is there a judge in Ohio that would consign them to prison, or a constable that would execute such a decree? Then should the ladies submit and take imprisonment, for rest assured it will not be long; then every man in Ohio, who has a spark of manliness in him, would burn with shame, and the free men of this state would rise in their might, and say, This traffic in death shall be crushed out."

Subsequent to this Dr. Lewis modified his view in this respect, and counselled obedience to the laws. The doctor continued: —

"It is safe to say that three fourths of the men and nineteen twentieths of the ladies are in favor of strong temperance measures, if they could be got at without entangling side issues. But why is not this sentiment put into action? A has a business; his eye is on that. B has a shop; his eye is there. C and D have farm and merchandise; and they go their ways, saying, 'It's a pity, a great pity that men will debase themselves; but it always has been so, and always will.' But let them see a band of women praying, singing, pleading with the rum sellers, and all at once this latent sentiment springs into life. The man and the citizen is shamed, and the Christian and patriot alarmed, for their country, and every one is impelled to do his best. And that is why I justify this mode of fighting intemperance. I know it is not nice. It would be much pleasanter for those ladies to sit at home and talk about the evils of intemperance. But must they sit at home while brothers perish? No; they must come out and waken the moral sense of the community. Why, we are not talking to convince people of the evils of intemperance. That would be a pure waste of time. We want them to act — act on what they already know."

Next day the temperance party started on its travels. It consisted of Dr. Lewis, the noted Van Pelt, who went along in the double capacity of lecturer and "horrible example," and four members of the press, representing the Cincinnati dailies and the New York Tribune. The destination was Xenia, where a rousing mass meeting was to be held the same night. When the cars reached Loveland, Dr. Lewis was handed a despatch asking him to step off at Morrow, and give the laborers some advice and encouragement. He answered yes, and at three o'clock the whole party alighted. A prayer meeting was then in progress at the door of Max Goepper's saloon. It was a strange picture to look upon. At one door of the saloon was a woman with hands raised in prayer; at another, the proprietor was placidly smoking a cigar, and trying to force a smile of contempt and unconcern, while all about were moving trains and hundreds of bystanders.

The meeting came to order, and Van Pelt was loudly called for. Thereupon the converted rum seller came forward, and, with a preparatory clearing of the throat, launched out upon the first temperance speech of the tour. Barring the unreportable mistakes of grammar, and twisting of the king's English, he spoke substantially as follows: —

"Ladies and Gentlemen: As by request I will give you a little of my experience as a saloon keeper, and then pass on to some arguments to show that the ardent is one of the greatest curses of the land, and that the labors of these women are destined to sweep it out of our midst. As a saloon keeper I could bring up many dreadful acts during my experience. When I look back, I can't see how any man can keep up the business of selling liquor. I will suppose myself in my own saloon. I will pass behind the bar with a smile, meeting my customer with a decanter; and, as he gulps down the liquid poison, I look at the man; I see that God has endowed him with all the strength of manhood; that perhaps he has been raised in good society. Then I look at him after a few years have passed. See his emaciated form and tattered clothes! Could one believe that he was once the pride of the society of the place? And this is but a case out of ten thousand. Many have I thus started on the road to ruin, and led on down the broad way. Now, when he thinks of this, is there a man who can stand and deal out these liquors? It is hard for me to follow my own experience. When I look back, it seems as if only a monster could do the things I have done. Yet men are doing this every day.

"Now, to our dear sisters who are laboring in the cause, I will say that they have the greatest reason to labor on. Take a mother who has pleaded with her erring son, and then just when she has persuaded him to leave his wickedness, a tempting companion, or a saloonist, leads him astray again. How many such cases there are! Why, then, shouldn't our sisters and mothers work in the cause? I don't believe there is a saloon keeper in the United States but that believes he is shortening the lives of his fellow-creatures just to fill his own coffers. We might enter into arguments to show the saloon keepers that they are wrong; but they are already satisfied of that."

He was listened to with great interest by the crowd, who were curious to hear the man whose wickedness had given him a reputation almost national. Dr. Lewis then spoke a few feeling words, and all adjourned to the Methodist church, where both Lewis and Van Pelt again made speeches.

The party arrived in Xenia in time to face an immense audience assembled to hear the noted temperance apostles in the City Hall. This meeting we reproduce at length, as a good representative of its class during the whole campaign.

Van Pelt was the first speaker. After some general arguments in favor of temperance, in which he was not very successful, he proceeded with an inside view of the campaign in New Vienna, from the saloon keepers' standpoint, telling how they met often to consult; how they waited for the women to overstep the bounds of the law; how one after another of his colleagues went over, leaving him at last alone in the fight, and how, at length, he saw his wretched business in its true light, and resolved to give it up. He gave a sample of his bravado speeches to the ladies, day after day, and made the statement that Cincinnati dealers offered to supply him with liquors for a year, if he would only stick it out. By way of peroration, he told the story of his surrender, which produced a storm of applause. The climax was impressively related in the following words: —

"Then I told all the men to retire, for this was the ladies' victory. I would surrender to no man, but to them; and I took that old meat-axe that I s'pose you've all read of [laughter], that I had threatened the same ladies with, and knocked in the heads of the barrels, and let the old serpent flow into the gutter."

Dr. Lewis was then introduced to the audience, and plunged at once into the subject, by stating that he considered this the most important meeting ever held in Xenia; "and," he continued, "I feel a deep anxiety lest the little I have to say shall not be well said, for this movement of the praying women of Ohio has got beyond the direction of any one man; its control belongs only to God." Some startling statements from various judges were then presented as to the proportion of crimes caused by intoxication, the speaker having the testimony of nineteen eminent jurists, none of whom were temperance men. In a meeting he attended the other day, a clergyman had recommended the introduction of the light wines of France and Germany to suppress our fiery stimulants; "but," said the doctor, "I would not walk across the street to aid any temperance reform that did not plant its two feet square on the rock of total abstinence. [Applause.]

"Dr. J. G. Holland has stood for twenty years directly in the path of the temperance reformation of New England by his position on this subject. Said he, 'You are not going to work in the right way; men will have stimulants of some kind; the desire for them is as natural as for air and sunlight. In Southern Europe every one drinks his half pint or pint of wine daily, and is the better for it. Let us induce our people to use these stimulants, and all will be well.' At last Dr. Holland went to Europe; and what did he see? He is a man that prides himself on his consistency. A great deal of his time is taken up in proving that he does not change; that he thinks just as he did seventeen hundred years ago — more or less. But when he got to Southern Europe, he took the back track for the first time, so far as I know, in his life. Said he, 'God forbid that the drinking customs of my country should be changed for those of this land! Bad as they are there, they are worse here.' I too went to Southern Europe, where men use these light wines. And what is the secret of their demoralization there? The women drink!! every woman, as well as every man; and during the time I was there, I never heard a woman decline to drink, except because of sickness; and one hour after dinner you could see the effects of wine-drinking in the face and eye of every woman of the company. And it is only because the praying mothers and faithful wives of Ohio do not drink, that they hate, *loathe*, abhor the *deadly* stuff, that they fight it from their houses as the presence of death, that any such movement as this is possible."

A scathing criticism of moderate drinkers followed. "Who," he asked, "set the example which young drinkers follow? Evidently not the drunkards, the men who get drunk every time they get the means; for all classes look upon them as disgusting. Nor is it the middle class, who drink habitually, and get drunk occasionally; for in every family and social circle you will hear them spoken of thus: 'Mr. A. has a good bank account now, but if he goes on this way five years, it won't be so. Mr. B.'s credit is good to-day, but he will be a pauper in ten years if he don't let liquor alone.' No; no young man feels called on to imitate them. No; it is the nice, elegant fellows, who turn up delicate cut glasses, and sip the finest foreign wines; or the sturdy, honest old gentlemen, who take only pure Bourbon; and the families that keep a little cordial for sociability, or a bottle of brandy in the house 'for fear some one should be taken suddenly sick in the night.' These are the men who set the fashion, whose every word and motion was imitated. For it is but a few men who set the style for a place; it is but a small number of women who determine the fashion. And there are women, and in the best society, — to our shame be it said, — who serve as agents to recruit the devil's army of drunkards.

"Mrs. Colonel Smith smiles sweetly the 1st day of January, as she says to the innocent young man who calls, 'Take a glass of wine with me before you go.' And to that young man she is a very goddess, moving before him in trailing clouds of beauty. The woman who would thus let herself down to be an enlisting officer for the devil's army of drunkards should be tabooed, inexorably shut out from all respectable society forever." [Prolonged applause.] A series of interesting sketches followed, showing that the speaker could drop occasionally from the severe to the lively and amusing; but through them all ran one general moral: There is no safety but in total abstinence; and the moderate drinkers set the example which makes drunkards.

He then addressed himself to the question, "What shall be done?" Nothing had ever raised communities to such a height of moral sublimity as this women's temperance movement of Ohio. "Three hundred times," he said, "have I given temperance lectures in which I urged this movement, and never found the soil fit for it before. Now that it has come, I almost fear to touch it, lest I hinder. When I saw the women at Morrow praying in front of that saloon, I felt weak; too weak to add anything to the power at work; and I knew then why brother Van Pelt had surrendered. He must have been half crocodile, half tiger, and all devil, to have withstood it. Now, friends, the hour of action has come. I propose this plan: We want a chairman, four secretaries, and ten speeches of two or three minutes each by clergymen and leading citizens."

By unanimous vote of the audience, Dr. Lewis himself was made chairman, and Messrs. Dodds, Stern, Colonel Finley, of the Xenia Gazette, and the Rev. Mr. Marley named as secretaries. Short and pointed speeches were then made by Rev. Mr. Bedel, of the Baptist church, Rev. Mr. Ralston, of the Presbyterian, Rev. J. G. Carson, of the United Presbyterian, Rev. Mr. Morehead, Mr. Starr, Mr. Shaeffer, Rev. Mr. Yockey, and Rev. Mr. Marley. One or two hesitated somewhat before embarking in the Hillsboro' method of suppressing intemperance, but the expression of the orators generally, and the tone of the audience, were decidedly in favor of it. One hundred and fifty women enlisted on the spot, and the meeting adjourned in a glow of enthusiasm until morning.

At nine A. M. on the following day, the hall was

again crowded, mostly by women, who showed by their countenances that the enthusiasm of the night before had not been slept off. The work of organization was again taken up, and the list of volunteers increased to nearly four hundred. Dr. Lewis advised a division of forces into four bands, who should take separate districts of the city. The ladies then held a private meeting, and adjourned until afternoon.

Notwithstanding the work had been so auspiciously begun, the party of temperance missionaries went away with many misgivings in regard to Xenia, there seemed so many formidable obstacles to be overcome. It was the largest city yet attacked, having a population of nearly eight thousand. It was aristocratic, wealthy, and conservative. There was a very strong element in the religious community of United Presbyterians, who could not conscientiously sing a hymn, or allow a woman to speak in a church. How could ladies from these churches work harmoniously with Methodists and others? Then there were half a hundred well-rooted saloons to encounter. These and other difficulties seemed to many almost insurmountable. How they were swept away like chaff before the wind, will appear further along in this chapter.

Springfield was the next point of attack. It was approached with some fear on account of its size and the strength of the liquor interest. Up to this time the movement had not been attempted in any place containing more than four thousand inhabitants, and it was declared by many that if it strove to make conquests on a larger scale, it would inevitably meet with defeat. People, however, who had witnessed the marked and speedy results of prayer in the smaller places, were sanguine that the same method would prevail in the cities, if fairly tried. Springfield contains something like fifteen thousand inhabitants, being about double the size of Xenia.

It had one hundred and thirteen saloons, besides wholesale houses, breweries, and doubtful drug stores. As in Xenia, the ladies of the upper classes are slightly given to aristocratic notions, while the liquor sellers were so numerous as to form a society of their own, and otherwise unite for joint protection and resistance. It was, therefore, not a promising field for laborers for temperance according to the new plan, and many thought it would give a searching test to the efficacy of the moral method.

The subject of temperance had been agitated there some time before Dio Lewis arrived. Six weeks previous the movement had been set on foot mainly by "Mother" Stewart, under whose maternal supervision it had since remained. Weekly meetings had been held and moderately attended. The speeches were carefully elaborated, and the essays were of the most polished order, and all had a general tendency towards temperance; but somehow the cause did not thrive. A legal campaign had been vigorously pushed by Mother Stewart. A vain attempt had been made to persuade the City Council to use their power, under a city ordinance, to abate the saloons as nuisances. And at last, just before the arrival of the Dio Lewis party, some attempts had been made with the praying method. But the nice ladies held aloof, distrustful of such strange means: the doubting, and well-disposed, shook their heads and said, "It was of no use; whiskey had got too strong a hold," while the saloon keepers smiled a smile of good-natured contempt.

Things were about in this condition when Dio Lewis and Van Pelt came on the scene. The Opera House was crowded to hear the far-famed temperance apostles. On the stage were the whole party of itinerant speakers and journalists, together with Mother Stewart, Clifton

Nichols, editor of the Republic, who acted as chairman, and several of the ministers and dignitaries of the town. Van Pelt had his say first, and improved considerably on his Xenia performance. The doctor followed in an address which was, to some extent, the same as already reported. The following, however, in regard to adulterated liquors, excited some surprise and considerable applause among his hearers: —

"He did not sympathize with the wish for pure liquors; on the contrary, he considered the poison-compounder the friend of temperance. He did not know of any drug so deadly that it would not improve whiskey. He would bid the mixers God speed, if it be lawful to use the name of God in such a connection. There is no nonsense so pervading and injurious as this talk about unadulterated liquors. Men say, 'O, if we only had the pure liquors that our grandfathers had, we would live on as they did; it is this poison stuff that kills us off.' It is all nonsense. The reason liquor hurts us worse than our grandfathers is the difference in other physical conditions. They worked hard in the open air, lived on coarse food, and though they drank often, did live out three fourths of their days. The men who live in the open air now, who start with a good constitution and unusual physical advantages, can live as long. Be not deceived! Alcohol is poison — *it is poison — it is poison.* The more deadly it can be made, the better. If a man has become an habitual drinker, the sooner he dies, the less harm he does. Is it not better for him to go in a year or two, than to go on, a curse to himself and the world, for twenty? If the whiskey could be so mixed that it would kill a man in three days, it would be a glorious thing for temperance."

The speech was concluded in a blaze of enthusiasm, and the business meeting began. It was conducted in the same manner as the one at Xenia. Four secretaries were named by the audience — C. H. Shaeffer, O. G. Hoffman, T. J. Finch, and O. D. Hawk. These were to name one hundred ladies from the audience, who would take an active part in the crusade. While this work was going on, Mother Stewart was called to the front. She said, —

"God seems to be giving us the desire of our hearts, but we have a very peculiar warfare here. I cannot describe it. We never did anything until we started to work at the saloons. It seemed to me that we were only beating the air. Four months have passed since that poor woman came to me for help for herself and children against the rum sellers that were killing her husband. I told her to-day to come here to-night, and see if this meeting gave her hope; and she is in the audience. At last the people are interested; some actual drunkards, and young men, drinkers, but not yet drunkards, have taken my hand, and said to me, 'Go on, Mother Stewart; we do hope you will succeed.' Sometimes I have felt so discouraged I almost wished that God would lay me on a bed of sickness, for I might be an obstacle in the way of reform. Still we worked on. I felt, when that poor woman came to me, that our great reliance must be in prayer. The great question was, Could we succeed in that way in this city? At last we went forth, and then a host of friends seemed to spring out of the ground. The burden of this thing has been on my mind till I have felt that I could not live unless we went forward. We could not trust to other causes. The politicians admit that they are powerless. They are so entangled that they cannot act.

"On Monday two or three went out and prayed. Good women came and prayed with us; and at last, yesterday, we went to the saloons, twenty or thirty of us, and to-day more came — yes, seventy or eighty; and you all know the result. Many gentlemen have said to me, 'Those places must be closed;' but I felt almost in despair when I received a telegram from Dr. Lewis. As our band increased, there was a great crowd of men and boys, but they were very polite and respectful. They only seemed anxious to see and hear. To-day we visited the Lagonda House saloon; the proprietor treated us very kindly, but locked the outside door to keep the crowd out. He gave us the billiard rooms, and we had a very precious season there. At the next place I tried to talk, a crowd collected. The man came out and said, 'Get away; get away, every one of you; I don't want any trespassers; you shan't stand on my steps.' But I was never more composed. When I started down from the porch a hundred voices said, 'Stay where you are.' 'Go on, Mother Stewart, go on.' Then a policeman took the man in, and when we were ready to leave, he came out in good humor, and bid us good day."

Ten minute speeches being in order, John C. Miller, city solicitor, General Kiefer, Rev. Mr. Bennett, Rev. Mr. Spring, L. H. Olds, and others responded to calls; and, though some of them handled "this particular plan" a little gingerly, yet all were in favor of some decided movement on the subject at once. The enthusiasm on the subject of organization was not what it was at Xenia, and as soon as the meeting came to real business, the people seemed in a dreadful hurry to go home, and kept constantly leaving the hall.

Next morning, at nine o'clock, the Central Methodist church presented a more encouraging picture. It was nearly filled with ladies, who, by their coming, indicated that they were ready to take hold of the work. An executive and advisory committee were appointed to subdivide forces, arrange plans, and take entire control of the movement. The names of four hundred and fifty women, ready for the work, were reported. Dio Lewis and Van Pelt were present. The former acted as chief organizer, and the latter gave an account of his experience as a saloon keeper. Two or three men, belonging to good families in the city, but who had been almost ruined by intemperance, told the ladies that on the success of the movement depended their own salvation from rum.

The temperance party left for Lebanon in the afternoon, feeling that the work had been well organized and well begun in Springfield, and expecting to hear, very soon, of grand achievements in the cause. But such is the weakness of human judgment. In Xenia, from which little was expected, a week sufficed to revolutionize the town. In Springfield, which gave such fair promise, the movement dragged along for months with no great results.

There was a vague suspicion among the members of the temperance band that Lebanon was small game for half a dozen able-bodied men. From the account already given, it will be remembered that there was but a single saloon in town that had survived the terrors of the law, and the proprietor of that was selling in strict conformity with the law. But Dio Lewis had engaged himself to lecture there, and was determined to improve what opportunities for usefulness still remained. The keen scent of the reformer discovered three saloons and a distillery in the little squad of houses that make up Deerfield — the railroad station of Lebanon. It struck him that the ladies of the latter place, having no foe to overcome in their own midst, might do a little excellent missionary work in their degenerate suburb.

There was a large and fine-looking audience assembled in the evening to hear the doctor. Nate Woods, the only remaining saloonist, himself bought five dollars' worth of tickets for the lecture, and distributed them among his friends. Van Pelt orated in the customary style; Dr. Lewis was very entertaining and impressive; the usual five minute speeches were extracted from prominent men and ministers present, and the work of organization was commenced. While many were doubting whether so many ladies were needed to suppress the small whiskey shop that was left, and the two suspicious drug stores, Dr. Lewis sprang upon the audience the question of their interesting suburb — Deerfield. It was a surprise. The listeners pictured to themselves twenty wagon loads of Lebanon women descending from the steep hill upon the forsaken little town and its distillery. In prospect it seemed like the descent of Hannibal from the Alps upon the fair fields of Italy.

A meeting was held in the Congregational church next morning. Dr. Lewis acted as manager, and the usual company of women was enlisted for service. A disposition was manifested to supplement the work of the law by a little influence of the gospel, and then, when the last remnant of whiskey was rooted out of Lebanon, to push the victorious car over the hills to Deerfield, and redeem that place from its load of wickedness and misery.

Nate Woods was sought out by a reporter, and unbosomed himself for the benefit of the public. He regarded the situation as serious, and yet hopeful. He seemed to be laboring under the delusion that the temperance cause and the Rev. Mr. Burrows were identical, and gave a long history of the persecutions he had suffered at the hands of that gentleman. When asked what he would do when the women came, he said he would shut up his shop and go home till they got through. He had money enough, and could stick it out as long as they could.

"But suppose they swoop down every time you open up?"

"O," said he, "they won't do that. They'll get tired of this by and by, and go home and mind their own business. It can't last."

The next engagement of Dio Lewis was at Marysville; but after an exasperating drag of twenty miles through the deep mud, the train was missed by a few minutes, and the people of Marysville had to start the temperance movement unaided and alone. What was their loss, however, proved to be Franklin's eternal gain. That place had been among the first to enter upon the crusade against saloons. Six had yielded, after an ineffectual resistance, and the women were engaged upon the last and worst. It was kept by one Munger, who has achieved, in that locality, the reputation of a Van Pelt — unregenerated. While the ladies were praying about this place, the temperance party drew near and listened. A voice — that of a young woman, almost a girl — was raised in prayer. It was so sweet and pure a prayer that a reporter telegraphed it entire to the New York Tribune; so that thousands of readers in the east next morning saw in their paper the tender, pleading words of a "crusader" before an Ohio saloon.

On the 14th and 15th of February Dr. Lewis and Van Pelt were in Mt. Vernon, a manufacturing town of considerable size, north-east of Columbus. There were twenty-eight saloons there, and the custom of drinking had such a strong hold upon the masses that many, even of the good temperance people, thought it folly to waste any prayers for the regeneration of Mt. Vernon. It was past cure. But others had faith, and among them were ladies belonging to the very best society of the place. A large band organized and entered upon the work, with what remarkable success will be seen at the end of this chapter.

On the night of the 16th Dio Lewis was booked for Columbus, where a great mass meeting was to be held with a view to inaugurating the work there. All eyes were turned towards Columbus for the answer to the question, "Can this movement succeed in large cities?" It was a tremendous meeting in point of size, but the cold, critical lookers-on seemed to outnumber and paralyze the zealous advocates of the cause. As the seat of the state government, the city was overrun with politicians, who from the first looked with disfavor upon the woman's movement. The average politician, without the facilities of the dram shops, would find politics a dreary and unprofitable profession. These and certain other elements united to smother what little enthusiasm the ladies, in their private prayer meetings, had worked up. The verdict of the press was "failure;" and the majority of people, who depend on their newspaper for their opinions, straightway concluded that it was all up with the cities. They were mistaken, as the record of a succeeding chapter will show. With the Columbus ladies it was only hope deferred. The cold-blooded politicians, and some other disturbing elements, had checked, but by no means discouraged them. A great State Temperance Convention was appointed for the following Tuesday, and the meeting adjourned, after taking up a collection to cover expenses. One hundred dollars were called for, and the hats returned laden with nickels and coppers to the extent of eighteen or twenty dollars. The audience had sacrificed something over half a cent apiece!

From Columbus the doctor went to Washington Court House, where a grand thankgiving jubilee had been arranged to celebrate the final closing out of whiskey from the place. He was met at the depot by a brass band and half the people of the town. The reception took place in Music Hall, and was a memorable affair in the history of the little city. Mrs. M. G. Carpenter, wife of the Presbyterian minister, who had been one of the leaders in the movement, extended a welcome to Dr. Lewis in the following well-chosen words: —

"Dr. Lewis: In the name of the women of Washington I welcome you. Eight weeks ago, when you first came among us, you found us a people of willing hearts and generous impulses, fully alive to the evils of intemperance, but needing the magnetism of a master mind to rouse us into a determined resistance to its ravages. Yours was that mind. Your hand pointed out the way. You vitalized our latent activities; you roused us all, men and women together, and we have gone forth to the battle side by side, as God intended we should; ourselves perfect weakness, but God mighty in strength. He has given the success — not yet complete, 'tis true, but our faith is still unshaken. He sent you here; He put the thought into your head; He prepared our hearts to receive it; He has directed our steps. And now He has brought you among us again to gladden you with the fruition of hope long deferred — to see the seed, sown long ago by your mother, springing up, budding, and bearing fruit. Dr. Lewis, in behalf of this whole people, I again welcome you to the hearts and homes of Washington."

Dr. Lewis replied: —

"Madam and Friends: I cannot make a speech on this occasion. I may, perhaps, compare myself to an Indian on a visit to the city of Washington — from the frontier to the place where the battle has long been fought and won. I have always been on the frontier, always engaged in the battle of reform; and now, to find any thing really done, to find a town positively free from the curse of liquor selling, it seems that there is nothing for me to do. I feel as one without his working harness. But I will say this: None but God can ever know how much I owe to this town, nor how fortunate it was for me and for many that I came here. I will not say that this is the only community in which the work could be begun. The heroism and self-sacrifice displayed in other places, the moral force developed in Southern Ohio, would make such a remark invidious. Often have I tried to start this movement—once in particular, in one of the most moral towns in New England. Two United States senators came upon the platform to give the movement their sanction. We had as fine an audience as could be assembled, and I said to myself, 'At last we are going to succeed.' But it was a dead failure. I know not why. All the elements of success seemed to be there; but some invisible force was lacking. There is an invisible force at work in this movement. At last I came to you, and you delighted me by your work. You came out to meet me with music and words of welcome. But I come to thank you, to take you by the hands, to look into your eyes, and tell you how much I owe to you for being the first to cheer me with success. I am indebted to you for bringing out this plan. I am indebted to you a thousand times more than you are to me. But the hour of victory leaves me with little to say. I have never been able to visit the battle-fields after victory—have always gone on to new fields. I can only close by tendering you my earnest thanks."

Further festivities of a mild nature followed, after which Dr. Lewis took leave of the town that won the first complete victory under his system, and from there went to Springfield, Dayton, and Cincinnati, at which latter city he delivered a regular lyceum lecture. Sunday was spent in advising and encouraging the laborers at Hillsboro'; and on Monday the original party, Van Pelt excepted, found itself reunited and headed for Delaware, a quiet little city in Central Ohio, the seat of the Ohio Wesleyan University, and the home of Apollo and the Muses.

On Monday the women of Delaware had no thought of inaugurating the praying movement; twenty-four hours later they were thoroughly organized, and had entered upon the work in a glow of enthusiasm. Dr. Lewis was invited to lecture, not by the citizens, but by one or two students of the Chi Phi fraternity, who were also perfectly guiltless of any intention of improving the morals of the town. A large audience assembled in the Opera House to hear the lecture, and almost before they knew it, they were fairly imbued with the new idea. They came for an evening's entertainment, and went away pledged "crusaders." Next day a large meeting was held at the Williams Street M. E. church, where a permanent and effective organization was formed. Mrs. A. S. Clason was made President, and Mrs. Bishop Thompson Secretary. The most cultivated and influential ladies came promptly forward, and went to work with an intelligence of purpose and strength of determination that spoke the inevitable doom of the thirty-three saloons that flourished in their midst.

The temperance apostles reached Columbus next day just in time for the great convention, to which all workers in the cause had been invited. The proceedings of this and other conventions, during the progress of the movement, will be found in a succeeding chapter.

We have left the movement fairly inaugurated at a number of interesting points, some full of promise, and others of discouragement. It may be well to go back, and, in the light of subsequent events, review the progress of the work.

Xenia was the first place where Dio Lewis tried his skill as an organizer. The elements of opposition were so plentiful that a stranger, on the morning Dio Lewis left, would have said there was not a ghost of a chance of success. One week later the writer returned, and spent three days in the place. The very atmosphere seemed to be changed. The excitement was as intense as at any time during the war. In business, in society, on the streets, everywhere, temperance was the all-prevailing topic of conversation. Hundreds of women, divided into several bands, were praying daily before the saloons. The morning meetings in the churches were crowded with men and women, and the most intense interest was manifested in every part of the proceedings. While these meetings were in progress, the stores were closed, and business generally suspended.

It was remarkable, most of all, to notice how the barriers of society and denominationalism were broken down. All churches and all classes of society were united in the movement. People who, a week before, would have counted it a sin to sing out of any but Rouse's version, now joined lustily in the old Methodist hymns. One prominent member of the U. P. church remarked that she "had got all over her old notions about singing psalms, and women speaking in churches. If anybody wanted to discipline her, they might; she would speak or pray when she felt like it, and sing whatever was started." In society it was the same way. Every lady in town, except one, belonging to what is known as "the first circles," was active in the movement, and on the streets daily. That one was sick, and could not. The leaders, among whom might be mentioned Mrs. Monroe, Mrs. Finley, Mrs. Lowe, and others, seemed, from their good sense, high standing, and zealous devotion, admirably adapted to the great work before them.

There was one saloon, known as the "Shades of Death," which, in the early stages of the movement, was the centre of attack. Notwithstanding its notoriously bad character, its proprietor was a young man, named Phillips, who had been well brought up, and who seemed to have a few traces of self-respect remaining. Day after day the ladies had patiently prayed and pleaded with the man, but apparently to no purpose. Whenever they attempted to enter, he would thrust them out, good-naturedly, sometimes, but always determinedly. But one afternoon the church bells set up a deafening clamor. People rushed about the streets in great excitement, spreading the news that the "Shades of Death" had surrendered. Cheer after cheer rose upon the air from the vicinity of the saloon. Hastening to the spot with the crowds of people that were flocking in from all directions, the writer witnessed a remarkable scene. There had been an unconditional surrender on the part of the young saloonist, and a genuine "pouring out" of his liquors. The doxology had just been sung by the crowd, as though they intended it to be heard a mile, and special emphasis was laid upon the last word of the first line. The ladies, with tearful eyes but stout hands, had rolled out the barrels. One of them tugged away at a faucet for dear life, and when it would not come, she seized a stone, and went at it with an energy that soon sent the beverage reeking through the gutter. The mingled fumes of whiskey and beer filled the air, and people fell on each other's necks and wept. It was unanimously voted on the spot to encourage Phillips in any legitimate business he might undertake; and now a well-patronized meat market takes the place of the old traffic in whiskey. The same night two other saloons surrendered; next day, two or three more; and so on, day after day, until the whole forty were reduced to half a dozen, which still hold out, and will have to be brought to terms by law.

At Springfield the women continued the campaign of prayer; but somehow the cause did not seem to prosper. At Lebanon Nate Woods resisted for a while, but at length shut up his saloon, and left town to "wait till the storm should blow over." At Delaware the work was carried on vigorously. Part of the saloons yielded to persuasion, and the remainder were closed by the enforcement of the city ordinance.

Mt. Vernon was revolutionized almost as speedily as Xenia. It is a city of about the same size, and much the same characteristics. The women enlisted in large numbers, and soon became a power that nothing could resist. Saloon after saloon melted away before them. Ten days sufficed to reduce the number from twenty-eight to a dozen; and it was not long before all, except a few doggeries of the lowest character, were shut up. The leading saloon keeper, who was among the first to surrender, was one McFealey, known to convivial spirits throughout all that section of country. His place was a favorite resort for Kenyon College boys, who came down from Gambier to shake off the cares of learning and drown them in the flowing bowl. A few days after he had run up the white flag, a couple of correspondents walked in to interview him. They were met with a cordial shake, and, —

"Have a glass of ginger ale, or lemonade, gentlemen? We don't keep anything stronger now."

Over this mild refreshment, he explained how he conducted his business since whiskey was thrown overboard, and what he thought of the temperance movement.

"I don't know what it is to be converted," said he, "but from what I have heard people say, I think I feel something like that. I never was so happy in my life as since I quit selling whiskey. Before, I used to cross the street, when I saw a lady coming whom I happened to know, to save her the embarrassment of recognizing a saloon keeper publicly. Now all that feeling is gone, and I feel that I am as good as anybody."

He was running a restaurant and billiard room on the temperance plan, and so great had been the increase of

SALOON KEEPER SURRENDERS, AND SIGNS THE PLEDGE.

his respectable patrons, that he was doing a better business than he had ever done before.

And so the work was going on in scores of towns, of which there is hardly space here to mention the names. At the time Dio Lewis returned to the east, the telegraph and mails were bringing to the daily papers reports of progress from nearly every part of the state. Besides the hundreds of saloons closed, and thousands of individuals pledged to total abstinence, there were indirect results none the less important. A strong popular feeling was growing up against drinking in every form, and against the men who enrich themselves by the misery and degradation of their fellow-creatures. Individuals were being saved from habits of self-destruction; and perhaps more important than any of these, the minds of the young were moulded into a love for the principles of temperance.

CHAPTER XXIV.

THE MOVEMENT SPREADS TO INDIANA.—SHELBYVILLE THE FIRST POINT ASSAILED.—A JUVENILE SPREE THE IMMEDIATE CAUSE.—THE HOME OF THE AUTHOR OF THE BAXTER LAW.—NOBLE WORK OF THE QUAKER LADIES OF RICHMOND.—SUDDEN UPRISING IN FORT WAYNE.—HOW THE INDIANAPOLIS WOMEN DIRECTED THEIR ENERGIES.—PRAYER AND THE BAXTER LAW JOIN HANDS.

THE work so auspiciously begun in Ohio early spread into Indiana. The conditions being very similar, the plan of operations was but slightly modified. The ladies in Southern Indiana took to the praying method with much the same readiness and determination as their sisters across the line. They did not have the personal presence and counsel of the commander-in-chief, in consequence of which operations were begun in some places somewhat irregularly. The very important accessories of large numbers, of social prestige, and of a favorable popular sentiment, which were so marked in some of the Ohio cities, seemed wanting, to some extent, in Indiana. The pioneers in the movement, in the southern part of the state, were very largely Quaker ladies, who waited not for organization, or any pronounced backing on the part of the general public. They had faith to believe that God would send them numbers and strength as the work progressed.

The campaign in Indiana was inaugurated at Shelbyville on the 28th of January. The immediate cause of the uprising of the women was a drunken spree of a couple of youths between seventeen and eighteen years old, who belonged to the most pious and respectable families of the town. One of them purchased liquor on the plea that it was for family use, and, together with a comrade who was not so new to the business, they launched out upon a bacchanalian revelry that would have done credit to old and accomplished soakers. Their pursuit of pleasure led them to a house of bad repute, where their drunken orgies attracted the attention of the officers, who arrested them. Their pious mothers and friends were horrified at the excesses of the boys; and so great was the feeling upon the subject, especially among the women, that a "mothers' meeting" was held at the close of the prayer meeting on the evening of the 20th. The cause of the trouble was traced directly to the sale of intoxicating liquors, and, as in the similar case recounted by Dio Lewis, they resolved to devote their earnest and prayerful efforts to the suppression of intemperance.

The next morning another meeting was held. Soon after, a committee of ladies waited on Mr. Schrader, whose permit to sell liquor had just expired, and asked him not to renew it. He replied that he would quit if the others would; and so the ladies were led almost inevitably into the work of visiting saloons. But the saloon keepers all met them with the remark, "Go to the druggists. They are the ones that are responsible for the most drunkenness." Accordingly the women went to the drug stores, where tippling of a respectable kind was encouraged. There were six of them, and, with one exception, they positively refused to sign. It was understood that the traffic in liquors, wholesale and retail, formed the most profitable part of their business. Each one would throw whiskey overboard if all the rest would; but that was a promise which they knew they were perfectly safe in making.

On the 26th of January, over a hundred women met at the Baptist church, and organized the "Woman's Temperance Alliance," with the following named officers: Mrs. John Elliott, President; Mrs. Harrison, Vice-President; Mrs. Hattie Robbins, Secretary; and Mrs. Mattie S. Thompson, Assistant Secretary. An appeal to the public was drafted, asking for assistance in the good work of temperance reform. But this method was not deemed sufficiently speedy and certain, and it was resolved by a large majority to proceed to the saloons in a body. George Deprez was first to receive attention. He admitted them readily, and a prayer meeting was held. When talked with directly upon the subject, Mr. Deprez responded that he was a member, in good standing, of the Presbyterian church, and hoped thereby to obtain eternal happiness. Next day they proceeded to other saloons; but the proprietors generally met them at the door with the remark that their house was kept for other purposes than prayer, and, if the ladies wanted room for such exercises, they could have the churches and the highway.

But the band of praying women increased in size, and grew strong in faith and courage. They went on in the crusade against saloons from day to day, meeting with varying successes. A number of saloon keepers were induced to quit the business; men were led back from the very gutter into ways of sobriety; and a feeling was created in the public mind which will render the enforcement of the law a more certain and easy process.

The following incident is related as occurring in one of the saloons at Shelbyville: A man went in to get a drink of whiskey. While standing at the bar, the wife of the liquor seller called her husband to come to dinner.

"What have you got for dinner?" he asked.

"Roast goose," she replied, naming several other good dishes.

"Have you any apple-sauce?" he inquired with interest, adding, "I like apple-sauce with roast goose."

"No, but I will soon have some," was the answer.

And the man at the bar, waiting for his dram, thought to himself, "What has my family for dinner to-day? This man has roast goose and apple-sauce, and my family have none. I will furnish no more money for him to buy roast goose and apple-sauce."

About two weeks later, Jeffersonville was seized by the same epidemic. Two hundred ladies formed an organization, and began the usual street operations. They were followed by crowds that sometimes became so noisy as to compel them to suspend their efforts for a time. In Muncie, Kokomo, and many smaller places, the movement was started in a similar way.

In Richmond, a staid Quaker city of twelve or fifteen thousand inhabitants, the work was quietly inaugurated late in February. A few determined Quaker ladies first started the street movement, but they rapidly gained in numbers until all the churches were represented in the ranks. Richmond is the home of William Baxter, author of the Baxter law, and is therefore a good point from which to view the effects of that enactment. It will be remembered that the law provides that no man may keep a saloon or sell intoxicating liquors until he has secured the signatures of a majority of the voters in his ward or township to a petition asking for such saloon. He is required to furnish bondsmen, who shall be liable for any violation of the law on his part, and, furthermore, the property on which the liquor is sold is liable, as under the Adair law in Ohio. As may be readily seen, not one saloon keeper in twenty can comply with all of these conditions and carry on a profitable business.

The consequence is, that in that city, out of the thirty-one registered saloons, but a single one was licensed under the Baxter law, the business of the other thirty being carried on in direct violation of it. The law is ineffective in the cities, simply because it is almost impossible to secure direct evidence against any of these places. Men who drink will not swear to it, and thus dry up the source from which they expect to get more. And if by any means a witness is secured, he is bought off, if there is money enough in the treasury of the liquor sellers' association to do it. It is very different, however, in the country districts. There hundreds of saloons were closed up by the law, and will remain closed as long as it exists. A majority of the voters in country townships is generally found to be opposed to whiskey selling, while, from their detached locations, the whiskey sellers cannot combine to override the law.

At the present writing, all the druggists are pledged, and about two thirds of the thirty-one saloons mentioned have either succumbed to law, or to the prayers of the women. Not less than seven of these yielded to the simple influence of prayer, and some of them are now zealous advocates of temperance. The finest saloon in Richmond was kept by one McCoy. It was called "The Continental," the word being displayed in a many-colored arch over the door. But McCoy surrendered to the ladies, and now a cross-bar, underneath the arch, bears the word "Market." Twenty gentlemen subscribed fifty dollars each, and loaned him that amount to set him up in business. August Woeste poured out his liquors unconditionally, and was rewarded with the proceeds of a public supper given in his establishment.

Thomas Lichtenfels, however, surrendered under the most interesting and dramatic circumstances. He had always prided himself on selling strictly according to law, had a regular license under the Baxter bill, obtained without fraud, and never sold to drunken men or minors. As the lower class saloons surrendered, one after another, their customers centred upon him; and, though he was taking in money twice as fast as ever before, he felt a growing disgust at the character of his patrons. At length the ladies began to visit his saloon, and remain some time each visit. One afternoon he undertook to shut them out, and half a dozen who had entered were imprisoned from four o'clock till nine P. M. with the rudest crowd the city could furnish. The rowdies exhausted their resources in attempts to frighten and browbeat the ladies without actual violence; and for a while it looked as if they would not hesitate at that. They called for beer as fast as two persons could hand it out to them, quoted Scripture in blasphemous mockery, and parodied the songs sung by the ladies. Finally they raised a cloud of tobacco smoke so dense and sickening that it drove out two of the ladies, but the others stood it like heroines. They did not attempt any religious exercises, but continued most of the time in silent prayer. Before the evening was over, the proprietor was heartily ashamed of his patrons. Precisely at nine o'clock he announced that the "time had come to shut up, according to law" (the Baxter bill directs that all saloons shall close at that hour), and turned off the gas. He followed the ladies into the street, shook hands with them all, and said, "This is the last day I will open a saloon; this is too much for me." The next day he did not open, and is now preparing to move West.

Fort Wayne has a population of about twenty-two thousand, and there is probably not a city in the state that does a larger liquor business, in proportion to its size. The Germans compose about one third of the population, and are, almost to a man, bitterly opposed to the woman's movement. Then, in addition to this, the Christian people of the community were indifferent and inactive on the subject of temperance long after their brethren and sisters, all about them, were in the field. But at last there was an awakening. Though it came late, the city was aroused from centre to circumference. For twenty years the dram shops had ruled the town, and there were not a hundred respectable people to contest their sway; but almost in a day all this was changed. The first public meeting was held about the middle of March, and within a week there was a powerful central organization, and branches extending into every ward in the city.

The plan of operations adopted by the women differed in some essential particulars from that generally followed. Instead of praying in saloons and on the streets, they resolved to hold regular morning prayer meetings in the churches, and then start out upon the work of the day. That work, it was decided, should consist of visits to every citizen, to secure the pledges of voters not to sign any more petitions for permits under the Baxter law, not to lease property to liquor sellers, and to refrain from drinking themselves. They also circulated the druggists' pledge, which was largely signed. As can readily be seen, this course, persistently carried out by the active organizations in every ward, soon rendered it impossible for a saloon keeper to renew his permit, according to the requirements of the law. A lawyer was employed to give his whole attention to the business, and thus prevent the perpetration of any frauds by the saloon keepers, many of whom had already forfeited their licenses by selling liquor on Sundays and after nine o'clock at night. Committees were appointed to gather evidence, and the men put their hands in their pockets liberally to back any prosecutions that might be begun. Under this strange combination of the law and the gospel, the influence of the whiskey element gradually wasted away. The Sundays—hitherto a boisterous holiday — became quiet, and the nights were once more free from the sounds of revelry. Unable to renew their licenses, and afraid to continue selling without them, the dram sellers are one by one dropping off, and seeking other employment. If this work, so energetically begun, is patiently and persistently carried forward, there is no doubt that the curse of intemperance, if not wholly swept from the city, may at least be restricted to very narrow limits.

The Christian women of Indianapolis became interested quite early in the campaign. The first to move in the matter were Quaker ladies, but they were soon reenforced from other denominations, and the movement acquired a strength that was felt and acknowledged. The high respectability of those connected with it will be seen from the following list of officers of the "Woman's Christian Temperance Union:" President, Mrs. Delitha Harvey; Secretary, Miss Auretta Hoyt; Corresponding Secretary, Miss Gertie Holliday; Treasurer, Mrs. Carrie Evans. There are also prominent in the work Mrs. Hannah T. Hadley, Mrs. Elizabeth Jenkins, Mrs. J. Trueblood, Mrs. Bartlett, Mrs. Bayliss, Mrs. Wingate, Mrs. Boggs, Mrs. Townsend, Mrs. Stagg, Mrs. W. A. Holliday, Mrs. Israel Taylor, and others. While prayer was to be relied upon as the chief weapon in the warfare, these ladies determined not to employ it in the same manner as their sisters in the Ohio cities. The direction which the movement took was towards the County Commissioners, before whom came the petitions for saloons, under the Baxter law. These documents are examined by them, and, if found satisfactory, the permit is at once issued. But this system had, in the large cities, and especially in Indianapolis, degenerated into the most notorious farce. Under the old law, every liquor seller was compelled to pay a round sum for a license. Now, all he had to do when he wanted a new permit, or his old one renewed, was to hire a man to go out and get the required number of signatures; and it was remarkable how readily that number was always obtained. The graveyards were generally well represented, and the list was further ornamented with the names of plenty of fictitious persons, non-residents, minors, and others, with an occasional property-holder or two thrown in to give character to the thing. When these palpably fraudulent lists were presented to the commissioners, there was no one to call in question their genuineness, and they were generally passed upon without any objection being raised.

Here, the ladies perceived, was an opportunity for usefulness. They could be present at the examination of these petitions, and, with very little evidence, expose their fraudulent character. Accordingly, one day, the sedate commissioners were surprised in their deliberations by a band of these women, who came in in the interests of temperance. The session was opened by prayer, permission to pray having been granted, and then the batch of documents passed under the scrutiny of these zealous women and their legal adviser, with the most alarming results to the whiskey fraternity. Out of twenty-four petitions presented, only four stood the test, and were passed upon.

The ladies then turned their prayerful attention to the enforcement of the existing provisions of the Baxter law, especially those in regard to liquor selling on Sunday and after nine o'clock at night. As in most of the large cities of the country, the saloons hardly made a pretence of closing on Sunday; and as for the nine o'clock provision, a good share of the money taken in passed over the counter after that hour of night. The temperance movement had not proceeded far before there was a public sentiment which demanded of the city authorities the execution of the law in these respects. An order was issued to that effect, and the result was, the next Sunday was the quietest ever known in Indianapolis.

Three objects, then, were the aim of the women of Indianapolis — first, to arouse public sentiment; second, to persuade men, by the power of Christianity, to give up the sale and use of intoxicating liquors; and, third, to enforce the Baxter law. To illustrate how successful they were in their first object, a union mass prayer meeting, held early in March in the Academy of Music, was crowded to excess, and upwards of a thousand people were turned away unable to get in. A similar meeting was in progress at the Third Presbyterian church, and was crowded in the same manner. A month before, it would have been difficult to get together a corporal's guard to talk or hear about temperance. Though the movement took a somewhat legal turn, it never for a moment lost its eminently religious character. Every meeting, for whatever purpose called, was opened by prayer, and, in most of the meetings, religious exercises were the chief feature. At present, the organization of the women has reached almost absolute perfection. Its ramifications extend into every ward, street, alley, and house in the city; and so well do the ward associations fulfil their mission, that the men who sign petitions and those who circulate them are getting to be a distinct race. Those engaged in the movement belong to no particular religious sect or political party. Episcopalians and Methodists, Democrats and Republicans, all stand upon a common platform, and battle with a com-

These features, which are so prominent in the capital city, are characteristic, to a greater or less extent, of the work throughout the state. At Lawrenceburg, Union City, Bedford, Madison, Greenfield, Wabash, Warsaw, Lafayette, Kokomo, Logansport, Terre Haute, and in scores of the smaller towns, the praying method and the Baxter law have joined hands. The deficiencies of the one are supplemented by the strong points of the other, and the result is a combination so powerful that few of the saloons can stand up against it. It will require the most persistent watching on the part of the women to see that the demands of the law are fully met; but they have pledged eternal vigilance and prayerfulness, which alone are the price of their liberty. If this work in Indiana is carried forward for a few months longer with the same wisdom and zeal that have characterized it thus far, popular sentiment on the subject of temperance will reach a point where most of the saloon keepers will find it profitable to go out of the business.

CHAPTER XXV.

THE WOMAN'S MOVEMENT IN THE LARGE CITIES. — DIFFERENT CONDITIONS IN CITY AND COUNTRY. — THE EXPERIMENT FIRST TRIED IN DAYTON. — HEROISM OF THE PRAYING BANDS, AND INSULTING CONDUCT OF THE MOB. — EXCITEMENT PRODUCED BY THE CAMPAIGN IN COLUMBUS. — DISCOURAGEMENTS FROM EVERY QUARTER. — PRAYER MEETING IN THE CAPITOL. — HOW THE MUNICIPAL CODE WAS SAVED INTACT. — THE CRUSADE IN CLEVELAND. — CINCINNATI A FORMIDABLE POINT. — THE THREE STAGES OF THE MOVEMENT THERE. — INTENSE OPPOSITION OF THE LIQUOR SELLERS AND GERMANS. — THE CHURCHES PUT TO GOOD USE. — PROCLAMATION OF THE MAYOR, ETC.

EARLY in the progress of this remarkable movement, the problem of the large cities began to excite interest. "The praying plan will do well enough for small towns," people said, "but when it comes to the large cities, — Cincinnati, Cleveland, and Columbus, — why, it's folly to think about it!" On the other hand, many enthusiastic friends of the cause firmly believed that it would triumph everywhere and under all circumstances, and would soon sweep the whole curse of liquor from the land. Then there was a large middle class, who believed that just so far as the movement went, it would do good, and that therefore it was the duty of all to give the women every encouragement, and make the reform extend as far as possible. If it was effective in driving out the saloons and reforming drunkards in the small towns, it would be a great work; and if anything could be done in the cities, there was so much the more to be thankful for.

It will very readily be seen that the conditions of success in a small town and in a large city are very different. In the former, the saloon keeper forms a part of the social fabric, and is more or less dependent on the esteem of his more respectable fellow-citizens. Unless he is on good terms with his neighbors, he is doomed to an isolation that soon becomes positively unendurable. Whiskey sellers are much like other men in human instincts and pride. The taunts thrust by schoolmates upon their children, and the moral aversion of the community to themselves, cut more deeply than is generally supposed. In the city, on the contrary, the saloon keepers are so numerous as to form independent business and social combinations. If the better class of people look down upon them, it makes very little difference with their profits, or enjoyment of life. They are courted and paid by politicians. They are winked at by the authorities. They wear good clothes and drive fine horses, and the pleasures which wealth can purchase amply compensate for all the loss of social prestige.

There are other things which render success less difficult in the country towns. There the women know the character and surroundings of each of the saloon keepers with whom they have to deal, and can therefore approach them more intelligently, and consequently more effectively. The ladies themselves, also, are acquainted with each other, and readily unite in the work. But in the cities, society is divided up into grades and cliques, which can no more combine than oil and water. Ladies hardly know their next-door neighbors, and are always afraid of them until they become well acquainted. Then the ramifications of the liquor interests are so widespread, and have so important an influence in all branches of trade, that business men are afraid to declare their principles. And so it is impossible for temperance men to separate themselves from all restraints, and unite themselves in opposition to the power of whiskey.

In view of all these facts, the friends of the cause awaited the result of the experiment in the cities with beating hearts. It early became apparent that that experiment would be made. Dio Lewis boldly declared that one hundred women from each church, in any city, bound together by the same Christian faith and zeal, would drive out the rum shops just as speedily and as surely as had been done in Washington and Wilmington. God's arm was not shortened, that it could not save big towns as well as small ones, and prayer was just as effective ascending from the stone pavement in the city as from some obscure cross-roads in the country.

The first city of any size to begin the women's crusade was Dayton. The work had just been inaugurated in several cities of intermediate size, such as Xenia, Mt. Vernon, Springfield, &c., when Dio Lewis came there. Dayton is a manufacturing town of about forty thousand inhabitants, laid out in broad, beautiful streets, and built up with substantial residences and business blocks which betoken wealth and luxury. How many of those handsome stone fronts were reared on the tears and groans of widows and orphans, any old citizen can tell. Large distilleries in the city and vicinity have been a prominent source of the wealth concentrated there. Add to this that the people were conservative and aristocratic, and the result would hardly seem favorable for the introduction of the praying plan of overthrowing saloons, of which there were over five hundred.

But the movement was started. A little band of temperance women began to pray together, and it was not long before their numbers and spirit had grown too large to be contained within narrow church walls. A temperance mass meeting was held in Music Hall, presided over by Dio Lewis, and on the next day, February 20, a permanent organization was formed. A vice-president from each church in the city was appointed, who formed a committee for the arrangement of work. It was decided, however, not to move at once upon the saloons, but, by prayer and private endeavor, to make a more thorough preparation for the task of regenerating the morals of the city. After a few days spent in this manner, a number of ladies went quietly, in small committees, to many of the saloons, and gave the proprietors an opportunity to yield gracefully in advance. But there was not much inclination thus to yield. More vigorous measures, therefore, became necessary. After a few more mass meetings and days of prayer, two hundred women were enlisted for active service, and the band felt strong enough for an aggressive move. On the morning of the 6th of March, two companies were designated, under the leadership of Mrs. Weakley and Mrs. J. Harry Thomas, respectively, to visit the saloons. There were twenty-two in each band, and they started out with a firm step; but beneath their water-proof cloaks their hearts throbbed anxiously. The rain was falling steadily, and as the women huddled together under their umbrellas, and offered up their earnest prayers, the crowd recognized their heroism by decorous behavior. Saloon after saloon was visited, services generally being held before the doors; and at last one man, who had a light stock of liquors, offered to surrender if they would pay him first cost. The vile compounds were then emptied into the gutter, amid much rejoicing. In the afternoon the two bands exchanged territory, so that the same saloons received two visits.

The excitement now began to increase. The bands increased in numbers, and more favorable weather brought out great crowds of people to witness the strange spectacle of women actually praying on the streets. The rabble began to grow turbulent and threatening. Saloon keepers saw the matter was putting on a serious aspect, and fought every inch of ground by the most unscrupulous means. It soon came to be known that the visit of the ladies to a saloon meant free beer and whiskey at that place, and there "the boys" rallied in force, like vultures over a dead carcass. The result was, more drunken men on the streets than had been seen since the Fourth of July; and, as if this roundabout warfare was not sufficient, direct insults were heaped upon the ladies. The voices of prayer and song were drowned by those of ribaldry and blasphemy. Bits of bologna and crackers were thrown at the kneeling women, who bore these indignities meekly and with no word of reproof. One of the worst elements in these noisy mobs was the women, mostly of foreign nationalities, who joined their screaming to the shouting and swearing of their male relatives.

The result of this unseemly mocking and jeering was to inflame the public mind, and bring thousands out to the evening mass meetings, where reports of the day's proceedings were read and commented upon. Under such dire persecutions the bands steadily increased in size, and grew more determined. Says a correspondent, —

"The women form for action near the curbstone, and are speedily encompassed by the crowd, who watch with varying manifestations and emotions. Lines of men file into the bars to quench real or affected thirst, and the clink of foaming glasses chimes in with the soft, pathetic notes of the worshipping women. But the plaintive voice of prayer, when the women on bended knees supplicate the mercy of God, produces an instant and indescribable hush even in the bar-rooms; and as the eloquent pleadings ascend, the influence quickly strikes the nearest rank of spectators, and penetrates to the outermost rim of the ragged semicircle formed about them. There are moments, when the women weep and pray, that their influence is thrillingly impressive, and men even who do not approve of the saloon devotions are unconsciously but irresistibly affected. Excepting among the depraved, there is not the remotest suggestion of levity in the scene. It is touchingly solemn."

For nearly a month, operations on this plan continued with little variation. As the novelty wore off, the crowds of spectators decreased somewhat, and the opposition seemed to be dying out. But it still had a most vigorous life; and when, on the 6th of April, the municipal election came on, the work of the bummers was brought to the surface. The whiskey candidate for mayor (Butz) was found to be elected over the temperance candidate (Houk) by a large majority; and whiskey councilmen were put in office, to see that no troublesome McConnelsville ordinance should vex the peace of the saloon keepers. This was taken as a verdict for free whiskey; and next morning, when the women reported at Grace church for active duty, they were astounded by the following proclamation, which emanated from the Board of Police Commissioners: —

WHEREAS it has become apparent to this board that the visits of the recently organized bands of ladies to the various saloons in the city, and the occupation by them of the sidewalks and streets for religious exercises, have, on several occasions, attracted large crowds of riotous and disorderly persons, who assembled in the vicinity in such numbers as seriously to threaten the peace and good order of the city, and materially to obstruct the free and proper use of both the sidewalks and the streets; and,

Whereas it is, by the laws of this state, unlawful for any person or persons, by agent or otherwise,

1. To sell, in any quantity, intoxicating liquors (except wine manufactured of the pure juice of the grape, cultivated in this state, beer, ale, or cider), to be drank in or upon the premises where sold, or in or upon any adjoining premises connected therewith;

2. To sell any intoxicating liquors whatever, without exception, to minors, unless upon the written order of their parents, guardians, or family physician;

3. To sell intoxicating liquors, of any kind whatever, to persons intoxicated, or in the habit of getting intoxicated; and,

Whereas, all places where liquors are sold in violation of these laws are declared public nuisances, and, upon conviction of the keeper thereof, are required to be shut up and abated as such; therefore

Be it known, that orders have been issued to the police force of this city to prevent the use and occupation of the streets and sidewalks as aforesaid, and to give special and careful attention to the enforcement of the said laws, and make prompt arrest of any and all persons violating the same.

By order of the Police Board.

WM. H. SIGMAN,
Mayor and ex officio President Police Board.

A council of war was held, and it was decided best to desist, in deference to the law, but to call upon the authorities to execute the law so appropriately quoted in the latter part of the proclamation. And so, after twenty-five days of unwearied labor in the interest of temperance and humanity, the "crusade" was brought to a sudden end. Operations, however, were by no means suspended. The method was merely changed, and at the present writing the campaign is being vigorously pushed in every direction but that of street "crusading."

In Columbus, the movement passed through a great many critical preliminary stages before it came to street praying. Mention has already been made of the serious obstacles encountered in this city, as the political centre of the state, and of the interest felt in the cause at the capital city, throughout the state. From the first, everything seemed to go wrong. About the middle of February, an immense mass meeting was held under the direction of Dio Lewis; but for some reason the clergymen of the city developed a decided antagonism to the great temperance apostle, and would not work harmoniously with him. Prohibitionists kicked out of the traces because law was not the objective point. The newspapers took grounds against the movement. Prominent citizens withheld their means and influence, and when a man did come to the front, the cry was raised, "It is a woman's movement. Let it alone, or you will spoil it." Bad advice was heaped upon the movers in the work, and bad blood was developed at almost every step.

All this hindered, but did not discourage, the faithful and persistent women. They held their women's meeting, turned out to the mass meetings, and filled the churches when temperance sermons were preached. When the prohibitionists and preachers got into a wrangle, they calmed the troubled waters by a prayer, and one of the soothing old hymns. The women's daily prayer meetings were kept up with increasing interest, and at last, in the face of all discouragements, they decided that the time had come to go forth and grapple with the monster in his very haunts. Without any previous announcement, one hundred and fifty women issued forth from the First Presbyterian church, on the afternoon of the 3d of March; and while the deep-toned bell tolled, took their way, in a long and solemn procession, up High Street. In five minutes it seemed as if half the people in town were on their track to witness the strange sight. The great retail liquor estab-

SINGING OUTSIDE THE SALOON.

lishment of Glock & Stevenson was passed by, and the column came to a halt before the American House, one of the leading hotels in the city. Four ladies — Mrs. S. V. Dessellem, Mrs. H. C. Lewis, Mrs. N. J. Miner, and Mrs. W. W. Bliss ascended the broad steps, and were received in the parlor by the proprietor and his clerks. The bar-keeper was summoned, but no promise to quit could be extracted from him. Two large saloons in the immediate vicinity were entered, and impressive services held. Then the procession filed into the Neil House, and marched back to the office. Neither the proprietor nor bar-keeper was in, and the column moved on, followed by a crowd of two thousand or more. Other places on High and Broad Streets were visited, and the ladies returned to the church to pray and talk the matter over.

The second day of the campaign commenced amid great excitement. The women were upon the streets in increased numbers and with reinvigorated courage. In the afternoon, three hundred of them filed out of the First Presbyterian church, and amid the ringing of bells, moved upon the saloons. The throng of excited spectators increased at every moment, until it was difficult for the police to clear the way before the advancing column. Saloon after saloon was visited. Wherever they were admitted, they prayed and pleaded with the saloon keeper, and when they were shut out, a prayer and song were offered on the steps. The vast crowd surged and crowded about the praying women, and occasionally became noisy and threatening. At length the second day's work was done, and the ladies returned to the church, where continued prayer had been offered up while they were upon the street.

Next day the immense crowds induced a change of programme. The force was divided into four good-sized bands, each going in an opposite direction. During the afternoon, one of the squads encountered a crowd of Germans at a beer saloon on West State Street, who had evidently prepared for their coming. The bar-keeper met the ladies at the door, and refused to sign the pledge. The ladies then began to sing, and immediately a shrill cornet within struck up "Shoo Fly," which was continued, with ingenious variations, all through the prayer. The building was filled with men and women, who yelled and cheered, and even spit upon the kneeling women. The chief of police, who was present, made a speech to the crowd, commanding order. The ladies then moved on to the next saloon, while the able-bodied cornet man sarcastically played, "Home, Sweet Home." As soon as they were gone, the crowd of loafers came together and held a mock prayer meeting, at the conclusion of which all were invited in to drink.

While the ladies were kneeling in prayer at the next place, a beer wagon drove up, and the stalwart German driver shouldered a keg and marched through the circle into the saloon, at which bold achievement the men, women, and children set up an unearthly shouting and screaming. Among the results of the first few days work were one or two saloons closed, and all kinds of liquor banished from the restaurant at the Union Depot. Many signatures were also added to the citizens' pledge, and among them that of James G. Bull, democratic mayor of the city. Many of the men who signed the pledge were notoriously hard drinkers.

This method of operations was continued, day after day, with no marked success. Tremendous mass meetings were held in the great City Hall, and abundant sympathy with the cause was exhibited. But, somehow, it did not prosper. No man of recognized ability and force came forward to champion the movement and secure for it aid and support among the men. There was also no one among the ladies well adapted to the leadership of the forces. Their numbers dwindled from day to day; the excitement subsided; side issues were raised; and within a month the crusade in Columbus was practically at an end. Not many saloonists had quit, but over four thousand persons had signed the total abstinence pledge.

On the 20th of March, one hundred and twenty-five ladies formed in procession and marched to the rotunda of the State House, where they took possession, and sang and prayed for an hour. The members of the General Assembly left the halls of legislation, and formed a circle about the prayer meeting. Hats were removed, and respectful attention paid, but the effect of all this labor upon subsequent legislation was not apparent.

Early in April a bill was introduced into the General Assembly to so amend the municipal code as to take away from town or city corporations the right to prohibit the sale of ale or beer, and the keeping open of tippling houses within their limits. This was known as the Pearson bill, the aim of which was to knock the bottom out of the hundreds of ordinances similar to that of McConnelsville, which were going into effect all over the state, and working such fearful havoc among the saloons.

As soon as this bill was before the House, both parties rallied their forces for the struggle. Delegations of beer venders poured into the capital to see the bill through, and counter delegations of crusaders were sent to preserve the laws intact. Here, again, the Columbus ladies paid their respects to the legislature. When it was known that the bill had come up for discussion, the alarm was given. Bells were rung, and in an hour the hall was filled with female advocates of temperance, who watched the words and vote of every member with exasperating closeness. The bill never passed, and for this the friends of temperance everywhere are indebted to the prompt action of the women of Ohio, and especially of Columbus. On Saturday, the 18th of April, it being the last session of the House, three hundred women staid with the members until midnight, and had the satisfaction of knowing that they had put a quietus on the schemes of the liquor sellers for a year, at least.

Cleveland was seized suddenly by the epidemic, and experienced a violent attack. The city is nearly three times as large as Columbus, and is the seat of a large liquor trade. The inauguration of the "temperance crusade," therefore, stirred the whiskey elements to the lowest dregs. The devotees of Gambrinus learned when the ladies were going to make their first advance, and were on hand in an immense mob to receive them. March 19, four bands started out, one on the east and three on the west side. One of the latter bands, while going up Pearl Street, was followed by a fierce and excited crowd, who assailed them with yells and insulting remarks whenever they attempted to sing or pray. The rabble finally became entirely unmanageable. The ladies were threatened with violence, and one or two of them were quite seriously injured. A number of men who interfered to protect the ladies were severely beaten, and a policeman, in attempting to keep the mob back, was struck on the head with a brick and nearly killed. The ladies, at last, escaped from the howling populace and returned home in safety.

These barbarous demonstrations of course excited indignation in the minds of all good citizens, and many, who had been opposing the movement of the women, were now driven to take sides with them. Neutrality was changed to sympathy, and sympathy grew into support; so that the liquor sellers, next day, found their opponents strengthened, rather than weakened, by the violent treatment they had received. The crusade was renewed with increased numbers. An angry and threatening crowd followed them, and when a policeman attempted to arrest one of a crowd of roughs, a fight ensued, in which the police were obliged to use their clubs vigorously. For a while a riot seemed imminent; but re-enforcements from the police headquarters prevented an outbreak. During the excitement the German brewers organized a procession of lager beer wagons, in which sat men on beer kegs, drinking as they moved along.

That same night both parties to this irrepressible conflict were warned by a proclamation from Mayor Otis to "abstain from all such assemblages on the streets of the city as would tend to disturb the peace of the community, as such assemblies were in direct violation of an ordinance of the city." It was announced that if any attempted to molest citizens in the orderly exercise of lawful rights, whether in the streets or elsewhere, it would be at their own peril. This ambiguous document, like Belshazzar's warning, or a Delphic oracle, had to be interpreted before it could be determined to whom it applied. The judge of one of the courts came to the rescue, and decided that the mayor could legally prohibit the assembling of the ladies to pray on the street before a saloon; but if they were admitted inside, the laws of the city could no longer reach them, and they could carry on their devotions untrammelled by law.

With this lucid exposition of legal restrictions as a guide, the ladies went on with the visitation of saloons. The mayor's proclamation was strictly observed. Wherever they could persuade a dram seller or liquor merchant to let them in, they prayed and sang, and pleaded with him to give up the business; but where they were denied admittance, they passed quietly on. The proclamation and the emphatic expression of public sentiment in favor of protecting the ladies, had the effect to allay the excitement, and prevent any further demonstrations of violence. Some of the wholesale liquor establishments on Water Street allowed the crusaders to come in, and for a while the voices of prayer rose on the air with the fumes of rye and Bourbon.

For several weeks this plan of operations was kept up; but owing to the restricted field of labor, the ladies found that little could be accomplished beyond obtaining names to the citizens' pledge, and exerting an influence privately. Popular interest subsided as the novelty wore off, and at last the beer jerkers were allowed to carry on their avocation unmolested by praying women.

Cincinnati was a point which the crusaders hesitated to attack. It loomed up before them as an impenetrable barrier to their complete success. The general belief was, that the women would not be rash enough to attempt any movement with the country plan of praying in saloons. If they should, people predicted the gravest consequences to the peace and good order of the city. Even the most sanguine friends of temperance trembled for the result of the battle, when they made a survey of the field. To begin with, there were between three thousand and three thousand five hundred regular places where liquor was sold. There were scores of heavy wholesale houses, the aggregate annual trade of which amounted to thirty-three million dollars, or more than double the value of the immense pork trade of the city. Millions of capital were invested in this vast business. The money made by the breweries and distilleries built scores of massive business blocks and elegant private residences. Banks and business men were largely dependent on whiskey money for the conduct of their trade. Many of the wealthiest men in the city were whiskey dealers, and their rank in society was high.

Then, too, the habits and sentiments of the people were not a pleasant subject of contemplation for a temperance reformer. One third of the population were Germans, educated to the use of beer and wine from their youth up. Every movement in the interest of temperance was regarded by them as an interference with their personal rights, and an abbreviation of the liberties which they were led to expect in coming to this land. Those who entertained opposite views were looked upon as Puritans, fanatics, and bigots. To change all this condition of affairs would seem like overturning the very foundation of things. Social drinking among Americans, also, was quite prevalent. The wealthy and aristocratic families in the city and suburbs had their cellars stocked with choice wines and liquors, which figured conspicuously in the hospitalities of the house. Prominent business men, lawyers, physicians, and politicians took their occasional or regular dram, as they had done for years. Young men, with plenty of money, consumed vast quantities of choice drinks at the high-toned places; while in the common beer saloons gathered thousands of laboring men and mechanics, to spend, for beer and whiskey, a good share of their weekly earnings. Well authenticated cases are cited of industrious Germans who spent regularly a full half of their pay for their daily supply of barley juice.

So much for one side of the picture. What was there on the other? A few hundred men and women, who realized the terrible evils of intemperance; about twelve thousand church members, who could generally be counted on the side of temperance, though some of them rented property to liquor sellers; a carefully elaborated state law, which was as dead as though it had been enacted in China; and perhaps what was more than all, the inspiriting example of the scores of small towns throughout the state, reports from which crowded the daily press. To inaugurate the woman's temperance crusade on such a basis, to all human calculation, seemed the height of presumption. But it was done, and at the present writing (late in April) the movement is still in progress.

The honor of taking the initiatory step belongs to the ministers of the Methodist Episcopal church, which has led the van in so many great moral reforms. At their Monday morning meeting, about the first of March, these clerical gentlemen unanimously decided that the spiritual and temporary interests of society demanded a great temperance reformation, and indorsed the woman's movement as the best means of effecting this great work. A call was made for a meeting of the ministers of all denominations, which took place on the following morning. A large number of clerical gentlemen of all stripes of belief were present. Views were interchanged, and plans proposed, and the result of the meeting was to unanimously determine upon a mass meeting of friends of the woman's temperance movement, to be held at Wesley chapel, on Thursday evening following. A committee of two from each denomination represented was appointed to make arrangements for the meeting, and prepare rules for its government. The mass meeting was largely attended. Many came out of pure love for the cause, and many others from motives of curiosity, expecting that a crusade was to be organized at once. Speeches were made by a number of women, ministers, and citizens generally, all of whom with one voice called upon the women of Cincinnati to organize and push forward the work begun by their sisters throughout the state. It was decided to appoint a woman's meeting next day at three o'clock, at the First Presbyterian church, and the assemblage broke up in a glow of enthusiasm.

The woman's meeting was attended by about three hundred. They were not from the wealthy and aristocratic classes of society; nor did they represent the opposite extreme. They were well-to-do, intelligent, thoughtful ladies, many of whom had been prominent in charitable and Christian enterprises. There were also a few among them whose plain garb and pale, sad faces told the story of personal sufferings from the evil they longed to suppress. The burden of their prayers was, that they might be guided with wisdom, that every word might be spoken in love and gentleness, and that only the spirit of kindness might prevail in their efforts with the liquor sellers. A deep feeling of earnestness and piety prevailed. The only business done was to appoint a committee of six ladies to have charge of the organization of a league. The names of all those who would volunteer for personal service were enrolled, and made a lengthy list.

Then followed a series of temperance mass meetings, held in the evenings at the principal churches. Popular interest in the cause was exhibited by the hundreds and thousands of persons who flocked in to these meetings, and listened eagerly to every word that was said for temperance. At the second regular mass meeting, the wholesale druggists of the city, through Mr. Burdsal, reported that they had voluntarily agreed to sell no spirituous liquors except to physicians and druggists, and not to them when there was any reason to believe it would be used as a beverage. One of the hotels — the Henrie House — also reported that its bar should be ever thereafter discontinued; and that, to this day, bears the honorable distinction of being the only "temperance hotel" in the great city of Cincinnati.

This era of mass meetings continued, unmarked by any special incident, until the 10th of March, when D. M. Bleaks, keeper of an extensive saloon on Fourth Street, near Plum, and formerly chief of police, surrendered, on solicitation of a couple of ladies who went quietly to him with the request to close. This gave much encouragement to the women about entering upon the great work. It was, after mature deliberation, decided best not to begin at once with the visitation of saloons by large bands, but to go in separate committees of two or three, and talk privately with the liquor sellers. To facilitate the work, the city was divided into twenty districts, each embracing about six squares. Two ladies were appointed to have charge of each district, the understanding being that they should first canvass their territory thoroughly, and plead with the liquor sellers to yield.

This visitation by committees was properly the first stage of the street work in Cincinnati. The first day they started out in this manner, there was a tremendous sensation. As the two or three elderly ladies passed quietly along the street, arm in arm, the cry of, "Temperance women," was raised, and soon they found themselves in the midst of a dense crowd of women, children, and rowdies, who howled and surged about them as though they were an invading army, or some wonderful show on wheels, instead of a couple of weak and inoffensive women. Some of the committees experienced more difficulty than others; but all were treated in the most barbarous and insulting manner, and received scarcely a word of encouragement from any one. It was a weary and thankless task, and, when day after day of this trying labor brought no results, it was determined to adopt some more effective plan.

By this time organization had been more thoroughly

completed. Advisory and executive committees were appointed, to have entire control of the plans and movements of the league. The following officers wers elected for permanent service: President, Mrs. Chas. Ferguson; First Vice-President, Mrs. W. H. Malone; Second Vice-President, Mrs. W. H. Allen; First Secretary, Mrs. E. L. Johnston; Second Secretary, Mrs. E. G. Dalton; Treasurer, Mrs. Dr. E. Williams.

One incident that occurred early in the campaign gave a new impulse to the movement. The brewers of Cincinnati loaded up wagons with beer, organized a force of five or six hundred able-bodied Germans, and marched to the relief of the saloon keepers in the adjoining town of Madisonville, who were besieged with the temperance band. When the ladies assembled in the church, the Cincinnati crowd, by concerted action, formed before the door, and with music and beer thought to break up the proceedings. Not succeeding, they began to pour into the church, to overawe the few feeble women inside. But fortunately several German ministers from Cincinnati were present, and preached the gospel of Christianity and temperance to the intruders in a manner wholly unlooked for. The scene was dramatic and impressive; and so well did the women and ministers improve their opportunity, that some of those who came to scoff were actually moved to tears. Mrs. Wells, a remarkable little woman, who afterwards attained quite a reputation for her pure and simple eloquence, did most effective service at this crisis. The effort to overawe Madisonville ladies was a failure, but it aroused the Cincinnati ladies to the necessity of giving their liquor sellers and drinkers enough to occupy their attention at home.

The second stage of the work in Cincinnati was the crusade, after the approved country style. The plan of visitation by committees was given a fair trial, and found to be wholly ineffective. It was necessary either to abandon the movement altogether, or else rally more strength, and visit the saloons in bands of sufficient size to command some respect. The latter plan was immediately adopted. Subordinate leagues began to be organized in different parts of the city, and the change of tactics gave new life to the mass meetings which were still regularly continued. The street crusade was fairly inaugurated on the morning of March 26, when thirty-five women arose from their knees in the Ninth Street Baptist church, and volunteered to go with Mrs. Ferguson to one of the fashionable Fourth Street saloons. It was known as the "Custom House," and was situated next door to the Merchants' Exchange. The time chosen for the visit was about half past eleven o'clock—just the hour when the business men on 'Change were wont to step in next door to "take something." The band of women descended upon the place so suddenly that some of the honorable merchants who were inside had no chance to escape, and were compelled to sit for half an hour and listen to the praying and singing. They would have given several barrels of pork apiece to have been able to crawl through a knot-hole; but they were fairly caught, and put on a bold front.

The news of this sudden raid spread through that part of the city, and in a few minutes the whole square from Main to Walnut Street was packed full with people, stretching their necks in a crazy endeavor to catch a glimpse of the women behind the green shade. The services over, they were invited to come again next day; which invitation they promptly accepted. They then pressed their way out through the crowd, and returned to the church, where prayer had been offered up constantly while they were out.

Four other bands, numbering from thirty to sixty each, went out the same day, exciting the greatest commotion in their respective districts. The one which attempted some missionary work in the German beer saloons on Freeman Street met with the most shameful treatment. The crowd rushed in pell-mell after them, mounting chairs, tables, and each other's backs, and keeping up a continuous shouting, yelling, and laughing. When the ladies in one part of the room began the sweet strain, "Rock of Ages," the Germans struck up "Die Wacht am Rhein," and the two choruses mingled together strangely on the air.

The scene next day near the Merchants' Exchange was more exciting than the first. A crowd of two or three thousand persons surged and swayed about the little nucleus of praying women, who were refused admittance to the saloon, and held services on the walk in front. Amid the yells of the mob, and the cries of "Keep back" from the policemen, rose the fervent, eloquent prayers of Mrs. Ferguson, Mrs. Leavitt, Mrs. Glenn, and Mrs. Stewart, and the strains of the well-known hymns could be heard above all the noise and commotion. The proprietor of the saloon mounted a curb-stone, and addressed the thirsty crowd with, "This way, gentlemen; walk in and get your drinks; there goes another fifteen cents." The excitement increased, and the pushing and jostling of the crowd made many tremble for the safety of the dauntless band.

A lieutenant of the police appeared on the scene, and said, "For God's sake, ladies, stop this! you will create a riot!" A scissors-grinder, who had been hired to go through the crowd ringing his bell, was stopped, when he came near the ladies, by some man. A fight ensued, and the scissors-grinder was arrested. Another man, who tried to create a disturbance, was arrested, but, at the urgent solicitation of the ladies, was released by the authorities.

In Fulton — a remote corner of the city, lying far up the river — the crusade was begun early, and prosecuted with vigor, squads of ladies going out daily in street cars from the city to re-enforce the little band. Their labors were rewarded, after a few days, with the first, and almost the only, "pouring out" during the whole course of the movement in Cincinnati. Richard Manley, who kept a beer saloon and billiard-room on Front Street, broke in upon the hymn they were singing one morning, with, "Hold on a minute — I'll give up." He then told the ladies that his whole stock was at their disposal, and that he himself would help to throw the vile stuff into the street. With beaming faces the ladies rolled out the beer barrels, knocked out the fawcets, and sent the contents reeking through the gutters. The bottles upon the shelves were brought out, and dashed upon the pavement, before the eyes of the gaping crowd that stood about. After the saloon had been emptied of everything that could moisten the throat, or make glad the heart of man, the proprietor thought of some fine old Catawba, stored away in the cellar. This was soon hunted up, and shared the fate of the rest, the conscience-stricken saloonist saying, if he owned all the liquor between there and Columbia, the women might have the whole of it.

This campaign of active street work was just beginning to bear promising fruits, when it received a sudden and unlooked-for check at the hands of the mayor. The bands of women were increasing in numbers, and the rabble was gradually diminishing in numbers and growing less dangerous, when Mayor Johnston, at the instance of the Board of Aldermen, sent in to one of the morning meetings, about the last of March, a quasi-proclamation. He "respectfully urged that the women would desist from any further interference with the rights and privileges of the business community, and adopt some other mode of accomplishing their desires, which was not so objectionable." His imperative duty demanded of him the enforcement of the ordinances with which the ladies had come into collision. The document created quite a commotion, and was at once referred to the Advisory Committee, with instructions to consult with lawyers upon the questions involved, and report at the next meeting. The decision of the committee was, to abide scrupulously by the ordinances of the city, and cease praying upon the streets; but to call upon the mayor, in turn, to enforce *all* the ordinances. They argued that a technical trespass of theirs should not be dealt with more severely than the open and constant violations of the law on the part of the saloon keepers.

Then began the third stage in the movement. In response to inquiry as to what they might do, the mayor had told the women they might meet in the public squares of the city, and pray all they liked, or even in the saloons, if the proprietors were willing to admit them. Here the ladies saw an opportunity for usefulness, and were prompt to avail themselves of it. The bands continued, as before, to meet in the Ninth Street Baptist church in the morning, and in the afternoon to send forth from the headquarters of the various leagues as many volunteers as were available. These bands went to the market spaces and public squares in their district, and there preached the gospel of temperance and Christianity to the crowds that gathered. Saloons were called at on the way to and from these services; but the liquor sellers, as if by concerted action, uniformly refused them admittance, and they passed on, without infringing on the majesty of the law.

The labors of the day ended, the bands took their way

back to the church from which they started out, great crowds of the unwashed following at their heels. The doors of the church were thrown open, and the street rabble rushed in, filling all available space. This was probably the most successful feature of this stage of the work in Cincinnati. In these meetings, men, women, and children heard the gospel of peace who had never been inside of a church before. One young man, who was thus led in, acknowledged to the ladies that it was the first time he had ever heard the story of Christ. Pledges were always ready at the desk, and hundreds — almost thousands — of men and boys, in the course of these meetings, voluntarily walked forward and took upon themselves the pledge of total abstinence. Some failed to keep it, and yielded to subsequent temptations; but many did not, and now bless the "praying women" for their deliverance from the terrible curse of intemperance. Among the leagues which did the most effective service in this direction, was that having its headquarters at Finley chapel, and led by Mrs. S. K. Leavitt, Mrs. Alfred Hill, and others; that of the Ninth Street Baptist church, in which Mrs. Whitredge, Mrs. Ferguson, and Mrs. Dr. Dalton were prominent; that of St. Paul's Methodist Episcopal church, led by Mrs. Glenn and Mrs. Bishop Clark; that of York Street, headed by Mrs. Hudelson, Mrs. Robbins, Mrs. Moore, and others; and that of Wesley chapel, in which Mrs. W. I. Fee and Mrs. George B. Beecher took an active part. These bands varied in size from day to day, but were generally all on the streets at the same time, and numbered in the aggregate from one hundred and twenty to two hundred and fifty.

At the present writing this method of operations is still observed. The authorities having shown no disposition to enforce the ordinances of the city against saloon keepers, the ladies do not adhere strictly to the mayor's orders, but sing and pray wherever the spirit moves them. Generally, however, devotional exercises are confined to the market-places, and the infringements upon the sacred rights of saloon keepers are of short duration, and somewhat rare occurrence. What the next stage of the movement will be, it is impossible to predict. It still has a strong and vigorous life, which is a sufficient guarantee that, in some form or other, its influence will be felt for years. But the test has been applied, and it cannot be denied that for the redemption of large cities from whiskey, the woman's movement is a failure.

CHAPTER XXVI.

THE MOVEMENT IN THE EAST. — ON THE PACIFIC COAST. — IN THE SOUTH AND WEST. — WORCESTER THE TRIAL POINT IN NEW ENGLAND. — THE WESTERN PLAN DISCARDED. — THE INTEREST IN NEW YORK CITY. — INFLUENCE OF THE CRUSADE FELT IN CONGRESS. — DESCENT UPON THE MARYLAND LEGISLATURE. — GREAT RESULTS IN PHILADELPHIA. — DISGRACEFUL SCENE IN CHICAGO. — IN GENERAL.

It is hardly an exaggeration to say that, within three months from the time the first prayer was made in the streets of Hillsboro', the Woman's Temperance Movement had spread over the entire country. The temperance columns of the daily papers, in a single day, contained despatches from Kansas and California on the west, from New York and Massachusetts on the east, and from Michigan and Wisconsin on the north, while even the Southern States gave evidence of an awakened interest in the subject. But the farther the movement got from its source, the less it seemed to have of its original force and vitality. As the originator of the plan was wont to observe, the Ohio Valley was about the only soil in which the thing would grow. In other states it took on new and strange forms, and generally, after passing rapidly from one experiment to another, died out after a few weeks' agitation.

Considerable interest was excited in the success of the movement in the East, where temperance legislation for the past twenty years has been so prominent a subject in politics and morals. In the course of his second tour through Ohio, Dio Lewis announced that he was about to return to inaugurate the work in Massachusetts, and declared his belief that Worcester could throw off the horrid incubus in three weeks, and Boston in as many months. For various reasons, Worcester was selected as the first point of attack. A mass meeting was held on the evening of March 2, under the direction of Dio Lewis. There can be no doubt that the meeting was a success. Many went there with positive prejudices against the praying plan, and many others without the least confidence in its success; but Dr. Lewis worked with such peculiar tact, and told the story of the crusade in Ohio with such good effect, that the whole audience soon reached a state of enthusiasm that was a surprise to themselves. It was soon apparent that there were several hundred women in the audience ready for vigorous work. The signs were so encouraging that the over-sanguine orator predicted that within two weeks the thirstiest man in Worcester must drink water, or go dry. But then came a two days' season of debate and deliberation, during which the warmth of their enthusiasm cooled off very perceptibly. After talking the matter over long and earnestly, it was decided to be impracticable for the conservative East to adopt the peculiar method of the unconventional West, and a compromise was agreed upon. Instead of praying in saloons until the keepers would close up, the women determined to go in smaller bands, and work by private and personal appeal, not only with the liquor seller, but with the owner of the property which was rented for the sale of liquor. Hotel keepers and druggists were to be proceeded with in a similar way.

This mode of operations, it will be perceived, was in marked contrast with the Ohio way of doing things, and yet it was an indication of a deep and genuine temperance revival. Eastern people generally approved the plan as much better than that of marching through the streets in large bands; and it was generally believed in the West that the Ohio plant would not bear transplantment into a climate so uncongenial. This, then, practically settled the question, not only for Worcester and Central Massachusetts, but also for all New England. No doubt some good has been accomplished by the method of operations chosen; but there have been no reports of surrenders of saloon keepers, or of any pouring out of liquors. Boston was left to enjoy her thirty-five hundred dram shops in security, and the prediction of Dio Lewis went unfulfilled. The refined tastes of New England could not tolerate such Western vulgarisms.

Boston, however, deserves the credit of some good resolutions. The next day after the Worcester meeting, the Total Abstinence Society of Boston passed the following: —

"*Resolved*, That inasmuch as the women and children are the chief sufferers of the untold evils of intemperance, it is eminently appropriate that the female sex should take the most active part in the efforts of the day for the suppression of this universally acknowledged immorality; and we look with deep interest on the women's movement in regard to temperance reform, and cherish the hope that a divine Providence will direct and rule over it for good.

"*Resolved*, That, in the opinion of this board, no great success in the temperance reform can be expected till the Christian church and ministry take a decided stand on the side of total abstinence."

Dio Lewis first appeared in New York city on the last day of February. Very little temperance excitement had preceded him, and the mass meeting at Association Hall was not an astounding success. An admission fee was charged, although Dio Lewis gave his services free. Nothing was done at that meeting, or indeed at any subsequent time, towards an organized crusade, on Western principles. The general influence of the revival in other parts of the country, however, took a strong hold on the popular mind. Vicar-General Turner, at St. James Cathedral, in Brooklyn, a week later, referred to the temperance movement, and urged his congregation to give it all the aid in their power. This is one of the few instances in which the crusade was sanctioned by high authority in the Catholic church. The agitation of the question in the city was continued for a month or more, in a variety of ways. Once or twice, a small number of ladies in Brooklyn quietly began a saloon visitation, but this phase of the work never grew into any prominence. Meetings of clergymen and friends of the cause were held from time to time, and the customary resolutions passed, reciting the evils of intemperance, and the necessity for some action for their suppression.

At a meeting held in the Hanson Street Methodist church, on the evening of March 12, Dio Lewis took charge for five minutes, in true Western style. He called for all the men who believed in Christian women and their work to get up. Hundreds jumped to their feet, while applause shook the house. He next called for the women who thought intemperance a curse, and who were willing to help rid the country of it, to rise. A multitude of women were on their feet instantly. He then called for all the men and women who were ready to unite in the work to get up, whereupon nearly the whole audience arose, amid great enthusiasm. Dr. Lewis pronounced it "magnificent." The Rev. Dr. Steel, jumping up, said, "It is magnetic;" while the Rev. Dr. Fulton, walking up and down the platform, cried, "Glorious! glorious!" But, as far as heard from, nothing ever came of it.

Strange as it may sound, the influence of this temperance movement was felt even in the halls of Congress. On the 2d of March, Judge Lawrence, of Ohio, introduced into the house a bill which provides that in the territories of the United States, and in the District of Columbia, every husband, wife, child, parent, guardian, or other person who shall be injured in person, property, or means of support, by any intoxicating liquor, in person, or in consequence of the intoxication, habitual or otherwise, of any person, shall have the right of action, in his or her own name, against any person or persons who shall, by selling or giving intoxicating liquor, have caused intoxication, in whole or in part, of such person or persons, for all damages sustained and exemplary damages; and the owner or lessee, or person or persons, renting or leasing any building, or persons having knowledge that intoxicating liquors are to be, or are being, sold thereon, or who shall knowingly permit intoxicating liquors to be sold in such building or premises, shall be liable for all such damages, severally or jointly, &c.; all of which is substantially the Ohio Adair law transplanted into national legislation.

The following, partaking somewhat of the nature of a joke, was presented to the Senate, March 18, by Senator Carpenter himself. The letter was referred to the Committee on Finance, and ordered "to be printed."

NEW YORK CITY, March 18, 1874.

To Senator Carpenter, President of the Senate:

As the tidal wave of the temperance crusade will soon reach Washington, on behalf of the army of women who are alive to the movement, we ask you to join our ranks. Your high position, your well-known eloquence, and your championship of women, mark you as a man to step to the front. We want you and Senators Chandler and Sprague to inform the committee to receive our praying band at the bar of the Senate. Congress is beginning to recognize this leading reform. The bill just passed to investigate drunkenness proves this. Will you read this appeal to the Senate, asking permission to receive our band under the escort of your chaplain?

Yours, in behalf of the crusaders,

MRS. P. R. LAWRENCE.

About a week later a mass meeting was held, under the auspices of Dio Lewis, at which General Leggett, Commissioner of Patents, was one of the principal speakers. Meetings of clergymen were also held on various occasions, but nothing resembling the woman's praying movement was attempted in the city of Washington.

Annapolis, the quiet seat of the Maryland legislature, received a visitation of women about the middle of March, much in the Western style. A bill was before the legislature to allow townships and wards to determine for themselves whether they should allow liquor to be sold within their limits — in other words, a local option law. Baltimore became interested in the question. An immense meeting was held in favor of the proposed measure, and, shortly after, a delegation of one hundred ladies started by steamer for the capital city, to present a memorial to the legislature in favor of local option. When the steamer arrived, the House was in session, and the ladies were furnished with seats in the lobbies. Shortly after, the House, in order to rid itself of the crusaders, adjourned, and most of the members left the hall. The ladies then took possession, sang a hymn and the doxology, and adjourned themselves. The memorial was then presented to the Senate, where it was received and read. Shortly after the adjournment of the House, a brass band appeared to serenade the ladies; but their attentions were cut short by order of the President of the Senate. A temperance mass meeting was then held in the hall of the Capitol; and soon after, the ladies returned to Baltimore by the steamer.

The Pacific coast was not exempt from visitation by the temperance revival. A regular, organized crusade was entered upon by the women of San Francisco early in March. Their visits were mainly confined to corner groceries where liquor was sold; and in a few days six of these were reported closed, as far as the whiskey business was concerned. The women also appeared before the Board of Supervisors, and presented a petition for an increase of the licenses paid by the liquor sellers. Mayor Otis gave his indorsement to the movement soon after it was begun, and wished the ladies success in all their efforts against intemperance. But the most unique feature of the movement in California was a bill passed by the General Assembly, making it a misdemeanor for a person to accept an invitation, or invite another, to drink at a public bar.

In Pittsburg, Pa., the ladies organized, and pushed forward the work with considerable energy. Many other towns in Western Pennsylvania became aroused, and inaugurated the street praying movement. In Ithaca, Lockport, Elmira, and a large number of cities and villages in Western New York, the temperance revival was, for weeks, the all-absorbing topic. From Iowa, Minnesota, and Michigan, reports came of the same work going on. Even from Louisiana came words of congratulation and encouragement to the "noble Christian women, throughout the country, in their uprising against the gigantic vice of the age." In Leavenworth, Kansas, the men went with the women to pray in the saloons, and consequently the whole party was very badly treated.

In Philadelphia, the work was begun quietly, and carried forward with very little noise, but a great work was accomplished. The saloon keepers took the alarm, and were advised by the Supreme Council of the Liquor Dealers' Association to close all their dram shops on Sunday. Some twenty, who failed to heed this injunction, were arrested by the police, and heavily fined. If reports are to be trusted, the labors of the women were rewarded with greater results in Philadelphia than in any other large city. At a temperance meeting held in Horticultural Hall about the middle of April, the following statement was made by Mrs. Dr. Elizabeth J. French, regarding the great work which had been going on. It took the outside public, and even the Philadelphians themselves, by surprise.

Saloons visited,	406
Refused admission to,	2
Expelled from,	7
Church members who had rented property for saloons, agreeing to rent them no more,	38
Churches opened to the "band,"	212
" refused,	2
Saloons closed,	367
Pledges signed by saloon keepers,	281
" " " bar keepers who resigned,	80
" " " drunkards,	1,613
Children sent to Sunday school,	411
Converted,	200
Members of the praying band,	24,870

Chicago developed more fierceness and bitter hostility between the two factions — or, at least, on one side — than any other of the large cities in which the work was commenced. The women began visiting saloons early in March; but this method of operations met with intense opposition from the saloon keepers and their adherents, and was at length abandoned, without having produced any marked results. Efforts in the cause were not, however, wholly given up. The whiskey element having attained the ascendency in city politics, a proposition was made in the City Council to repeal the Sunday saloon-closing ordinance. This aroused the whole body of women who were at all interested in the temperance cause; and, on the afternoon of the 15th of March, five hundred of them met at the Clark Street Methodist church. One hundred of the number were appointed a committee to present to the Council a remonstrance, signed by sixteen thousand women of the city; and while they were out on their mission, the rest remained in the church to pray. On their way to the City Hall, the delegation was followed by a constantly increasing crowd of men and boys, which became almost a mob before they reached the doors of the Council Chamber.

The ladies were allowed to come in, and their memorial placed on file; but the repeal ordinance was passed, in their very faces, by a vote of twenty-two to fourteen. Then came the trying ordeal. The defeated ladies rose to depart, headed by a posse of police, who strove to break a way through the howling and groaning mob, who assailed them as they passed with the foulest epithets. The ladies, who were the wives and daughters of the most respected citizens, hid their faces in their hands, and hurried on through the gantlet of filth. A reporter of a morning paper thus described the scene: —

"But when the open air was gained, the situation in no wise improved. Egress was had by the door in the rear leading to the alley next to the Grand Pacific. Thousands were crammed into this space — a howling menagerie. The police cleared the sidewalk, but the crowd lined the verge, and poured a volley of blasphemy and obscenity at the procession of ladies. When Lá

Salle Street was reached, other thousands were awaiting their approach, and these howled even louder than those who greeted them in the alley. The noise was positively hideous; and this hooting, yelling, blasphemous mob, and five thousand roughs, the very offscourings of the saloons, flanked and followed them clear to the door of the church. Jostling them on the way; spitting tobacco juice on their dresses; pulling at their chignons; in some cases tripping them up; knocking off the hats of their escorts, — brothers, husbands, or sons, — giving the latter kicks, cuffs, and digs in the ribs; and all the while the hooting, yelling, howling continued, and not infrequently members of the procession would sink to the ground, swooning from very fright."

The Chicago Times, in speaking editorially of this disgraceful affair, used the following vigorous language: —

"The onset of a howling mob of ruffians upon a committee of respectable ladies that visited the Council Chamber last Monday night, to remonstrate against the repeal of the Sunday tippling law, cannot be characterized in the terms of condemnation that it deserves. It was the most vile and disgraceful demonstration of the spirit of ruffianism ever witnessed in this city. Probably not another city in any civilized country on the globe has ever witnessed, in time of peace, a performance so unspeakably brutal. An invading army of barbarians, licensed to commit any manner of outlawry, could hardly have exhibited towards a body of decent and well-behaved women a more disgusting temper of diabolism. It was the outspew of the slums, and groggeries, and brothels; it was the grand army of pimps, loafers, blacklegs, thieves, and drunken roughs, marshalled to defend scoundrelism and indecency against the protest of virtue. The ruffianly conduct of the performers was certainly worthy of their thoroughly brutal-

It would be impossible, within the limits of an ordinary volume, to give anything like an adequate review of the woman's movement in half of the towns and cities where it was inaugurated. And the story, if told, would only be a repetition of the same features, with merely a change of incidents and surroundings. The writer has aimed to present, as briefly as possible, an outline of the work in the most prominent cities, and in the smaller towns in Ohio, where the movement first attracted the attention of the country. Each peculiar phase has been described but once, although it may have appeared at many of the points referred to. The full history of this remarkable temperance revival cannot be written until the movement has subsided, and time enough has elapsed to allay the excitement, and trace out the main influences set at work to their results. The two following chapters will supplement this review of the external features of the movement by giving some insight into the spirit and purposes of those most actively engaged in it.

CHAPTER XXVII.

LICENSE VS. PROHIBITION. — THE PROHIBITIONISTS TRY TO CAPTURE THE WOMAN'S MOVEMENT. — LICENSE VIGOROUSLY OPPOSED BY THE LADIES. — THE FIRST GRAND CONVENTION IN COLUMBUS. — PROHIBITION STATE CONVENTION AT MT. VERNON. — SECOND WOMAN'S CONVENTION. — MASS MEETINGS IN CINCINNATI FOR AND AGAINST LICENSE. — GRAND WOMAN'S ANTI-LICENSE CONVENTION IN CINCINNATI.

THE woman's movement had not proceeded far before the old controversy regarding license and prohibition was renewed with fresh interest. The prohibitionists, who had been a steadily increasing political party in Ohio for several years, made an early attempt to capture the movement and appropriate its results. They had been vainly striving for years to accomplish by law what the women were now doing by moral force. They saw the important bearing of the new reform upon their efforts, and promptly came forward to further the cause and carry it in their arms. This disposition was apparent in the first convention, at Columbus, where an attempt was made to set the two factions, of workers by prayer and workers by legal force, by the ears. The latter, however, claimed to be in full sympathy with the gospel method, only they wanted to supplement it with a little law. They were anxious to hitch on the praying movement as a powerful auxiliary to their struggling political party.

But the women refused to form any entangling alliances. They hoped to conquer by love, and not by force; but if they failed, and had to resort to harsher measures, there were already sufficient laws lying idle on the statute-book to break up nine tenths of the saloons in the state, if once carried into execution. Whatever motives or feelings may have been developed later in the progress of the movement, the ladies, in its early stages, as a rule, never thought of law, or politics, or woman's rights. They worked with an eye single to the suppression of intemperance, and that by moral means. As to the right of women to vote, and of the state to govern individual action by prohibiting every man from selling liquor, the ladies paid not the slightest heed, so that they were not easily hitched on to the prohibition car. Dio Lewis, when asked for his advice, placed himself in square opposition to prohibition. It had failed, he said, utterly, in Boston, and the question could only work mischief if introduced at that stage of affairs in the woman's movement.

The question of license, also, soon grew into prominence. But whereas the ladies generally refused to have anything to do with prohibition, they were not slow in giving emphatic expression to their sentiments against license. The progress of the controversy on these points, however, may be better traced by a brief review of the principal mass meetings and conventions held, pro and con.

The first general convention was held in Columbus, February 24. It was called by Dio Lewis, without any reference to license or prohibition, but simply as a means of interchanging experiences and congratulations, and establishing a uniform basis of operations throughout the state, where the movement had been begun. It was held in the City Hall, and attended by not less than fifteen hundred delegates, mostly women, from the various fields of labor. The general tone, as well as the results of the convention, are summed up in the following platform, which was unanimously adopted: —

"*Resolved*, That the success of the Ohio woman's movement in behalf of the temperance reform has given us substantial assurance that the traffic in and use of intoxicating drinks can and will be removed from the state and nation.

"*Resolved*, That in the prosecution of this work we rely on divine assistance, secured through fervent, persistent, and importunate prayers to Almighty God, offered in faith in the Lord Jesus Christ, and with hearts filled with love for souls.

"*Resolved*, That faithful and persistent prayer must, as an inevitable result, be accompanied by efficient, personal, and organized work.

"*Resolved*, That, in addition to contributions of money, generously and freely given, it is recommended to the men aiding in the woman's effort to suppress intemperance in our communities, and to the women who carry on the work, to avoid all envy, hatred, malice, and uncharitableness, bitterness of speech, and denunciation of the men engaged in the liquor traffic; to cultivate their acquaintance and kindly feeling, and by all honorable and practicable means to assist them to change from a business injurious to society, to some other calling remunerate to themselves and beneficial to the community.

(Signed)

MRS. E. D. STEWART, MRS. M. W. BANES,
SARAH POLLARD, C. M. NICHOLS,
MISS LIZZIE T. MCFADDEN, H. S. FULLERTON,
MRS. H. J. SHARP, J. M. RICHMOND,

Committee.

Two days later, the regular State Convention of the Prohibition Party was held in Mt. Vernon. Of course the woman's movement formed the principal subject for consideration. No one opposed it, but, as the last of the following resolutions will show, they were not willing to leave it to itself: —

"Whereas the manufacture, sale, and consumption of intoxicating liquors is in open violation of the law of God, and antagonistic to the moral, social, and political well-being of society; and

"Whereas the Christian women of Ohio are seeking to eradicate this evil by the instrumentality of prayer to Almighty God, and Christian, womanly entreaty with liquor sellers against their destructive traffic; therefore,

"*Resolved*, That we, as delegates to the State Convention of the Prohibition Party of Ohio, in convention assembled, do hereby congratulate the noble self-sacrificing women of Ohio in their success, and assure them of our sympathy and co-operation with them, and all other agencies of the temperance reform.

"*Resolved*, That we will not only unite our prayers with our sisters to Almighty God, but we will call upon our brothers in Ohio to assist in making permanent the benefits of this moral uprising by the execution of law against all engaged in the liquor traffic, and to seek through the ballot-box the speedy enactment of such prohibitory laws as shall extirpate the evil of intemperance from our state.

"S. L. ROBERTS."

The following letter from Dio Lewis, representing the views of the friends of the woman's movement generally, was received with the most severe denunciations from some of the speakers of the convention, among whom were Dr. Porter, of Columbus, and Rev. John Russel, of Michigan: —

"COLUMBUS, February 24.

"*To the President of the Prohibitory Convention at Mt. Vernon.*

"I cannot suppose that your convention will take any interest in my opinion about prohibitory law; but as I have been at work for some time with all my heart and strength in the cause of temperance in your great commonwealth, you may, perhaps, permit me a word.

"In my humble opinion no law could be more just, or more justifiable, than that which would remove the source of a large part of all our poverty, misery, and crime. The prohibitory liquor law, thoroughly enforced, would, I have never doubted, contribute more to the wealth of the state, and the welfare of society, than all the other laws of our statutes put together. But if this law be enacted before public sentiment is prepared to enforce it, it must divert the attention of temperance men from the vigorous and undivided employment of those moral influences which alone can give development and power to public sentiment. I affirm that its influence in New England has been disastrous up to this time.

"If the great social and moral revolution now in progress in Southern Ohio is not disturbed, but encouraged, within six months a prohibitory liquor law could be as easily enforced in this state as the law against theft.

"Will not the convention which meets in Mt. Vernon on the 26th, and which I believe will contain a large number of the truest friends of temperance in the state, give a word of hearty approval of the 'Woman's Temperance Movement?'

"Trusting the convention may pardon this intrusion, I am, sir, and gentlemen,

"Your obedient servant,

"DIO LEWIS."

On the 17th of March, another State Temperance Convention assembled in Columbus. But it was a state convention only in name. There was no necessity for it; and the call was so ambiguously stated that when the few delegates assembled they could find nothing to engage their attention. The entire day was spent in discussing the object of the convention, and at the last moment an attempt was made to clear up the muddle by a series of resolutions; but they were tabled, and the convention adjourned without even giving its reasons for coming together.

The most important event, and one which brought the matter of license anew before the people, was an immense mass meeting in favor of a well-regulated license law, held at Exposition Hall, Cincinnati, Saturday evening, March 28. The attendance was very large, probably reaching upwards of five thousand. The larger part of the audience was composed of Germans, and prominent wholesale and retail liquor dealers, who were present in large numbers. There were also many prominent business men and well-known citizens present, who, taken together with the high character of the speakers, gave a tone of respectability to the meeting. Speeches were made by Judge Whitman, Judge Taft, Emil Rothe, Rev. M. Lilienthal, George F. Davis, S. A. Kittredge, James H. Laws, and O. J. Dodds. The meeting was presided over by George F. Davis, a temperance man. It was opened by prayer, and mainly confined to arguments in favor of a "judicious license law" to regulate the traffic in liquors. An occasional side thrust was directed towards Dio Lewis; but in the main the woman's movement was treated with respect. The following resolution, which was adopted without dissent, has, at least, the merit of brevity. It was the text upon which half a dozen lengthy speeches were made.

"*Resolved*, that it is the sense of this meeting that a judicious license law meets the wants of the times, and affords the best solution of the question of traffic in intoxicating liquors."

Out of the many speeches delivered on this occasion, we give a few brief extracts from that of Judge Alphonso Taft. It embraces, substantially, the arguments used by all.

"If men are permitted to drink, some men must be permitted to sell. The right to drink and the right to sell go together. A judicious law to regulate, by license, the sale of liquors, would close at once more than half of the drinking places in Cincinnati, and at the same time improve the character of those which should remain. It would limit excesses, and to a considerable extent restore a respect for and observance of the laws on the subject.

"The principle of imposing a moral guardianship, by law or otherwise, of good men or good women over their fellow-citizens, in the exercise of their tastes in innocent things, has usually provoked rather than repressed excesses. Free agency is a principle of God's moral government. All attempts by men to defeat the fair operation of that principle have failed.

. . . . . .

"I cannot doubt the humane and religious motives of those engaged in the present temperance crusade in the city. But it seems to me that they are not quite satisfied with God's plan in dealing with moral subjects. His plan is too slow, and allows too much liberty. They would have a certain fixed control delegated to good men and women over the unwary consciences of their fellow-men. One effect of their well-meant zeal is to punish the innocent and excuse the guilty. The man who drinks to excess is the object of their complacency, while the rest of the world are charged with the guilt of his excesses. This is not a fair distribution of human responsibility.

. . . . . .

"Signing a pledge I regard as useless, and it tends to depreciate a man's self-respect. As a motive it has no meaning. To do or not to do a thing which concerns one's self, for no better reason than that he has promised to himself, or to persons who have no right to exact such a promise, is trifling with his own independence. If a thing ought not to be done, stop doing it. A promise or a pledge makes it neither better nor worse.

"It is an objectionable feature of the present crusade that it intrudes religious observances upon those who do not ask them. Prayer for or with those who desire it is commendable; but when forced upon the unwilling it is a mockery of God, as well as of the victims on whom it is forced."

This mass meeting of course created a necessity for another of an opposite nature. The anti-license portion of the community felt called upon to make its voice heard. The license men had provided able speakers to sustain their views, and turned out an immense crowd to hear them; yet there were numbers and eloquence on the other side which only needed an opportunity for public expression, to make their influence felt. The meeting was called for Thursday night, April 9, in Pike's Opera House. Meteorologically considered, it proved to be the worst night of the season. A cold rain and snow rendered the streets almost impassable; yet the building was well filled. Friends of the cause turned out as a religious duty, and made up a large and enthusiastic audience. Hon. C. W. Rowland presided, and he, with the Hon. Will Cumback of Indiana, Hon. E. D. Mansfield and Rev. Dr. Walden, made the speeches. The stage was filled with prominent gentlemen, and with a choir of singers backed by a full brass band.

The following resolutions, which were unanimously adopted, gave expression to the sentiment of the meeting: —

"*Resolved*, That what society acknowledges alike injurious and dangerous to its interests should be neither protected nor encouraged by law.

"*Resolved, therefore*, That the traffic in intoxicating liquors should not be licensed, and that the Constitution should not prevent the legislature from restraining, limiting, or suppressing it.

"*Resolved*, That the existing laws, or others that the legislature may pass to diminish or suppress the evils of this traffic, should be strictly enforced in all respects."

One of the most interesting and argumentative speeches was that of the venerable E. D. Mansfield. We append two or three of the concluding paragraphs, which contain, in a nutshell, the principal reasons why most Christian people are found on the anti-license side.

"The third idea is, that they will make this business respectable. They have three thousand funnels now, in this city, to run the liquor out of, and they think by the license system they can reduce the three thousand funnels to one thousand funnels. But do you think there will one drop less of liquor run out of those one thousand than out of the three thousand now? Not a bit of it. You will never find a brewer or a distiller going to any public meeting to reduce his own business. No common sense man would do it. The thousand funnels, if they are reduced down to a thousand, will run more liquor than the three thousand. They will make it more respectable — that is, by enlarging it, they think it will be more respectable. How respectable an aristocracy of drinking-houses would be! [Laughter and applause.]

"Did you ever hear of such a thing in regard to drinking-houses? Did you ever hear of such an aristocracy and such respectability? [Laughter.] Can you conceive of such an idea? Now I will tell you what it looks like to me. It would be like a gentleman who finds his garden full of snakes, and they begin to multiply until it becomes very uncomfortable, and he wonders what he will do with them. He hardly knows what to do; but at last a thought seizes him. He says, 'I will license them!' [Laughter.] License snakes in a garden! And for what reason will he license them? 'Why,' he says, 'the garter snakes will all be killed, and all the rattlesnakes will be left.' [Renewed laughter.] I never got hold of such an idea as these people got when they declare they are going to kill all the little saloons, and leave the big ones to bite and poison worse than ever.

"I know of only one reason why there should be a license law. It will put some money into the treasury. But what sort of money will it be? The Anglo-Saxons, our ancestors, had a compromise with every crime, upon which every one of them could be paid out. Murder, suicide, and every crime could be paid for if you put the price high enough. Everything of the kind was committed and paid for. Now, if we go on and license every evil in society, we shall be just where they were. We shall be commuting and compromising with murder, suicide, death, and ruin, and every dollar that goes into the treasury will groan and exclaim as its victims roll along to the grave, rattling over your streets, 'Murder, suicide, paupers.' Every dollar in your treasury will tell of crime commuted, and the groans of ruin and destruction will go up to the God of Sabaoth, who hears and loathes all crime. [Great applause.]"

About this time the constitutional convention, which was in session in Cincinnati, came to the question of license or no license in the new constitution. The division of the members on the matter was very nearly equal; those from the country districts generally opposing, and those from the cities generally favoring, license. The question presented itself in various forms to the convention, and is not, at the present writing, disposed of. The following is the proposition of Judge West, which excited much discussion both in temperance and anti-temperance circles. It is designed to be submitted as a separate article to the electors, for ratification or rejection, and if ratified to stand in lieu of Article XV. of the present constitution.

Section 1. Except in compliance with, and upon the terms and conditions prescribed by law, no person shall traffic in or sell intoxicating liquors within this state.

Sect. 2. Laws shall be passed to prevent the evils and compensate the injuries resulting from the sale or furnishing of intoxicating liquors, and from the intoxication consequent thereon.

Sect. 3. County commissioners, township trustees, and municipal authorities, shall have power severally to restrict or prohibit the traffic in, and sale of, intoxicating liquors within their respective jurisdiction, and to impose thereon terms and conditions other than and in addition to those prescribed by law.

Sect. 4. Nothing in this constitution shall be construed as denying to the General Assembly the power to restrict or prohibit the manufacture and sale of intoxicating liquors, or to regulate the same in any manner not consistent with the provisions of this article.

In view of the importance of this matter, in the new constitution, a call was issued for a third grand convention of the Women's Temperance Leagues of Ohio, to give an emphatic expression of opinion on the license question. The convention met on the 22d of April, and was the largest and most important of the series. The extent to which the organized temperance movement had now spread in the state, may be judged from the fact that one hundred and forty-one different leagues, in seventy-three different counties, were represented by delegates. The Ninth Street Baptist church — the place appointed for meeting — proved entirely inadequate in size, and the convention adjourned to Wesley chapel, — the largest church audience-room in the city, and capable of holding over two thousand people. During the whole of the sessions of the convention this church was crowded — sometimes almost to suffocation.

The first subject for consideration, after the body was organized, was, of course, the license question. A committee was appointed, consisting of one from each county in the state, to draft a memorial to the constitutional convention, indicative of the feeling of the temperance people of Ohio generally, and the women's leagues in particular. After deliberation, the committee returned an article which they offered as a substitute for the proposed article in the constitution. With the exception of the first section, it was substantially the same as that submitted by Judge West. The first section, however, provides that the state shall not, in any way, license the traffic in intoxicating liquors.

The debate which followed on the report revealed a great unanimity of sentiment against license in any form; but there was considerable difference of opinion as to the best manner of bringing the matter before the constitutional convention. But the report was finally adopted, amid great enthusiasm, and a large committee of ladies was appointed to convey the memorial to the constitutional convention, where it was received and laid on the table for future consideration. The debate on the second and third sections of the article was interesting, as showing the position of the delegates in regard to prohibition. A few of the most radical were for the complete and eternal prohibition of the traffic by state laws. They argued that it made no difference whether the general public was prepared for it or not; it was the duty of every temperance man to declare for the total annihilation of alcohol. The large majority of the convention, however, and those of the most sober sense, believed that it would be folly to demand a prohibition law now, when the public sentiment is not able to carry into execution the laws that are already upon the statute-books. In other words, a little law, well enforced, would be better than a sweeping prohibitory law, which it was absurd to suppose could be carried out, especially in the large cities.

Another important, but somewhat chimerical, project before the convention, was that of memorializing Congress to abolish the revenue from all intoxicating liquors, used as a beverage, including native wines, ale and beer, and thus withdraw the apparent support of the government from the traffic. The debate was continued with great skill and pertinacity by both sides.

"In God's name," said Mrs. Weitzel, of Middletown, "let us not recognize by law the great evil; let us wash our hands clean of participation in the wrong, if we expect a just God to reward our labors in this cause. Women themselves often, very often, have to pay this tax. Their husbands' liquor bills are sent to them to pay from their hard earnings at the needle or wash-tub. If you increase the tax, you increase their already heavy burdens; you take from them and their needy children the bread from their mouths and clothing from their backs."

Another speaker wanted the convention to consider two facts: —

1. That Congress has no power, under the Constitution, to authorize the manufacture of ardent spirits, or the vending of them in the different states, and has no power to prohibit the same.

2. That many men have large amounts of money invested in the liquor business, and that Congress simply lays its hands upon the property, and says it shall pay a certain revenue. This lessens the profits of the business, and checks the sale. If Congress lets the traffic

alone, it would simply offer a premium to and facilitate this nefarious business. He thought whiskey should be more heavily burdened with tax than any other kind of property.

The subject was finally referred to a committee, who reported in favor of postponing further consideration of the matter until the next convention. A compromise was, however, struck, in voting to ask Congress to prohibit the importation of intoxicating liquors. The remainder of the time of the convention was devoted to hearing brief reports from delegates, concerning the progress of the work in their several districts. They generally indicated no abatement of interest in the cause throughout the state, but a more fixed determination to shut up the saloons, by all available means of law and love. Allusions to the former method were more frequent than in the first convention, showing that the gospel plan is, to some extent, losing its distinctive character.

CHAPTER XXVIII.

SOME ACCOUNT OF THE OPPOSITION TO THE WOMAN'S MOVEMENT. — BITTER ARTICLES AND ABSURD STORIES PUBLISHED IN THE GERMAN PAPERS. — A SPECIMEN OF BEER DRINKERS' RESOLUTIONS. — ATTITUDE OF THE CATHOLICS. — ARCHBISHOP PURCELL'S LETTER. — A MANSFIELD PRIEST'S ANATHEMA. — DR. J. G. HOLLAND IN OPPOSITION, ETC., ETC.

IN the foregoing chapters, the progress of the woman's movement has been viewed mainly from the orthodox temperance stand-point. The intense opposition which it excited has only been referred to incidentally, in the course of the narrative. The character of this opposition, however, is in some cases so extraordinary as to render a more extended notice of it necessary to the completeness of this history. We therefore give place to a number of extracts from the articles and speeches of the anti-temperance press and orators.

The following correct translations of some of the articles published in the German papers of Cincinnati appeared in the Cincinnati Gazette. The movement was first treated by these papers in a sarcastic and humorous way, as in this extract from an early editorial in the *Volksfreund*: —

"The women's war against the saloons, in the various southern counties of our state, is still in full bloom. By companies the banded 'water virgins' march from saloon to saloon, fall upon their knees, and fight 'King Alcohol' and 'Emperor Gambrinus' with singing and praying, so that the windows rattle. In Greenfield, Highland County, they boast that they have already prayed and sung down eight saloons; and the other six they hope to capture soon. Of the four druggists, two have signed the pledge; the other two, as most incorrigible sinners, continue to make opposition, but will undoubtedly finally have to surrender. A German saloon keeper, by the name of Hiens, had declared his willingness to sell no more whiskey, and to restrict himself to the sale of beer and ale. But to such a capitulation the managers, with and without hoop skirts, will not consent; they demand an unconditional surrender; that is, to water, tea, coffee, and snuff. The temperance law they do not for the present design to invoke, but will endeavor to capture peaceable citizens by labors of love and a glib tongue."

But the "labors of love and a glib tongue" continued to spread and achieve such great results, that the humorous was changed for the impartial and philosophical tone. Witness an editorial from the *Volksblatt:* —

"The temperance movement of the women in the interior of the state seems not yet to have reached its culminating point, but continues to spread to other localities that have, up to this time, been free from the mania. In larger cities, like Cincinnati, Cleveland, Toledo, Columbus, Dayton, &c., such excesses, of course, would be impossible; but in the rural districts, and smaller towns and villages, they have full sweep, and but few will dare to think of resistance or opposition. Under these circumstances, those who are affected thereby seem, for the most part, to have come to the conclusion to let the storm expend its fury. Movements of this kind are usually of but short duration. The more violent they are in their first assault, the sooner will they come to an end. The Know Nothing movement, for instance, which in 1854 and 1855 bore all before it, and at first seemed irresistible, soon afterwards lost itself in the sand, without leaving a trace behind. The present woman's movement is evidently destined to the same fate, for the excitement and strain upon all the powers are too great to be of long duration."

The movement refusing to die out, in accordance with the prediction of its enemies, the beer-drinking editors began to show their tempers. The *Waechter am Erie*, published in Cleveland, relieved itself thus: —

"There is, in our view, a distortion and ugliness in this whole farce which is disgusting to us, and seems like a profanation of prayer; for in reality this movement to pray away the drinking saloons is nothing else than a lynch procedure. Behind the psalm-singing women stand the gentlemen heroes of the slipper; and gallants, too, if necessary, adopt other measures, if the soft, pious cooing should prove unavailing. The whole offers in the tedious winter months — and insufferably tedious it is in such nests — a somewhat exciting and amusing entertainment; and then one can get his 'bitters' anyway in the drug store, or it can be bought from one or the other of the large places on the sly. The saloon keepers are not to be blamed if they retreat from these houndings. Who can, for any length of time, bear the howling, and this folly in the mask of morality and virtue? No; more annoying than a swarm of mosquitos, worse than a bed full of bed-bugs, is such a woman's siege; and in some places they have made the thing very comfortable for themselves by planting a movable tabernacle, with stove and chairs, before the saloon, in which from early morning till late at night 'the good work' is carried on in the most comfortable manner, interchangeably with tattle. Think of the condition of a saloon keeper who receives a visit of this kind. Is he not in a worse case than a sensible man in the midst of a swarm of fools?"

A correspondent of the *Volksfreund*, writing from Portsmouth, says, —

"The temperancists here are beginning to be the plague of the land. Not content with howling against all devotees of the spirituous in their public prayer meetings, they now make raids upon the saloons, and by singing pious hymns seek to induce the beer and whiskey sellers to leave the broad road of vice, and to close their saloons. Even the most unyielding and determined must, under the application of such a moral torture, eventually become tractable, and be glad to dispose of his supply of whiskey to his tormentors for a consideration. Thus they bought of a beer saloon keeper of this place, 'Dutch Michael,' the whole stock of whiskey he had — about four gallons — for thirty dollars, and then sprinkled the street with the precious stuff. If any one takes a drink to strengthen his stomach, then these camel-swallowers and gnat-strainers set up a howl; but if the city treasury is robbed of the insignificant sum of ten thousand dollars, they hold their tongues, and cover the crime with the mantle of Christian charity."

But still the praying went on, and the saloons melted away before the advancing women, like the frost before the sun. Then the German editors began to get mad about it. The movement was always referred to as the "prayer pest," and the tone of editorial articles was somewhat like the following, which was published in *Die Gegenwart*, of Covington. In speaking of the Methodists, whom the editor holds responsible for all this temperance agitation, it demands that they should all be hung to lamp-posts, and swept from the face of the earth, for the following reasons: —

"In the first place they undermine the morals of the people. They furnish more rascals, great and small, counterfeiters, adulterers, perjurers, and bank swindlers, than all the other sects put together. They are the founders of the Young Men's Christian Association, the principal school of all gallows birds and swindlers. S. Colfax, former Vice-President of the United States, the greatest perjurer and scoundrel of the nineteenth century, is a Methodist, and the father of the Young Men's Christian Association. General O. O. Howard, Chief of the Freedmen's Bureau, who has swindled God and all the world, is a Methodist. The suit of the Methodist Book Concern in New York, which it took years to decide, and in which all those who were interested were convicted of perjury, is an evidence of their wickedness; the many complaints against their ministers for adultery, seduction, and other crimes, are an evidence of their immorality. We could furnish evidences by the thousand, if we had the room.

"Secondly, they trample the doctrines of Christ under foot, and make a mockery of prayer and religion. They boast to the world that they believe in Jesus, and at the same time they fight for Satan and his kingdom. Christ, when he instituted the holy supper, took the cup of wine, *drank of it himself*, and gave it to his disciples to drink, saying, 'This do in my memory.' *The Methodist church of America resolved that they would use no wine at the communion, because it is a sin.* Now, we ask every sensible man whether this pack prays to Him who said, 'This do in my memory,' or whether they pray to him who said to Christ, 'All this glory will I give thee if thou wilt fall down and worship me.' The answer was, 'Depart from me, Satan.' We say, Methodist, do not name the name of Christ, for you do not believe on him. We pronounce every Methodist, or other hypocrite who says that wine drinking is a sin, and at the same time professes to believe the doctrine of Christ, a mean, sneaking liar; for every man who declares that the commands and doctrines of Christ are a sin, is a fool and an ass, if he says that he believes in Christ.

"And now, thirdly, the greatest crime of the Methodists is this: That in their churches they adopt resolutions that are inimical to the liberties of the people. They send hundreds of petitions to the various legislative bodies, as Methodists, in order to pass laws according to their taste and for their benefit, and to the injury of the rest of the people. They come together in their churches, and conspire, and discuss, and resolve how they may attack the property, and business, and the lives of their fellow-men. They come forth from their churches in troops, and interfere with the business of our countrymen, threaten them with death, and deprive them of their liberty. They pray that their God may strike the saloonists and their families dead. (Very Christian — is it not?)

"Is this right? is it Christian? is it humane or citizen-like? We say no.

"We say to this band, Halt! for your hour has come. *Become a man and a citizen, or you must be destroyed.* We fed the South with powder and lead, when it attacked the rights and the existence of this country. Just so must this rabble be punished. We are not at all afraid to write against this band because a few Germans are to be found among them. These should keep away from them, or leave them and become decent men. It is sad, but true, that among the German Methodists there are some who are not exactly the best of brethren; but then, they may yet be converted, and return again to the bosom of humanity. May the light shine upon you."

It is but fair to say that the tone of the more influential German papers in Cincinnati never became so bitter as the above, although many false and exceedingly unjust statements were published. The following is a single instance: After the ladies had been engaged for some time in the crusade in Cincinnati, the *Volksfreund* one morning came out with the charge that the leader in prayer of one of the bands was seen so drunk during one of the services that she could scarcely rise from her knees when the prayer was ended, and reeled away to the church in the most disgraceful manner. This seemed too grave a charge to pass over in silence, and a committee of gentlemen was appointed to wait on Mr. Haacke, the editor of the paper, for his authority and proofs. He refused to give either, but repeated the charge. At length the truth of the matter came out. A ragged and dirty Irish woman one day came staggering into the circle of kneeling women, in a state of intoxication, knelt with them, and afterwards followed them to the church. The German readers of the *Volksfreund* never got the benefit of the correction, and to this day believe that one of the leading praying women was out on her mission too drunk to walk!

Another absurd story, which was started with still less foundation, was to the effect that the women engaged in the movement were paid regularly for their services, at the rate of three dollars a day. It was in vain to deny this ridiculous charge to any of the less intelligent Germans; they had read it in their papers, and therefore it was gospel. Admitting the truth of the statement, it would have been an expensive campaign for somebody. Five hundred dollars would have been needed every night for weeks and months to pay off the bands for their venal prayers and songs.

Having given considerable space to reports of temperance meetings, it might be of interest to produce a representative of another class. The following resolutions, adopted by a large anti-temperance mass meeting held at Hamilton, in March, show the sentiment entertained by the beer drinkers, in regard to the woman's movement: —

"*Resolved*, By all the German citizens of Hamilton and suburbs, —

"1. That we organize in order that we may be better able, after deliberation, to cope with this nuisance, and that we adopt such lawful measures from time to time as are necessary to secure us our just liberty and rights.

"2. That we never will permit that our religious and social liberties, and especially the latter, be infringed upon or taken from us under the cloak of a religious movement, by which religion itself is only disgraced and mocked.

"3. That under temperance, according to its proper meaning — an expression to which, with many other misused words, its true meaning ought to be restored — we understand moderation in the use of spiritual liquors, a matter which we highly appreciate, and whose opposite, 'drunkenness,' we deeply despise, and for whose abolishment we are ready to do all in our power, and for which we shall strive with all our influence.

"4. That we consider the movement known as the women's whiskey war an unlawful one, and that a hypocritical attack is made by it upon social liberty, and a sacrilege is committed upon religious exercises, especially the exercise of prayer, which, as private devotion, was by the Founder of Christianity himself emphatically destined not to take place at the street corners, but in the solitude of a closed room. To term it in short words, we can call it nothing but lunacy, and a fanatical swindle.

"5. That we in this movement recognize a total revolution of the Christian, social orders, by which the man is the head of the woman, and not the opposite. We recognize in it an aberration of the women from God's destined path of duty in which man and woman can be satisfied, and that they ought to consider that Christianity first raised the woman to an equal being with the man, but surely not to the end that man should become the slave of their notions and imbecile ideas.

"6. That we, as citizens of German descent, without difference as to religion, will use every means in our power to secure and hold for ourselves the liberties which the Constitution grants.

"7. That we look upon all advocates of the movement as enemies to religion and social liberty.

"8. That we will give no candidate, be it for state, county, or city office, our support or vote who takes part in the movement.

"9. That these resolutions shall stand and be carried into effect as long as the now raging temperance mania exists, and until these imbecile women, as we wish, for their own good, may soon prove the case, become sensible again, and are prepared to return to their own respective duties.

"A saloon keeper in Seven Mile will apply to-morrow, through Van Derbeer & Symmes, for an injunction against temperance visitation in that village."

Reference has once or twice been made to the attitude of the Catholics on this question of women praying down the evils of intemperance. In some towns the Catholic priest came out decidedly for it; in others he was favorably inclined, but afraid of the consequences of his espousing the cause. Generally, however, the movement met with determined opposition from the authorities in the Catholic church. Archbishop Purcell, whose word is law in Catholic circles, was early appealed to to define his position in the matter, which he did in the following letter: —

"St. Paul, in his instructions to the Romans, and through them, to all Christians, advises them 'not to be more wise than it behooveth to be wise, but to be wise unto sobriety.' Rom. xii. 3.

"The undersigned takes this occasion to answer the numerous applications made to him for sympathy and co-operation in the crusade against intemperance.

"He does not now, for the first time, express publicly his sympathy with the object, if not with the means adopted by the crusaders, or his readiness to co-operate with every legitimate and wise effort for the suppression of intemperance. Scarcely has he ever had the spiritual care of a congregation, as priest or bishop, without warning those who heard him of the temporal and eternal evils resulting from excess. In sermons and pastoral letters he has insisted on the necessity and exhorted to the observance of holy temperance, going so far in one of those letters, many years ago, as to express the wish that not one of his flock were a low, disreputable saloon keeper. For ten years he practised total abstinence, hoping, by example, to induce those whom his words reached not, to shun the vice that leads to every other vice. He is even now totally abstinent. This he considers pretty good; but he cannot go to the excess suggested by some of the lady league. He cannot instruct or preach that it is a sin for a day laborer, who has to carry the hod, on a broiling hot day in July or August, up a steep ladder to the third or fourth story of a building, to restore his exhausted strength by a glass or two of beer. This he would consider cruel. If the toiler has the physical endurance and the will to do without the beverage, in the name of God let him do it. And if he cannot take this refreshment without drinking to excess, let him abstain altogether, or quit the hard work, or die — for it is better so than to be a drunkard.

"Again, the archbishop cannot ask a clergyman to blaspheme the divine Author of our religion by asking him why he made wine at Cana, in Galilee, to recreate guests at a wedding. Why he instituted the Eucharist, the Lord's Supper, partly in wine, of which he commanded the apostles to drink. Why Jehovah's Holy Spirit teaches us in the Bible that God made 'wine to cheer the heart of man.' Psalms ciii. 13. And the vine to ask why it should desert its 'wine that cheereth God and men.' Judges ix. 13. Why did the dying patriarch, under the influence of divine inspiration, wish his son 'abundance of wine?' Why, again, does the Holy Ghost tell us that it is 'hurtful always to drink water, or wine, but to mix them is pleasant, or sometimes to drink one and sometimes the other'? 2 Mccb., last verse of the Old Testament.

"But God, they object, did not make the wine. We have shown that he did make it. Neither did he make the bread, except in the miracle of the loaves in the desert. But he made the grape and the wheat, from which wine and bread are made, the one by a process not much simpler than the other. Catholics, then, go to the Bible, and they understand it; and with the blessed Book before them, we cannot with bell, book, and candle, with praying and psalm-singing in the mud, excommunicate those who drink, or those who dispense the liquid which God has made to be used with moderation and thanksgiving. This, then, is the verdict of the Word of God: Use, do not abuse; and if you cannot use without abusing, use not at all.

"Some few years past, three or four Protestant clergymen called on the archbishop to ask his co-operation in an attempt to abate the nuisance of the grog-shops. He told them that when there was the question of the licensing, or absolute prohibiting, of the sale of inebriating liquors, he earnestly recommended the imposing of as heavy a fine, or license, on the venders of such liquid as they could bear, and inexorably to close, by all the penalties known to the law, those vile bar-rooms where bad liquor is sold to minors, drunkards, men or women, who are now the pests of the community, a disgrace to their families, and teaching by word and example the broad way to perdition. This, he conceived, would be the most effectual check to the evil we deplore. It would diminish, perhaps, by two thousand the three thousand 'spiracula ditis,' those craters of hell, by which our city is in peril of combustion; and it would pay the city much, if not all, the expense of the workhouse and other institutions which honest and sober citizens are now shamefully taxed to support.

"All which is respectfully submitted to all whom it may concern. † J. B. PURCELL,

"*Archbishop of Cincinnati.*

This letter was ably replied to by Dr. J. G. Holland. We quote one or two brief extracts: —

"Besides, would it not be well for us to remember the women who engage in this crusade are working in the only way that Providence has left open to them? Who are they? They are the mothers, wives, sisters, and daughters of men whom they have seen, year after year, dropping into the graves of drunkards. They have suffered worse than death that the rum seller might live. They have seen their loved ones become sots, idiots, madmen. They have seen their fortunes squandered; they have found themselves disgraced; they have been cursed, beaten, bruised; they have seen their peaceful and happy homes turned into places of fear and torment. Boys that were nursed on the bosoms of some of them have been transformed by drink into fiends. Men whose kiss of love and loyalty honored them with wifehood, have degenerated into beasts. For these, through weary, suffering years, they have prayed. Nay, they have knelt with them, and held up their weak and imbecile hands while they prayed for themselves. Day after day they have done this, as men have gone to their business through temptations that beset their path at every corner, and have received them at night only to cover them from sight with shame, and sink back into their old despair. The sorrows through which these women have walked have been simply immeasurable. No words of mine can describe them; no words of any man can exaggerate them.

"They have looked to the leaders of the church for help; have they had it? They have looked to the politicians for help; have they received it? They have asked for laws, which were easily made to satisfy their clamor; have they been executed? They have been pure and abstinent themselves; has their example been of any avail? They have pleaded with all the eloquence of love with those who have broken their vows to cherish and protect them, to forsake their vice, and have received only curses or promises not worth a straw. What, in God's dear name, was there left for them to do, but just what they are doing, and what you condemn? Who have driven these women to this great necessity? Who have forced them into a position from which all their natural instincts dissuade them? Who have made their crusade absolutely necessary, in order to save the men of the present generation from going to ruin? Men, and men of influence, with shame be it said! If the leaders of the Christian church had done their duty, and the leaders of state and national politics had done theirs, there would not be a dram shop to-day between Canada and the Gulf. The whole business has thus been left to God and the women; and the latter are praying in the churches and in the street, and pushing on their divine and peaceful crusade, because the men of America have failed to do their duty. Shall a Christian man, in high station or low, lift his voice against them? Rather let him hide his head in shame and self-contempt.

. . . . . .

"You say that you, or those for whom you speak, cannot, 'with bell, book, and candle, with praying and psalm-singing in the mud, excommunicate those who drink, or those who dispense the liquid which God has made to be used with moderation and thanksgiving.' What is this liquid? Is it wine? That is the liquid you talk about; that is the liquid the drinking of which you find justified in the Bible. But whiskey is not wine. Whiskey is the liquid that burns up stomach, brains, morality, industry, prosperity, life. Whiskey fills a hundred thousand homes with misery, and is poisoning the blood of the generations. Whiskey fills the poorhouses, and hospitals, and prisons. Whiskey is associated with nearly every crime committed in your community. It is the grand, fiery fountain of the national woe and crime. This is what the women of Ohio are seeking to banish; and they know that with it must go that which all the national experience has proved will be used as a cover for the baser liquid."

But while men of high position and great influence were carrying on the discussion with courtesy and moderation, some of the smaller fish strung together a series of bitter denunciations, and imagined they had thereby settled the question forever. The following short extract from an open letter by the Catholic priest of the flourishing city of Mansfield, Ohio, deserves a place among the literature of the campaign, as a sample of its kind:—

"The woman's temperance movement is absurd in its nature, in its concomitants, in its advocates, and in its efforts. Neither signing a pledge nor the screams of crazy women will help so much as to make one man temperate. Suppose that our Mansfield ladies fill with their prayerful screams, and their 'Come to Jesus,' and their glorys, and their amens, our narrow Main Street. How many of the saloon keepers and their visitors will be moved to pledge themselves in sincerity to abstain? Will they call upon the professional drunkard, or upon those who use with reason of beer and wine? The first class will be as much moved as Balaam's ass to pass the narrow gate. The second class will look upon you as a set of bigots and lunatics, and with great reason; for how do you dare to call upon men to abstain from what they do not abuse, and use with reasonable moderation or temperance? To try to deprive others of their rights is nothing else than despotism and Puritanism, which seems to be a boon Ohio has inherited from the New England States.

. . . . . .

"This is pharisaism, Puritanism, hypocrisy, pure sectarianism, intolerance in the name of a false God, whom the reformation and its ignoble upholders, the preachers are setting on their self-fabricated altars, and whom everybody should adore or perish.

"A. MAGENHANN."

We had hoped to give extracts from some of the leading speeches of the campaign in opposition to the movement, including the disgraceful one delivered by Judge Safford before the liquor sellers and drinkers of Chillicothe; but space forbids. Enough opinions of representative men and papers have been cited to show the animus of the forces arrayed against the temperance cause. It is only when these utterances, and the resistance which they provoked, are taken into account, that the grand results which the women achieved can be properly appreciated.

www.ingramcontent.com/pod-product-compliance
Lightning Source LLC
LaVergne TN
LVHW021318110826
845150LV00003B/611

* 9 7 8 1 4 2 5 5 5 7 4 8 5 *